100 Questions
Every First-Time
Home Buyer
Should Ask

100 Questions Every First-Time Home Buyer Should Ask

with Answers from Top Brokers from Around the Country

ILYCE R. GLINK

TIMES BOOKS

RANDOM HOUSE

Library of Congress Cataloging-in-Publication Data

Glink, Ilyce R.
100 questions every first-time home buyer should ask : with
answers from top brokers from around the country / Ilyce R. Glink.
p.   cm.
Includes index.
ISBN 0-8129-2283-2
1. House buying. 2. House buying—United States. I. Title.
II. Title: One hundred questions every first-time home buyer should
ask.
HD1379.G58 1993
643'.12—dc20   93-30570

Manufactured in the United States of America
9 8 7 6 5 4 3 2
First Edition

To my husband, Sam,
my mother, Susanne,
and the memories of
Dad, Dukey, and Leon

Preface

A s the title implies, this is a book for first-time home buyers. It could also be used quite successfully by anyone who hasn't bought property in the past few years. Or buyers who bought homes within the past few years but had trouble with their brokers, the negotiation process, the inspection, the closing, or any of the other dozens of pieces that go into the complex game called real estate. But first-time buyers are a breed apart. Brokers say the moment first-time buyers walk into the house of their dreams, and realize it is affordable, a moment of complete satisfaction settles in on their face: it is the thrill of achieving the American Dream.

The idea for this book came to me as I was writing an article for the Your Place section of the *Chicago Tribune*. The article was supposed to be about the questions first-time buyers ask. The brokers I interviewed told me all first-time buyers ask the same questions—over and over again. I easily culled a dozen questions from my interviews with brokers. And then another dozen. And over the years I added to that list. But one thing came through loud and clear: Not every first-time buyer remembers to ask every question. And in real estate, those unanswered questions often turn into curve balls.

100 Questions Every First-Time Home Buyer Should Ask leads you through the maze of purchasing property by answering the questions that pop up at different checkpoints along the way. I've tried to phrase the questions in the way you would ask them and think about them. And I've tried to explain the answers in a way you would understand and recognize. There are two ways to use this book: You can read it cover to cover, starting with the introduction. Or you can pick it up when you have a question, find your question, and read the answer. I recommend you do both.

Good luck. And happy house-hunting.

Ilyce R. Glink
Summer 1993

Contents

100 Questions
Every First-Time
Home Buyer
Should Ask

Introduction

S o you want to buy your first home. Well, you're not alone. According to the most recent report published by Chicago Title and Trust, the nation's largest title insurance organization, more than 2 million first-time buyers bought property last year. In many areas of the country, first-time buyers accounted for more than half of all home buyers. And those numbers are expected to increase each year for the foreseeable future, primarily since most first-time buyers are two-income families who are free to buy the moment they have saved enough money for a down payment; they, unlike the rest of the home-buying population, are not already tied down to a property. They do not have to sell before they buy.

In other words, you're not alone. There is some comfort in that. There are approximately 2 million other first-time buyer families who are about to embark on the same voyage you'll be making. Like you, they're going to be learning the language of real estate, with an entirely new vocabulary. You will learn to be selective in choosing a new home, smart in negotiating for that home, careful in inspecting it, and adept at piecing together the details for closing on it.

Real estate brokers and sales agents will tell you there is nothing like working with a first-time buyer. Why? In part, first-time buyers have a naïveté that is genuine and enjoyable. One broker from Florida says working with first-time buyers is like taking your children to Walt Disney World for the first time. Their excitement is contagious. It's easy for a broker to get excited about working with someone who's excited about the prospects of home ownership. Once you've bought and sold your fourth, fifth, or tenth house, looking for a home can become commonplace or even a chore: It isn't fun for you and it isn't fun for your broker. First-time buyers, for all their questions, for all the hand-holding brokers do, reinvigorate the process of purchasing real estate. When first-time buyers step into the home of their dreams, and realize they can afford it, their faces light up. And rightly so. There are very few things that will give you as much satisfaction as owning your own home.

Who Is the First-Time Buyer?

Would you recognize yourself in the following description? According to a study called "Who's Buying Houses in America," completed by Chicago Title and Trust, nearly 73 percent of first-time buyers are married couples. The average first-time buyer is around thirty years old. On average, it takes nearly three years for first-time buyers to save for a down payment, and almost 78 percent of that down payment comes from savings. Better than 10 percent of first-time buyers receive all or part of their down payment from parents or relatives.

The median income for first-time buyers tops out at over $55,000, with the average first-time buyer's home priced close to $120,000. The average down payment is almost 15 percent of the purchase price (remember, you *can* buy a home with as little as 5 percent down). And most first-time buyers choose thirty-year mortgages. More than 17 percent of first-time buyers opt for new construction. Eighteen percent of first-time buyers purchase condominiums. The rest choose single-family homes and town houses.

Jim, a longtime Chicago broker, has worked with hundreds of first-time buyers in his years of brokerage. "First-time buyers are sophisticated, motivated people with money to spend," he says. "But they're sophisticated enough to know they need education and guidance. They know that while they're nervous about making the biggest purchase of their life, they know that education is an antidote to fear."

Are You Ready to Buy a Home?

Think about that for a moment. Are you really ready to make the commitment required by home ownership?

The answer is more complicated than you might imagine. There is a chasm of difference between a home owner and a renter. Renters are free to pick up and move at a moment's notice, provided their lease is up or they find someone to sublet their rental apartment or house. Home owners, while able to list their property for sale, are more vulnerable to the changing tides of the marketplace, and usually must wait for their property to sell before moving on.

Renters rent for many reasons, including: They haven't saved up enough money for a down payment; they are in a job that may require them to move from location to location; they are unsure where they want to live; they are unmarried; they believe they can make more money in investments other than a home; they don't want to be tied down; they think they can't afford what they really want; or, they are uneducated about the benefits of home ownership.

If you ask home buyers why they bought, they might tell you: It's part of the American Dream; their parents told them it's the best investment they can make; they've saved up enough money for a down payment; they've decided where they want to live and want to settle down; they see it as an enforced savings plan; they're tired of "throwing" money away on a rented apartment; they don't want to deal with landlords; or they want a place to call their own.

The Psychology of Home Ownership

As you can see, there is a strong psychological barrier between owning and renting.

Frank and Julie have rented an apartment in Chicago for more than twenty years. Susanne, a residential real estate broker and Julie's friend, asked her why she still rents, when in the past twenty years she could have bought a house or condo and probably paid off the mortgage. Instead, twenty years later, all Frank and Julie have to show for their $240,000 in rent (twenty years × $1,000 average per month × 12 months per year) are rent receipts. But Julie said she and Frank never could agree on where to live. He wanted to be downtown near his work and she thought they'd eventually move to the suburbs. They liked their apartment building and thought if it went condo, they'd buy then. There was always some excuse not to buy.

Are you psychologically ready for the responsibilities that come with buying and owning a home?

Buying a home means more than simply making a monthly mortgage payment. It also means paying taxes, maintenance costs, and insurance premiums. If you buy a condo, town house, or co-op, you're also taking on the added responsibility of monthly assessments for maintenance of the commonly held property. If you're a home owner, you shoulder the burden of home maintenance yourself. If the roof leaks, you have to fix it. If the boiler breaks, you must replace it. There is no landlord to call.

As a home owner, you also shoulder the burden of real estate taxes. You become one of those home owners who support the local school system, fire and police departments, and city government. Buying a home means you're also buying into your local community. And if someone wants to put a trash dump next door to your house, you'd better be out there fighting against it to protect your property's value.

And you may be there for a long time. Although today, the first-time-buyer market is considered the "hottest" market—meaning there is the greatest amount of demand for homes generally priced under $150,000—that could change. If it does, that two-bedroom condo you bought in a bidding war three years ago could sit for 60 to 120 days before you receive a single offer. Becoming a home owner means you are somewhat subject to the whims and tides of the market. Renters can leave at the end of their lease, or they can sublet their unit. Home owners must either rent out their homes or sell. Neither is an attractive option when under pressure.

But there are lots of benefits to home ownership that compensate nicely for any hardships. In addition to having a place to call your own, you receive support in the form of tax breaks from the federal government, affectionately known as "Uncle Sam." You may deduct the interest you pay on your mortgage, and take a deduction for your real estate property taxes. If you work out of your home, there are a number of tax benefits, including a deduction for the costs associated with owning and maintaining the portion of the home you use exclusively for business. When you sell the home, you can roll over any profit you may have into your next purchase, provided it costs as much or more than the home you just sold. When you reach the age of fifty-five, you can take a onetime tax-free exemption of $125,000 off your home profits.

But perhaps the best reason to own a home is that traditionally, it has been an excellent financial investment. In the past thirteen years, home prices have increased, on average, more than the rate of inflation. In addition, paying down a mortgage offers home owners an enforced savings plan. Every payment into the bank is part mortgage interest and part mortgage principal. That little bit of principal is called home equity and it adds up over time. When you sell the home it becomes cash in your pocket.

If you've already decided you're "in the market" to buy a home, then this book ought to help. It will tell you what questions you should ask, and then will answer those questions in easy-to-understand English. There are no stupid questions in the complex game of real estate. There are only questions that never seem to get asked.

Women in Real Estate

I am often asked what changes I see taking place in the real estate industry. A major change in the past generation is that more women are purchasing real estate by themselves. There are more single mothers, divorced mothers, and single women who have good jobs and who have become aware of the financial benefits of home ownership. They too want to buy their piece of the American Dream.

But women often face special challenges when purchasing property alone. The decision to buy seems fraught with peril, and the fears that couples have about their purchase seem multiplied when sitting only on one pair of shoulders. The financial responsibility is, of course, borne by one, not two. Not all of the female members of this current generation of first-time buyers—who are in their late twenties and early thirties—have been taught that they *can* purchase and maintain property by themselves. These fears and insecurities are often reinforced by naïve or prejudiced brokers who sometimes forget that they must see beyond the curves; that the person they are showing around is first and foremost a first-time buyer. Not a woman. Not a man.

Today, women have more opportunities for involvement with real estate than ever before. In earlier, less enlightened times, women had little opportunity to purchase real estate for themselves, and were in fact prohibited from owning or inheriting real estate in most of the world. Unfortunately, this kind of rampant discrimination continues to flourish in places, including England to some degree, where daughters cannot inherit their fathers' titles of nobility.

In numerous instances, women have encountered severe and disheartening discrimination and prejudice when trying to buy or sell real estate. When my husband, Sam, and I were shopping for a loan, we went first to the bank where my family has had numerous accounts for more than fifty years. The loan officer (a woman!) looked first at my husband's robust salary and then at my smaller freelance-writer's income. With a withering look, she said, "Your income doesn't matter. Only your husband's counts." And she continued the meeting addressing him only. I was humiliated and ashamed. And at that moment, as I think happens with anyone who experiences hateful prejudice, bias, or bigotry, a little bit of me withered up and died. Unfortunately, this sort of thing happens all the time. Recently, a professional woman who makes an excellent six-figure salary complained that when she took over the bidding process after her fiancé left town, their broker didn't believe she had "really been given the authority to make an offer and counteroffer." This successful first-time buyer was insulted, and rightly so. There are thousands of these cases. I'd like to be able to say that the discrimination is occurring with less frequency, but I'm not sure it is. And it's more than a little ironic that the discrimination persists since many women are employed within the real estate industry as brokers, agents, loan officers, and appraisers.

Your job is to remove any obstacle that stands in the way of your ability to purchase property. Let your broker know that you have the authority and financial wherewithal to make an offer and follow through on it (but don't tell too much about your finances). Don't be afraid to admit what you don't know, but don't appear too weak and indecisive either. Don't let the broker take advantage of your time or good nature, and be confident about asserting yourself. Remember, you have the money. You're doing the buying. You've got all the cards.

Of course, if you find yourself talked down to, or treated badly, don't hesitate to confront the managing broker about the situation and ask for help. You can also switch brokerage firms if you feel that your needs aren't being met. Remember, there are hundreds of real estate brokers who are happy to help you feel good about the process and about yourself, and will just as happily collect their share of the commission.

Minority Discrimination

Any discrimination is deplorable. That said, it's best to acknowledge that the world isn't a perfect place and we must do what we can to achieve our goals despite these obstacles. Minorities, and particularly African-Americans and Hispanics, receive the brunt of the worst kind of discrimination. Study after study has documented that African-Americans seem to be rejected for home loans twice as often as Caucasians.

So far no one has been able to pinpoint the exact reasons, but there are some good guesses. Some say loan officers "redline" a specific neighborhood or town, meaning they don't make loans in certain areas because there is a high rate of default. Others say loan officers simply don't like to make loans to minorities. Whatever the reason, if you're a minority or a woman, you may have to work twice as hard to get your loan. Just remember, it's worth it. However, if you feel that you're being discriminated against, contact your local office of the Department of Housing and Urban Development (HUD) to file a complaint.

PART I

Looking for a Home: House, Condo, Co-op, Town House

HOW DO I KNOW WHAT I WANT?

Should I Make a Wish List? What About a Reality List?

First, let's talk about what exactly constitutes a wish list. A wish list is nothing more than a list of everything you've ever dreamed of having in your house: marble kitchen countertops, a wood-burning fireplace, three-car garage, four-person whirlpool, the best school district in your state, a five-minute walk to work, four bedrooms, a master suite with his and her closets, and vaulted ceilings. You get the picture.

The best brokers in this business will ask their first-time buyers to create a wish list detailing everything they'd love to have in a home, including:

- *Location.* Think about where you like to shop, where your children will attend school, where you work.
- *Size.* Think about number of bedrooms you want, the size garden, the extra room you may need to expand, where you will do the laundry, storage space.
- *Amenities.* Think about the garage, kitchen and bathroom appliances, swimming pool, fireplace, air-conditioning, electrical wiring, furnace, hardwood floors.

On the first pass, many of the items may seem to be in conflict with each other: You want to be close to a transportation network so it's easy to get around, and yet you want a quiet and peaceful neighborhood. You might want to walk to work, but when you come home, you want your home to be silent and secure. You want a wide variety of shopping, and yet you also need to be close enough to your health club to use it on a regular basis. You want to take advantage of the city, yet live in the suburbs.

But that's what a wish list is all about. If you're honest about what you want, the inconsistencies and conflicts will come out. Most first-time buyers are confused by all their choices. First-time buyers take on that "kid in a candy store" quality: Many have difficulty choosing between different styles of homes. One broker says she always has a few first-time buyers each year who need to see at least one of everything in the area: a California ranch, an old Victorian, an in-town residence, and several new subdivisions. It takes a tremendous amount of time, which is wasted if the buyer decides ultimately to go with a loft.

Some brokers also use a tool to help their clients define their needs as well as their wants. They call this the reality list.

Joanne, a real estate sales associate in New Jersey, says she asks her first-time buyers very specific questions about what they need to survive in their first home. "I just know their pocketbook will not allow them to have everything they want. I tell them they will begin to get what they want with their second home. Not the first."

Here are some of the questions Joanne might ask:

- How many bedrooms do you need?
- How many children do you have or are you planning to have?
- Is a garage absolutely necessary?
- Why do you need a home with a basement?
- Do you use public transportation on a daily basis?
- How close to work do you need to be?
- Does driving on a major expressway or in traffic make you crazy?

By asking specific questions about your daily lifestyle, Joanne and other brokers are able to center in on the best location and home size and amenities for your budget. They can read between the lines on your wish list.

Wish and reality lists have another use. By prioritizing the items on these lists, a good real estate agent can tell which items you might be willing to trade off. For example, if the first wish on your list is to have a four-bedroom, two-bath house, and the thirty-eighth item is a wood-burning fireplace, then the broker knows you would probably prefer a four-bedroom, two-bath house without a fireplace to a four-bedroom, one-bath house with a fireplace.

The bottom line is this: Unless you win the lottery, or are

independently wealthy, you're probably going to have to make some trade-offs when buying your first house.

Sometimes you're going to make a mistake. When Sam and I bought our first home (a vintage Chicago co-op built in the 1920s), we didn't own a car. Our wish list included a parking place, but it was low on the list, maybe around the twentieth item. A wood-burning fireplace was pretty high on the list, about number five. You can guess what happened. When we inherited a car a few years later and began hunting and pecking for parking spaces on the street, we were sorry we didn't have a space to park the car. But not as sorry as when we tried to sell our unit, and discovered that most buyers in our area won't even consider a building that doesn't have parking. Fewer people cared about the fireplace, although we loved it. On our next wish list, you can bet that having a parking space or a garage will be near the top of our list.

How Do You Make a Wish List?

Brokers say the best wish list should include everything you want in a home, such as location, schools, shopping, and distance to work. If your initial list says "nice house, four bedrooms," try asking yourself these questions to stimulate your true desires.

- How often do I go to the city? Suburbs? Country? Where would I rather be?
- How long do I want to spend driving to work each day?
- Do I have frequent guests? Do I need a separate guest room?

- Will my children take a bus to school, walk, or will I have to drive them?
- How far away is my church?
- Do I want a big garden?
- Must I have a garage? Two-car? Three-car?
- How far away is the airport?
- What is my favorite form of recreation and how far away from it am I?
- Where does my family live? Where do my friends live? How far away from them do I want to be?

Questions of lifestyle are crucial components of a wish list. Do you and your spouse like to stay in on Saturday nights? Or do you prefer to be close to the "action"? And will that change over the years? Are you a single woman or married with six children? Do you travel frequently? Do you own a car? Do you own, or are you contemplating purchasing, a boat in the near future? Will you want to be within fifteen minutes of the marina?

Once you get the information down on paper, try to organize it into a concrete sentence: "I want a four-bedroom, three-bath home with a large garden, fairly new kitchen, loads of closets, a wood-burning fireplace, two-car garage, within a fifteen-minute commute to the office and church, down the street from the high school, in such-and-such location."

That's a start. Now, prioritize the items in your wish list, and think about which items you would trade off for others. For example, would you give up a wood-burning fireplace if it meant having a two-car garage? Could you get by with a smaller house if it means you'd be in a better school district? Would you prefer to be closer to work even though it means giving up a large garden? What if you had to live in a condo but could walk to work?

Now for your reality list. Write down everything you can't live without for the next five years. If you're a single woman, your reality list might include:

- Two bedrooms (that's really for sale purposes; it can be much easier to sell a home with two bedrooms than a home with one bedroom, which we'll get to in a later chapter);
- Two bathrooms (same reasoning as above);
- Parking space or attached garage;
- Outdoor living space of some sort (could be a garden or patio);
- Second floor or higher;
- Within a twenty-minute drive to work.

Now your broker has something to work with. He or she can take your wish list and begin to match it to homes listed in your local multiple-listing service.

Are the wish list and reality list worth the time and effort? Brokers say yes. Even though a good broker will spend an hour or two divining the same information, writing up a wish list and a reality list will help focus your mind on what you really want. An honest wish list is a road map to finding the house of your dreams. You may just have to buy and sell a few homes before you actually get there.

What Does "Location, Location, Location" Really Mean?

"Location, location, location" is what industry professionals call the broker's maxim. During the days, weeks, and months you'll be searching for a home with a broker, you're likely to hear this phrase at least once, if not a dozen times. What does it really mean?

Brokers say the key to buying and selling successfully is linked to the location of the home. You can change everything about a home *except* its location. Think about it: You can paint, decorate, gut the interior of the house, replace the asphalt shingles with slate, put on new siding, add a deck, repave the driveway, and plant flowers. The only thing you can't do is move the home to a different location. (It's true that there are mobile homes, prefab homes that come from a factory and are placed on a lot, and homes that are moved from one location to another to prevent them from being torn down. That's not what we're talking about here. You're not going to move an apartment from midtown Manhattan to New Jersey. And you're not going to take your 150-year-old brick town house from Boston's North End and move it to Newburyport, Massachusetts.)

If the house of your dreams is located next to a railroad yard, you probably want to go back to sleep. A poor location will severely limit the property's ability to appreciate in value and will hamper your ability to sell the property quickly when that time comes. (There's a reason that house is priced so low . . .)

Ed, a real estate attorney, bought and sold several homes before he bought the one that backed up to Chicago's famous elevated train tracks, known as the "El." It was an 1880s brick two-story house with a nice yard that desperately needed some TLC. But it backed up to the El. Trains run by there every ten to fifteen minutes. The whole house shakes. But Ed didn't think it was a problem—"You get used to it; I hardly ever hear it anymore"—and bought the house. He proceeded to completely renovate it, and even put in a sauna. When he decided to move to Texas, he put the house on the market. Two years later, it was still for sale, waiting for someone who wanted to spend several hundred thousand dollars buying an overimproved house in a good neighborhood, but in a very poor location.

What is a poor location? Defining *poor* is often a matter of taste. To brokers, *poor location* means difficult to sell because it is located:

- Next to a railroad yard;
- Near a toxic waste or municipal garbage dump;
- On top of, or next to, a freeway, expressway, or interstate highway;
- In the center of nightlife activity;
- Near a busy intersection;
- Next to a high school;
- In the midst of gang territory;
- In a run-down block or neighborhood;
- In a city, town, or suburb having significant budget problems.

Of course, plenty of people can turn what might normally be called a poor location into a positive. If you buy a home in a run-down neighborhood that is surrounded by yuppie housing, you might be able to turn a nice profit as the neighborhood improves over the years. Being located next to a noisy high school may mean you can keep an eye on your children throughout the day.

A good location, on the other hand, is one that allows the owner to thoroughly enjoy every aspect of his or her home. It will be located close, but not too close, to shopping, restaurants, work, transportation, good schools, etc. A good location is one that you can sell easily to someone else, giving you additional flexibility. If, when you're looking for homes, you're faced with a choice between a beautiful home in a lousy location, or a slightly smaller, less beautiful home in an excellent location, which one will you choose?

How Do I Choose Where to Live?

This is a problem for many buyers, not just first-timers. In part, the answer will be decided somewhere between your pocketbook and your wish list. Neighborhoods being what they are, you can almost certainly find something in your price range in an area in which you want to live. For example, I'm sure you could find an affordable one-bedroom condo in a suburb of $1 million homes. But if you need three bedrooms, that expensive suburb will most likely be out of your price range. The point is, you can find something affordable in nearly every neighborhood. Whether it meets your needs is another story.

The first thing to do is to find a suburb or neighborhood that offers homes that meet your needs, at a price you can afford. Sometimes the easiest way to find what you're looking for is to cross out options that don't work for one reason or another. Start by asking your broker to cross match your price range with your reality list. That should instantly narrow your choices to maybe several suburbs or neighborhoods. Now take a close look at these areas, and apply some of the features of your wish list: Is one in a better school district? Is another closer to work? Does one have more character or better shopping? Is one located on a golf course? Is one nearer your parents or in-laws?

Once you've narrowed down your choice of areas to two or three suburbs, neighborhoods, or even streets, take an extensive driving tour of these areas. Get out and walk around. Sit on a bench and watch the people go by. After all, these might be your future neighbors. Start looking at some houses in the neighborhood. If you begin to see homes you like in an acceptable, affordable neighborhood, you're on the right track.

QUESTION 4
How Long Do I Plan to Live in My Future Home?

This might be one of the most important questions in this book. Why? The answer directly affects the size and type of home you buy as well as the type of mortgage you'll eventually choose. Times have changed drastically since our parents bought their homes. Chances are, unless they've retired or are in professions where they are required to relocate to different parts of the country from time to time, your parents are still living in the home you grew up in. My mother, Susanne, has been living in the same building for more than twenty-five years. It was the first and only apartment she and my father purchased. And she will probably be there for some time to come. However, statistics from the National Association of Realtors (NAR) reveal that today, on average, people live in their homes for only five to seven years. That's it. Then they move.

How are you supposed to know how long you're going to live in your house? I suppose there is no way to know for sure, but there are some general guidelines. If you're a young single person who wants to get married, and it seems likely you might, then you'll probably only stay in that two-bedroom condo five to seven or less years. If you're a young, married couple who wants to have children, you'll probably move in five to seven years, once your family starts to grow. If you're married, or a single parent, or divorced with a couple of children, it's likely that after two to three moves, you're ready to settle down for a while. You might find a house in a good school district and decide to stay there ten to fifteen years, until your children are through with school. Once your children are grown and out of the house for good, you might decide to sell your big house and move to a smaller condo or a senior center. And then you might retire to a sunny, warm clime.

National statistics tell us that the average family will move five to seven times in their lifetime. In addition to accommodating fluctuating family sizes, buying and selling homes is one of the best ways to accumulate wealth. By purchasing a home, fixing it up, and selling it every five to seven years, you should be able to increase the size of your equity significantly over the course of your lifetime.

Knowing how long you plan to live in your house is also crucial to choosing the correct mortgage. If you're only going to live in the home for five years, you may want to choose an adjustable-rate mortgage (ARM) since that might allow you to maximize interest rates. If you're going to stay in the house for fifteen years, you might want a fifteen-year fixed mortgage; when you sell the house, you'll own it free and clear and have a sizable amount of cash for your next purchase. (If you have additional questions on mortgages, turn to the financing section of this book beginning with Question 51.)

Take a look at your prospects for change, then decide where you are on your lifeline:

- Is marriage, a life partnership, or living with someone else a possibility within five to seven years?
- How many children do you plan to have during the next five to seven years?
- Are your children near or at school age? Have you chosen the school district you want for them?
- Is it likely you'll be transferred for your job within the next five to seven years?
- Do you have an aging parent in another part of the country who may require your close supervision or attention?

QUESTION 5

What Are the Different Types of Homes?

Your home is supposed to be your castle. But unless your name is Windsor, it's unlikely you'll end up living in one.

There are several basic types of homes that are commonly available in all parts of the country. If you decide to buy a home, you will probably end up choosing from among a condominium, town house, cooperative apartment, and a single-family house. Or you might get a hybrid or a variation on one of these housing types. There are numerous differences between each of these home types, from the rights of ownership to the way the property is maintained. As the saying goes, it's all in the details; knowing the differences between these types of homes is key to making a successful choice.

Condominium

Usually found in urban centers or densely populated suburbs, condos (as they are commonly referred to) became popular in the 1970s when state legislatures passed laws allowing their existence. An apartment building is converted to a condominium by means of a condominium declaration (often called a "condo dec"). This declaration divvies up the percentage of ownership, defines which areas are commonly held by all owners, determines who is responsible for the maintenance of the property, and states the condo rules.

One of the most important things to remember about a condo is that you don't actually own the unit you live in. You own the air space inside the walls, ceiling, and floor of the unit, possibly the plumbing within your unit, and perhaps a parking space. With your neighbors, you also jointly own the common elements of the property, which may include the roof, plumbing, common walls, lobby, laundry room, garden area, or garage.

Condos don't always look like tall buildings. Condo developments can take the form of town houses (see page 27), duplexes (condos stacked two by two), or four-plexes (condos stacked four by four, also known as "quads"). Suburban condos tend to stretch out (longer than higher). City condos tend to be in mid- or high-rise buildings.

Maintenance: A condo association raises money for maintenance of the common elements through monthly assessments. The building's expenses are tallied, then divided by the percentage of ownership, and then divided by twelve. So if your annual share of building maintenance cost is $1,200, you will pay $100 per month in assessments in addition to the costs of your mortgage and real estate taxes.

Note: If you choose to buy a condo or a co-op (see below), you must understand that the lender will take into account the extra monthly payments you'll have to make and will readjust the amount it is willing to lend to you. For example, the lender might tell you that you can purchase a $160,000 house or a $130,000 condo.

Cooperative Apartment

Before there were condos, people owned their units by buying shares in a corporation that owned the building in which that unit was located. As my friend David puts it, if you own a condo, you own real estate that you can use to secure a mortgage. If you own a co-op, you own shares in a corporation that owns the real estate in which your apartment is located. The shares give you the right to lease your unit from the corporation. You pay a monthly assessment (often called lease payment or rent) based on the number of shares you own in the corporation.

One sticky issue with co-ops is control. For many years, co-op boards used their power to reject potential buyers at will to keep a firm grip on who moved into the building. Unfortunately, a little of that unpleasantness continues to this day, particularly in swanky neighborhoods and in buildings whose owners have "attitudes." In addition, co-op rules often require a higher cash down payment (between 20 to 30 percent), and sometimes refuse to allow purchases financed with a mortgage. Fortunately, many co-ops have relaxed this restriction in recent years. If you're looking for an abundance of co-op units, try New York City, although there are a fair number spread out over the rest of the United States.

Maintenance: Like a condo, your monthly assessments cover the general maintenance of the property. But because the corporation pays real estate taxes on the property as a whole, your share of the taxes is normally included in your monthly assessment. That means your assessment is going to look pretty steep when compared side by side with a condo building assessment notice. Remember, the co-op assessment includes property taxes.

Note: Aside from New York City, many brokers, especially those new to the business, have trouble understanding the concept of co-ops. They may try to tell you that co-ops aren't a good investment, or try to steer you away for some other reason. Like any type of home, a co-op can be an excellent investment. Sometimes co-op prices are below that of a comparable condominium apartment partly because brokers may not understand them and partly because co-ops typically require a larger down payment, which makes them unaffordable or impractical for many first-time buyers. On the other side, if you own a co-op, it may take you longer to sell, on average, than a condominium.

Town House

A town house development can take several different physical forms, but it usually looks like a group of slender houses attached into a long row. Generally, you share a wall in common with each of your neighbors.

The difference is in the way the property is held. Most row houses built in the first half of this century are held "fee simple," meaning you hold legal title to your home and the land it sits on, and are responsible for the real estate taxes even though you share a common wall with your neighbors. Some town houses may be held as condos, but most are a hybrid, falling somewhere between condos and single-family homes.

Maintenance: Town house developments often have a home owner's association that manages the common elements of the property. You pay a monthly assessment covering the maintenance of the common elements, which may include the roof, common outdoor, recreation, or parking areas, and any laundry facilities.

Single-Family Home

Far and away the most common form of home is the single-family detached house. Available in all shapes, sizes, and prices, the most common feature among single-family homes is that the house sits by itself on its own piece of property.

Maintenance: You, the home owner, are responsible for all of the expenses associated with ownership and maintenance, including real estate taxes, garbage removal, water, and sewage.

What Are the Advantages and Disadvantages of Buying a Home that Needs Renovation? How Much Improvement Should I Plan to Put In? And What Do Brokers Mean by "Overimproved"?

Brokers like to say there are three kinds of homes.

First, there is the "move-in-condition" home. There's no decorating or renovation required. All you have to do is move in your furniture and start living.

Second is the home that's in "good condition." When you hear brokers refer to a home like this it generally means the home's "bones," or structure, are in fine shape, plus the amenities and appliances are in good working order. The drawback to a home in good condition might be the decor. You may need to repaint the walls, strip the floors, or replace the carpeting.

The third kind of house is what a broker refers to as a "handyman's special." With a handyman's special you can expect to see anything from a home needing minor repairs to a home that requires a gut job to be livable.

When it comes to the question of the advantages and disadvantages of buying a home that needs renovation, the answer depends on how much money you have to spend. Most first-time buyers have limited cash reserves. Usually the down payment is a stretch, let alone finding money to decorate or renovate a home. Also, fewer people today have the time or know-how to actually do much of the renovation themselves, so renovating or decorating can be expensive options. If the option of buying a new home is available to you, buying new construction can be cheaper and easier in the long run.

If you have the time and cash to put into renovating a home, however, there are significant advantages to be gained: You might be able to purchase a bigger home in a better neighborhood; and brokers say one of the best ways to maximize your investment is to buy a home that needs work and fix it up.

But there are also disadvantages to fixing up a home. Renovating and decorating create mess and chaos; understand ahead of time that during the period of the renovation your house will never be clean. Construction and renovation almost *always* cost more, and take more time, than you plan for. And more than one relationship has been known to end over the turmoil and tumult of construction.

When you look at a home that needs renovation or a gut job (taking a house to its structural bones or guts), you need to understand exactly how much work would be required and acquire a realistic ballpark estimate of how much that work will cost.

Remember: Unless your broker is also a contractor, his or her estimation of how much renovation work costs will likely be dead wrong. Do not rely on his or her estimate. Instead, hire a contractor or architect to tour the home with you before you make an offer. A contractor's or architect's ballpark estimate of renovation and construction costs will be close enough for you to decide how much you want to pay for the home. Just remember, when renovating expect the unexpected, and add 10 to 15 percent to your expert's ballpark estimate. Renovation almost always costs more than you think it will.

For example, if you're in a neighborhood of renovated homes that sell for $175,000, and you see a house that requires a new kitchen, new electrical wiring, repainting, refinishing of floors, and three new windows to make it livable, you must take into consideration the cost of construction and subtract that from the list price. If the house is listed for $175,000 and you figure the renovation will cost $30,000, then the effective list price of that house for you should be $145,000; you might offer something in the high $120,000 range. If, however, every house in the neighborhood needs similar renovations, then $175,000 for the house might be an appropriate price.

Another problem with renovation is that buyers sometimes think they can buy a cheap house and create the house of their dreams. When the time comes to sell the house (in five to seven years), they find they have a white elephant: a house whose value far outstrips the other homes in the neighborhood. This is called "overimprovement." You can overimprove a house to the point where you will never be able to get your money out of it. Try to avoid the situation of selling a $400,000 house in a $100,000 neighborhood.

Daniel recently bought a house that needed a new kitchen. He loves to cook, so he put an $18,000 kitchen in a $160,000 house, and planned to do other repair and renovation work. One day his broker stopped by to say hello and look at his construction work. After admiring his beautiful new kitchen, the broker cautioned Daniel not to spend so much money that he would want to ask more than $250,000 for the house. "The neighborhood won't support a house that's worth more than that. I'll have trouble selling it," the broker told Daniel. He hasn't overimproved his house yet, but he must be careful where he spends his renovation dollars.

First-Time Buyer Tip: If you're thinking about buying a home that needs renovation, be careful to consider what other homes that have been renovated are selling for in the marketplace.

HOW DO I LOOK FOR A HOME?

How Do I Find the Home of My Dreams?

There are two ways to find the right home. Either you can work with a real estate broker or you can do it yourself. Since most of this book is slanted toward buyers who work with brokers, let's spend a few minutes examining how you can find a home on your own and why you might choose to do it that way.

If a seller chooses to sell a home without the help of a broker, it's called "for sale by owner." You might also see the acronym FSBO, pronounced "fizz-bo." Home owners choose to sell their homes themselves for two reasons: They think they can, and they won't have to pay a commission to the selling broker.

You'll find FSBOs listed in your local newspaper's real estate classified advertisements under "Houses for Sale." You might also find them listed in alternative newspapers, weekly or monthly neighborhood newspapers, and local magazines. One of the best ways to find a FSBO is to walk around the neighborhoods you've targeted as being acceptable. FSBO homes usually have a sign posted outside letting prospective buyers know they are for sale.

If you decide you want to tour the inside of a FSBO, simply call the telephone number in the advertisement or on the sign and make an appointment. The home owner will then give you a tour of his or her home. This can be awkward, as you should be looking for every fault and every reason *not* to buy the home. And yet you don't want to insult the home owner, just in case you *do* want to buy the home.

Why would you want to look for a home yourself? Some buyers feel they'll get a better deal from a seller who does not have to pay a commission to a broker. They believe the seller will negotiate down to at least the 6 to 7 percent that would have been paid in commission. Other buyers like FSBOs because it makes them feel as if they are seeing everything that's out there on the market. Of course they aren't because the majority of homes for sale are listed with brokers in a computerized system called a Multiple Listing Service. Access to the MLS is restricted to member brokers and their clients. One caveat: If you're going to buy a home that's a FSBO, be sure you get a good real estate attorney to help you draw up the contract and an excellent home inspector who will thoroughly scrutinize the home.

You can also shop for new construction by yourself, although it may be easier and less time consuming if you go with a broker. New-construction developers will tell you that you don't need a broker, but they will pay the commission to a broker should you choose to use one. If you don't bring a broker with you to the model, and if you don't protect your broker by signing in under his or her name, the broker who represents the developer effectively becomes your broker and may even earn extra commission on your purchase.

Once in a while, the developer will lower the cost of the new construction by the amount that he would have paid in brokerage commission fees. More likely, he'll give you extra upgrades for free or at a reduced cost. Beware: A good broker might be able to extract the same concessions—that's what negotiation is all about. Again, be sure you have a good real estate attorney if you choose to go it alone. (Although it isn't common to hire an inspector for new construction, it's a good idea to have an inspector or someone familiar with new construction to look over the property *before* you close. If you purchase new construction before it's built, it's an excellent idea to have someone familiar with the process to check up on the construction frequently, and to point out any mistakes or shoddy workmanship while the home is still under construction and the errors can be remedied.)

If you decide you don't want to look for a place to buy by yourself, your other option is to use a broker. Brokers come in all different shapes, sizes, and personalities. The benefits of using a broker can be significant.

First, a real estate broker is supposed to be your eyes and legs, prescreening homes on the market and selecting the ones he or she thinks might be right for you. The broker is supposed to do your legwork and walk through these homes to further eliminate ones that won't work for your needs. Finally, a good broker will make your appointments for you, chauffeur you around from showing to showing, help you understand the good and bad about a house, provide you with enough information to determine an offer, and then present your offer to the seller and selling broker. A good broker will educate you about the process and the local real estate market.

By tapping into the local multiple listing service, brokers can pull up all kinds of information, including:

- A list of all homes available in your price range;
- The home's amenities, square footage, most recent tax bill, number and size of bedrooms and bathrooms;
- How long the home has been listed for sale;
- The original price plus any price reduction;
- The home's address and the broker's phone number;
- Other pertinent and interesting facts and figures.

Remember, brokers are only as good as you let them be. If you choose to use a broker, you'll have to learn the difference between conventional, buyer, and discount brokers. You'll also learn how much to tell your broker and when complete honesty may not be entirely appropriate.

QUESTION 8
What Is the Difference Between a Real Estate Agent and a Real Estate Broker? What Is the Difference Between a Realtor® and a Real Estate Broker?

Real estate professionals go by a few different names, although the distinction shouldn't matter much to you, the first-time buyer. The only caveat here is to make certain the broker or agent you choose to work with is a licensed real estate professional. All real estate brokers and sales agents are licensed and regulated by each state. Most states have laws that require brokers and agents to post their licenses in a visible place.

What is the difference between a real estate broker and a real estate agent? To the average home buyer or seller, there isn't too much. Before a broker can take the state brokerage examination, he or she must have started out as a sales agent, completing the required number of hours of classes and passing an examination. To become a broker, an agent must take additional classes, have a specified amount of experience in the field, and pass another exam. Both agents and brokers can assist you equally well in the purchase of property.

Having a real estate broker's license confers certain privileges, including the right to open, run, and own a real estate office, and to work independently of an office. A real estate agent must work for a broker, who is responsible for that agent's actions.

Is it better to work with a broker than to work with a sales agent? Not necessarily. Although it seems that a broker may have more experience or be more knowledgeable than an agent, that is not always the case. Plenty of sales agents have chosen not to become brokers because they have no intention of ever running their own office. The experience and knowledge of an agent who has been working in an area for fifteen years will far surpass that of a brand new broker. You should find the most experienced professional to work with you, regardless of whether he or she is an agent or a broker.

What is the difference between a broker who is a Realtor and a broker who is not? A Realtor is a broker or agent who belongs to the National Association of Realtors (NAR) and subscribes to that organization's code of ethics and conduct. There are around 2 million real estate agents and brokers in the United States, of which around 750,000 belong to the NAR.

Is it better to work with a Realtor than a broker who is not a Realtor? Not necessarily. Again, you want to find the best, most knowledgeable, and most reliable broker or agent. Don't worry about titles, designations, and how many letters follow his or her name.

QUESTION 9
How Do I Choose the Right Broker?

Finding a broker or an agent who meets your needs and personality can be tougher than it sounds. Those buyers who have the worst experiences are often those who just walk into or call their neighborhood shop and ask for anyone at random. That is *not* how you find a good agent or broker. That is how you find a big headache.

Connie is director of career development and advertising for a real estate firm located in Overland Park, Kansas. She has her broker's license and has sold real estate for more than nine years. Connie believes every buyer, but especially a first-timer, should carefully interview several agents and brokers. Here are some of her recommendations: "Have them describe to you how they go about assisting a buyer. Try to get a feel for the agents' philosophy on working with buyers. Try to get a feel for their background and experience level. And be sure to ask them for a résumé. If you're thinking about letting someone represent you in the transaction, I think it's reasonable to expect to see a copy of their résumé."

Connie says she would be leery of any agent who lets you walk into his or her office and then immediately bundles you into his or her car and shows you homes. "They need to interview you," she says. "And first-time buyers generally need an education on the purchase process and understanding what their options are in transactions."

Although Connie recommends working with a heavily experienced agent, she says that sometimes brand-new agents offer excellent service. "That depends on their training and support. It can be a good situation. But more often than not, the more experienced the agent, the more transactions he or she handles in a year, the more situations they're confronted with, the more insight into the closing process they will have."

In addition to looking for an experienced agent, try to find one who suits your personality. If you're an early bird, don't choose someone habitually late. If you're allergic to smoking, don't choose a smoker. If you're extremely organized, don't choose a broker who is constantly losing his or her keys. Over time, or on long days of multiple showings, these little personality quirks will make you crazy.

How do you find a good broker or agent? As in choosing a doctor or an attorney, most people are referred to a broker by their friends or a family member who has recently bought or sold a home and had a good experience. Although it's certainly wise to interview a broker who is referred by someone you know, also interview several other agents who frequently work in your area. Aunt Jeanne's suburban agent may not be the most effective agent to help you find a downtown loft.

It's also important to find someone who won't push you into making a decision before you're ready. You want a broker who will tell you the facts and will help you compare the differences between properties, but you don't want someone who will scare you or pressure you into purchasing a home. Unfortunately, some brokers and agents do pressure buyers to buy. If that happens, you must be tough enough to back away from that pressure and find yourself a new agent. You can also talk with the agent's managing broker about the situation; one of the managing broker's jobs is to smooth out the bumps between agents and buyers.

QUESTION 10

What Is a Seller or Conventional Broker? What Are the Seller Broker's Responsibilities to Me?

First, you should understand there is a significant difference between a seller broker, also known as a conventional broker, and a buyer broker. Buyer brokers represent the interests of the buyer (see Question 11). Seller brokers represent the interests of the seller.

A broker works for the person who pays his or her commission. A seller broker means the seller is paying the commission. A buyer broker means the buyer is responsible for paying the commission (although sometimes the seller may pay a buyer broker's commission; for more information see Question 11).

Since buyer brokerage has only recently caught on around the country (and is not yet offered everywhere), most brokers are still seller or conventional brokers. When a seller broker brings the buyer to the deal, he or she is also called the subagent. Even though they'll take you, the buyer, around to see houses, and appear to work in your best interest, they're still seller brokers. Being a seller broker means he or she has a fiduciary responsibility to the seller, rather than to you, the buyer. The seller broker is required by law to represent the seller's best interest—not yours. These distinctions have caused a tremendous amount of confusion for buyers, who quite naturally assume that the person taking them around and showing them about houses works for them.

Let's be clear on one point: If you haven't hired a buyer broker and signed an exclusivity contract with him or her, you're working with a seller or conventional broker. But confusion amongst buyers still persists. To counteract some of this, many states have adopted an "agency disclosure" law that requires brokers to disclose to the buyer whom they represent. In some states, brokers and agents must make that disclosure in writing. If you live in a state that requires a written disclosure form, you might get something that looks like the following. (See Appendix III for a complete form.)

When you sign the form, you're saying that you understand that the broker or agent works for the seller's best interest and not for yours.

If you're a buyer working with a subagent, there are certain things seller brokers may not do according to the law (which varies slightly from state to state). In general, he or she:

- Cannot tell you what to offer for the property. Because
they work for the seller, they're supposed to help the
seller get his or her list price. You will almost never pay
the list price for property so that's a conflict you will
have with the seller broker.
- Cannot tell you which home to buy if you are deciding
between two. A seller broker works for each seller and
may work for multiple sellers. That's confusing, but if
you like two homes, the seller broker technically works
for each seller, and so should not help you choose one
home over the other.
- Cannot point out the defects of a home, unless they are
hidden, material defects. The seller broker cannot say
anything or do anything that will influence you not to
buy a property. Hidden material defects must be disclosed, however, because they are not visible to the
naked eye. For more information on seller disclosure,
see Question 42.
- May only provide you with comparable data upon request. Seller brokers must provide you with all the infor-

mation you need to come up with a reasonable offer. Ask your seller broker to provide you with a list of "comps" detailing how much other homes in the neighborhood, similar in size and amenities to the one you like, sold for in the past six months. Also ask the broker to provide you with a list of current like listings and their list prices. It's important to know the difference between the asking and sales prices of homes in the area.

Of course, some seller brokers provide you with all these things anyway. It's understandable why they do it: A broker relies on referrals in order for his or her business to grow. If everyone refers two buyers or sellers, the agent's or broker's client list pyramids, and after a few years he or she could have a client list numbering in the hundreds. Seller brokers *want* you to have a good experience buying a home. They *want* it to be easy. They *want* you to like them. They *want* you to refer your friends to them. Before you start believing that conventional brokers won't be able to help you buy a home as effectively as a buyer broker, let me reassure you that is not always the case. For dozens of years conventional brokers were the only game in town. They've helped millions of buyers successfully purchase homes.

Many seller brokers pride themselves on being full-service firms, and since they have every incentive to close the deal—after all, they get paid only at the closing—the broker should be delighted to provide you with the names of various mortgage brokers, inspectors, and attorneys. (Always get several recommendations for each service. That way you can properly interview the prospective attorney or inspector and choose the best person for the job.)

The various changes in state laws governing brokers who are

subagents of the seller require that you be more aware of the shifting nature of the relationship. However, a good broker (whether buyer or seller) will be responsive to your needs. That puts the onus on you to be well informed about what you want and how you intend to get it.

Remember, you want to work with the very best broker you can. A great seller broker may be a better choice for you than a lousy buyer broker.

QUESTION 11
What Is a Buyer Broker and Should I Use One?

We've established that the broker works for the one who pays the commission. Traditionally, that's the seller. But for an increasing number of buyers, the conventional broker's role poses a conflict of interest. They ask: How can a broker have my best interest at heart when he or she is being paid by the seller? How can a broker help me find the best property at the best price when he or she is bound legally and financially to serve the seller's best interest?

If you find yourself having these qualms about traditional brokerage, you may want to consider buyer brokerage. You find a buyer broker you want to work with and then sign an exclusivity contract that states that you will not look for a house with another broker for a specified period of time. The buyer broker will hunt for homes that are appropriate for your needs and budget. He or she will negotiate every facet of the contract, striving to get you the best price and terms. Some buyer brokers will even help you find the best mortgage and home owner's insurance with the most favorable terms. Then the broker will represent you at closing.

Tom Hathaway, cofounder, president, and chief executive officer of The Buyer's Agent, Inc., a nationwide network of buyer brokers based in Germantown, Tennessee, says his brokers offer twenty-six services to their clients, including negotiating the best price for the home, finding the best mortgage, and hiring the best inspector.

If you're wondering how a buyer broker might treat you differently from a seller broker, you're not alone. If the seller broker breaks the law by providing you with insights and information about various sellers and their homes and advises you on which house to bid and on how much to offer, then there may not be a great difference in service. (Then again, the seller broker could be liable to the seller for breaching his fiduciary duty to the seller. But that's not your concern.)

On the other hand, a buyer broker is completely on your side, bound by contract to provide you with all the information you need to buy your dream home at the lowest price possible and on the most favorable terms.

Sharon, a sales agent in west suburban Chicago, says: "When I'm working for the seller, my job is to bring in the best offer. When I'm working as a buyer broker, I feel free to give that kind of advice as well as to suggest different pricing [strategies] my clients may offer."

Experts say buyers generally have trouble with two facets of buyer brokerage: the exclusivity agreement and the payment for services rendered. When a buyer opts for buyer brokerage, he or she is asked to sign an exclusivity agreement. According to most of these contracts, the buyer agrees to work only with the buyer broker for a certain length of time. If the buyer purchases a home within the exclusivity period, he or she will owe the broker a fee. Sounds simple enough, but buyers, who are used to changing agents at will, sometimes find the idea of exclusivity disquieting. If you feel that a ninety-day exclusivity period is too long, offer a thirty-day term that is renewable. A good buyer broker will understand your nervousness (you're not the first to feel this way) and should be happy to make you feel comfortable; thirty days will be enough time for you to decide if you like the buyer broker's service.

Payment of fee is another issue—especially for first-time buyers who are often short on cash—although it is the fee that guarantees the buyer broker's loyalty. Buyer brokerage fees can be paid either as a flat payment, hourly, or as a percentage of the purchase price of the home.

In the real world, however, the buyer broker's compensation often ends up being paid by the seller. What happens is the seller's agent agrees to split the commission with the buyer broker, just as the seller's agent would agree to split the commission with a conventional broker.

Do buyer brokers ever pressure their clients to buy something if their exclusivity contract is about to expire? Most brokers say no, but first-time buyers Dawn and Bill don't agree. They say they've had a nasty experience with a buyer broker who applied enormous pressure and even took the couple to court. (The judge threw the broker's case out of court and forced him to pay both side's legal fees.)

There are many reasons to choose to work with a buyer broker, but the most obvious one is hardly ever mentioned. Because the buyer broker is paid by the buyer, he or she is free to bring the buyer to any property that is available, including those that are for sale by owner. Mark, an architect who purchases homes for rehabilitation and resale, has used both conventional and buyer brokers. Recently, he made an offer to purchase a for-sale-by-owner home with his buyer broker. "The property wasn't listed in the multiple-listing service. A conventional broker wouldn't have even found it."

Is a buyer broker the right choice for you? That depends on

how comfortable you are with the concepts of exclusivity and being responsible for the broker's commission. If Mark bought the FSBO property, he would have had to pay his agent's commission. More buyers, especially first-timers, are choosing buyer brokers because they like having someone represent them. Some companies who transfer employees from one location to another and pay their moving costs, ask the relocation company to give their employees a buyer broker option.

As when making any selection, interview a buyer broker and a seller broker and decide who will help you the most.

What Is the Typical Real Estate Commission?

Although this is more a question for sellers, it can be important for buyers to be aware of how much commission is actually being paid. By law, there is no standard real estate commission. If you ask seller brokers what is the typical commission in your area, they should tell you it's negotiable. And technically it is. But more often than not, sellers will offer to pay around 6 percent of the sales price of the property to their broker, who then splits the commission in half with the subagent, who brings the buyer to the table.

If you hire a buyer broker, the buyer broker will negotiate a commission up front, either hourly, a flat fee, or a percentage of the sales price of the house. The average is around 2.5 to 3 percent, depending on the price range in which you're shopping. Buyers should be aware of the commission rates and whether it is a buyer's or seller's market in their area. If they are in a seller's market, commissions might be below what is typically acceptable for that area. If the commission is normally 6 percent, it might be 5.5 percent or less, since the demand is high for the seller's property and the seller broker doesn't have to work too hard.

If it is a buyer's market, you might find the seller offering more than the typical commission to entice brokers to bring their buyers. If the typical commission is 6 percent, you might see the seller offering 7 percent, with 4 percent going to the subagent who brings the buyer. Although most agents won't try to sell you a piece of property just because it has an extra-high commission attached, they might bring you to see it.

QUESTION 13
What Is a Discount Broker? And When Should I Use One?

Discount brokerage is an emerging trend, whose success has been encouraged during these recent recessionary times. Currently, not every area has a discount broker.

The basic concept is this: The discount broker gives you the names and addresses of properties for sale from the local multiple-listing service (MLS), but you do all the legwork, look at every home that might possibly be right for you, work out your own mortgage, present your own contract, submit your own counteroffer, arrange for your own inspectors, do your own walk-through, and make your own follow-up calls. If you do all the work, then the discount broker will give you a portion of the commission he or she receives.

Why should the discount broker receive anything if you're doing all the work? Good question. To begin with, the discount broker has access to the MLS, which lists all the property for sale in the area. That's where you find out all the information about homes for sale, such as their size, price, and number of bedrooms and bathrooms. It's a very useful list to have, but access is strictly limited to member agents and brokers and their clients. By sharing the commission with the discount broker, you're essentially buying access to the local MLS.

Discount brokerage firms give back up to 50 percent of their share of the commission at closing. On a $100,000 property, your share might be as much as $1,500. That $1,500 might well pay the points for your mortgage, or cover the cost of repainting the interior of the house after you move in. And while $1,500 may not seem like it's worth the effort, discount brokers say that there are those home buyers, particularly first-time buyers, who need every nickel to buy a home and are willing to put in the time and effort needed.

Here's how it works: The realty company that works with the buyer typically receives about half the commission the seller pays to his or her listing agent's company. If the commission is 6 percent, each side gets 3 percent. A discount brokerage buyer splits his or her 3 percent commission with you, minus any "extras." The "extras" are where the buyer has to be careful. The discount brokerage firm puts a price tag on every service it provides for you, including every telephone call or each showing. Usually a minimum number of showings is included in the deal, but if the broker shows you any additional properties, the fees for these pay-as-you-go services are deducted from your portion of the commission.

For example, there is a discount brokerage firm in Chicago that charges between 1 and 4 percentage points off the commission refund for each service it performs for you. So if you need the broker to place a follow-up call to your lender, the company would reduce your refund by 1 percent for each call. If the total possible refund is $1,500, each phone call would cost you $15.

The general caveat for real estate services holds true here also: Don't necessarily use the first broker you find. Try to find more than one discount broker, then interview each at length. Ask for a résumé and references, and then call those people and ask them how much time they put into their home purchase and how much money they received back from the broker. Discount brokerage is best used by buyers who have a clear idea of what they want, or who have been through the process before. But first-time buyers who are willing to put in a little "sweat equity" might be able to save some money.

QUESTION 14

How Much Should My Broker Know About How Much We Can Afford to Spend on a Home?

Mark and Amy recently discussed their search for the perfect home on Long Island. Like most first-time buyers, they had a general idea of the process, but only a vague concept of the fine lines the real estate world has drawn between broker-seller and broker-buyer relationships. As discussed earlier in this book, all brokers are obligated to work on the seller's behalf, except where the broker is a buyer's broker, meaning he or she has a written fiduciary responsibility to the buyer. The reason is clear. The seller pays the commission of both brokers, the one who lists and shows the property, and the subbroker, who brings the ready, willing, and able buyer to the table.

Mark and Amy found a beautiful house in a tiny, wooded community on Long Island, about an hour and a half from Manhattan. The house was listed at $350,000. They put in a low-ball offer for $260,000, but told "their" (a seller broker) broker they would go as high as $300,000.

That was a strategic mistake. By telling the broker they were willing to go spend as much as $300,000 for the property, they were precluded from getting the property for less. (As it turned out, they didn't buy that house.)

Why? "Their" broker was obligated to bring the seller the $260,000 offer, but should have also informed the seller that the buyers would go as high as $300,000. If the seller had responded favorably to the lower bid, he or she might have been persuaded to sell the property for less than $300,000. But once informed that the buyers would go as high as 300,000, the seller has no incentive to make the deal for less than that.

If, as required by law, the broker actually told the seller that Mark and Amy were willing to bid as much as $300,000 for the house, then their effective bid would have been $300,000 rather than $260,000.

How can you protect yourself? Often, the best course of action is to be selective in what you tell any seller broker. Never tell your broker the top price you'd be willing to pay for a piece of property. Always assume that whatever financial information you convey to the broker will be transmitted to the other broker and ultimately to the seller. Play your cards close to the vest.

How Do I Know if My Broker Is Doing a Good Job?

Whether you use a buyer broker or a seller broker, the first objective of that broker or agent is to assist you in finding a property that's suitable and affordable.

A broker or agent is doing a good job if he or she listens closely to your wants and needs and asks you thoughtful follow-up questions that prompt further explanation. Whether or not the agent is doing a good job becomes more apparent once you start seeing some homes. Do the homes you're being shown match up with what you've told the broker you want and need? Do they match up with the priorities on your wish and reality lists? If your broker is totally off the mark, then he or she might not have been paying attention. Or perhaps you didn't communicate effectively and honestly with your broker.

Here are some clues to help you know if your broker is competent:

- Do you feel the broker is paying attention to you? Or does his or her attention wane when you are speaking?
- Does the agent ask you a lot of questions? Has the agent ever asked you why you're looking for a four-bedroom home or one that has an exercise studio? By asking, the agent may be able to better understand your motivations.
- If you've worked with the agent several times and all the properties you've been shown were not even close matches to what you had hoped to find, you might have a problem.

- If you're working with a buyer broker and the seller suddenly seems to know your every move during the negotiation, your agent might be spilling the beans and breaking his or her fiduciary duty to you, the buyer.
- If your broker never returns your phone calls, that's a clear signal that he or she is not being conscientious.

If you decide that your agent hasn't done a good job, or has mistreated you in any way, don't hesitate to file a complaint with the agent's managing broker. If you are not satisfied with the response you receive from the managing broker, feel free to file a complaint with the state agency that regulates real estate professionals. In any case, unless you have signed a buyer brokerage exclusivity agreement, you can always find another broker. And if you can't break your exclusivity agreement, it is for a limited duration, and no one can make you work with someone you don't like. Simply wait out the expiration of the contract.

QUESTION 16
How Can I Help in the Search for a Home If I Use a Broker?

Brokers across the country say the most important thing you can do is be *honest* about what you really want in a home and what you actually need. Most buyers think they're being honest, but they may not turn that into usable information for the broker. You can say you need a four-bedroom house, but if you don't tell the broker that you need that fourth bedroom for an office, you're not being as helpful as you could.

After honesty, brokers ask that buyers be flexible with their time and responsive to their calls. If a broker agrees to spend an entire Saturday with you and sets up a day of showings, it's extremely frustrating if you decide to cancel on Saturday morning. (Of course, if there's an emergency, communicate that to the broker and reschedule.) If a broker calls with an urgent message about a property, call back immediately. You might have received an answer to your offer. Or a new, hot property might have come on the market in the neighborhood you want.

Brokers also like loyalty. If you've taken up six months of a broker's time, and things are going well, it's not appropriate to suddenly switch to your relative or to a discount broker. Legally, of course, you have the right to switch at any time. But if you want your broker to treat you well, you must return the favor. If you want to use Aunt Edna because she'll give you a portion of her commission back, use her for the entire process. Don't waste another broker's time.

You can help your broker find properties you might like by looking through the real-estate-for-sale ads in the local paper. If your broker has a good handle on the local market, he or she has probably seen most of the properties for sale. But if you see something interesting in the paper, ask about it.

Finally, you can help your broker by trying to learn everything you can about the neighborhood you've chosen. Walk around and try it on for size. Visit the local grocery store, dry cleaners, schools, and parks. Drive around at various times of the day, so that you can experience "rush hour" traffic. Get a feel for the people who live and work there. Educate yourself rather than relying on your broker for lessons.

How Should I Interpret the Home Description in the Local Newspaper? Or in Broker Listing Sheets?

The key to understanding real estate ads is to assume that the broker is putting the best face on a bad situation. That's not to say that brokers are being dishonest. Most of them aren't. But if Mr. Jones's apartment has a four-inch-wide view of Lake Michigan sandwiched between two towers, Mr. Jones's broker will undoubtedly put "lake view" somewhere in his or her ad. Brokers know that most people want to have a good view from their windows—even if they're going to be away at work during the day and won't see it until night. (Actually, I've always been amazed at people who want to have a view of Lake Michigan or any other body of water because at night it's completely black and you can't see anything anyway.) Usually the more expensive property is congregated around whatever view is the star attraction: In Chicago, it's Lake Michigan; in Boston, it's the Charles River; in San Francisco, it's the bay; in New York . . . well, in New York, everything is expensive. But the buildings that overlook Central Park are *really* expensive.

So in reading an advertisement, how do you distinguish between an apartment that really has a great view from one that has a six-inch-wide strip of blue? How can you tell a home that's really in move-in condition from one that needs to be completely redecorated? That's the tough part. But remember: The broker will usually be very specific about a true feature. If the kitchen is new with top appliances, the ad may say "gourmet kitchen with top appliances." If the view really does include Lake Michigan (or Central Park, or the Bay, or whatever), it will say so.

Here's a list of key phrases to watch out for and what they may mean (in a tough, cynical world):

Phrase	*What It Might Mean*
Fantastic View	Could be the best view of your life; or there might be little, if any, view, and you might have to crane your neck out the window to see it.
Treetop View	The apartment is about four floors up. During the summer your view may be blocked by the leaves.
Just Renovated	Probably needs a minimal amount of redecorating.
Move-In Condition	May be in pristine condition, or you may need to paint.
Needs Work	Could mean anything from new paint and carpeting to major structural renovation.
Handyman's Special	Probably a gut job; it's likely the home needs serious renovations and may even be unlivable.
Bright and Sunny	Maybe it has a southern exposure, or maybe every room is painted bright yellow.
Dollhouse	A word brokers use to describe a home that is too small to accommodate a growing family; it may also be too small to accommodate a single person.

Phrase	What It Might Mean
Oversized Rooms	Don't expect Queen Elizabeth's great hall; could mean truly large rooms or anything over nine by nine feet.
Street Parking	The broker is telling you the home doesn't come with a parking space and that you can park easily on the street. If the home is located in a congested metro area, don't believe it. It isn't always easy or desirable to park on the street.
Deeded Parking Space	You get a parking space. It could be indoor (garage) or outdoor, but it's yours.
Round-the-Clock Security	Could mean a twenty-four-hour doorman (though brokers usually say this), a nighttime security person patrolling the premises, a television security system, or a buzzer system.
Newer Mechanicals	Could've been replaced last year or five years ago. You may have to replace expensive mechanical systems within five years.
Newer Roof	You may have to replace the roof within five years.
Needs New Roof	The roof probably leaks. Check for water marks during the inspection. Does the roof need a "tear-off," where several layers of old roofing must be pried off and replaced? Or could you (for a lot less money) add another layer of asphalt shingles?

Phrase	*What It Might Mean*
Oversized Lot	In Chicago, which has one of the smallest lot sizes in the country, an oversized lot could mean something as small as 30 by 125 feet. (The standard lot size is 25 by 125 feet. The phrase usually means you're getting a little extra grass.)

The concept of square footage requires a bit more explanation. As you tour different homes, brokers will give you a listing sheet for the property. On it you will see that the size of the unit is given in square feet. A square foot is a two-dimensional square measuring one foot by one foot. Homes are measured the same way. But the truth is, the square footage given can be a little deceptive. If your sheet says a house has two thousand square feet, you may assume it's a big house. But when you get there, it may not feel that big. Why? Because a home's square footage is supposed to be calculated by measuring the exterior perimeter. So in addition to losing the interior wall space, you also lose the exterior wall space. Although it doesn't sound like much, it can be.

Brokers want you to think you're getting the most for your money, so they'll put down the largest number for the home's square footage that they can get away with. In my building, a vintage co-op built in the 1920s, I've seen our unit listed as low as seventeen hundred square feet to a high of twenty-three hundred square feet. Six hundred square feet is an entire apartment in New York!

SELECTIVITY — HOW DO I IDENTIFY WHAT I NEED VERSUS WHAT I LIKE?

How Do I Become Selective When Choosing a Home and How Do My Wish List and Reality List Help Me?

Joanne set up ten showings for a couple who were first-time buyers. The couple went to the first home and fell in love with it. They wanted to make an offer on the spot. But Joanne, an agent in Pompton Plains, New Jersey, has a policy: Never let a first-time buyer buy a home at the first showing. "First showings are all about emotion," she says. "You have to get some distance and some perspective before choosing the right home."

Joanne showed the rest of the homes to the couple. They liked three of the ten, including the first. And then they had to choose. The issue of selectivity is very tough for first-time buyers. Nearly every home is going to look a lot better than the cramped one-bedroom apartment you've been renting for the past five years. But it's important not to jump at the first house that appears to meet your needs. Why? Because in addition to meeting your basic needs, you might also be able to get a few things you want.

Relatives and friends help lend perspective. Mike, a sales associate in York, Pennsylvania, says family members can help first-time buyers become more selective about a home, especially if they come to the first showings. If they come to the first showing, they feel as if they're part of the process. "If they come only for the second showing, they feel compelled to find something wrong with the house," Mike explains.

Listening to other people's advice is part of learning how to be selective. But selectivity is also about defining your own tastes and trusting your own judgment. It's about putting aside emotion in favor of reason and logic.

You start the process by determining how much you know about the type of home you'd like to buy. Let's say you aren't sure whether to live in a condo or buy a ranch. Have your real estate agent show you a wide variety of homes, say a ranch, a Victorian, a condo, a town house, and a new-construction subdivision. Compare the styles and feel of each environment. Once you've identified which housing style you like best— maybe it's a new-construction subdivision—have your broker set up showings of a handful of houses that fall into your price range and size and amenity requirements.

Next, you need to compare what you like and dislike about each of the homes you've seen. After each showing, Joanne provides her buyers with a listing sheet with a photograph of each home. "When we get back in the car, I immediately ask them to write down what they liked and didn't like about the house. After they've seen five or six homes, I ask them to throw out two or three," Joanne says.

Joanne recommends you look at the properties that come closest to your needs and wants. Then begin to eliminate those that don't add up. Try to keep the list of homes you love to no more than two or three. If another "fabulous" home comes up, compare it to the others you love and try to sort out which are the new top two.

Selectivity isn't easy because it forces you to make decisions about what you like and don't like. Also, the issues aren't clear cut. Each home will have pluses and minuses: One may be in a good school district, the other might have four oversized bedrooms and a nice backyard. Your wish list and reality list can help. If you've been honest about your priorities and understand that reality will temper the amenities you'll get with your first home, the lists should help you step back and take most of the emotion out of the decision.

QUESTION 19
When I Go to a Showing, What Should I Look For?

The most important thing you can do at a showing is not to look at the house as a home but as a house: four walls, floor, and a roof. Brokers say that first-time buyers often get caught up in the moment. There's a rush of attention thrust upon you, with brokers willing to do almost anything to get you to like them and their properties.

Mary, a sales agent in San Antonio, Texas, says she tries to have people look dispassionately at the homes that are for sale. She tells her first-time buyers to inspect everything, every nook and cranny, every corner of the house. Pick up rugs to inspect the condition of the floor, she recommends. Open every door. Poke through the closets. "I actually prefer to show a vacant house rather than one with furniture in it because by the time the buyers get halfway through, they're looking at the antique sewing machine, not the bones of the house. Inevitably, conversation turns to the great bedspread or grandfather clock," Mary says.

On your first showing, you are looking for a home that meets your basic needs:

Is it in the right location?

Does it have enough bedrooms and bathrooms?

Is there enough storage space?

Is there parking?

Is it safe?

If the home meets the basic requirements, then start to look for how many wish list items it includes:

Is there an extra bedroom and/or bathroom?

Is there a double vanity in the second bathroom?

Is there a garden or deck?

Is there a separate laundry room?

Is there a basement or crawl space?

Is the garage attached?

Can the kids walk to school?

Is there a wood-burning fireplace or a gas fireplace?

What is the condition of the house, its appliances, roof, foundation, walls, mechanicals, wiring, etc?

Start with the general items, then get more specific.

First-Time Buyer Tip: If you're having trouble remembering which home had more of the features you want, or are finding it difficult to rank the homes based on their amenities, try this simple rating system. Assign five points to each item in the top five spots on your wish list and reality list. Assign one point to the remaining items on each list. As you go through each house, check off all the features it has on the wish list and reality list. Add up the points and put that number at the top of the listing sheet. It should help you nonemotionally rank the homes. If you want to be more specific, make a few copies of your wish and reality checklists and attach the checked-off copies to the listing sheet.

QUESTION 20
How Can I Remember Each Home When I've Seen So Many?

It's difficult to keep all the homes straight in your head, particularly if you've toured more than ten houses. Brokers know that after seeing five to six homes, buyers tend to start confusing homes. That's why brokers suggest you limit your favorite homes to two or three.

Here are some tips to help keep each house organized in your mind:

1. Keep a written log. You can include the date you saw the house, time of the showing, and who was there (your broker, the seller broker, the owner, your mother, your father-in-law, etc.).
2. Photocopy and enlarge a map of the areas in which you're most interested. As you go through an area, use a yellow highlighter to mark the streets you've looked

at. Use a different-colored highlighter (red, blue, or green) to mark the various homes you've actually seen in the area.

3. Put the listing sheet given to you at each house to good use. Choose a few specific or spectacular or memorable things (lime-green kitchen, beautiful greenhouse, attached four-car garage, sauna in basement, pine floors, plastic wood paneling in basement) about the house and write them down on the back of the listing sheet. Draw out the floor plan.

4. Staple a completed wish and reality checklist to the listing sheet.

5. A picture is worth a thousand words. Invest in, or borrow, a Polaroid instant camera and a few packs of film. An interior and exterior photo of each house will surely jog your memory later that evening, or even a few weeks later. Be sure to mark the photo with the address of each house. Better yet, staple it to your listing sheet. (Be sure to ask the listing agent for permission to take an interior photo. You do not need anyone's permission to take an exterior photo.)

6. If you're buying the home with another person (spouse, girlfriend, boyfriend, business partner, child, parent, etc.), be sure the other people involved have a chance to write down what they think about the house. If you have children over the age of eight, they will have definite likes and dislikes about a house. I'm not telling you to rely on their judgments, but they should certainly be included in the process, perhaps at the second, or third, showing.

How Do I Know When It's Time for a Second Showing?

Sales agent Joanne says a lot depends on the buyer's reaction to a home. If a home appears to meet a buyer's needs and the buyer has an emotional reaction to it, Joanne will immediately set up a second showing. Brokers say you'll know when you're ready for a second showing. It usually happens after you've seen four to five houses, and despite doing everything suggested above for remembering which house is which, you can't seem to place that one house. Or you'll find that you still like a certain house best and want to go back for an extended look. Brokers may schedule first showings twenty minutes apart so that you can see five to six homes in a morning or afternoon, including travel time. Fifteen minutes should be enough time for you to decide whether the home is a possibility or an impossibility. You'll say either maybe or forget it.

Second showings are longer, starting at about a half hour in length. During a second showing you want to reconfirm that the things you liked about the house the first time are still appealing. Or you may decide that the house really isn't right, and cross it off your list. If you do like the house, the second showing is where you should begin to examine the home's structure and mechanicals. Although you will hire a home inspector for a professional inspection, each inspection will set you back between $150 to $300. If you know what to look for, you can spot problems early on in the game and save yourself some money.

Here are some things to keep in mind:

- *Overall impression of the exterior.* Does the house seem in good shape? Is it sound? Step back: Are the lines of the house straight? Does the roof sag? If the house is brick, is the mortar between the bricks cracked or chinked? Is the paint peeling? Is the aluminum siding dented, dirty, or in good shape?
- *Roof.* Are the shingles curling or lifting? Ask the owners how old the roof is and if there have been any problems. A new roof should last between fifteen and twenty-five years. If the house has a tile or slate roof, it could last for fifty years or more, but might be overwhelmingly expensive to fix or replace.
- *Windows and door frames.* Are they in good shape? Are there storm windows? Has the caulk dried out and pulled away? Are they cracked? Does air come in?
- *Overall impression of the interior.* Does the home appear to be sound? Do the wood floors creak when you walk on them? Are the stairs shaky? Is the kitchen or bath linoleum tile peeling or bubbled? Are there discolored patches on the walls or ceiling? Are there other signs of leaks? Is the plaster cracked? Is the paint or wallpaper peeling? Are the walls and ceiling straight? Do doors, cupboards, and drawers open easily?
- *Attic or crawl space.* Is there insulation? Has it been laid properly? Is there a fan? Are there air leaks? Is there poor ventilation?
- *Plumbing and electricity.* Turn on all faucets and showers and bathtubs. Is everything working? Do they drain well? How is the water pressure? Does the water have a funny smell? Does the home use city water or have its own well? Do all the lights seem to work? Check the

fuse box or circuit breaker. Are there enough electrical outlets, or is everything connected with extension cords? Are there enough telephone jacks?

- *Basement.* Are there cracks in the walls or foundation? Does it smell musty, stale, or damp? Does the basement leak? Is the house in a flood plain?
- *Mechanicals.* How old are the hot water heater and furnace systems? Is there an air-conditioning system or are there window units? How old are the window units and do they come with the house? Ask to see the heating, electricity, and water bills.
- *Pests.* Is there evidence of termites? Cockroaches? Mice? Check any wooden beams for tiny holes or piles of sawdust.

Second showings take the selectivity issue we discussed earlier one step further. In a second showing, you should sit down on the furniture and try to imagine living in the home. You should look around and think about where you would put your furniture. How would you feel about coming home after a hard day's work? Where would you relax? Can you see yourself cooking in the kitchen? Will your television hutch fit in the living room? Is the bedroom quiet enough for sleeping? Open the windows and listen to the sounds of the neighborhood. Are there noisy wind chimes? Children? Dogs? Dump trucks? Airplanes (is the house in a flight path)? Traffic? Other noises?

At this point, you might be able to make up your mind about a house. For some first-time buyers, the second showing clinches it and they make an offer. However, a lot of first-time buyers need a third, or even fourth, showing.

Third Showings

After living in our co-op for a few years, Sam and I decided to sell and buy a house. We put the apartment on the market and a couple came and looked at it on five separate occasions. The rule of thumb is, if you don't have a contract in hand when you come for the *fifth* showing, don't come at all. If you ask for a third showing, the brokers and the seller are going to think you're really interested. They're going to expect you to make a serious offer. (Our five-timers never made an offer to purchase our unit, and we eventually took it off the market.)

If the third showing comes and goes and there's no offer, the seller is going to begin to get impatient. If you then call and ask for a fourth showing, the brokers will have to persuade the seller to go along with it. It's a lot of work preparing for a showing. The seller will have to clean up the house, pack everyone off, and basically clear the decks. It's a major maneuver, because most of our homes don't look like those featured in *Architectural Digest* or *House Beautiful*.

By the time you ask for a fifth showing, the seller has given up on you and is more interested in the next buyers who are scheduled to come through the door. If you do put in an offer after a fifth showing, the seller may not treat it very seriously, especially if it's a low-ball offer, just because you've wasted his or her (and everyone else's) time.

I can hear you howling, "But I wanted to be sure! It's a big investment—the biggest investment of my life!" All that's true, but five showings is a great inconvenience to a seller, particularly if there is no offer. Still, take your time. Be sure. As you become more familiar with it, the process of buying a home moves faster.

Buying a Home on the First Showing

Some brokers say first-time buyers don't really need second or third or fourth showings. They say, if you've been honest with the broker and honest with yourself in filling out your wish and reality lists, the broker will lead you to several homes that will work for you.

Sales agent Mike says he tries to eliminate the need for second showings by picking homes that most closely match the buyer's needs and wants. He does, however, encourage second showings if the buyer initially sees the house at night. "If I've done a good job," he notes, "they'll be ready to make an offer after only two outings. My first-time buyers rarely need to see more than ten properties" to find one they love.

When Do I Know I've Found the Right House?

Here's the most important thing you can learn about buying a home: *There is more than one right home.*

This is such an important concept that I'm going to repeat it: There is more than one right home. Sometimes buyers are so overcome with emotion that they become fixated on one particular property. They focus all of their energy and attention on this property and either may not get it, or may overpay for it.

There is more than one right home. When you go out looking, try to retain a little bit of perspective. Don't get emotionally involved with the seductive process of buying a home (it's spending money, a lot of money). Real estate attorneys routinely advise their clients *not* to fall in love with property. "It's not wise because if you fall in love with a house and then you have the inspection and something's terribly wrong, you're going to want to buy the house anyway and that may not be in your best interest," says one attorney.

Sometimes brokers will seem to encourage you to fall in love with a house. They'll say things like, "Isn't it beautiful?" or "I could spend my whole life here" or "You'll be so happy here" or "Don't you just love this place?" Of course they want you to fall in love with a house. You'll buy it. They'll receive their commission and go on to the next first-time buyer. You, on the other hand, will end up spending the next five to seven *years* in that home. But despite the admonitions *not* to fall in love with a home, *not* to become fixated on one particular piece of property, people do it all the time. Including me. I fell in love with our vintage co-op with a wood-burning fireplace. We could have bought a new-construction house we saw on a huge lot (for Chicago) in a nice neighborhood that in the first five years went up significantly in value. But no, I was completely enamored with this twenty-four-hour doorman, no-parking building. I saw all the pluses, and none of the minuses, a typical symptom of "first-timeritis."

There is, however, a difference between falling in love with something you've seen and recognizing that you could buy a piece of property and successfully live there for whatever length of time.

Sales agent Joanne says she can tell when her buyers find the right house by the look of joy on their faces. "If they sit down on the couch, it's a good sign. If they're trying to decide where to put their furniture, it's a very good sign. If they've got a special glow on their faces, it's the right house."

In a few years, the home that's right today may seem small and cramped for your growing family. You'll change, and as your fortunes increase, today's dream home may seem like a starter home: You'll reset your sights on that golf course development, or a better neighborhood or school district. Your cozy kitchen will suddenly seem too small for your growing family. Where did all the space go, you'll wonder. And then it will be time to find your next dream house.

AFFORDABILITY — HOW DO I KNOW WHAT I CAN AFFORD?

QUESTION 23
How Much Can I Afford?

How much house can you afford? The answer most real estate experts give is this: If you can afford to rent and have cash for a down payment, you can probably afford to buy. But the easiest way to find out how much you can afford is to get prequalified. You can either do it yourself or stop by your local lender and ask them to prequalify you.

If you have the lender prequalify you, you do not need to tie yourself in by paying an application fee and actually applying for the mortgage. You can save that until after you've found the home you want to buy and then you can comparison shop to find the best mortgage deal. Lenders will be delighted to prequalify you in a preliminary way, with no obligation, because it means they get an opportunity to pitch their wares to you.

Prequalifying is a relatively painless process. They'll ask you a few simple questions about your debts and assets and then apply some debt-to-income ratios that have proven successful over the years. And then they will tell you a number, which is the amount of mortgage you can support with your income, assets, and liabilities.

Or you can figure out for yourself exactly how much house you can afford to buy. Let's do a quick calculation. If you are paying $600 per month in rent, and you assume the home you're buying will require around $100 per month in real estate taxes and insurance, you're left with $500. Multiplied by twelve, that annual rent payment of $6,000 can pay a $60,000 mortgage, if you assume the interest rate is 10 percent. If you assume an interest rate of 8 percent, that $6,000 annual rent payment can support a $75,000 mortgage.

The two percentage points less make a huge difference. The following chart shows how sliding interest rates can drastically affect how much house you can afford to buy. At 4 percent interest (the beginning rate of some adjustable-rate mortgages (ARMs), $500 per month in rent can support a $150,000 mortgage, excluding real estate taxes and insurance.

Interest Rate	@$500/Month	@$750/Month	@$1,000/Month
4 percent	$150,000	$225,000	$300,000
5 percent	$120,000	$180,000	$240,000
6 percent	$100,000	$150,000	$200,000
7 percent	$ 85,714	$128,571	$171,429
8 percent	$ 75,000	$112,500	$150,000
9 percent	$ 66,666	$100,000	$133,333
10 percent	$ 60,000	$ 90,000	$120,000
11 percent	$ 54,545	$ 81,818	$109,090
12 percent	$ 50,000	$ 75,000	$100,000

Real estate experts tell us home buyers can buy more "house" than they think. The last three years have been the most affordable for home buyers in the last thirty years. Mortgage interest rates have fallen from their high of 18 percent in the early 1980s to 10 percent in the late 1980s to well below that today.

If interest rates are 10 percent, you can afford to buy something that costs somewhere between two (if you're conservative) to two and a half times your income. This assumes you have 20 percent in cash to put down on a house and little long-standing debt (like the car you bought with a loan or any credit card debt). If interest rates fall to 8 percent you may be able to buy a home that costs more than three times your income.

For example, if your combined family income minus debt payments is $50,000 per year, and interest rates are at 10 percent, conventional wisdom suggests that you can afford to buy a house that costs around $100,000. If interest rates are 8 percent, your $50,000-per-year income might stretch far enough to buy a home that costs between $150,000 and $190,000, depending on how much you can put down in cash.

How do mortgage companies specifically determine how much you can afford to pay for your mortgage? Mortgage companies, called "lenders," have developed debt-to-income (the amount of debt compared with your income) ratios through trial and error through the years. All lenders more or less follow the same ratios. They've determined that you can afford to pay between *28 and 36 percent* of your gross income in debt service. That means that altogether, your mortgage principal and interest payments, real estate taxes, insurance, car loan, and credit card payments may not exceed 36 percent of your gross income.

In the last few years, however, several of the largest mortgage investors (who control the way mortgages are made) have somewhat relaxed this debt-to-income ratio. The Federal National Mortgage Association (Fannie Mae), the nation's largest investor in home mortgages, is a private corporation federally chartered to provide financial products and services that increase the availability and affordability of housing for low-, moderate-, and middle-income Americans.

At the beginning of the 1990s, Fannie Mae decided it would extend the upper limit of the debt-to-income ratio of 28:36 to 38 in some cases. That upper limit has even reached 39 and 40 percent of gross income in very special circumstances, particularly where state and local government funds were being used to help provide the down payment. Although the extra 3 to 4 percent doesn't sound like much, this is ground-breaking stuff. Suddenly, if your family's gross income minus debts is $50,000, and interest rates are 10 percent, you could buy a house worth $125,000 to 140,000, a significant difference in many communities.

Figuring Out How Much Loan Payment You Can Carry

Down payment aside (see Questions 59 and 60), brokers say you should only spend between 25 and 33 percent of your monthly gross (before taxes) pay on housing. Here's a chart to help you figure out how much loan payment your income can carry:

1 Gross monthly income from all sources: _____
2 Divide by four (25%) or three (33%): _____
3 Subtract present monthly debt service:
   credit cards   _____
   car loans   _____
   charge accounts   _____
   other personal debt   _____
   Total debt   _____
4 Equals maximum monthly payment   _____

71

Let's say your gross monthly income is $5,000 ($60,000 per year). Divide by four ($1,250) or three ($1,667). Let's say you have a car loan ($150 per month) and you're paying off a credit card balance ($100 per month):

$$\$1,250 - \$250 = \$1,000 \text{ or } \$1,667 - \$250 = \$1,417$$

In this example, you'd be able to spend between $1,000 and $1,417 per month on your principal and interest payments, real estate taxes, and insurance. If real estate taxes are $100 per month ($1,200 per year) and insurance is another $50 per month, that will leave you between $850 and $1,267 to spend on a mortgage.

Here's how to calculate the amount of the mortgage you can afford to carry: Multiply the net amount you can spend ($850 to $1,267) by twelve (for an annual mortgage amount), then divide that number by the current prevailing interest rate (say, 8 percent for a thirty-year fixed-rate loan).

25 percent of gross income: $850 × 12 = $10,200 ÷ .08 = $127,500
33 percent of gross income: $1,267 × 12 = $15,204 ÷ .08 = $190,050

So how much house can you afford? Assume you add a 20 percent down payment to each of these mortgage amounts (divide $127,500 or $190,050 by 5 and add that number to the total).

$$\$127,500 + \$25,500 = \$153,000$$
$$\$190,050 + \$38,010 = \$228,060$$

According to these calculations, on a $60,000-per-year income, assuming you have 20 percent to put down in cash, you'd be able to afford a home that costs between $153,000 and $228,060.

The 8 percent interest rate allows you to purchase a home between two and a half and nearly four times your income!

Use this chart to figure out the approximate price you can afford to spend on a home:

	25 Percent *Gross Monthly Income*		*33 Percent* *Gross Monthly Income*
GMI	_____		_____
÷ 4 =	_____	÷ 3 =	_____
monthly			
debt	− _____		− _____
	= _____		= _____
× 12	= _____	× 12 =	_____
current			
rate of			
interest	÷ _____	÷	_____
	= _____	=	_____
	(amount of mortgage you can afford)		(amount of mortgage you can afford)
down			
payment +	_____	+	_____
	= _____	=	_____
	(approximate purchase price of house)		(approximate purchase price of house)

Finding the Comfort Level

But just because you can afford to spend up to four times your income doesn't mean you have to. It's extremely important to find a level of payment that's comfortable for you and your family based on how you like to spend money. Although you may be technically able to afford a $150,000 home, making those interest payments might mean your family will have to give up other luxuries like summer camp or new clothes for school. Remember, no one says you have to spend every nickel you have on your home.

Figuring Out Your Budget

Finding your comfort zone is most easily accomplished if you're on top of your expenses. If you know what you spend, you know which expenses can be redirected toward paying the costs associated with home ownership (see Question 24).

The first thing to do is figure out where the money goes each month. Use the following Monthly Expenditures Checklist to help you determine what you're spending your salary on each month. Be honest. If you routinely spend $16.99 a week on the newest CD, put them in. If you rent two videos per week, put it in. If you eat lunch out with your friends four days a week, put it in. Later on, when you're trying to figure out how to save enough money for a down payment, you'll know exactly where to make the cut.

Are your monthly expenditures more than your monthly after-taxes take-home pay? Are the two numbers closer together than they ought to be? Look over the list and begin to determine which expenses can be eliminated or cut down.

First-Time Buyer Tip: Let's go back to getting yourself prequalified for a moment. A new wave of technology has produced another way for you to get prequalified: It's called *Com-*

Use this checklist to figure out exactly where your money goes each month. If you have other expenses not listed, add them at the bottom.

Expenses	*Amount Spent per Month*
Rent	_____
Electricity	_____
Gas	_____
Telephone	_____
Auto Loan Lease Payment	_____
Auto Insurance	_____
Health Insurance	_____
Renter's Insurance	_____
Savings/Retirement Contribution	_____
Grocery Bills	_____
Weekly Transportation	_____
Restaurants/Ordering In	_____
Entertainment	_____
Health Club/Working Out	_____
Child Care/Baby-sitters	_____
School/Tuition	_____
Children's Expenses (lessons/camp clothing, etc.)	_____
Housecleaning Expenses	_____
Vacations (divide your annual expense by twelve to find out the monthly expenditure)	_____
Books/CDs/Records/Tapes	_____
Newspaper/Magazine Subscriptions	_____
Laundry/Dry Cleaning	_____
Gifts	_____
Major Purchases (stereo/computer)	_____
Furniture/Decorating	_____

Expenses	Amount Spent per Month
Clothing	_____
Sundries/Drugstore Items	_____
Miscellaneous Expenses	_____
Other	
_____	_____
_____	_____
_____	_____
_____	_____
_____	_____
Monthly Total	_____

puterized Loan Origination, also known as CLO. With the expanding capabilities of computer technology, some brokers have elected to install computer systems in their offices that can prequalify you for a loan in minutes. Some brokers, along with the National Association of Realtors (NAR), tout CLOs as being the one-stop-shopping wave of the home-buying future. And maybe they are. But for now, while CLOs are *unregulated* and are in their infancy, there are a few caveats of which you should be aware:

- Many CLOs only feature the mortgage packages of *one* lender. While it may seem as if you are choosing among several different mortgages, in fact the same lender is providing them. There is no competition, and the mortgage company and broker *view you as a captive audience.* If the CLO features only one lender, it is likely you will pay more than market rate (sometimes a *lot* more) for your loan. The idea, of course, is that you'll feel comfortable knowing this particular lender has approved your loan and you may be more likely to apply to this lender for your actual mortgage, rather than shopping the market.

- Even if three or four lenders are featured on the CLO, it may not be enough to foster true competition and produce the best and least costly loan package for you. Mortgage experts recommend that buyers *use CLOs only if the system allows all local lenders to make their products available through it.*
- The broker may ask you to pay a fee for the CLO service. The fee can be small (around $25) or large $100 or more). The idea here is that you're paying for the ease of doing everything in one place. Be aware, however, that the broker may have a financial arrangement with the mortgage company or companies that are displaying their products. If the broker owns a piece of or all of the mortgage company, the broker is no longer a disinterested third party looking out for your best interests. In that case, the broker may have another purpose: to fatten his or her own bankbook.

The process of looking for a home and shopping for a mortgage is stressful, arduous and time-consuming. I'm all for one-stop shopping to expedite the process, but I strongly believe the best person to prequalify you for a loan is an independent lender. Not your broker, particularly if you're working with a broker who is a subagent for the seller. If you honestly fill out the prequalification chart on page 71, you'll have a pretty good idea of how much you can afford to borrow to purchase your new home. If that seems complicated, give a local lender a call. Or better yet, walk over and spend a few minutes with a loan officer.

QUESTION 24
How Much Will It Cost to Own and Maintain a Home?

In the movie *The Money Pit,* Tom Hanks ends up throwing his life savings into renovating his home. Maintaining a home often feels the same way. Calculating the costs of home ownership appear to be easy: If you can afford your mortgage, insurance, and real estate taxes, you can afford to own a home. Unfortunately, that's not usually the case. There are costs of home ownership hidden from renters that can lighten the wallet and break the bank.

Calculating these costs is a lot tougher than predicting your mortgage payments because they're variable by nature and given to change. If PITI—principal, interest, real estate taxes, and insurance—are the fixed costs involved with owning a home, utility payments are semifixed, and everything else is a variable.

Here are the basic expenses you will be responsible for when you actually buy your home:

- Mortgage payments of principal and interest, paid monthly;
- Real estate taxes, paid annually or in two installments
- Home owner's insurance, usually paid monthly with the mortgage, but sometimes paid separately from the mortgage in an annual or semiannual premium;

- Assessments (see Question 25);
- Electricity;
- Heating/cooling/hot water;
- Gas;
- Trash and garbage collection;
- Water and sewage (may be separate or billed together);
- Repairs and maintenance of the interior and exterior of the home;
- Landscaping and grounds maintenance;
- Snow removal (for those living in colder climates).

How much do these items cost? For some, like landscaping, water, and the utilities, the answer depends greatly on season and usage. Your mortgage and insurance payments will likely be fixed and remain the same. Utilities will go up and down with the seasons and will likely drift higher. Repairs and maintenance of the house depend on the condition of the home. If the boiler is on its last legs, you may have to pay for a new one outright.

Real Estate Taxes

Real estate taxes are another matter. From every corner of the United States, home owners cry out that their property taxes are too high. Formulas for calculating property taxes differ from state to state, but the general feeling is that you can expect to pay anywhere between 1 and 3 percent of the market value of the home.

For example, if your home has a market value of $100,000, it's likely that you might pay anywhere between $1,000 to $3,000 per year in property taxes, depending on where you live. In Chicago, if you own a $120,000 condo in the Gold Coast (the fanciest part of town), you might pay up to 70 percent more in real estate taxes than the person who owns a $120,000 bungalow on the city's northwest side. Is it fair? No.

First-Time Buyer Tip: You can't escape property taxes, but you can fight them. See Appendix II for useful information on how to lighten your property tax burden.

General Maintenance

What kinds of specific expenses might you encounter in your first few years of home ownership? General maintenance and upkeep of the home can be expensive and brokers say would-be home owners often forget to consider the basics for the exterior and interior of the home. Cold-weather and warm-weather climates exact their own peculiar punishments on a home. Severe winter weather can wreak havoc on driveways, gutters, the roof, and exterior paint, not to mention the time spent shoveling. Depending on the amount of snow, you may want to invest in a snowblower. (Or consider joining your new neighbors to pay for snow removal during the season.) In addition, your driveway may need a coat of sealant from time to time to prevent cracking. Landscaping and a garden are year-round issues. If you live in the far South, your garden will require constant care and attention to avoid becoming a jungle. In the North, you'll have at least three seasons of gardening.

Another maintenance concern is the exterior upkeep of the home. Brick homes may need expensive tuck-pointing to keep the walls from leaking. Clapboard or shingle houses need painting every few years to stay weather tight, and may require new boards from time to time. Even homes with aluminum or plastic siding have portions that require some painting or, at the very least, washing. (Aluminum or plastic siding tends to be the cheapest alternatives in the long run, as they require little maintenance beyond the occasional cleaning, experts say.) Repairing or patching the roof can be an ongoing expense, as a particularly severe winter or windstorm can rip shingles right off the roof. If you live in the house long enough, you will one day have to replace the roof, though a new roof should last twenty years and usually comes with a warranty.

First-Time Buyer Tip: If you're purchasing an older home, a good broker or inspector should point out the age of the home and remind you that you might have to replace that roof or other appliances and mechanical systems within the next five years.

Maintaining the interior of a home can also be expensive. Older windows may need recaulking or a new sash. You may want to purchase storm windows to improve energy efficiency. Bathroom tiles may need regrouting. Older homes may need rewiring, a new hot water heater, or a new furnace right away, but depending on how long you plan to live in the house, odds are you'll replace most of the major mechanical systems. Even newer mechanicals require yearly upkeep, however, as filters need to be changed and systems need to be cleaned. Although basements and attics might seem like ideal storage facilities, they require maintenance as well. Basement walls may require treatment for mold and cracks. Attics may need extra insulation. Other issues may arise as the house—especially a new home—settles.

A good inspector should help pinpoint upcoming maintenance expenses associated with the home, including any pest problems. (For more on inspectors and the inspection process, see Question 43.)

QUESTION 25

What Are Assessments? Do All Town Houses, Condos, and Co-ops Have Them?

Assessments are fees that you, the owner, pay for the upkeep of property held jointly with other owners. You will pay an assessment if you choose to buy a condo, co-op, or town house. If your single-family home is located in a particular type of subdivision that has common property (like a private playground, security gate, clubhouse, etc.), there may be a home owners' association that will assess you for a share of the maintenance of that common property. Regardless of the type of property, your proportionate share of the upkeep of the property will be assessed based on your percentage of ownership. If you own 1 percent of the property, then you will pay 1 percent of the upkeep.

Many different areas and amenities may be part of the common area, including a parking garage or parking spaces, recreational amenities (clubhouse, health club or workout facilities, tennis courts, private lake or lagoon), land, the roof and exterior walls of condos, town houses, and co-ops, lobby, security, doormen, etc.

How do you pay an assessment? Assessments are usually billed monthly by the home owners' association. Some single-family home owners' associations bill on a yearly basis. Whenever it comes, the bill is expected to be paid promptly, and if it is not, the association is entitled to bill you for late fees and even to take you to court to force you to sell your home to pay for late assessments.

If you're thinking about buying a town house, condo, co-op, or single-family house that would require payment of an assessment, you should be aware that the lender will consider the assessment to be another fixed expense (like paying down a car loan or credit card balance) and will include the assessment in the debt-to-income ratio. That means you will have less money to spend to buy a home.

For example, if you have $1,000 per month to spend on housing expenses and the monthly assessment of the condo you've had your eye on is $200, you really only have $800 to spend on your housing expenses.

Another thing: Assessments usually go up. Every condo, co-op, or town house association has a board of directors that oversees the costs, repairs, and maintenance done to the property. They have the power to impose "special assessments" to pay for large-scale capital improvements, including a new roof, new deck, new elevators, new windows, tuck-pointing, and a hundred other things.

How can you protect yourself? Before you close on a condo, co-op, or town house, it's a good idea to request copies of the last two to three years of budgets and board minutes to familiarize yourself with ongoing issues of maintenance, problems, and long-range planning. Reading board minutes can be like reading a juicy gossip rag. You won't know the people, but if you move in, they'll be your neighbors.

Reading the board minutes will quickly get you up to speed on any major capital improvements the board may be planning. In that case, it may give you an advantage in negotiating the price of the home. If you read the minutes and find out that the board is planning to levy a three-year special assessment to cover the cost of windows that were replaced five years earlier, you should try to get your seller to lower his or her price to at least recoup some of that cost. (After all, the seller enjoyed the use of those windows for five years.)

PART II

Putting Together the Deal

MAKING THE OFFER

How Do I Decide What to Offer for the Home?

If you've been prequalified by a lender, your broker, or you've figured it out for yourself, you already know your uppermost limit. That's the number you can't go beyond. However, what you can afford to spend has nothing to do with how much a seller is asking for his or her house. The seller wants the most money possible. You want to pay the least amount of money. The rest is subject to negotiation.

But it's important to determine how much a house is worth *before* you make an offer. (This would seem obvious, but there are plenty of buyers who get caught up in the heat of the moment and just offer up a number.) The answer lies with your broker, although you'll have to proceed on a slightly different course depending on whether you use a buyer broker or a seller broker.

If you're using a buyer broker, and I'm assuming he or she is competent, it should be relatively easy to ask the buyer broker for "comps" (comparable values of like properties that have recently sold in your neighborhood). If you're working with a seller broker, he or she is required by law in most states to provide you with everything you need to make an informed decision on how much to offer. However, you may have to specifically request that the seller broker provide you with recent sale comps, as well as the listing prices for similar homes in the neighborhood.

What are comps? Comps are homes that are similar in size, location, and amenities to the one on which you want to bid that have recently sold. Comps give you an idea of what other sellers have been paid for their homes. Finding out the listing prices is also important, because comparing the list prices with the sale prices tells you exactly what percentage of their sales price sellers are getting. (As an aside, study after study has found that homes sell, *on average*, for 6 percent below list price. But that assumes the home is not overpriced. If a home is well priced it is listed a bit above what comparable homes in the neighborhood have sold for.)

Here's how it works: Let's say House A was listed at $100,000 and sold for $96,000 (Seller A received 96 percent of his list price); House B was also priced at $100,000, and sold for $95,000 (Seller B received 95 percent of her list price). Home A and Home B are nearly identical homes in more or less the same good physical condition. Seller C, however, put a few extras into his home, such as a wood-burning fireplace and upgraded carpet. His home was priced at $110,000 and he received $104,000 (Seller C received 95 percent of his list price).

You come and look at House D, which is in the same condition as Houses A and B, but Seller D is asking $110,000 for her house. Based on the sales prices of other homes in the subdivision, how much would you pay for the house? Although Sellers A, B, and C received around 95 percent of their list price, their homes were competitively priced. Seller D's home is not competitively priced.

If you know the most you want to offer Seller D for her house is $95,000 (95 percent of $100,000, which is where the house should be priced), you have to make a decision about how much lower than that you want to offer initially.

Unless you're in a heated situation where several parties may be bidding on the same house you want, or if you're in a tight seller's market (meaning that sellers are getting almost exactly what they want for their properties in a very short amount of time), *you'll never offer the list price for a home.* What you do is offer between 5 to 10 percent below the maximum price you want to pay for the home. So if you've decided you're not going to pay any more than $95,000 for Seller D's home, then you may want to consider an initial offer of $90,000. That's called negotiation (see Question 34).

Know what you want to pay for a property *before* you make your first offer. And instead of emotion, that decision should be based on logic and reasoning. If you can't get a clear idea of how much to offer based on the comps your broker has provided to you, then ask him or her for another set of comps. If you're working with a buyer broker, you should feel free to ask what he or she would pay for the house. Buyer brokers, because they have a fiduciary responsibility to you, the buyer, should be forthcoming with how much they think a property is worth. If your seller broker is less forthcoming ask how much he or she would allow his or her children to pay for the home. Remember that he or she has a fiduciary responsibility to the seller.

According to a strict interpretation of the law, the seller broker can't do anything but suggest you pay list price.

QUESTION 27
How Do I Make an Offer?

There are three basic pieces to an offer: the address or description of the property, consideration or the price you are prepared to pay, and the date on which the closing will take place.

A valid offer can be written on anything, including a paper napkin, and can read as follows: "I, Ilyce R. Glink, offer to buy 1 Willow Lane for $125,500, to close on July 13, 1994."

Although property has been bought and sold this way for centuries, making an offer today is usually a bit more complex. In some states, it's customary for the broker to use a "contract to purchase" form when making an offer. In other states, the broker has a preprinted "offer for purchase" form. Whichever form is used, you will generally sit with the broker and discuss all sorts of issues such as contingencies (see Question 30), earnest money (see Question 29), and any requests you may have for personal property (such as appliances, lamps, attached bookcases, etc.) before filling in the form. After you fill in the form, and sign it, your broker will then present the offer to the seller and his or her broker. If you are buying a FSBO, you will have to make the presentation yourself. If you don't understand the contract and its implications, don't sign it. Consult a real estate attorney first.

Typically, buyers represented by brokers do not attend the offer presentation. But sometimes they wait downstairs. Leo and Genna looked at fifty homes on Chicago's North Shore before they found the one they wanted to buy. Because there was so much interest in the property, they decided right on the spot (at the first showing) to make an offer. They sat at the kitchen table with their broker and drew up the offer, then waited while the broker went upstairs to present the offer to the sellers. These first-time buyers knew almost immediately how much they were going to offer for the house because they had seen so many similar homes in the neighborhood and knew at what prices they had been sold over the previous six months. That knowledge enabled them to act fast when the time was right.

Sometimes, getting what you want hinges on how quickly you're able to act under pressure. Even at its best, making an offer can feel like a pressure cooker. Don't allow yourself to be sucked in to a point where you're no longer able to rationally discuss the offer and its implications. If you're finding yourself dragged along by the current, perhaps against your will, take a time-out. Remember, there is more than one right house for you. If you're the typical home owner, you're going to move between five and seven times in your life. There will always be another house. If you fall prey to the notion that this home is the only one for you, you may offer too much for it, thereby making it an imperfect choice.

What Goes into the Actual Offer to Purchase or Contract to Purchase?

Offer to Purchase

The offer to purchase is usually a much simpler document than a contract to purchase. Why? Because the contract to purchase must get much more specific about the property description, fixtures, exclusions, and all the necessary legal language for property transfer, rights to sue for specific performance (if the buyer or seller backs out of the contract on a whim), damages, brokers' fees, etc.

Every city and state will have its own real estate or Realtor (member of the National Association of Realtors) association that provides standard form contracts for the purchase and sale of real estate. *Although the contracts are similar, real estate law varies from state to state.* Just remember that it is likely these contracts are written from the seller's perspective (most brokers are seller brokers, not buyer brokers) and as a buyer you're going to want to look over the forms carefully and probably hire a real estate lawyer to help you sort them out. (See Questions 39 and 40.) If you're purchasing a FSBO, your attorney should have a contract you can use.

Let's look at an offer to purchase real estate contract which starts out like a letter. It is addressed:

To: _____
    (seller and spouse)

There is a place for the date of the offer. Then:

The property herein referred to is identified as follows:

Here you would fill in the address of the property.

I hereby offer to buy said property, which has been offered to me by _____ (fill in name of seller's broker), as your broker, under the following terms and conditions:

The contract now allows you to check off whether you will pay for the property by check or cash. Next comes how much you will pay for the property, and in what stages:

$ _____ is paid herewith as a deposit to bind this offer.
$ _____ is to be paid as an additional deposit upon the execution of the purchase and sale Agreement provided for below.
$ _____ is to be paid at the time of delivery of the Deed in cash, or by certified, cashier's, treasurer's or bank check.

Next comes a statement that tells the seller that the offer is only good until a certain time on a certain date. The seller has until that time to accept the offer or the offer for purchase becomes invalid. The seller may counteroffer and then further negotiation would take place.

Then the seller is notified that the offer is contingent upon the execution of the standard purchase and sale agreement.

Next comes the closing date:

A good and sufficient Deed, conveying a good and clear record and marketable title shall be delivered at 12:00 Noon on _____ 19 _____, at the appropriate Registry of Deeds, unless some other time and place are mutually agreed upon in writing.

After another paragraph, in which the buyer promises to forfeit his deposit if he or she does not fulfill his or her obligations, and one that says "time is of the essence," there is a space to write in any additional terms and conditions, or to attach any riders.

Finally, the document is signed by the buyers, and the receipt for deposit at the bottom of the page is filled out.

The standard purchase and sale agreement form from the Greater Boston Real Estate Board is four times as long as the offer to purchase form. (See Appendix III for a complete form.) Real estate attorneys say that most buyers never read the contract. *But you should.* Although each contract will vary by state or even city, most points will be similar.

The following section walks you through the contract, point by point:

1. *Parties.* Fill in the name of the seller and buyer.
2. *Description.* Give the address, title reference, and description of the property. For example: "the land with the buildings thereon, numbered 391 Waverley Avenue, Newton, Massachusetts, Middlesex County,

being shown as Lot B on a 'Plan of Land in Newton belonging to Katherine F. Cameron,' E. S. Smithe, Surveyor, dated May 1914, recorded with Middlesex South Registry Deeds Book 4741 and more particularly described in deed to Seller dated May 27, 1977, recorded at Middlesex South Registry Deeds in Book 13200, Page 450."

3. *Buildings, Structures, Improvements, Fixtures.* This is a general list of the buildings, structures, and improvements that are included with the sale. You should delete, exclude, or add anything appropriate. In particular, list items that the sellers could take with them, but should be part of the deal, like the dishwasher, washer, dryer, and refrigerator. Some of these items will be decided based on local custom. For example, in downtown Chicago, all appliances stay with the house. In the northern and western suburbs, refrigerators, washers, and dryers generally go with the sellers to their new home.

4. *Title Deed.* Specifically note any restrictions, easements (rights other people may have to use your property or otherwise restrict your use of the property), rights, or obligations that you are willing to accept on your title and delete those that you are not. Your attorney will help you with this.

5. *Plans.* The plans should have already been approved and recorded in advance by the seller and they should comply with all laws, allowing a clear transfer to the buyer.

6. *Registered Title.* There are some states that have a registration system for title.

7. *Purchase Price.* Fill in amount and write out the amount to be paid as a deposit, the amount of the es-

crow (that is, money held in trust by a third party) "upon execution of this agreement," and the remainder at closing.

8. *Time for Performance: Delivery of Deed.* State the time, date, and place for closing.

9. *Possession and Conditions of Premises.* Says that the buyer receives full possession free of tenants and occupants at closing, that the property does not violate any building or zoning laws, and that the buyer shall be entitled to inspect the premises before closing.

10. *Extension to Perfect Title or Make Premises Conform.* Gives the seller thirty days to correct any problems with the property's title.

11. *Failure to Perfect Title or Make Premises Conform.* Should the seller fail to deliver good title, your money will be refunded.

12. *Buyer's Election to Accept Title.* If something impairs the property's title, such as a mechanic's or tax lien, you can elect to take the property as is, subject to the lien, and deduct the lien amount from the purchase price. Should a disaster occur, such as a fire, you can elect to take the home as is and be compensated from the insurance proceeds, or take a reduction in the price of the home to cover the damage.

13. *Acceptance of Deed.* Acceptance of the deed at closing means that all duties and obligations under the contract have been fulfilled by the seller.

14. *Use of Money to Clear Title.* The seller may leave behind money at closing to pay off any liens against the property.

15. *Insurance.* The seller promises to maintain a certain amount of insurance. The amount is usually nego-

tiated, but should be sufficient to cover the cost of restoring the property after a fire or other disaster.

16. *Adjustments.* List of expenses (like water or assessments) and taxes that must be prorated for the portion of the month or year the seller owned the house until closing. You will be credited at closing for these expenses. (See Question 94.)

17. *Adjustment of Unassessed and Abated Taxes.* Taxes that have not yet been assessed for the year are usually prorated based on the prior year's taxes according to a local formula.

18. *Broker's Fee.* Spells out who gets the commission and how much.

19. *Broker's Warranty.* Names the brokers and warrants that they are licensed.

20. *Deposit.* Spells out the escrow agreement and who will receive the interest on the account.

21. *Buyer's Default and Damages.* If the buyer fails to buy the property, the seller gets to keep the escrow money.

22. *Release by Husband or Wife.* The spouse agrees to release any claim. Omitted if seller is divorced or widowed.

23. *Broker as Party.* Says the brokers are a part of the contract.

24. *Liability of Trustee, Shareholder, Beneficiary.* Included if one of the parties is represented by a trustee, otherwise omitted.

25. *Warranties and Representations.* Whatever promises the seller makes to the buyer regarding the conditions of the property.

26. *Mortgage Contingency Clause.* Standard on some con-

tracts, otherwise added as a rider. (See Question 31.)

27. *Construction of Agreement.* Legal language that sets up the contract as a contract.

28. *Lead Paint Law.* In Massachusetts, if a child under the age of six resides in any residential premises where paint, plaster, or other material contains dangerous levels of lead, the owner must remove or cover the paint to make it safe for children.

29. *Smoke Detectors.* In Massachusetts, the seller agrees to provide a certificate from the local fire department stating the property is equipped with smoke detectors. In Illinois, you must provide a certificate saying your water bill has been paid.

30. *Additional Provisions.* The place for any additional riders.

(See Appendix III for a complete contract.)

Contract for Single-Family Home

CHICAGO TITLE INSURANCE COMPANY • ILLINOIS FORM A '

Real Estate Sale Contract

1. _____ (Purchaser)

agrees to purchase at a price of $ _____ on the terms set forth herein, the following described real estate in _____ County, Illinois:

(If legal description is not included at time of execution, _____ *is*

___ed to insert thereafter.)

_____ , and

× _____ , together with the following property presently located thereon: *(strike items*

... wnings; (c) outdoor television antenna; (d) wall-to-wall, hallway and stair carpeting; (e)

... lectric, plumbing and other attached fixtures as installed; (h) water softener;

transmitters; (l) radiator covers; (m) indoor and

96

Condominium Contracts

The difference between purchasing a condo and purchasing a single-family home is slight; when you purchase a condo you are buying real estate plus an interest in the common areas managed by the home-owners' association. Sometimes real estate sales contracts for condominiums contain special provisions that are not applicable to single-family houses. For example, some condo boards have the right of first refusal when a condo unit is sold. This allows the board to purchase the unit if it decides that is in the best interest of the condo building. In a sales contract, the seller will agree to procure the release or waiver of any option or right of first refusal. (See Appendix III for a complete contract.)

Contract for Condo

CHICAGO ASSOCIATION OF REALTORS®/MLS
REAL ESTATE SALE CONTRACT — CONDOMINIUM

1 TO: _____ SELLER   Date _____
2   I/We offer to purchase the condominium unit known as: _____
3 located at: _____
                    (Address)   (City)   (State)   (Zip)
4 together with its undivided interest in the common elements and accumulated reserves, together with the following, if any, now in the
5 unit, for which a Bill of Sale is to be given: screens; storm windows and doors; shades; venetian blinds; drapery rods; curtain rods;
6 radiator covers; attached TV antenna; heating, central cooling, unit air conditioners, ventilating, lighting, and plumbing fixtures;
7 attached mirrors, shelving, interior shutters, cabinets and bookcases; awnings; porch shades; tacked down carpeting; draperies;
8 refrigerator; range; dishwasher; disposal; and also _____ .
9 1. Purchase price $_____
        _____nest money $_____ in the form of _____
        _____, to be increased to 10% of purchase price within _____
        ___t money shall be returned and this contract shall be void if not accepted by Seller on or before
        ____ shall be deposited by _____
        _____d escrow account in compliance with the laws of the State of Illinois. An
                                        ____ as follows (STRIKE THROUGH

97

Co-op Contracts

When you purchase a co-op, you are not really purchasing real estate. You purchase personal property in the form of shares in the corporation that owns the building. You become a tenant and pay "rent" (monthly maintenance assessment fee) for the right to live there. Co-op contracts are entirely different from condo or single-family contracts. (See Appendix III for a complete contract.)

Contract for a Co-op

REAL ESTATE SALE CONTRACT—CO-OPERATIVE APARTMENT

QUESTION 29
What Is the Earnest Money? Who Holds It? When Do I Get It Back?

The earnest money is an amount of cash that the buyer puts up to show he or she is serious about purchasing the property. The money represents the buyer's commitment to buy and acts as an unofficial option on the property. After receiving an earnest money check, the seller will usually stop showing the property, and wait to see if the buyer can get a mortgage. Earnest money is important to the transaction because it shows the seller that the buyer is operating in good faith (hence the name, "earnest"). The bigger the deposit, the more reassuring it is to the seller, who thinks, "This buyer is serious." It also ties the buyer to the property and keeps him or her from looking for additional properties.

On the offer to purchase, the earnest money is also called a deposit. Usually the buyer offers 5 to 10 percent of the sales price of the house in cash as the earnest money. That amount is large enough that it will make any buyer think twice about walking away from the house on a whim. If you don't have 10 percent in cash, then put down 5 percent. Sometimes a buyer will attach a $1,000 check to the offer to purchase to show initial good faith. The rest of the deposit, or earnest money, is due when the contract is signed by both parties, or shortly thereafter.

Who holds the earnest money? The money typically goes into an escrow account held by the seller broker, but this is largely a matter of local custom or it can be negotiated. The buyer usually receives the interest on his or her money.

When do I get the earnest money back? If the sale goes through, the earnest money plus interest is often used as part of the cash down payment and is paid to the seller. If the sale does not go through for some reason covered by a contingency in the contract (if, for example, the buyer could not get a mortgage), the seller should sign a release of escrow and the earnest money will be refunded to the buyer. The earnest money should also be refunded to the buyer if the sale does not go through because of a problem on the seller's side. If, however, the buyer is at fault, return of the earnest money may be subject to negotiation.

What if the seller won't sign the release of escrow? If there is a fight between the buyer and the seller over the earnest money, the broker holding the funds might turn them over to the real estate commission for mediation or local courts for litigation. Ask your broker to explain your state law and local customs regarding this matter.

When We Make an Offer, What Contingencies Should We Include?

A contingency allows you to back out of the contract for a specific reason. There are typically three contingencies that accompany a contract to purchase: financing or mortgage; inspection; and attorney approval. Each of these is explained in the following three questions.

There are many other contingencies that might appear in a contract for purchase, including:

- Sale of your prior residence (but not for first-time buyers);
- Admittance to certain clubs (for example, if you are buying a home near a private golf course, you might make the purchase contingent on your acceptance to the club);
- Approval by the condo or co-op boards;
- Pest inspection, asbestos, radon, lead, water (may be separate contingencies or lumped under inspection);
- Compliance with building code.

You can have almost any contingency you like, but remember, having contingencies, including mortgage, inspection, and attorney approval, could give the seller grounds for refusing your contract. (See Appendix III for sample contigency forms.)

QUESTION 31
What Is a Mortgage or Financing Contingency?

A mortgage or financing contingency gives you a way to back out of the contract to purchase if you cannot get a lender to give you a mortgage commitment. The contingency will generally require you to be specific about the type of mortgage you are seeking and will require you to seek mortgage approval within a specified period of time, generally forty-five to sixty days. You must be reasonable about the mortgage's parameters, and usually you must agree to look for a mortgage at the current prevailing rate of interest.

The contingency is meant to protect you in case you can't find financing. Here is the mortgage contingency from the Greater Boston Real Estate Board:

> In order to help finance the acquisition of said premises, the BUYER shall apply for a conventional bank or other institutional mortgage loan of _____, payable in no less than _____ years at an interest rate not to exceed _____. If despite the BUYER's diligent efforts a commitment for such a loan cannot be obtained on or before _____, 19 ___ , the BUYER may terminate this agreement by written notice to the SELLER(S) and/or the Broker(s), as agent for the SELLER, prior to the expiration of such time, whereupon any payments made under this agreement shall be forthwith refunded and all other obligations of the parties hereto. In no event will the

BUYER be deemed to have used diligent efforts to obtain such commitment unless the BUYER submits a complete mortgage loan application conforming to the foregoing provisions on or before _____, 19 _____ .

(Provided courtesy of the Greater Boston Real Estate Board.)

The mortgage contingency should be included in the contract. If it is not, be sure to ask your broker or real estate attorney to add it as an addendum to the contract.

QUESTION 32
What Is the Inspection Contingency?

This contingency gives you the right to have a house inspector come and examine the property before you close on the purchase. Again, the purpose of the contingency is to protect you from buying a home that may have serious hidden structural problems or material defects. When you add an inspection contingency to the contract, you'll want to make sure it covers both the home and the property on which it sits. You might also want to have a separate contingency for each of the following:

- Radon
- Asbestos
- Lead
- Toxic substances
- Water
- Pests, including termites, mice, rats, roaches, etc.

Generally, the inspection contingency will require you to have your inspection within five to ten days after the offer is accepted by the seller. Otherwise, you may lose the right to withdraw from the contract.

Here is a sample inspection contingency addendum:

The BUYER, may at his own expense and on or before _____ , have the property inspected by a person engaged in the business of conducting home inspections. If it is the opinion of such inspector that the property contains serious structural, mechanical, or other defects, then the BUYER shall have the option of revoking the Offer by written notice to the SELLER and/or the Broker, as your agent, prior to the expiration of such time, which notice shall be accompanied by a copy of the inspector's opinion and any related inspection report, whereupon all deposits made by the BUYER to you shall be forthwith refunded and this Offer shall become null and void and without further recourse to any party.

(Provided courtesy of the Greater Boston Real Estate Board.)

Sometimes buyers hope that the inspection will turn up small, fixable problems with the property so that they can get additional money from the seller at closing. The real purpose of the inspection contingency, however, is to protect you from purchasing property that may have serious, expensive, or unfixable problems. Like the mortgage contingency, the inspection contingency should be either in the contract or attached to it as a rider or addendum.

What Is the Attorney Approval?

Before you sign any contract or offer, be certain you consult with someone who can advise you about the purchase and its legal consequences. In some states, that's the real estate attorney's job. In others, the broker will advise you. The attorney contingency or rider essentially gives your attorney the right to make changes to the contract.

First-Time Buyer Tip: If you are working with a seller broker and that broker is the person who is supposed to advise you of your legal rights under the contract, there may be a serious conflict of interest. If you have any qualms at all about being counseled by your real estate broker or sales agent, consult an attorney. Spending between $250 to $750 for an attorney is a small price to pay when you're making the biggest investment of your life. As all the fees and costs are pinching your wallet, try to imagine how expensive and time consuming it would be if something *really* went wrong.

First-Time Buyer Tip: Do not assume that just because you have an attorney rider that your attorney can remove you from the deal if you suddenly discover you have made a mistake in the offer (usually offering too high a price for the home). Although some attorneys do try to cover for their clients' mistakes by rejecting the contract, this is unprofessional. If you have any questions about the offer or contract, consult an attorney *before* making the offer or signing your name.

In some states, the offer for purchase is worded in such a way that there is no need for an attorney approval rider. It would say something like, "This offer to purchase is subject to a contract that is agreeable to both parties." If you aren't sure whether or not your offer is worded in that way, it is best to attach an attorney rider.

Here is a sample attorney approval contingency:

It is agreed by and between the parties hereto as follows: That their respective attorneys may approve of, make modifications, other than price and dates, mutually acceptable to the parties. Approval will not be unreasonably withheld, but, if within _____ days after the date of acceptance of the Contract, it becomes evident agreement cannot be reached by the parties hereto, and written notice thereof is given to either party within the time specified, then this Contract shall become null and void, and all monies paid by the Purchaser shall be refunded. In the absence of written notice within the time specified herein, this provision shall be deemed waived by all parties hereto, and this contract shall be in full force and effect.

(Provided courtesy of the Chicago Association of Realtors.)

NEGOTIATING THE CONTRACT

QUESTION 34
How Does the Negotiation Process Work?

Negotiation, no matter what is being negotiated, is about give and take. The person who holds the stronger hand usually gets to give less and take more, but in a successful negotiation, both sides end up compromising. In a house sale, that's really what you want. You don't want the seller to take you for a ride, nor do you want to ride the seller, or he will begin to like you a lot less and it will make the move a lot more difficult for him. Emotions run high anyway in something as personal as selling a home, and when negotiations get tough, emotions become embittered arms at war.

Unlike a judge's settlement, where both sides may end up profoundly unhappy with the result, a successful house negotiation can leave everyone feeling like winners. And that's the goal: As a buyer, you want the sellers to feel they are getting a fair price for their home. You want them to bask in the glow of having made a good deal so that they will be nice to you when you want to tromp through with the inspector, your spouse, your friends, your decorator, and your parents. You want that niceness to extend through to the closing, so they do not make you crazy with all kinds of little mishmash at the end. You want them to like you so that the sellers will feel good about selling their home to someone who will love it as much as they have. At the same time, you also want to feel as though you paid a fair price for the home. There is nothing worse than finding out the day after you've signed the contract that you overpaid for the house. There is nothing worse than fighting with the sellers over items you thought were included with the price, but that they intend to take (stealing, you may call it). The nastiness can leave a bad taste in your mouth. And in your home.

So how do you negotiate fairly? How do you end up with good feelings on all sides of the table? First, enlist your broker's (or attorney's, if you choose not to work with a broker) help in keeping everyone's emotions at bay. Brokers are good at this. It's probably one of the most important parts of their job. They must present your offer as something worthwhile, not insulting. You must rely on them to make you seem like a serious buyer.

Once you write up the offer with your broker, it's up to him or her to present the offer. This is the first step of the negotiation. The broker will take your offer and present it to the sellers and, usually, the sellers' broker. This can take place in an office, but usually your broker will go to see the sellers in their home, where they are most comfortable. And then, perhaps over a cup of coffee, your broker will tell them exactly how much you are willing to pay for their home, the conditions under which you'll purchase the home, and when.

Sometimes it doesn't happen like this. Once in a while, especially if the sellers are out of town, or if they work odd hours, an offer will be communicated over the telephone or by fax. But usually it is done in person. After all, as my mother, Susanne, the agent, likes to say, this is a very personal business. When your broker leaves, the sellers and their broker will discuss the offer. Unless it is a full-price offer or they are quite desperate, they will almost never take your first offer. Everyone understands that the first offer is a little bit (or quite a lot) below what you expect to pay for the property. The key to a successful negotiation is to remember that it's a psychological game.

Here's how it works: Let's say the home is priced at $100,000. You think that's close, but maybe a slightly higher price for the home than you think is fair. You offer $90,000, or 10 percent less than the asking price. The sellers now assume you'll be willing to compromise somewhere in the middle, say $94,000 to $96,000. The sellers then make a calculated guess: Are you willing to go up to $96,000? Or will you only go up to

$95,000? Or will you stop at $94,000? If the sellers want to cut to the chase, they may instruct their broker to present a "split the difference" counteroffer. That means that you'd pay $95,-000 for the property.

Sometimes negotiations get tough. If the sellers think the $100,000 price is fair and don't want to go much lower, they may come back in much lower increments, say $1,000. Then you have to decide if you also want to match those increments or make a final offer. Making the last offer is like saying "I call" in a card game. The sellers might come down $2,500 and say that $97,500 is a final offer, take it or leave it. Or you might put in a take-it-or-leave-it offer of $95,000, and put the ball in the sellers' court. If you turn the negotiation into a power struggle, it could quickly turn nasty. Better to keep things on a more even pace, if not downright friendly, to keep the negotiations moving ahead step by step.

But that doesn't mean you shouldn't play up your strengths. If you can't afford to pay more than $95,000, have your broker tell the sellers that you are making your very best offer and while you can't be more flexible on the price, you really love the house and would be more flexible on the closing date. You're never going to know what the sellers' hot points are. They may be much more concerned about the closing date than the extra $5,000. They may also be more interested in turning their home over to people who really love it.

The Low-Ball Bid

If you decide you love a home that's either too expensive or way over your budget, you have a choice. You can either walk away and say you'll come back to it later in your life, or you can make a low-ball offer. Although there is no one set definition of a low-ball offer, several things can be said to describe one: First, it is usually more than 10 percent below the asking price of the home; second, sellers usually find them insulting, which means the seller's broker must plead with them to reconsider and make a counteroffer; third, it gives a decidedly negative cast to the negotiation process.

Sometimes a low-ball offer works and other times it doesn't. A lot depends on the presentation of the broker and the desperation of the seller. For example, if you decide to offer $80,000 for a home priced at $100,000 and enclose with your offer comps of other like homes in the neighborhood that recently sold for $75,000, the seller may consider your offer. But if you offer $50,000 for a house that's well priced at $100,000, it's the nice seller who would even dignify that offer with a response. As the buyer, you have the right to make whatever offer you want. And your broker must present that offer to the seller. But that doesn't mean you won't tick off the seller.

What Is a Bidding War?

A bidding war is when more than one buyer is interested in purchasing the same home. Usually the seller broker will ask for bids from the interested parties. The broker will then present the bids to the seller, who will decide which offer to respond to. What often happens is that you'll find out there is another interested party and your broker will encourage you to make your very best bid. That is, no negotiation. If you want to offer $95,000, then that's what you put in the bid. If you think the other party is going to offer $95,000, and you really want the house, you can offer a little more.

First-Time Buyer Tip: The one problem with the negotiation step in the home-buying process is that it's extremely pressured. Your broker will tell you to stay close to the telephone so that you won't miss The Call. You'll be on pins and needles, wondering if your bid is going to be accepted or rejected. Try not to get so worked up about your bid that you can't concentrate on anything else. Take a walk. See a movie. Get your mind off of it.

And I can't stress this point enough: Remember that if you lose this home, you *will* find another that you'll love as much or more than this one.

QUESTION 35
How Do I Make a Counteroffer?

A counteroffer is what happens after the initial contract is presented. You make the offer. The seller responds by making a counteroffer. Any response from you or the seller, after the initial offer presentation, is by definition a counteroffer. Making a counteroffer is actually simpler than making the first offer because you are in the driver's seat. A counteroffer means that the seller has responded to your offer. Responding to your offer means that the seller believes you are a serious buyer and that your offer is valid.

Before responding to the seller's counteroffer, make sure you understand the psychological implications behind it. In making your counteroffer, you can either match the decrease in price with an equal increase, or jump up more to make the seller feel better about the deal. The choice is yours. When you've decided how much to offer in this next round, talk to your broker. It's usually unnecessary to draw up an entirely new contract, although customs vary from state to state and county to county. At this stage, the broker usually modifies the existing offer and calls the seller's broker, who relays the new offer to the sellers.

QUESTION 36
What Is a Home Warranty? What Kind Can I Get for New Construction? What About a Previously Owned Home?

The concept of a new home warranty sounds pretty good: If something breaks, the foundation cracks, or the roof leaks, all you have to do is call an 800 number and someone will come out and fix it for free. Sounds too good to be true, and in most cases, it is. Although home warranties should work this way in theory, in practice there are often extra headaches and extra expenses you will incur on the road to fixing your problem.

There are two types of home warranties: a home owner's warranty for new construction, and a home owner's warranty for previously owned homes. Let's look at new construction first.

New construction can be a completely different animal. Usually you're working with a developer, who often hasn't even built the home you want to buy. Many times you can pick out your own style of home, decor, cabinetry, floor coverings, appliances, and bathroom fixtures. You may even have a choice of options, including a basement, sun room, attic, two- or three-car garage, extra bedroom, and the upgrades: carpet, floor coverings, cabinetry, fixtures, etc.

In the past, developers of new construction provided a home owner's warranty backed by one of two or three organizations that created a pool of money that covered structural problems with new homes. It worked pretty well until a rash of undercapitalized, sleazy developers built shoddy homes and didn't put in enough money to cover the problems. That left one of the organizations short of funds and unable to pay the claims. In the past few years two other warranty companies stepped in to fill this gap and have again recently begun providing home owner's warranties for new construction.

But real estate attorneys say reputable developers of new construction will often back up their own work, and this should be one of the criteria on which you select a new home. Usually, the developer will provide a door-to-door warranty for one year on nearly everything in the home. Part of this warranty is covered by the manufacturers of your new appliances and mechanical systems. The developer might also extend the warranty to five or ten years for specific major components, such as the roof, hardwood floors, or fireplace. It's important to know exactly what your developer will warrant when you are buying a new home. If the developer refuses to warrant anything, watch out. That refusal might mean that the developer is sleazy or has built a shoddy project or has something to hide.

First-Time Buyer Tip: When buying new construction, check out homes built by the developer to see how the homes have stood the test of time. See how happy the home owners really are. If you're buying in an established—or semiestablished—subdivision, knock on doors and ask the owners what they like and dislike about their home. Ask about everything from how well the mechanical systems work to how quickly the developer fixed items on the punch list (a list of items not finished to your satisfaction by closing). Check out other, older subdivisions the developer has built and see what complaints, if any, turn up. Check for complaints that may have been filed against the developer with your local chamber of commerce, Better Business Bureau, and your local state's attorney's office. Remember, "the best defense is a good offense." Find out ahead of time what you're up against.

The time to reaffirm that your new home has a warranty is in the negotiating phase. Your attorney can step in and request a new home owner's warranty, then make it a condition of buying the home. At the very least, not having a home warranty for new construction means you have no recourse (other than expensive litigation) should something go wrong.

What other kinds of warranties are available? Most first-time buyers will be buying previously owned homes, those that are up for resale. About twenty years ago, several companies began providing home warranties for pre-owned homes. Although this type of home owner warranty was slow to catch on at first, it has grown by leaps and bounds in the last few years, fueled by our increasingly litigious society and some recent court rulings that have placed more responsibility on the seller to disclose problems in the home. More than 500,000 home owner warranties were purchased last year, about half of which were for homes in California. In other parts of the country, the number of home owners who purchase warranties ranges from 8 to 20 percent.

Unlike new construction warranties, which cover all types of problems, including expensive structural problems, home owner warranties for previously owned homes are actually service contracts—many people confuse them with insurance and, in many states, they are actually regulated by the state department of insurance—where the warranty covers any costs to repair or replace a broken appliance or plumbing system over and above a deductible, also called a service fee. Home owner warranties do not, however, cover preexisting problems. If the appliance works on the day of closing, it's covered. Otherwise, it's not. But these warranties don't cover everything in your home. Most important, they do not cover structural problems, such as a crack in the basement or a leaky roof. Industry experts say they are designed to cover those appliances that are in working condition when the home is sold.

The typical policy covers the furnace, air conditioning, kitchen appliances, water heater, trash compactor, electrical system (fuses and interior wiring), and interior plumbing. But there are serious exclusions. For example, if a pipe bursts because something gets stuck, it's covered. But if a pipe bursts because it freezes, it's not covered. Commonly, separate warranties must be purchased for refrigerators, washers, and dryers.

Usually the seller purchases a home owner's warranty, which is paid for out of the closing proceeds. All that you, the buyer, are responsible for is the deductible, which the industry likes to call the service fee. Are home warranties worth it? "If you look at a home in terms of the kinds of things that can go wrong in the first year, it's a pretty good deal" for the buyer, says Mike Rosenfeld, of the Home Warranty Association of California. "It's inevitable in a [resale] house, some things are going to break down. Water heaters can explode. Furnaces can go out. Air conditioners can break. Without a home warranty, you'd probably spend one thousand dollars to repair a furnace or twenty-five hundred dollars to replace it," he adds.

While a home warranty offers some protection against some problems, you are still responsible for the deductible or service fee, which on some home warranties can run as much as $150 per service call. Most home warranties have deductibles, or service fees, that range from $35 to $150.

First-Time Buyer Tip: In some states, home warranties are completely *unregulated*. In other states, the department of insurance regulates the home warranty. If the home you are considering comes along with a home warranty, check out the company for any reports of nonpayment of claims. Also, check for complaints that have been filed with the Better Business Bureau, your state's attorney's office, and the attorney general's office.

QUESTION 37
What Does the Contract Really Say and What Are My Obligations Under It?

The real estate contract, also called a purchase and sale agreement, contains certain provisions that deal with the transfer of title to property between two parties. It also has certain provisions that deal with what happens to the property if it's destroyed before the deal is closed.

Price and title (the actual ownership interest in a house) are most important. What are you buying? With a house, you are usually buying a house on land with things in it. With a condo or town house, you are buying the space between the walls, floor, and ceiling of a building with things in it. The sellers are supposed to deliver to you title to the house or condo or town house. How are they going to guarantee and deliver good title? If they are including personal property in the sale, like a washing machine, are they giving it to you with good title?

Before we get into the meat of it, let's have a definition of good title. Good title means the property's title is free of defects, easements, liens, mortgages (except your own), and free from any matters that would impair your use of your home as a residential dwelling. The basic elements of a contract include: the assurance of good title, the deed, conveyance (that is, transfer to your ownership) of personal property like bookshelves or light fixtures, how you're going to pay for the property, and where the closing is going to be. Other elements of the contract are of slightly lesser importance.

Of all the basic issues, title is the most important. This example may illustrate one problem. Let's say you're looking at a house in the Indiana Dunes. You see a house and agree to pay $200,000 for it. So the seller has you sign a contract. But if you don't know anything about the title to that house, you don't know what rights the seller is selling to you. The seller might be selling you a house on leased land that may only have five years left on the lease. In the Indiana Dunes, the federal government, which owns the land, recently made a decision not to renew the leases for land upon which some homes sit. Those home owners, some of who recently paid big bucks for vacation homes on the beach, are out of luck. If you bought one of those houses for $200,000 and only had ten years to live there, that's a steep $20,000 per year. Plus, you'll never be able to resell the property and recoup your investment. A purchase and sale agreement usually provides that the seller must give the purchasers a warranty deed. That deed warrants that the seller has good title to the property and that he or she will defend you against others who may claim to have an ownership interest in the home you are buying. If the seller has only a leasehold interest in the property, then he or she can sell only that leasehold interest, and not title to the property.

Under the contract, you are obliged to purchase the property, for a certain amount of money, at a certain time, provided the seller guarantees good title.

QUESTION 38
What Should I Sign Without Having an Attorney Review It First?

You can sign any contract, as long as it contains the absolute right for your attorney to review the document and approve it. If the contract or document does not contain that absolute right, then do not sign it unless you're sure you understand all the provisions contained within the document. As I mentioned before, most attorney riders give your attorney the limited right to cancel the contract on the basis of your attorney's review of the contract. If you're going to use a real estate attorney, and you're not sure you understand the terms of the contract you're signing—for example, if you're not sure if there is an absolute right for your attorney to review and approve the document—then show it to your attorney *before* you sign it.

QUESTION 39
Do I Have to Have a Real Estate Attorney? Do I Need a Real Estate Attorney?

No state will require you to have a real estate attorney. In fact, real estate professionals in some states actively discourage the use of an attorney, instead encouraging buyers and sellers to rely on real estate brokers and the local title company to close the deal. Whether or not you need a real estate attorney depends on how familiar you are with the workings of the real estate industry. I've talked to attorneys and brokers all over the country and they overwhelmingly recommend that first-time buyers use attorneys.

There are several reasons for this. Real estate attorneys:

- Act as another layer removing emotion from the deal;
- Can negotiate the finer points of the deal for you;
- Can protect you from getting a bad deal should the negotiation turn nasty;
- Can work with the brokers to organize and finalize details of the closing;
- Can explain the legal consequences of the deal and any terms you may not understand;
- Are a good buy for the money, as you can usually get them to work for a fixed fee;
- May be able to get you a reduced fee from the title company (which works on volume);
- Track all the little details that ensure a smooth closing;
- Provide you with a closing book that neatly organizes all the documents involved with your house closing.

You may think you're making a smart move by cutting out your real estate attorney and saving yourself the fee. But when you consider a $60,000, $100,000, or $200,000 investment (which is the cost of your home), it isn't so smart. On a $100,-000 home, the attorney's fee is minuscule, and on a bad deal, that fee could save you a tremendous amount of heartache as well as money to fix whatever problems crop up.

How Do I Find a Real Estate Attorney and How Much Should He or She Charge Me?

Not all real estate attorneys are competent, let alone good. And it's important to find one who will help, rather than hinder, the deal. Finding a good real estate attorney is like finding a good broker. First, you should ask your broker and friends for recommendations. You want someone experienced, someone who has handled a minimum of fifty closings within the past three years. After you get several names, call them up and ask them how much they charge and what they will do for that fee. Don't be embarrassed to ask about fees. It's crucial that you know how much you're getting for your money.

Some attorneys (especially those in medium or large law firms) charge by the hour. Others (especially solo practitioners) charge a flat fee. Try to find someone who will charge you a flat fee for his or her time. That way if there is a problem with the closing, you won't be charged for all those extra hours.

Looking solely at how much attorneys charge for their services is not necessarily the best way to choose your attorney. For this, the biggest investment of your life, ask yourself if you feel comfortable telling this person all the intimate details of your financial life. It's vital that you feel comfortable with, and perhaps even a bit close to, your attorney.

If a deal is really complicated, you will almost certainly need an attorney. Sam once worked on a house closing that seemed pretty ordinary until he found out there were ten lenders. He had to negotiate a separate deal with each lender until they were all satisfied. The extremely complicated closing took ten hours. Someone at the closing called it the "hour per lender" deal.

Once you hire the attorney, the general idea is to let him or her do the job. If the attorney advises you on certain points, believe him or her. If he or she tells you to do something, do it. The attorney knows the ins and outs of real estate law much better than you do.

Note: Hiring a real estate lawyer is *not* the same thing as having your Uncle Harry, the tax attorney, do your real estate closing. Real estate law is specialized and while Uncle Harry may be a whiz at writing wills, or leasing airplanes, or finding creative places to put your money, he may help get you nailed to the wall in two minutes if he doesn't truly understand the finer points of real estate law.

Should I Close at the Beginning, Middle, or End of the Month and Why Does It Matter?

When you choose to schedule your closing will be a point of negotiation between you and the seller. The issues you need to consider are personal timing and money. Here are some points to help you clarify why timing is everything:

1. Set the closing date according to when your current lease ends. If you're living in an apartment, it's foolish to close when you still have six months left on your lease, unless you can easily sublet your apartment or you have an escape clause. If you close at the beginning of a month and your lease expires at the end of the month, and you don't need to do any work in your new home, you'll be paying double rent for one month, which can be costly.

2. If you close at the beginning of a month, the lender will require you to prepay the interest on your loan from the day of closing to the end of the month. Therefore, the cash you would need at closing will be more than what you would need if you chose to close at the end of the month. For example, if you close April 15, you'll have to prepay your mortgage from April 15 to April 30. If you close April 30, you only pay one day's mortgage interest.

3. If you're trying to decide whether to close December 31 or January 2, remember that you get to take deductions for your house in the year that it closes, even if it's on the last day of the year. If you close December 31, the points you pay at the closing on a purchase, plus any prepaid interest, are deductible on your income tax statement for that year. But you should make sure if you choose to close on December 31 that these deductible costs will be greater than the standard deduction allowed to you by the IRS. Talk to your accountant or someone familiar with these real estate tax issues to find out how they might affect your situation.

Note: Mortgage interest and principal payments are paid in arrears—that is, you pay on July 1 for money you've borrowed in June. If you close April 15, you would pay a half month's mortgage interest in cash at closing. You would then pay nothing until June 1, when you would pay the interest for the month of May. On July 1, you pay interest for the month of June. And so on. The reason for this is that your loan payments are computed at a certain rate and that rate remains constant, like a fixed-rate loan. The lender must manually compute the amount of interest from the day of closing to the end of the month.

First-Time Buyer Tip: If you decide to close at the end of the month, which is the day your lease expires, be sure you have a back-up place to live just in case you don't close on the property—even if it means moving back home with the folks for a few nights.

QUESTION 42
What Is Seller Disclosure and How Does It Affect Me?

Seller disclosure is one of the more recent phenomena of residential real estate. Essentially, seller disclosure requires the seller to disclose any known material latent defects in his or her property. That means the seller must disclose if his or her property has any hidden or unseen defects that could adversely affect the value of the property.

Buyers like seller disclosure because it tells them up front about the condition of the property. Some sellers like disclosing the defects, because it protects them from buyers discovering the defects during an inspection and then asking for money to fix the problems. Other sellers don't. They feel uncomfortable with this formal process of baring their home's soul, so to speak. As a buyer, you want to find out everything you can in advance about the condition of the home. If you run into a seller disclosure form (and it is increasingly likely that you will), the seller might say the price of the house takes into account these problems. Then you will have to decide if the house is worth the asking price if it also needs a new roof and a new furnace or air-conditioning system. Remember, anything can be negotiated.

Here's a little bit of recent history to explain the hoopla over seller disclosure: Although it seems as though state law would already cover seller disclosure, for the most part it does not. State law in Illinois prior to 1993, for example, was silent on the issue. In effect, that meant if there was a defect hidden in the house and the seller knew about it but didn't say anything to anyone about it, then the buyer was stuck with the problem. Caveat emptor: Buyer beware. If, however, the seller told his or her broker about the hidden defect, the broker was obligated to inform the buyer.

By 1992, only California and Maine had some sort of formal regulation requiring sellers to disclose any hidden material latent defects in the property. In 1987, California passed a law that codified the questions the seller must answer. In addition, the agent for the seller, the buyer, and the seller himself or herself must sign off that they have reasonably inspected the property and disclosed any defect. In Maine, the broker is required to ask specific questions that the state has designated. The broker is required to gather this information at the time the property is listed and provide this information in writing to the buyer prior to, or during, the preparation of an offer.

The National Association of Realtors (NAR) would like to see some form of seller disclosure mandated by every state. According to the NAR's legal counsel, one of the largest areas of controversy in the process of buying and selling homes is the failure to disclose defects in property. The majority of lawsuits after closing, where buyers are unhappy, involve the alleged failure to disclose some condition affecting value or desirability. The finger is usually pointed in the direction of the broker first, and then to the seller. Because the NAR protects the interests of brokers, it feels sellers, rather than brokers, should shoulder the responsibility for disclosing defects in their house.

As the NAR's attorney said: "The agent has the duty to disclose factors that he can observe with a reasonably diligent inspection. The broker doesn't live there. [Seller disclosure] forces those issues to be addressed."

In 1992, Coldwell Banker, a national real estate company, announced a new policy that required all sellers listing property with the company to fill out and sign disclosure forms. Although some sellers aren't thrilled with the prospect of having to fill out a form that asks specific questions about the house, land, and neighborhood, buyers are generally glad to have it. If you are not working with a Coldwell Banker agent but like the idea of a seller disclosure form, ask your broker if his or her firm has one. If not, you can use this Coldwell Banker seller's disclosure statement as a guide and ask the seller to answer specific questions about the condition of the property *before* you make an offer to purchase.

Coldwell Banker Seller's Disclosure Statement asks specific questions about the condition of the home, land, and neighborhood. (See Appendix III for a complete form.)

QUESTION 43
Do I Need a Home Inspection? How Do I Find a Reputable Home Inspector?

The quick answer is YES! Except in the rare situation, such as buying a home from your parents that you have lived in and know intimately, smart brokers always advise their buyers to have the home inspected by a professional inspector or someone you know is knowledgeable about construction matters and issues involved in residential properties. But that doesn't

SELLER'S DISCLOSURE STATEMENT

1. Seller(s) Name(s):_____

    Property Address:_____
    Is each individual named above a U.S. Citizen or resident alien? Yes ☐ No ☐
    Approximate Age of Property:_____ Date Purchased: _____

2. **NOTICE TO SELLER**
    Each Seller is obligated to disclose to a buyer all known facts that materially and adversely affect the value of the property
    ~~~~ that are not readily observable. This disclosure statement is designed to assist Seller in complying with
    ~~~~ Buyer in evaluating the property being considered. The listing real estate broker,
    ~~~~ctive agents will also rely upon this information when they evaluate, market

    ~~~~ Seller and is not a

(Coldwell Banker Seller's Disclosure Statement asks specific questions about
the condition of the home, land, and neighborhood. Copyright 1991, Coldwell Banker Residential. Reprinted with permission.)

excuse you from looking carefully over the home before you
get to the inspection stage. Remember, the inspector will
charge you between $150 and $300 or more for each inspection. By keeping a sharp eye out for the following, you may be
able to spot some major problems and eliminate a potential
property before paying an inspector. Watch out for:

- *Wet, clammy, sticky, smelly basements.* A damp feel to a
  basement can hint at water seepage caused by improperly graded soil, or an improperly laid foundation.
- *Cracks in the basement.* A visible crack line in the interior
  of the basement or on the exterior foundation could
  point to more-than-normal settling. Or the house may
  have been built on new landfill, a hill, or an improperly
  graded site. It could also point to an area prone to earthquakes or earth movement.

- *Poorly fitted duct work.* Heating and cooling systems can be problematic, especially if the original work was done in a slipshod way. Check the duct lines to see that they fit snugly and securely.
- *Discolored spots on walls and ceilings.* Discoloration could be the result of a water problem, either a leak from the roof, walls, or pipes. Also, beware of a fresh paint job, particularly in the top floor of the house. It may be covering up a problem.
- *Improperly fitted skylights.* Now extremely popular, skylights are usually one-piece preassembled units that are popped into a hole in the roof. Check for discoloration, peeling paint, or other signs that the skylights were improperly fitted or may be leaking.
- *Damp attic.* Poor attic ventilation can lead to moisture being trapped in the upper recesses, causing dry rot or condensation.
- *Insulation.* Does the house have adequate insulation? If not, you could be looking at a fortune in heating and cooling expenses. If the home has insulation, ask about the R factor (the higher the number, the better) and be sure the insulation is facing the correct way.
- *Sloppy masonry work.* Has the home owner tried to patch up the masonry him- or herself? It could be a sign of a larger problem. If you're looking at new construction, sloppy masonry and detail work can mean that other work was also done in a slipshod way.
- *Do-it-yourself electrical work.* Proper electrical wiring is a must to avoid future problems that could be costly to fix as well as a serious safety concern.

There are thousands of potential hazards when purchasing a home, and most buyers have no idea where to begin to look for problems. That's why it's so important to have the proper inspections completed before the expiration of the inspection clauses. First, you never know a home unless you've lived in it. Second, most people aren't particularly familiar with the structure and mechanicals of a house, town house or condo. The roof may look fine to your eyes, but a house inspector may see peeling shingles and notice water marks from leaks on the ceiling. Third, a house inspector can be yet another voice helping you to distance your emotions from the purchase of the home.

Once you've received the right to have the home inspected, you have to find the inspectors. If you look in your local telephone book, you'll find dozens, if not hundreds, of people calling themselves "professional home inspectors." Some of them are, some of them aren't. Some of the most qualified home inspectors are members of the American Society of Home Inspectors (ASHI), a nationwide, nonprofit professional association founded in 1976. ASHI only admits as members those home inspectors who have performed at least 750 home inspections according to the ASHI Standards of Practice, or 250 inspections in addition to other licenses and experience. Applicants must also pass a written exam, receive approval on at least three sample inspection reports, and perform a satisfactory home inspection before a peer review committee.

Where can you find a good inspector? Ask your real estate broker for a list of suggestions. When you call:

- Compare fees (they should range from $150 to $500, depending on the size of the home).
- Ask what's included in the fee and how long the inspection should take (generally around two hours for a thorough inspection of a moderately sized property).
- Compare telephone manner (the inspector should be courteous and knowledgeable).

- Ask for a list of specialized inspectors you might call (for radon, asbestos, electromagnetic power, water quality, pest control, etc.).
- Ask if the inspector is bonded, licensed, and insured.
- Ask if the inspector is a member of ASHI or another professional inspection association.
- Ask for references, and then call them.

Once you've found your inspector, have him or her come out before the expiration of the right-to-inspection clause in your contract. You will usually have about five days from the time you sign the contract to have your inspection. Don't wait until the last day in case it's raining or the inspection needs to be rescheduled.

First-Time Buyer Tip: Never have the inspector come in the dark or when it's raining or snowing, because you want him or her to inspect the entire property, exterior and interior spaces. Daylight makes the process easier. Also, if the inspector balks at inspecting the basement, crawl space, attic, garage, or anything else, you may want to call his or her supervisor, or simply find a new inspector. It could be that the inspector isn't doing his or her job.

At the end of the inspection, or perhaps the next day, the inspector will give you a report of what's wrong with the house. If you're smart, you'll go to the inspection and walk around with the inspector. Ask a lot of questions as you go along. The inspector should be happy to explain everything to you. It's an excellent opportunity to learn about the home you're buying and what to watch out for in the future.

If a qualified, licensed, and bonded house inspector tells you the property may need $20,000 worth of repairs within the first five years, it should change the way you think about it. Is the property still a bargain? Should you look elsewhere? Can you afford to buy a home that will need such a substantial cash outlay within such a short period of time? Is the house a great deal anyway? (If your contract has an inspection contingency, you should be able to terminate the contract and get your earnest money back. Then you can search for another home.)

QUESTION 44
Should I Test for Toxic Substances, Including Radon, Lead, Asbestos, Electromagnetic Power, and Contaminated Water?

You've already asked for the right to have a professional inspector inspect your house. And you've asked for the right to have your home inspected for pests. Have you thought about having an inspector test for toxic substances? Once a rare addition to contracts, toxic substance inspections—including radon, lead, water, and asbestos—have become a regular part of most real estate contracts. Unfortunately, most home inspectors are not qualified to do specialized tests for toxic substances. You must therefore find separate inspectors who specialize.

Here are the major toxic substances for which home buyers are inspecting:

Radon. A study in 1989 by the Environmental Protection Agency stated that twenty-two thousand deaths a year are attributed to radon, a gas that seeps through cracks in the house or foundation from the earth. According to an EPA pamphlet, "Radon is the second leading cause of lung cancer in the U.S., after cigarette smoking. As you breathe it in, its decay products become trapped inside your lungs. As these products continue to decay, they release small bursts of energy that can damage lung tissue and lead to lung cancer. It's like exposing your family to hundreds of chest X-rays each year." Of the home buyers and home owners who actually check for radon, the EPA estimates around 20 percent will find an unacceptable level.

Although you can purchase an EPA-listed radon gas test kit in your local hardware store, it's best for new home buyers to have a professional inspector perform the test, *which requires two to four days exposure in the home.* Radon emissions can be fixed, either by sealing the cracks or installing an air system that sucks out the gas from beneath the home.

For more information on radon, call the EPA's hotline at (800) SOS-RADO.

Asbestos. If you're buying new construction or anything built since the mid-1970s, you needn't worry about asbestos. If you are buying an older home, it is likely there is some asbestos in the house.

Asbestos is a microscopic airborne fiber that is ingested through the nose or mouth; it lodges in the lung and can cause lung cancer. If not disturbed, the threat from asbestos is minimal, if any. You can have an asbestos specialist come out and tell you if there is asbestos in the home and how much it will cost to have it wrapped or removed (the two ways to abate the threat). Lori, a first-time buyer in Chicago, said she wasn't deterred from buying her home because of asbestos. She and the seller agreed at closing to give her a cash credit (a payment to the buyer at closing) equal to the price it would cost to remove the asbestos.

For more information on asbestos, contact your local OSHA (Occupational Safety and Health Administration) office of the federal government, or your local office of the federal Consumer Product Safety Commission.

Lead. High levels of lead in paint and water have been connected with mental and physical development problems. Lead is a problem when eaten or inhaled. Lead paint is most often found in older homes (its use has been banned for more than twenty years) and can simply be covered up. In HUD homes, or those financed with an FHA mortgage, lead paint must be removed or covered over. A test by an outside agency can run between $100 and $300, depending on the number of samples tested.

High levels of lead in water is another problem, particularly in old homes and apartment buildings. If pipes that were soldered together with lead begin to corrode, lead particles can be released into your water supply. If the water is contaminated at the source (from your local city or municipal water supply), you may want to consider buying a filtering system, or looking for another home in a different area.

For more information, call your local office of the federal Consumer Product Safety Commission.

Electromagnetic Radiation. One of the most recently discovered hazards is electromagnetic radiation from high-voltage power lines. Although only a few, early studies have been done, they seem to show an increased rate of cancer and other unusual diseases in people who live in homes that are located directly underneath high-voltage power lines. Power companies deny the link, but you may simply want to avoid the risk. There is no way to fix the problem; you must simply find another house.

There is a test for electromagnetic radiation, which can cost between $100 to $250, depending on the house.

First-Time Buyer Tip: Real estate attorneys advise that the language you use in your contract should state that the "sale is contingent upon satisfactory results of the tests." You don't want the language to say that you have the right to have the tests but not the right to back out of the deal if the house fails to pass the tests.

QUESTION 45
What If the Inspectors Find Something Wrong with the Home I Want to Buy?

It's likely that your home, toxic substance, or pest inspector will find something wrong with the property you want to buy. Remember, that's their job. Once a problem is found, you have to ask yourself two questions:

- Is the problem fixable or unfixable?
- At what price is the problem fixable?

Here are some unfixable problems: The house sits on a fault line; the house is in a flood plain; the home's foundation is severely cracked; the house's water supply has been contaminated by the local dump; the house is located under electromagnetic power lines. Almost everything else is fixable. But is it affordable or smart to try and fix it? Is the house worth it? You can fix a leaky roof or replace it entirely, but is the house worth its $100,000 price plus $5,000 for a new roof? What if the house also needs a new furnace and hot water heater? What if it needs upgraded electricity for a clothes dryer? What if the pipes are old and leaking?

If your inspectors find something wrong with the house, you have two options: You can either withdraw from the contract (provided you have the right inspection contingency) or renegotiate the purchase price to reflect the cost of fixing the items marked on the inspection list. If you decide to withdraw from the contract, have your attorney write the letter. If you decide to go ahead, but want to renegotiate the purchase price, talk to your broker and your attorney about what may be customary for your area.

QUESTION 46
What Do I Do if the Seller or Broker Has Misrepresented the Condition of the Home?

If you find out from the inspection that the seller or broker has misrepresented the home, you have the option of walking away from the home and reporting the broker's conduct to the state agency that regulates real estate professionals. In that case, consider yourself lucky not to have bought what could easily have turned out to be a lemon of a house. There's nothing more frustrating than living through one crisis after another. If you find out after you close on the home that the seller or broker has clearly misrepresented the condition of the home, or did not disclose everything they knew about the property or should have known about the property, you can take them to court; but be prepared to prove that they did have knowledge of the problem or should have had knowledge.

When we bought our co-op, the seller and the seller broker told us that everything was working in the unit. We forgot to test the dishwasher (always run all the appliances) before closing. The first night we were in the apartment, we decided to turn on the dishwasher. Nothing happened. Sam reached down under the sink and turned the water back on (the sellers had apparently turned off the water to the dishwasher). The next morning we found out why. The dishwasher leaked all over our new downstairs neighbors' kitchen, ruining their window shade. We were furious. Obviously, the sellers knew that their dishwasher leaked, which is why they turned off the water. Still, it cost us only $150 to replace the window shade plus $60 for the plumber to replace the hose. We wrote a nasty letter to the sellers and felt much better.

POSSESSION AND OTHER PARTS OF THE OFFER TO PURCHASE

QUESTION 47
What Is Possession?

Possession is when you actually take control of the home. Most buyers take possession of the home at closing. The keys and other security devices are handed to the buyer from the seller, who has moved all of his or her belongings from the home. At that moment, you have the right to do anything you want with your house.

Sometimes possession is given either before the closing or after. Let's say you need a place to live or want to renovate the home prior to the closing. The seller might let you take possession early by a few days so that you can move in or get started on your remodeling. Usually possession issues involve the seller wanting to stay in the house after closing (see Question 48).

Possession and the closing date are closely linked. Sometimes, they're used as negotiation points when money isn't the primary issue. In one case in California, a first-time buyer made a full-price offer for a woman's house, but the woman was having trouble accepting the offer. She hadn't found a place to move her family and was worried. The buyer stretched out the date of the closing, in exchange for a few thousand dollars off the sales price, and the deal went through.

QUESTION 48
What if the Seller Wants to Stay in the House after Closing?

There are two issues to consider here. First, if you don't mind that the sellers are there, say, if you have a little bit of time left on your lease, then you might want to charge them a reasonable rate for the extra time. This "reasonable" rate should cover your daily expenses. Second, if the sellers have overstayed their welcome, and you see that you're going to have to force them out, then you should make them pay dearly for each extra day they stay. How do you know which it's going to be? If the sellers haven't indicated they'd like to stay past closing when you negotiated the contract, and then they announce at closing they're going to stay for a while, you may have a problem. Real estate attorneys generally advise buyers to refuse to close unless the seller has moved out.

In cases where the seller asks to stay in the home after closing (either because the seller's purchase of another home is a couple of days later, or the seller is arranging a move to another city), you can give them the couple of days (a set number) for a modest fee that will cover all of your expenses of ownership. But when those days are up, the sellers should pay a fee that encourages them to move out fast. An amount of money large enough to convince the sellers it's time to move should be held in an escrow account at closing, in addition to the daily fees they will owe you.

There are a couple of ways to calculate the per-day fee: You can charge the same prices as the local hotel, or you can find out the going rent for the home and divide by thirty. In any case, you want the seller to understand that staying in the home will be a very expensive proposition. Should all else fail, and the seller continues to stay in your new home, you may have to take legal action. Consult your attorney for more details.

Of course, in some areas of the country, it's customary for the seller to retain possession *at no cost* for three to five days after closing. Your broker should be able to advise you on local closing customs.

When Is the Right Time to Terminate the Contract?

If you want to terminate the contract because you're feeling buyer's remorse (see Question 50), you can't. That's the tough part about the real estate game. The rules say, when you sign the offer, and it's presented and the sellers accept, then you have a deal. Unless your inspector finds something wrong with the home, or your attorney rejects the contract, or your lender won't grant you a mortgage, you're pretty much stuck.

Some unscrupulous buyers will have their attorneys summarily "reject" a contract if they get cold feet. That's not really fair to the sellers, who have allowed you to tie up their property during the negotiation process. In addition, the sellers may be able to sue you for specific performance, that is, living up to the deal to which you signed your name.

You may be able to walk away from the contract at other times, if you are willing to forfeit your deposit, or earnest money. Most first-time buyers have little cash, so the idea of giving up 5, 10, or 20 percent of the purchase price seems a little steep. But it has been done many times before. In this case, the earnest money is either split between the seller and the brokers, or the seller gets to keep it all.

What Is Buyer's Remorse and How Do I Cope with It?

Buyer's remorse is the sinking feeling in the pit of your stomach that you've made a terrible mistake. It usually occurs the minute, day, or week after your broker presents your offer to purchase or you sign the purchase and sale agreement. It keeps you awake at night, tossing and turning in a cold sweat, as you wonder how you're going to make the payments and you agonize over your choice. Did you make the right one?

Pam, a broker in Rock Hill, South Carolina, says if a first-time buyer has buyer's remorse, the only person to blame is the real estate agent. "If the agent has truly done her job and qualified those people, and found out what they really wanted in their first home, then they should be happy," she says. "But if the agent turns a blind eye to their insecurity about buying a home and doesn't try to help them understand the process, it can be very tough."

Buying a home is such an emotional process that first-timers often get overwhelmed. Pam says brokers should be understanding and help you make sure you're making the right decision for the right reason. Brokers should be able to read the personality of that buyer and make sure that the decision is not 100 percent emotion, zero percent common sense. Pam says that she often helps her distraught first-time buyers with something she calls "The Ben Franklin Close": Make a list of everything you like about the house and then everything you would change. This will help you make a rational decision by seeing the pluses and minuses of a home."

What's the cure for buyer's remorse? As the sages say,

"Time heals all wounds." Give yourself six months in your new home. If you still hate it, you can always turn around and try to sell it. Chances are, after six months to a year, you'll be settled in and feeling a whole lot better.

PART III

Financing

THE PROCESS OF APPLYING
FOR A MORTGAGE

What Exactly Is a Mortgage?

If a person agrees to lend you money, it's likely he or she will ask you to put up something to collateralize the loan. The collateral must be something of equal or greater worth than the amount of the loan so that the lender feels secure in giving you the money. Here's a formal definition: A *mortgage* is a loan for which you pledge the title to your home as the collateral. The lender agrees to hold the title (or agrees, in some states, to hold a lien on your title) until you have paid back the loan plus interest. The lender gives you the money, and in exchange, you agree to make monthly installments of principal and interest, home insurance, and real estate taxes, which most people somewhat mistakenly call the mortgage payment.

140

The history of mortgages is interesting. Before the Great Depression in the 1930s, we didn't have mortgages the way we know them today. Back then, people paid cash for their homes. Or they would take out very short "balloon" mortgages, on which they would pay interest for maybe five years, and then owe the entire balance in one huge "balloon" payment.

When the stock market crashed in 1929, most people lost their life savings and were unable to pay back their mortgages. So they lost their homes. In fact, many people were unable to pay their real estate taxes and they, too, lost their homes. In 1930, so many people in Cook County (the county in Illinois that includes Chicago) couldn't afford to pay their real estate taxes (less than 50 percent paid), that the city cancelled the year's real estate tax collection. That's why Cook County collects its real estate taxes a year in arrears. In other words, Cook County home owners paid their 1993 taxes in 1994.

At the end of World War II, many returning veterans had money to spend. The U.S. government decided the men were good risks and helped come up with a plan to lend them money to buy homes. The plan allowed them to borrow money for thirty years and pay it back slowly, with interest. The program was such a huge success that commercial lenders soon followed suit.

That was the beginning of the mortgage industry. Today, billions of dollars in mortgages are made every year and are sold on the secondary market. They are such a stable source of income (less than 4 percent of all mortgages fail or go into default) that investors—like huge pension funds—buy mortgages from banks, savings and loans, and mortgage brokers. This puts money back into the system to be lent again.

Some lenders do keep a small percentage of loans in-house. To find out if your mortgage will be kept or sold, ask the person taking your application what percentage of loans are kept or sold. Remember to ask if *your* loan will be kept or sold. If your loan is sold, another company may be hired to "service" the loan for the new investor. If your loan is not sold, you will continue to pay and deal with the local folks who gave you your loan.

QUESTION 52
How Do I Get Information on Mortgages?

Getting information on mortgages is easy. Sorting through the numbers gets a little tougher. Start the process by opening up your local paper and checking out the mortgage watch column. This column gives you a list of what mortgages are currently being offered and how much they cost. Next, ask your broker if he or she has any information on getting a mortgage. Walk into your local bank, savings and loan, or credit union and ask for their free information (they should have gobs of it).

Everyone has information, and it's usually free. Even the federal government has publications that deal with mortgages. Simply write to Consumer Publications, Pueblo, Colorado 81003 and request a catalogue. Then, order the real estate–related publications you believe will help you. A word of warning, however. These federal publications talk about mortgages in general. They're good as far as they go, which isn't nearly far enough. If you find you have questions after reading through one of these little booklets, call your local mortgage company and ask questions.

What Is the Difference between a Mortgage Banker and a Mortgage Broker? And How Do I Find a Good One?

The essential ingredient to a successful purchase is finding a lender you can trust to walk you through the process. Where do you find such a person? To begin with, it's important to understand that lenders come in all sorts of shapes and sizes, and they're called by different names.

Mortgage brokers are involved with the origination side of the business. They take loan applications, process the papers, and then submit the files to an institutional investor, typically an S&L or a bank or a mortgage banker, who underwrites and closes the loan. Mortgage brokers usually work with a wide variety of investors—who will buy your loan on the secondary market, providing mortgage bankers and brokers with an almost inexhaustible supply of money with which to make new mortgages—giving them the ability to offer a wide variety of loan packages. Some mortgage brokers seem to have more lending flexibility and can work with those folks who might otherwise have a tough time getting a mortgage.

Mortgage bankers go a step further. They too work within the origination side of the business, but they also get involved with servicing the loan and closing the loan in their own name with their own funds. If you went to a bank for a loan, the mortgage banker would take the loan application and lend you the money from the bank's own coffers. Once you closed on the loan, the same company might service your account, collect payments, and make sure your real estate taxes were being paid. Or the company might sell your loan on the secondary market (to the institutional investors) and then relend the money. Mortgage bankers make their money on actually making the loan. You pay fees and points, which the banker pockets, or the mortgage banker might make additional money on the spread between the rate on your loan and the going rate of loans in the secondary market.

So how should you select a mortgage company? You should pick a company based on experience, customer service, and recommendations. The one thing you *shouldn't* do is to make the decision based solely on which lender is offering the lowest rates. While rates are extremely important, there is a tremendous amount of competition in today's mortgage market. That means all mortgage brokers and bankers should be offering mortgages at competitive prices. If a company is offering a mortgage package that's well below market rates, you should beware. All mortgage companies generally choose from the same pool of institutional investors. A company offering abnormally low rates might make up the difference by increasing closing costs or tacking on additional settlement fees.

Richard Nash, president of North Shore Mortgage and Financial Services, located in Evanston, Illinois, reminds borrowers that the lowest rates do not necessarily mean you automatically get good service (in a perfect world, they might); and fast, efficient service is essential for a smooth closing. You want to make sure the lender you choose will be able to deliver the funds to close on your new home. Most lenders offer free preprinted pamphlets and booklets on the mortgage process. The federal government also offers free (or nearly free) booklets from the aforementioned Consumer Publications Office, Pueblo, Colorado 81003. (See Resources in Appendix VI for additional places to call or write.)

How Do I Choose the Right Lender for Me?

Choosing the right lender will take some time, effort, and lots of telephone calls. It takes work because lenders today offer a plethora of mortgage options that are individually tailored to each borrower's financing needs. In major metropolitan areas, there are dozens, if not hundreds, of mortgage brokers and bankers; in smaller communities, the numbers fall proportionately. Still, there should be ample choices and fairly stiff competition among lenders for your business.

First-Time Buyer Tip: Remember, when going to apply for a loan, you're in the driver's seat. You're giving them *your* business, not the other way around. If a lender seems condescending or doesn't treat you fairly or with civility, take your business elsewhere.

To find out the names of some mortgage bankers in your area, contact the Mortgage Bankers Association of America (MBA). Headquartered in Washington, D.C., the MBA is a national real estate finance trade association that represents more than twenty-two hundred mortgage companies, savings and loan associations, commercial banks, savings banks, life insurance companies, and others in the mortgage lending field.

Starting Out

The first thing to do when starting to look for your loan is to find out what is the current mortgage interest rate. You want to know the following information:

- The current interest rate lenders are charging for their most common mortgages;
- How many points (a point is 1 percent of the loan amount) they are charging to make the loan;
- The annual percentage rate (APR) of the loan (which adds up all the extra costs and fees and amortizes the cost over the life of the loan—see Question 65);
- What lengths of loans the mortgage company offers (7/23, 5/25, thirty-year fixed, fifteen-year fixed, five-year balloon, etc.; for more information on various mortgage types, see Question 73).

The easy way to get this information is to look in your local newspaper for the mortgage watch column or advertisements. Newspapers often track current lending rates because they know many of their readers either own a home or are interested in buying or selling. The mortgage watch column lists a handful of lenders (anywhere from five to more than a dozen) and their current mortgage offerings. A telephone number and address are usually provided. What you have to do to find the best lender is to clip the mortgage watch column for several weeks, compare the prices quoted for various loans, and call up the ones that seem to have the best deals. At this point, there is no way for you to tell which mortgage banker or broker will be able to give you the best service. All you can go on is price and product.

How do you find a good mortgage banker or broker? As with finding a good real estate broker, seek out recommendations from friends and family. Your real estate broker may have excellent suggestions, since part of his or her job is to help you arrange financing. If you have a real estate attorney, ask him or her for a few names. Once you receive several names, go to their offices and talk to the manager in charge. Look around—some new mortgage brokers actually work out of their home—and see whom you're doing business with. Find out how long the company has been in business. Ask them how many mortgages they have closed and for around how much money. It's important to work with a company that has a track record.

First-Time Buyer Tip: You should feel entirely comfortable with your lender and your loan officer. If you get a funny feeling at the office, leave and find another mortgage company. If you're concerned about its track record, or the way it deals with its customers, don't be afraid to approach your local Better Business Bureau, chamber of commerce, or attorney general. You can also call the Mortgage Bankers Association (MBA) of America to see if any claims have been filed. Finally, feel free to ask for references, and then call them.

QUESTION 55
Who Are the People Involved with Making the Loan?

Once you've begun to compare rates and mortgage products (see Mortgage Types), it's time to go and meet the people who will be guiding your loan through the approval process.

The *loan officer* is the person you'll be dealing with, your primary contact. The loan officer should be with you all the way through the process, from application to closing.

Typically, the loan officer will take down all the information and bring the information back to the office (if the application was filled out somewhere other than the office) and then the loan processor (the loan officer's partner) will order the appraisal, credit report, and title and then mail everything out. The loan is packaged up and then sent to the investor, who will make the decision whether or not to approve your loan. All the way through, your contact should be with the loan officer, the person you've dealt with from the very beginning.

Beware of hand-offs. There are companies that use a loan officer to take your application and then you must deal with other people you have never met to continue the process—the loan processor. You don't want that. You want to have confidence that the loan officer will handle the application through to the end, will care about your needs, and will make sure the deal gets done.

How Do You Know if the Loan Officer Is Doing His or Her Job?

Generally (and this includes extremely busy periods of low-interest-rate refinancing), the loan application shouldn't take more than three to four weeks in most areas for approval. Ask the loan officer how long the approval process should take. If you're hearing about delays in mortgage processing, if you're getting numerous requests for additional information, then you should start to get concerned. There's nothing wrong with a loan officer's calling to say that four pieces of documentation are missing from the file. But if you're getting multiple requests for documentation, then the loan officer didn't do his or her job in the beginning. Unless you have special circumstances, like if you're self-employed or you trade commodities, the loan officer should ask for everything right up front. And you should make every effort to give the loan officer all that is needed to get your home approved. It is wise to discuss any particular issues affecting your financial picture early in the process and preferably before you put down any money. Some of these issues might include credit problems, previous bankruptcies, divorces, recent job changes, etc.

How Do I Apply for a Loan?

Applying for a loan is different from getting prequalified. Getting prequalified before you buy property involves going to a lender and having the lender analyze your assets, liabilities, and income stream. From these items (which the lender may not see but may just take your word on), the lender comes up with a dollar amount you can borrow. When you actually get down to the nitty-gritty of making a formal application for a loan, things change. The lender will want to see documentation and proof that you actually have the assets and debts you say you have. You will sit down with the loan officer, who will ask you questions and write down the answers.

Having the following information can speed up the process significantly:

- Copies of all bank statements for the last three months;
- Copies of all accounts, including stock brokerage accounts;
- Most recent pay stub;
- W2 form for the past two years;
- If you're self-employed, your last two years of tax returns plus a profit-and-loss statement for the year to date.

There are some important decisions you'll have to make at the time of application.

1. *What type of mortgage should you choose?* At the time of application, you'll have to decide which mortgage type is right for you. (See Questions 72 through 80 for greater detail on different mortgage types.) The type of mortgage you choose will depend heavily on your personality and the amount of risk you're willing to take. You'll have to decide if you're the type of person who likes little risk (fixed loan would probably work well for you), some risk (a 7/23 or 5/25 might be the ticket), or a lot of risk (ARMs—adjustable-rate mortgages—are a good choice, and they even have built-in caps on how high the interest rate can jump each year and over the entire life of the loan). The loan officer should be delighted to go over the different mortgage products offered by his or her firm, and to counsel you on which one might be right for your situation.

2. *Should you float the rate or lock in?* When the lender asks you this question, he or she is really asking you if you want to lock in at the current rate, or take a gamble that the rates will drop a bit before you close on the loan.

   Here's how the float option works: Let's say you go in on Monday and fill out an application. The rate for a thirty-year fixed loan is 8 percent. You're scheduled to close in two months. You think interest rates are going to drop in the next sixty days, and so you opt to float your loan, meaning that at any point in the next sixty days you can call to lock in the rate. If rates drop, you'll get the lower rate. But if rates go up, you'll have to pay the higher rate. If, however, you think that mortgage rates can't possibly go lower than they are before you are scheduled to close, then it's in your best interest to lock in the rate of your mortgage. That means, whatever the mortgage rate is on the day you make the application, that will be the interest rate you pay on your mortgage.

Locking in or floating the interest rate has nothing to do with what type of mortgage you choose. You can choose to float the rate or lock in on all types of mortgages, including a fixed or adjustable-rate mortgage (ARM).

3. *How long should the lock be?* This sounds like the same question as above, but it's not. When you apply for a loan, the mortgage rate offered by the lender is only good for a specific amount of time. You have to choose how long you want the rate to last, while remembering that the longer the rate lock, the higher the rate will generally be.

Lenders usually offer to hold the rate for thirty, forty-five, or sixty days. You should base the length of the lock on when you're supposed to close on the loan. For example, if you apply for a loan twenty-eight days before you want to close, you might choose to hold the rate for thirty days. If you're going to close in thirty-eight days, you might choose to lock in for forty-five days. Lenders will rarely offer to hold a lock for longer than sixty days, but if you need to close quickly, they might manage to approve your mortgage and lock a rate for seven days. The shorter the lock, the more important it is to furnish your lender with everything he or she needs to get your loan going.

The reason lenders don't like to lock in rates for extended periods of time is that interest rates fluctuate daily and often change several times each day. With that much activity, it's difficult for lenders and investors to predict how much interest rates will change over the course of two months. To protect themselves, they limit the length of lock-ins. Just remember, the longer you want the lender to hold the lock, the more you'll pay for that privilege.

4. *How many points do you want to pay?* Another decision you'll have to make is how many points you want to pay at the closing. Most first-time borrowers don't realize there is an inverse relationship between the number of points (a point is one percentage point of the loan amount) you pay and the interest rate you receive. You'll probably have to pay something in points, but the more points you pay, the lower the interest rate. If you pay no points up front, you'll have a higher interest rate, and pay more over the life of the loan. Points are paid in cash (usually tough for first-time buyers to come by) at the closing, but the federal government allows you to deduct them from your income taxes during the year of the closing. Or you can amortize your points (pay them over the life of the loan) which will ultimately increase your rate.

When do you want to pay points? Let's say you decide to close on your home in November. That means you might only have one month's worth of mortgage interest to deduct in that year. However, if you decide to pay three or four points in cash at closing, you would have more to deduct for the year. If you decide to pay five points, the lender might lower your rate by a point and a half. That's called "buying down" the loan.

152

(Sometimes developers use a different sort of buy down to entice first-time buyers to purchase new construction. They'll "buy down" the rate for the first two or three years with cash. This doesn't have anything to do with paying more points up front in exchange for a lower interest rate, though they're both called the same name.) You receive two significant benefits from buying down your interest rate. The first is a larger deduction; the second is a lower interest rate for the life of the loan.

Here's how points work: If you need a $100,000 mortgage, each point is $1,000. If you decide to buy down your loan with five points, you will need $5,000 in cash at closing just to cover the points paid to the lender.

Good Faith Estimate of Closing Costs

Every time you put in an application for a loan, the lender is required by federal law (the law is called RESPA, for Real Estate Settlement Procedures Act) to give you a good faith estimate of your closing costs. That sheet of paper should detail every fee you'll likely pay, and add it all up for you. You may even be asked to sign the document, to prove that you've seen it.

First-Time Buyer Tip: Many first-time home buyers feel somewhat deceived by the good faith estimate because the actual costs at closing may be slightly or significantly different from the costs originally listed. A good lender should get very close to the actual closing cost numbers in the estimate. However, an estimate is an estimate. There may be last-minute costs that come up at closing. If you feel that the charges are unusually high, you or your real estate attorney can talk to the lender and renegotiate. If a charge seems unfair or completely outrageous, and it was not on the good faith estimate, you should refuse to pay it.

NOTE: Never walk away from an application without getting a copy of every document you've signed. It is extremely important to be able to document in writing every step in the application process. If your lender ever gives you trouble, you'll have to prove what was said and what was signed. Also, signing a document signifies that you've actually read it. Take the time to read all documents at the application, and don't be afraid to ask questions of the loan officer. Remember, you're not the first first-time buyer the loan officer has dealt with. And you won't be the last.

QUESTION 57
What Kind of Documentation Will I Need for My Application?

If you've spent months searching for the perfect home, the last thing you want are delays in the mortgage approval process. Unfortunately, a delay in getting approved for your mortgage can push back the closing or be a viable reason for the seller to cancel the purchase contract. One problem causing delays is documentation. Even after going through the pounds of paperwork during the mortgage application process, lenders often request more documentation.

According to one loan officer, most borrowers don't know

exactly how much detailed information the lender will need to approve their loans. Here is a list of documents your loan officer may ask for:

- All W2 forms for each person who will be a coborrower on the loan.
- Copies of completed tax papers for the last three years; include any schedules or attachments.
- Copies of one month's worth of pay stubs.
- Copies of the last three bank statements for every bank account, IRA, 401K, or stock account that you have. Bring a copy of your most recent statement for any assets you have.
- A copy of the back and front of your canceled earnest money check. Contact the bank if this has not yet come through.
- Copy of the sales contract and all riders. You'll also need both brokers' names, addresses, and phone numbers, and the same information for both your attorney and the seller's attorney.
- If you are selling a current residence, you will need to provide a copy of the listing agreement and, if the home is under contract, a copy of the sales contract.
- If gift funds are involved, the giver must provide proof that he or she had that money to give, such as a copy of the giver's recent bank statement. You must then show the paper trail for the money, including a deposit slip. The giver will have to fill out a gift letter affidavit, available from the loan officer, indicating that the funds were a gift and the gift giver does not expect repayment.
- Complete copies of all divorce decrees.
- Copies of an old survey or title policy for the home you

are buying, if available when you apply for the mortgage, or when it becomes available during the purchase process.

- If you are self-employed, you will also need to provide complete copies of the last two years' business tax returns and a year-to-date profit-and-loss statement and balance sheet with original signatures.
- A list of your addresses in the last seven years.
- If you have made any large deposits (i.e., larger than your monthly income) into your bank accounts in the last three months, you will need to provide an explanation as to where the funds came from with proof.
- If you have opened a new bank account in the last six months, you will need to provide a letter explaining where the money came from to open this new account.
- Addresses and account numbers for every form of credit you have.
- Documentation to verify additional income, such as Social Security, child support, and alimony.
- If you have had a previous bankruptcy, bring a complete copy of the bankruptcy proceedings, including all schedules and a letter explaining the circumstances for the bankruptcy.
- For a Federal Housing Administration (FHA) or Veterans Administration (VA) loan, bring a photocopy of a picture ID and a copy of your Social Security card. Also, bring proof of enlistment for a VA loan. (See Questions 78 and 79.)
- If you have any judgments against you, you will need to provide a copy of recorded satisfaction of judgment, and copies of documents describing any lawsuits with which you are currently involved.

What Types of Circumstances Might Foul Up My Loan Application? And How Can I Fix Them?

Lower rates have led to a crush of business at mortgage lenders' offices and, as a result, the application process may take longer than usual. The problem is that delays can force you to the wall on the occupancy of your new home and even threaten the terms of your loan, such as the interest rate and the fees the lender charges. It's vital that you, the buyer, stay on top of things from the day of application through the closing. There are often things you can do to help speed the mortgage loan process and meet that pressing deadline.

Any number of things can go wrong during the mortgage approval process: You or the lender can lose documents; the lender may demand more documentation; appraisals may be running late; or verification from banks or your employer may not be processed quickly enough. Mortgage experts agree that problems can surface with interest rates, points, or the up-front fees a lender charges to make a mortgage loan. In fact, they estimate that as many as 30 percent of all mortgage applications will face some problem with the interest rate or points.

The Rate Lock

To eliminate the uncertainty of changeable interest rates, borrowers may pay their prospective lender for the privilege of locking in a specific interest rate and number of points (a point is equal to 1 percent of the loan amount). The lock is good for a predefined time, usually thirty to sixty days. When you lock in your rate, you must close on your mortgage before the lock expires, or you lose the preset interest rate.

But the mortgage loan process can easily go awry, particularly when interest rates start to fluctuate. Lenders, nervous about their investments and eager to charge the highest interest rate possible, are not as eager to close on their loans as when interest rates are dropping. According to the director of consumer affairs for the Office of the Commissioner of Savings and Residential Finance, which regulates and monitors mortgage brokers, mortgage bankers, and financial institutions in Illinois, there are many ways for the lender to give you trouble. "The lender may give you a lock [on the interest rate] that is intentionally too short given the current market conditions," she says.

A reasonable lock period is sixty days. Lenders rarely agree to extend a lock to ninety days because of market volatility. But the director says lenders often "play the float" with your mortgage. Although you think you've locked in at a certain interest rate with a certain number of points, lenders will, in essence, gamble with the rate rather than actually lock it in, hoping that interest rates will slip further. If they do go down, the loan officer and the mortgage company will then split the excess between the current interest rate the rate you locked into.

If Rates Go Up

The problems start when interest rates begin to go up. If the loan officer has been playing the float with your loan, and the rate goes up, he or she will have to pay the difference between your locked-in interest rate and the current market rate out of his or her pocket to close on the loan. And because loan officers are loath to pay out, they will often find something "wrong" with your application at the last minute, forcing you to accept a higher interest rate or more points, says one loan officer.

There are a few concrete things you can do to guard against such situations and to ensure you get the mortgage loan you applied for within the time frame allotted in your application contract.

- Some experts recommend that buyers apply for two different mortgages at two different companies. Float the rate with one application and lock in the other. "If you have trouble with one of the lenders, you can always play each against the other," says one loan officer. Of course, this method of safeguarding will cost you an additional application fee.
- Get the lock commitment in writing. Never accept a verbal lock. "That way you'll have proof that the lender went against the bargain," suggests the Illinois attorney general's office.
- Make sure you receive copies of anything you sign during the mortgage application process before you walk out the door. Don't let the lender mail the papers to you.
- Make sure the lender hands you a good faith estimate of closing costs before you sign anything or pay anything.
- Don't make major lifestyle changes after the application has been made and before you close on the property. Don't buy a car. Don't increase your indebtedness in any way. Don't change jobs.
- Keep in direct and close contact with your loan officer. Experts say that if you aren't going to be approved for a loan, the lender should know in about two weeks, which is when the credit report comes back.

- Call your loan officer on a weekly basis. It should take about four weeks for the loan officer to receive all the information needed to send the application to the underwriter for approval. It should take the underwriter three to five days to approve the application and another three to five days to set the closing.

At the end of four weeks, call the loan officer and ask if there is anything else he or she needs to complete your application. If the loan officer says no, *immediately send a letter by certified mail which states that per your conversation, the loan officer requires no additional information.* Keep a copy for yourself as part of your paper trail.

If, after all this, the loan officer tries to back out of your locked-in rate agreement and force you to take higher rates and points than you originally agreed to, experts suggest you start yelling. Literally. The squeaky wheel gets the grease. If the loan officer tries to make you take a higher rate, you should contact the manager of his office. Have your attorney yell for a while, and drag out the closing. A few threats about sending letters to the attorney general's office, the Better Business Bureau, and other consumer-action organizations should get the loan officer to back down.

How Much of a Down Payment Will I Need to Buy My Home?

The amount of the down payment depends partly on your ability to pay and a great deal on the type of mortgage you choose.

The standard down payment is 20 percent of the sales price of the home. If the home costs $100,000, a conventional lender would require that you have $20,000 in cash for a down payment plus closing costs. The reason lenders ask for 20 percent down is that home owners with a larger equity stake in the home are less likely to default on the mortgage than those home owners with a smaller equity stake.

But lenders today recognize that 20 percent of the sales price is a tremendous amount of cash for most first-time buyers. As a result, several different mortgage options will allow you to put down significantly less. For example, first-time buyers commonly put down 10 or 15 percent of the sales price. Conventional lenders will allow a smaller down payment (anything less than 20 percent) if the borrower agrees to purchase private mortgage insurance (PMI) (see Question 83). Private mortgage insurance is paid monthly, along with your mortgage, until you have about 20 percent equity in the home.

If you choose an FHA loan, you can even get away with 3 to 5 percent down in cash. If you put down 3 percent, FHA will accept a community development block grant (CDBG) from your local municipality, if it is available and you meet required income guidelines, to make up the 2 percent difference. Or you may receive a gift of the 2 percent from a friend or family member (don't forget your gift letter).

Finally, if you can get a VA loan, you don't need to have any down payment at all. The nice thing about VA loans is that they are at a fixed interest rate set by the government, the fees are low, and there is no down payment required. To get a VA loan, you'll have to prove you're a veteran of the armed forces, honorably discharged. (See Question 79.)

In special circumstances, a higher down payment may be required. Some co-ops may require a 30 or 40 percent cash down payment to prove that the resident has the financial means to cover any capital expenses that may be required in the future. Requiring a high cash down payment is another way for the co-op to filter out those individuals they choose not to have in their building. Fortunately, most co-ops have done away with the higher down payment requirement in order to make the units more affordable.

Should I Put Down the Largest or Smallest Down Payment Possible?

The answer to this question depends largely on how much cash you have lying around. Generally, first-time buyers are squeezed to the hilt. If they can get together a 10 percent cash down payment, they consider themselves lucky. But if you have more cash available, there are two schools of thought on the size of the down payment. Some experts feel that you should purchase your home with the smallest down payment possible. This will leave you with some cash for emergencies, decorating, and any renovation work you may want to schedule. Or you can invest the money.

On the other hand, you may want to put down a larger down payment in order to cut down the size of your monthly mortgage payments—and save yourself the private mortgage insurance (PMI) costs. The more dollars you put down, the lower the cost of owning the home: You pay less interest. If you put down 20 percent versus 15 percent, and the difference is $5,000, you should strongly consider putting down the 20 percent because you'll also be saving the PMI cost, which can really add up.

QUESTION 61
What Are the Fees Associated with a Mortgage Application?

There are usually three fees you may be required to pay at the time of your mortgage application. The first is the application fee, which can run anywhere from $100 to $500. In addition, the lender may ask you to pay the appraisal fee ($200 to $300) up front as well as the credit report fee (around $40 to $60). These fees may be grouped together under the application fee. Many times the lender will apply part of the application fee toward the appraisal and credit report fees. If you're planning to apply for two mortgages (one fixed, one floating), it's best to try to negotiate the lowest up-front fee possible, or find a lender that has no application or up-front fees.

QUESTION 62
What Are the Lender's Fees I'll Be Charged for My Mortgage?

When times were simpler, lenders often charged home buyers a flat fee to close on a loan. But as interest rates have fallen and some banks have experienced financial troubles, most lenders have begun charging for many different services that formerly fell under the flat fee. Some mortgage experts say lenders have sought to make up their lost profits by nickel-and-diming buyers to death.

Not every bank calls every charge by the same name, which can make comparing lenders as tough as comparing apples and oranges. Lenders are supposed to make it easy for you to know and understand their costs of doing business. At the time of the application, the lender is required by the federal Truth-in-Lending Law to provide a written, good faith estimate of all closing costs. And it's supposed to accurately reflect your closing costs. Mortgage brokers recommend that you shop around for the best deals before actually applying for a mortgage. You should also not be afraid to negotiate lower fees, and to ask for detailed explanations for each one.

Here are some of the fees that lenders may try to charge you for the privilege of lending you money. The fees cited reflect ranges given by real estate experts across the country, though actual charges may be higher or lower, depending on your individual situation.

- *Lender's points, loan origination, or loan service fees.* The lender's points—a point equals 1 percent of the loan amount—may also be referred to as the service charge. The points are the largest fees paid to the lender and usually run between 1 and 3 percent of the loan amount. Occasionally, the points will run more than 3 percent, particularly if the borrower chooses to buy down the loan rate. COST: Usually zero to 3 percent of the loan or more.
- *Loan application fee.* The money charged by the lender to apply for the loan. The application fee is almost never refundable, which means you'd better be pretty darned sure you want a loan from a particular lender and will actually be approved for it. COST: Usually between $0 and $350.
- *Lender's credit report.* The lender may actually pull up two credit reports on you: The first will come just after you have filled out the application and paid the fee; if

there is a second report ordered, it will be pulled just before closing, to make sure you haven't made any enormous purchases or gotten into credit trouble during the elapsed time. Most first-time borrowers don't realize there may be two credit checks. However, you only pay once. COST: Usually between $40 and $60.

- *Lender's processing fee.* With this fee, the lender is trying to pass onto you some of the cost of doing business. The processing fee is the fee for processing the loan application. COST: Usually between $75 and $125.
- *Lender's document preparation fee.* The cost of preparing the loan documents for the closing. COST: $0 to $200.
- *Lender's appraisal fee.* This is the fee lenders charge you to have the home you want to purchase appraised. Lenders supposedly charge you exactly what they're being charged for the service, which is provided by an outside contractor. COST: Usually from $225 to $350.
- *Lender's tax escrow service fee.* This is a onetime charge to set up and service your real estate property tax escrow (see Question 67). COST: From $40 to $65.
- *Title insurance cost for the lender's policy.* Most times, the title insurer will have a flat fee for the loan policy that will be given to the lender. If you want a title insurance policy that will pay you if there is a problem, that will be an additional fee. COST: Between $120 and $300.
- *Special endorsements to title.* If the lender requires extra title endorsements, the buyer must pick up the cost. Some of these might include a condo endorsement, if you're buying a condo, a PUD (planned unit development) endorsement if you're purchasing a home in a development having specific zoning characteristics, an environmental lien endorsement (a statement to the

lender that the lender's mortgage on the property won't be affected if the government finds an environmental hazard on the property and files a lien against it so that the owners clean it up), a location endorsement (proves the home is located where the documents say it is), and an adjustable-rate mortgage endorsement. COST: $15 to $50 each.

- *Prepaid interest on the loan.* The per-day interest charge on the loan from the day of closing until the last day of the month in which you close. This is paid at closing because the lender has to calculate it by hand. After you pay, you then skip a month and begin to pay your regular monthly balance. This is because the loan is paid in arrears. COST: Requires separate calculation for each borrower.

Note: The above charges are only the lender's charges for doing business with you. For a list of all the closing costs you can expect, see Question 88.

QUESTION 63
What Are Junk Fees? And How Do I Avoid Them?

Mortgage brokers say that some of the lender's costs are legitimate. For example, it costs around $50 to run a credit check almost anywhere in the country. But some lenders create "junk fees" purely to increase profits. True junk fees are often difficult to identify because the lender has given them legitimate-sounding names, which can confuse borrowers. As one mortgage banker puts it: "When I see names like 'underwriting fee' and 'commitment fee,' I can tell that these types of fees are being beefed up. When you have an appraisal fee or a credit report fee, you know the lender is being charged by different agencies or companies to do actual things. Those agencies or companies charge the bank and the customer pays it at the closing. But what is an underwriting fee? If you don't underwrite the loan, you have nothing. Buyers should have the lender explain charges they don't understand, and negotiate to exclude certain extra charges. For example, it's ridiculous to pay for an underwriting fee."

Note: The time to negotiate lender's fees is *before* you pay the application fee. Once you've completed the application, it's too late to renegotiate. You've structured the deal and both you and the lender must live up to the application contract.

First-Time Buyer Tip: If you've got the moxie, it's not a bad idea to call several lenders and ask them to submit bids to you on a particular type of loan with all fees. If you ask ten lenders to do this, five might actually do it. Then you can go back to the lenders and pit one bid against another, knocking out those lenders who can't match the lowest terms. Using this method, you should end up with the best possible mortgage with the fewest possible points and fees.

QUESTION 64
What Is Truth in Lending?

Under the 1974 Real Estate Settlement Procedures Act (also known as RESPA), the lender is required in most circumstances, within three days of receiving your application, to give you or place in the mail to you a Truth-in-Lending statement that will disclose the "annual percentage rate" (APR) of your loan.

In many cases, the APR will be higher than the interest rate stated in your mortgage or deed of trust note because the APR includes all fees and costs associated with making the loan. In addition to interest, points, fees, other credit costs are calculated into the total cost of the loan. The Truth-in-Lending statement also discloses other pieces of useful information, such as the finance charge, schedule of payments, late payment charges, and whether or not additional charges will be assessed if you pay off the balance of your loan before it is due. This is known as the "prepayment penalty." Most states do not permit lenders to charge a prepayment penalty. Be certain to ask your lender if prepayment fees are legal in your state. If they are, asked to have them waived.

Some of the information that the lender is required to disclose may not have been finalized by the time the Truth-in-Lending statement is sent. In that case, the lender's statement will say it is an estimate. The lender will *always* provide you with a new Truth-in-Lending statement at the closing. If you want to know about the charges you'll be paying before the closing, you can call the lender and ask if all the estimates on the statement were correct.

QUESTION 65
What Is the APR?

APR stands for the annual percentage rate. Under the Truth-in-Lending law, the lender must tally up all the costs involved in making the loan and amortize them over the life of the loan. The APR is what the loan is actually going to cost you. It includes the interest rate, points, fees, and any other costs the lender charges for doing business. If you go to a bank and look at its percentage rate of interest, it will also have the APR for that loan listed. The difference might be considerable: If the interest rate a bank will charge you for your mortgage is 8 percent, the APR might be 8.75 percent or even higher.

The APR is excellent for comparing loans apples to apples. For example, if Lender A and Lender B each offers you an 8 percent, thirty-year fixed-rate loan with one point, you'll be able to use the APR for each loan to see which loan will cost more.

QUESTION 66
What Is a Good Faith Estimate?

Under the terms of the Real Estate Settlement Procedures Act (RESPA) of 1974, when you file your application for a loan, the lender must provide you with a Good Faith Estimate of closing costs. Usually the lender will give you the estimate before you leave the office after completing your application, but it may also legally send it to you within three business days. The Good Faith Estimate is based on the lender's experience of the local costs involved with making a mortgage in your area. Any cost the lender anticipates must be stated—except for a paid-in-advance hazard insurance premium (if any), or other reserves deposited with the lender (hazard and mortgage insurance, city property taxes, county property taxes, and annual assessments). The estimate may be stated as a flat dollar amount or a range.

The Good Faith Estimate form must be clear and concise and the estimates must actually reflect the costs you will incur. It is your right to question any estimate of any cost that is provided in a dollar range rather than a flat fee.

If the lender does keep some funds in reserve, they may or may not be included in the estimate. Be sure to add them into your calculations of closing costs. And remember, closing costs can change. It's a good idea to check with the lender a few days before closing to determine the accurate closing cost for each item.

What Is a Real Estate Tax Escrow?

A real estate tax escrow is an account set up by a lender. Into it goes the amount of money your lender tacks onto your monthly principal and interest payment to cover your real estate taxes. When the tax bill comes up, the lender takes the money out of the escrow account and sends it to the tax collector. A lender will also collect for your home owner's insurance policy (for noncondo and nonco-op properties), which are included in the fees you pay to the lender to hold in escrow for payment of your real estate taxes and insurance premiums.

Why don't most owners pay their own taxes and insurance? Historically, government institutions that developed the concept of the thirty-year fixed mortgage collected additional money for real estate taxes and home owner's insurance. The default rate due to unpaid real estate taxes was low. As private lenders moved into the market, they followed suit.

Today, every state has passed legislation that says that lenders may require real estate tax and home owner's insurance escrows. Real estate taxes are a priority item for lenders, as the lien for real estate taxes comes before the lender's mortgage lien. That means if you default on your loan, and the home is sold to pay your bills, your real estate tax bill is paid before anything else, including the lender's mortgage (commonly called the first mortgage). Therefore, it's in the lender's best interest to make sure that property taxes are always paid.

Skeptics will tell you that lenders require escrows because they're a large source of free money. Currently, only a dozen states require lenders to pay interest on escrow accounts, although there is national legislation pending that will force lenders to pay interest on all escrow accounts.

Lenders will tell you they must protect their investment (the first mortgage). They also make the argument that borrowers like being budgeted so they aren't surprised with huge tax bills. There's some merit to both arguments.

Federal legislation regarding escrows is worded to allow the lender the authority to withhold or impound money to cover taxes and insurance. There are limitations, however, that went into effect in the early 1990s. *Lenders are limited to withholding no more than two months' worth of cushion. And they must provide an itemized statement of monies coming into your account and bills that are paid, similar to a checking account statement.* In other words, if you pay $100 per month to cover your real estate taxes and insurance, your lender may only hold an extra $200—or two months' worth—in escrow.

Fine. So why doesn't your lender pay you interest on that money? Because they don't have to. According to the Mortgage Bankers Association of America (MBA), fourteen states—including California, Connecticut, Iowa, Maine, Maryland, Massachusetts, Minnesota, New Hampshire, New York, Oregon, Rhode Island, Utah, Wisconsin, and Vermont—have passed state legislation requiring lenders to pay some form of interest on escrow accounts. Recently, Connecticut reduced the interest rate lenders are required to pay on real estate tax escrows from 5.25 percent to 4 percent. New Hampshire reduced the required interest rate from 4 percent to 2.5 percent and will reevaluate the rate every six months.

Lenders argue that escrows are complicated and an extra burden to them. They say it's an expense to them to keep in touch with each home owner's bills, all of which are due at different times. However, lenders do charge a onetime escrow service fee that should offset some of these costs. Many lenders will insist that tax escrows are not on the negotiating table, no matter how much equity you have in a house. They may tell you if you are using an FHA or VA loan that an escrow is required under the terms of that mortgage agreement. That isn't quite true. Although both FHA and VA loans contain provisions for real estate property and insurance escrows, the lender has the option to waive it.

According to industry professionals, some lenders will not demand an escrow account if you have a low loan-to-value ratio. For example, if you put more than 30 percent down in cash, most lenders will cancel the mandatory real estate tax escrow clause.

In many states, lenders must waive the escrow requirement if you pledge a savings account with an amount that would be sufficient to pay your real estate taxes. By pledging the account, you can maintain control over payment of your taxes and receive interest on your money. If you suggest this option and the lender balks, do not hesitate to say you'll be happy to call the state's attorney to check on the legality of the issue. Faced with that threat, the lender should back down. The exceptions are federally chartered savings banks, which are not required to comply with state laws regulating this part of the lending process.

If you are successful in getting your lender to agree not to require an escrow account, you might find yourself hit with a onetime fee *not* to have one. That fee can run as high as 1 to 2 percent of the loan amount. Lenders say they charge the fee because they have to go in once a year to make sure the taxes have been paid on the property. The fee adds weight to the argument that lenders like escrows because it's a good source of free money.

Not all lenders charge for the privilege of paying your own real estate taxes and home owner's insurance premium. And you may want to find one who doesn't.

It's important that home owners realize their escrow accounts can easily go awry. There are lenders who have collected enormous sums of money from individual home owners. One attorney said a lender tried to collect two years' worth of real estate taxes from his client up front. This is, of course, against the law.

Sara, a first-time buyer who recently moved to the East Coast, said the lender to whom her bank sold her mortgage increased her tax escrow by 46 percent. They told her they needed several months' cushion. At first she refused to pay the overage, instead sending 8 percent over her normal payment. "I heard from everybody, from the computer people all the way to the president of the company. Finally they started returning my checks. After a few months they make it hard for you. I finally paid it," Sara said, adding that she had almost 30 percent in equity in her property.

What Is an Insurance Escrow?

According to federal law, lenders can require you to buy home owner's insurance to protect the home in case of fire, earthquake, tornado, or other catastrophe. To pay for this insurance, lenders often will require home owners to pay the insurance premiums in the form of monthly payments that are tacked onto the regular mortgage payments of interest and principal. The money goes into an insurance escrow. Once a year, the lender will dip into that fund and pay the insurance premium. Insurance is one of the four parts of PITI—principal, interest, taxes, and insurance—and is one of the basic costs of home ownership. Overall, the insurance escrow works like the real estate tax escrow, except that you never get rid of it.

How Can I Avoid Setting Up a Real Estate Tax or Insurance Escrow?

Lenders will generally forgo the real estate tax escrow requirement if you meet the following criteria:

- Have a low loan-to-value ratio and put up 30 percent or more in a cash down payment. Most lenders use a 30 percent cash down payment as the benchmark for deciding whether or not to forgo the requirement for a real estate tax or insurance escrow.
- Pledge an interest-bearing account. If you promise to keep a certain amount of money (enough to cover your

taxes) in an account at the lending institution, your lender should allow that instead of an escrow account. But you may have to use additional funds outside of the pledged account to pay your real estate tax bill.

If you don't meet either of those criteria, you'll probably have to have an escrow account for real estate taxes. However, when you've built up the required 30 percent equity in your home, you can try to end your real estate tax escrow.

Insurance escrows work almost the same way. Lenders almost always require an escrow account for insurance, and are allowed to by law. Still, you can make this a point of negotiation. Ask your lender what you would have to do to have this escrow waived.

QUESTION 70

What Should I Do to Make Sure the Mortgage Application Process Goes Smoothly? And What Do I Do if There Are Problems?

Sometimes it seems as if the mortgage process has been set up just to bring out the beast in all of us. It can be a brutal, ego-shattering experience, one that not too many people enjoy. The idea is to make the entire process go as smoothly as possible. You don't want to raise the hackles of your loan officer, but at the same time, you want to remind him or her that you're in control of the situation. There are some specific things you can do to make the process go more smoothly:

1. *Straighten out your finances.* David was a doctor and Denise was a second-year resident at a Boston hospital

when they decided it was time to buy a house. David was making nearly $100,000 and Denise was pulling in close to $35,000. They figured together they had a decent salary and should stop wasting money on rent and start taking advantage of some of the deductions of home ownership. But when they went to get prequalified, they were in for a rude shock: Together, David and Denise had a *negative* net worth! They both had around $80,000 worth of school loans to prepay, plus they had a car loan and credit card payments. The loan officer told them it would be very difficult for them to be approved.

Realizing the loan officer was probably right, David and Denise went about paying off some of their loans. They made it a priority to pay off their credit card debt and their car loan. They consolidated their school loans and refinanced them at lower rates. They made sure their payments were made on time. They put off buying that second car and canceled their planned vacation to Europe and instead chose to drive around New England. When they went back to the loan officer six months later, their financial portfolio was much improved. The loan officer gave his approval and David and Denise started looking for a home. When they found one four months later, they sailed through the mortgage application process.

2. *Give your credit record a checkup.* Everyone has heard the horror stories: Your mother, sister, neighbor, or friend goes to buy a home only to discover that the credit report contains negative or inaccurate credit information. Somewhere along the line his or her credit history has been tampered with. Instead of having a clean re-

cord, he or she has an $80,000 outstanding bill for a liver transplant (or a lease on a Mercedes, a student loan, or something equally improbable for your particular life). The loan officer looks at the outstanding bill and gives you a choice: Clean up the credit problem or no loan. Some choice. And you've probably heard how difficult it is going to be to get your credit history cleaned up. Maybe so, but it's important to try nonetheless.

Here's what to do: First, order a credit report on yourself. There are several credit companies that will do this, including TRW and Equifax. You will find them listed in your local yellow pages under "credit reporting agencies." For less than $20, the credit bureau will send you your credit report. Some may even send it for free. It's the same information lenders will receive. What this does is give you a first look at any problems or discrepancies that have sprung up.

Let's backpedal a moment and talk about credit bureaus. In this computerized, big-brother-like world we live in, credit bureaus generally have exchange agreements with companies who provide credit, like credit cards (Visa, MasterCard, American Express, and others) and department or retail stores (including Bloomingdale's, I. Magnin, Marshall Field's, Spiegel), as well as banks, credit unions, and savings and loans. On a daily, weekly, monthly, or semiannual basis, these companies electronically send all their information to the credit bureau, which stores it in a mammoth database and updates the records of each person on file. When you go to a store like Limited Express and sign up for its credit card, it calls the credit bureau (to do a credit check) to be sure you have enough funds to pay your bills. Banks do it the same way. When you go to file an application for a mortgage, the lender wants to know how many debts are outstanding, and what your track record is in paying them. Credit bureaus provide that information.

They can even tell if you've been paying your taxes. Mark and Marlene were first-time buyers in the Seattle area. They had been looking for a home for several months and finally found the house of their dreams. Since they had been prequalified (not preapproved, which is a much more involved process), they knew they could afford it, and they had the cash for the down payment. But when they went to file an application, they were rejected by the lender. The lender pulled a credit report on the couple and discovered that they had "forgotten" to file their taxes in the two previous years. When he went back to the couple to inform them that they had been rejected for the loan, they were shocked at the news. The lender simply didn't want to have anything to do with them. After all, if they could forget something as significant as their federal taxes, how would they deal with a monthly mortgage payment?

So let's say you've ordered your credit report from TRW and it turns up an erroneous $80 bill from a hospital you've never been to. You realize that this isn't your bill. What do you do? You could go to the credit bureau, but since they didn't originate the information (remember, all the information is sent to the credit bureau from the companies giving credit), they probably won't be able to help you. In fact, you may find the credit bureau's response to be particularly distressing and frustrating. Instead, go to the source of the problem—in this case, the hospital. Ask them to pull up the payment record and try to work out whose bill it actually is. (Or if it turns out to be yours, pay it.) There should be some identification other than name that can easily solve the problem, like a Social Security number, the male/female check box, age, race, etc. Once you prove that the bill is not yours, the hospital (or other credit originator) should correct its computers. (This happened to a Chicago woman whose name was the same as her mother's. Even though the Social Security numbers were different, she had a heck of a time getting the report cleared up because the credit bureau computer kept confusing the names.)

Of course, it may take some time for that correction to work its way through the company's computers all the way through to the credit bureau. If you've started the process before you've found a home, you shouldn't have too much trouble. On the other hand, if you've gone to a lender because you've found the house of your dreams and then discover your credit is in jeopardy, you may want to get a letter from the credit originator that explains there has been a mistake and it has been corrected. You want to get your name cleared up as quickly as possible.

Now, if you discover that someone else has been using your credit to purchase property, cars, furs, jewels, etc., you will probably have a big problem. If this is the case, consult your attorney or the state's attorney's office.

3. *Gather the information the lender needs ahead of time.*

Question 57 discusses in detail the types of information lenders may require for processing your loan application. It's a very good idea to gather this information ahead of time and organize it so that it's easily accessible. If you know ahead of time that you'll need complete copies of your past two or three tax returns plus a current pay stub, or a current profit and loss if you're self-employed, you'll be able to have that information on hand when the lender comes calling.

4. *Get a current copy of the lending guidelines for Fannie Mae, Freddie Mac, FHA, and VA.* Although it may seem that the lender's primary job is disqualifying mortgage applicants, the reverse is true: The lender wants to qualify as many applicants as possible (lenders make their money by approving loans) but is restricted by the rules and regulations of a larger, more powerful body—the secondary mortgage market. If you understand that the secondary mortgage market (which will ultimately buy your loan, repaying the lender who will then make another loan), actually controls the lender, it's easier to understand why the lender must ask you again and again for more documentation. Usually if the lender asks you for more documentation, it means that he or she wants to approve your loan, but there are obstacles (like creditworthiness) that must be cleared up.

If you understand up front what your lender is going through, it may help smooth the process. Call your local Fannie Mae (Federal National Mortgage Association), Freddie Mac (Federal Home Loan Mortgage Corporation), FHA (Federal Housing Administration), and VA (Veterans Administration) offices and request a copy of their current lending guidelines. If you can wade through the morass, you will learn just how complicated it is to approve a mortgage loan.

5. *Qualify your lender.* Just as you shop for a broker and a new home, it's very important to shop for a lender. And not all lenders are created equal. Loan products, services, style, and personal attention vary greatly. Look for a lender that is best qualified to meet your needs. Look for someone exceptionally well trained and thoroughly knowledgeable in the mortgage type you want to use. Look for someone who is seasoned in the business and can guide you through with a practiced hand. (See Question 54 for more specific information.)

First-Time Buyer Tip: Most first-time buyers don't know that if they receive money from their parents as a gift toward the down payment, they need a letter from their parents stating that the money is a gift and does not need to be repaid. In addition, if your parents or relatives are going to give you money, it's a good idea to have that money in your account six months before you actually go to apply for a loan. Banks will look at your monthly balances for the past six months. The higher the balance, the more likely it is that you'll be approved for your loan.

QUESTION 71
What Are Some Tips for Getting the Best Loan at the Most Favorable Rates?

The first thing to remember is that the best loan may not be the cheapest loan. You want a loan that is going to work for your personal financial situation and that may mean paying a bit more up front for a lower long-term rate, or paying nothing up front for a higher rate. Either way, lenders now offer so many different financial products that it's easy to find the creative solution that's best for you.

But once you find it, there are some things you can do to get that loan at the best price possible.

- Pick up a newspaper and find the mortgage watch column. For loans under $203,000 (loans over this amount are called jumbo loans, and are often considered special cases), everyone should be fairly competitive. Pick the lenders who seem to offer the lowest rates and have them bid on your business.
- Remember that interest rates change daily. If you decide to float your loan, watch the bond market activity closely. If rates seem to be dropping, react quickly and call in your lock. Then get the confirmation in writing.
- Points also change frequently. Martha and Ken watched as the number of points required on their loan rose to four and a half and then fell back to two. They locked in at two and a half points.
- Consider using a mortgage broker. They usually have access to more than a dozen investors, and their job is to do the shopping around for you. Mortgage brokers can offer a wide variety of choices, but don't be afraid to tell them about other mortgage packages you've discovered elsewhere. Let them offer you a better deal.
- Don't be afraid to negotiate for lower fees. Ask for detailed explanations of fees and speak up if you don't like something. Once you have a detailed listing of fees and charges from each lender, you can compare apples to ap-

ples, then go back to the lender and ask for the elimination of specific fees.

- Consult with your real estate attorney *before* you apply for a mortgage. Some first-time buyers believe a real estate attorney should be called in only if there is a problem. Others call the attorney *after* the deal has been negotiated. The truth is, your real estate attorney should probably be the first call you make after having your offer to purchase accepted, or maybe even before. Real estate attorneys who do a lot of house closings know the people at the title companies, they know the brokers, and they know the mortgage players. They can give you resources, point you in the right direction, and guide you toward a successful house closing.

MORTGAGE TYPES

QUESTION 72
What Is an Assumable Mortgage? How Is It Different from a Subject-to Mortgage?

Sometimes a broker will show you a property, then lean over and say, "And it's got an assumable mortgage to boot." The broker is obviously trying to tip you off to something, but you're not exactly sure what's going on. An assumable mortgage allows the new buyer to assume the legal obligation from the seller to make monthly payments of principal and interest to the lender. The lender, assured of getting repaid on the loan, then releases the seller from his or her liability.

How do you find out if a mortgage is assumable? Most conventional mortgages are not assumable, meaning that they have a "due-on-sale" clause built into the verbiage of the loan. A due-on-sale clause means that if you sell the home, you immediately owe all of the money to the lender. FHA mortgages are assumable, which is one reason brokers like to show first-time buyers FHA property. It's also cheaper to assume a loan than take out a new loan. When a buyer decides to assume the mortgage of the seller, you pay fewer closing costs and fees. It's also easier: Provided the buyer qualifies for the loan, there is less paperwork that needs to be completed.

If you purchase property that is "subject to" the existing mortgage, that means you can take over the loan obligation, but the seller remains liable for the mortgage amount. There is no formal transfer of obligation or liability, as with assuming a mortgage. If someone tries to convince you to buy a property "subject to" a mortgage, make sure the lender can't call in the loan as a result of the transfer of title. If you purchase property subject to an existing mortgage, and the lender, upon receiving notice of the transfer of title, calls in the loan, you could be forced to pay the entire loan off immediately.

QUESTION 73
What Are the Different Types of Mortgages Available? And How Do I Choose the Right Type for Me?

Today, mortgage lenders around the country currently offer nearly two hundred different mortgage options. That's a lot of options! It seems overwhelming, but if you start to ask a few questions, you'll soon figure out that your lender is actually offering only six or seven basic mortgage types. It's just that in today's world of personalized banking, lenders say, everyone wants something that is made to order for his or her specific financial situation.

Choosing the right mortgage for you will depend on several factors, including your monthly income today and what you expect it will be in the future, the assets you currently hold, and how much debt you're carrying. Other factors can influence your mortgage decision as well. Do you want to pay points (a point is 1 percent of the loan amount) up front, or do you prefer to pay them over the life of the loan? Do you want to gamble that interest rates will stay low and get an adjustable-rate mortgage (ARM)? Or would you feel more comfortable paying a fixed amount each month?

Lenders offer a variety of financing options simply because today's home buyers want a cure for every ill. For example, if you plan to live in your house for only three to five years, you might consider a 5/25 (pronounced "five twenty-five") or a 7/23 ("seven twenty-three") mortgage, or a one-year adjustable- rather than a fixed-interest-rate mortgage.

Here is a quick description of the basic types of mortgages available in the marketplace. The following questions offer an in-depth explanation of these mortgages, along with suggestions as to which type of buyer might actually benefit from which type of mortgage.

- *Fixed-Rate Mortgage.* The original and most popular type of loan, a fixed-rate mortgage charges the same percentage rate of interest over the life of the loan. Home owners repay the loan with a fixed, monthly installment of principal and interest. Fixed-rate loans can be taken out in a variety of lengths, including ten-year, fifteen-year, twenty-year, and the ever popular thirty-year loan.

- *Adjustable-Rate Mortgage (ARM)*. Adjustable-rate mortgages have interest rates that fluctuate and are pegged to one-year Treasury bills or a specific index. The initial rate of interest is usually quite low, and then the rate bumps up between one and two points per year. There is usually a yearly cap of two points, and the loan also has a lifetime ceiling cap, usually around six points. The interest rate can also go down. In the late 1980s and early 1990s, ARMS proved to be the best deal around because interest rates sank and then stayed low. Home owners whose initial interest rate was around 5 percent now have loans at 6.5 to 7 percent.

- *Two-Step Mortgages*. These relatively new arrivals on the mortgage scene are usually called 5/25s and 7/23s, and they come in two different flavors: convertible (which converts the loan to a fixed loan for the remaining twenty-five or twenty-three years, respectively) and nonconvertible (which converts the loan to an adjustable-rate mortgage, also known as the ARM). They are similar loans with different numbers attached: the 5/25 is a thirty-year loan that has a fixed-interest rate for the first five years and then adjusts into a convertible or nonconvertible loan. The 7/23 is a similar thirty-year loan, except that it adjusts after seven years instead of five. Both of these loans can be amortized over the entire thirty-year period. They are considered more risky than fixed-rate loans, but they are significantly less risky than ARMS during the first five or seven years.

- *FHA Mortgage*. Preset spending limits are the hallmark

of an FHA mortgage. The loan amounts are set by the median prices of different cities within a particular area. In some rural counties in Illinois, for example, buyers can borrow up to $107,600. In more densely populated suburbs, the spending limit rises to $124,875. The best part about an FHA loan is the low down payment required: Only 5 percent need come out of your pocket. With some government programs, that amount falls to 3 percent. However, a steep mortgage insurance premium and other upfront costs are part of the bargain and must be considered when choosing an FHA loan. Also, FHA loans are assumable, which means you could simply take over the payments from your seller, saving a lot of cost and hassle.

- *VA Loan.* A VA loan is administered by the Department of Veterans Affairs in Washington, D.C., and is designed to help veterans of the U.S. Armed Forces buy homes with no down payment. In addition, veterans are not allowed to pay points to the lender, although they are responsible for some loan fees; that sometimes causes a problem because it's usually the seller who ends up getting stuck for the extra bucks. Only veterans who have served a specified number of days qualify for a VA loan. And you must get a certificate of eligibility from the Department of Veterans Affairs.
- *Balloon Mortgage.* This type of mortgage can be any length at all. There are balloon mortgages for which you make monthly payments of principal and interest, and others for which you pay only interest. In either case, when the loan comes due (after, say, five or seven years), the loan balance must be repaid in full. Balloon mortgages can be paid in one of two ways: Either the mort-

gage can be amortized over thirty or fifteen years, and you just pay the first five or ten years of the loan before paying it off or refinancing; or you pay only the interest on the loan (as opposed to interest and principal, which you pay when a loan is amortized) until the end of the loan period. For example, if you borrow $100,000 on a five-year interest-only balloon, the $100,000 is due on the last day of the five-year period. Throughout the five years, you'd pay interest only on the money.

- *Graduated-Payment Mortgage (GPM)*. The GPM was originally designed for first-time buyers because it offers reduced monthly payments early on in the life of the loan, which become larger as the loan progresses and, hopefully, the finances of the borrower improve. Most lenders have steered away from the GPM in recent years as two-step mortgages became more popular. In fact, FHA eliminated its GPM in 1988. The reason is that GPMs are complicated loans that require a tremendous amount of paperwork while 5/25s and 7/23s are relatively easy to package.

- *Shared-Appreciation Mortgage*. A shared-appreciation mortgage is a financial concept borrowed from commercial property transfers. The lender will offer you a below-market rate in exchange for a share in the profits of the home when it is sold. There are significant benefits to this, as you get all the tax benefits, and the lender doesn't make any money unless you do. On the other hand, if the home appreciates greatly, you could end up paying a lot of that profit to the lender. Shared-appreciation mortgages are most commonly coordinated by nonprofit associations seeking to help low-income first-time buyers become first-time home owners. They use community development block grant (CDBG) money to help make up the difference between what low- to moderate-income families can afford and what the competitively priced commercial products want to see on their borrower's balance sheet. (See Appendix VI for more resource information.)

- *Biweekly Mortgage.* The name for this mortgage product comes from the number of payments you make per month: two. Each payment represents half of what a regular monthly payment might be, but because you pay every other week, that adds up to twenty-six payments, or a thirteenth month. Making that thirteenth payment, no matter what form it takes, will significantly cut down the amount of interest you'll pay over the life of the loan. The trouble with biweeklies is that while they are easier payments to make (particularly if you get paid biweekly), the obligation to pay twice a month can be onerous, particularly if money is tight.

QUESTION 74
What Is a Fixed-Rate Mortgage?

The original and most popular type of mortgage is the fixed-interest-rate mortgage. The amount of the interest and principal repayment is amortized in equal amounts over the life of the loan. Many home owners like the financial security of knowing that they will pay exactly the same amount of money each month (excluding property tax or insurance payments to an escrow account) until the loan has been paid off in full.

Although the concept of fixed-interest mortgages hasn't

changed much, most lenders now offer borrowers a choice in how long a loan they want. While a thirty-year mortgage was, and is, the most popular length, ten-, fifteen-, and twenty-year fixed mortgages have recently become more popular as interest rates have continued to stay relatively low.

Because interest rates are low, borrowers are finding that the shorter loan length offers a significant financial advantage over the regular thirty-year mortgage: Home owners can save thousands of dollars in interest payments if they shorten the length of the loan by up to fifteen years. Of course, the shorter the amortization period, the higher the monthly payment. But the loan is amortized faster, so you pay less interest over the life of the loan.

For example, if you take out a $100,000 thirty-year mortgage at 8 percent interest, your monthly payments toward principal and interest would be around $730. If that same mortgage was fifteen years in length, your monthly payment would be around $940.

You'd end up paying $262,800 in principal and interest over the life of the thirty-year loan. You'd pay only $169,200— nearly $100,000 less—over the life of a fifteen-year loan.

	15-Year Loan	30-Year Loan
Monthly payment	$ 940	$ 730
Total payments	$169,200	$262,800

Who Would Benefit from a Fixed-Rate Mortgage?

Buyers on a limited or fixed income and those who do not like to gamble with interest rates are usually best served by a fixed-rate mortgage. Those buyers who can handle the higher payments and want to pay down their mortgage as fast as possible are best served by a ten-, fifteen-, or twenty-year fixed-rate mortgage. Still, people who choose a thirty-year mortgage for the initial lower payments and want to pay it off faster can make an additional mortgage payment per year—a thirteenth payment—and direct the lender to use that money to repay the principal (write it on the check). An extra payment a year will significantly lessen the amount of interest you pay over the life of the loan. If you make a thirteenth payment every year, beginning with the first, on a thirty-year mortgage, you'll effectively cut your mortgage nearly in half, and achieve nearly the same savings in interest as if you had a fifteen-year mortgage.

Be aware, however, that an extra payment per year does not relieve you of the obligation to meet your monthly payments. Moreover, the thirteenth payment does not lessen future monthly payments. It does alter the end balance on your account.

QUESTION 75
What Is an Adjustable-Rate Mortgage (ARM)?

An ARM is a mortgage with an interest rate that adjusts at specific times over the life of the loan—usually yearly, every three years or every five years. Adjustable-rate mortgages are attractive to a variety of buyers because their initial interest rate is much lower than those on almost any other type of loan. Interest rates on one-year ARMs tend to start out very low—sometimes as low as 4 or 5 percent—and increases in the rate are generally tied to an economic index, such as one-, three-, or five-year Treasury securities. When the time comes for your loan to adjust—either yearly, every three years, or every five years—a margin of between one and three percentage points is tacked onto whatever index the loan is tied to. This is how the lender comes up with your next interest rate.

Let's look at one index, the National Cost of Funds, which is based on the average cost of funds for savings and loans, as an example. Let's say the National Cost of Funds index is at 6.25 percent. If your lender charges a 2.5-percentage-point margin, your new mortgage interest rate based on that index would be 8.75 percent when the loan adjusts. ARMS are likely to fluctuate with the economy, though you can get an idea of how much your mortgage will adjust by keeping an eye on economic indicators, such as the prime interest rate and the interest rate the Federal Reserve charges banks. But even if the prime rate soars in the next few years, ARM holders are somewhat protected by a lifetime cap on their loan's interest rate. This cap, usually five or six percentage points over the lifetime of the loan, limits how much the interest rate can go up. With a six-point cap, an ARM starting at 5.25 percent could never go higher than 11.25 percent. Make sure your loan has an interest-rate cap.

ARMs, the lender likes to point out, can also readjust downward after the first adjustment period. In that case, the borrower could reap the benefit of his or her gamble for years. Let's say you need a $100,000 loan. You decide on an ARM, which has a starting interest rate of 6 percent. Let's say it's a three-year ARM with a two-point cap per year (meaning the loan can only go up two points a year) and a margin of two and a half points over the Treasury bills to which it is tied. For the first three years, your interest payment is $6,000, or $500 per month. At the end of the three years, let's assume the rate rises to 7 percent (just because the interest rate *can* go up two percentage points doesn't always mean it will). You will then pay $7,000 per year, or $583.33 monthly. (This example isn't exactly precise because I haven't amortized the numbers. But it works for straight interest loans. To create your own comparisons using amortized numbers, consult the amortization tables in Appendix V.)

Let's compare the $100,000 ARM with a $100,000 thirty-year fixed-rate mortgage at 8 percent:

Year	ARM	Fixed
1	$ 6,000	$ 8,000
2	$ 6,000	$ 8,000
3	$ 6,000	$ 8,000
4	$ 7,000	$ 8,000
5	$ 7,000	$ 8,000
6	$ 7,000	$ 8,000
Total	$39,000	$48,000

If you were the borrower in this example, and you had chosen an ARM over a fixed-rate mortgage, you would have saved yourself $9,000 over six years. But what if the ARM had increased over and above the interest rate of the fixed-rate mortgage? If you consider that most folks move every five to seven years, it's unlikely that the interest rate would have risen in that period of time to overcome the savings gained by using an ARM.

But let's say it does: You have a $100,000 ARM that adjusts every year and has a two-point annual readjustment cap with a lifetime cap of 6 percent:

Year 1: 5 percent interest rate = $5,000

Year 2: 7 percent interest rate = $7,000

Year 3: 9 percent interest rate = $9,000

Year 4: 11 percent interest rate = $11,000

Year 5: 11 percent interest rate = $11,000

Year 6: 11 percent interest rate = $11,000

The ARM would cost $54,000 versus $48,000 for a fixed-rate loan. Assuming that the ARM readjusted upwards at the maximum cap every year, it would have cost $6,000 more than the fixed-rate mortgage.

While that hasn't happened so far in the 1990s, it's impossible to predict long-term interest rates. In fact, if you bought your home in 1990, your ARM interest rate would have dropped the first year and held steady somewhere around 6 to 7 percent for several years.

Who Could Benefit from an ARM?

Buyers who have a higher debt-to-income ratio than normal, say 32 percent rather than 28 percent, might benefit from an ARM, particularly if they can show that they have good job and salary prospects for the future. Lenders generally will allow your housing expense—that is, mortgage principal and interest, private mortgage insurance, and property taxes—to equal no more than 28 percent of your monthly gross income (income before taxes).

For example, if your gross monthly income is $4,000, you could afford monthly mortgage and property tax payments of up to $1,120. All debt, including installment and revolving loans (credit cards, car payments), should not exceed 35 to 36 percent of gross income, most lenders say. Although conventional lenders have recently begun stretching the upper limit of the debt to income to thirty-nine, it rarely goes above that. So, although lenders never calculate a loan on the basis of future earnings, they might be willing to stretch the qualifications needed outside normal parameters if, for example, you are a fourth-year medical student with a guaranteed residency in the near future, or a third-year law student with a job offer.

(When lenders stretch the requirements for prospective borrowers, they usually keep the loan within the institution's portfolio, meaning they don't resell the loan on the secondary mortgage market. That way, they have additional lending flexibility.)

As with all loans, how long you're planning to stay in the home is particularly important. If you know you're going to stay in a home for only five to seven years, you may want to consider getting an ARM. Lenders acknowledge there is a strong probability that you will have a lower interest rate over the entire term of the loan than if you had chosen a fixed-rate loan.

QUESTION 76
What Is a Two-Step Mortgage?

These relatively new arrivals on the mortgage scene are hybrid cousins of the adjustable-rate mortgage (ARM) and fixed-rate mortgages. Called 5/25s ("five twenty-fives") or 7/23s ("seven twenty-threes"), they combine the relative steadiness of a fixed-rate mortgage with some of the risks and rewards of an ARM.

Two-step mortgages come in two varieties: convertible and nonconvertible. A convertible two-step mortgage means that a 5/25 or 7/23 loan has a fixed interest rate for the first five or seven years, then converts into a fixed-rate mortgage for the remaining twenty-five or twenty-three years, respectively. A nonconvertible two-step mortgage means that the 5/25 or 7/23 has a fixed interest rate for the first five or seven years, and then converts into a one-year adjustable-rate mortgage (ARM), which adjusts each year for the remaining twenty-five or twenty-three years of loan term.

Let's look at the convertible version in a little more detail. The 5/25, for example, is a thirty-year loan that has a fixed-interest rate for the first five years and then has a onetime adjustment that determines what the rate will be for the remaining twenty-five years of the loan. As with other thirty-year loans, it's amortized over thirty years. The 7/23 works the same way, but is set at a fixed-interest rate for seven years, and then adjusts once for the remaining twenty-three years of the loan.

Clearly, lenders have been keeping their eyes on the trends of home ownership. If the average home owner will sell his or her home every five to seven years, there is not as much need for thirty-year loans. Instead, these loans allow the home owner to start off at a much lower interest rate, which will then adjust once during the life of the loan. If you choose a 7/23, it's more than likely you'll move before the rate adjusts. If not, it's likely you'll move soon thereafter, allowing you to take full advantage of the first seven years of lower-than-average interest rates.

Just as with ARMs, the onetime adjustment for both of these

loans is tied to an economic index. The increase would be based on the status of the index at the end of the five- or seven-year term. On top of the index rate, the lender often tacks on a margin, usually in the neighborhood of one to three points. So if the index is at 5 percent at the end of seven years, and you have a three-point margin on your loan, your new rate would be 8 percent.

Let's compare the savings between a 5/25, a 7/23, and a thirty-year fixed loan. Let's assume the loan amount is $100,-000, and the interest rate is 7 percent (5/25), 7.5 percent (7/23), and 8 percent (thirty-year fixed). After five years, you would have paid $35,000 for the 5/25, $37,500 for the 7/23, and $40,-000 for the thirty-year fixed. If you move within five years and had a 5/25 mortgage, you would have saved yourself $5,000. Even if you stayed through the sixth year and the rate went up to 8 percent, you would still have saved $5,000 for the first five years.

Who Could Benefit from a 5/25 or 7/23?

First-time buyers who do not plan to stay in their homes for more than five or seven years would save thousands of dollars in interest by going with this type of loan, which has a lower initial rate than fixed-rate loans.

The idea is that you'll sell your home before or just after the rate adjusts upward. (The rate can also adjust downward, as those buyers who opted for an ARM in the past three years have happily discovered.) But even if you stay in your home ten years with a 7/23, the overall loan rate you pay may be far less than if you had chosen a fixed-rate loan. The rate on a two-step mortgage can be a full percentage point or more less than the rate on a thirty-year fixed.

Two-step mortgages have become extremely popular, as home owners (particularly first-time buyers) have begun to realize they don't need the long-term steadiness of a fixed-rate mortgage because, unlike their parents, they most likely won't spend thirty years in the same home.

What Is a Balloon Mortgage?

Before thirty-year fixed-interest-rate mortgages were invented (we're talking about pre-Depression era), everyone who bought a home and didn't pay cash had a balloon mortgage. Essentially, the buyer would borrow money at the exorbitant interest rate of about 3 or 4 percent for a short period of time, anywhere from one to five years. During the loan term, you would pay only the interest on the loan: You might pay it in monthly installments, semiannual installments, or as one annual payment of interest. At the end of the loan term, you would then owe the entire principal in full.

So if you borrowed $10,000 at 4 percent interest for five years, you would owe $400 in interest only per year, or $2,000 in interest over the life of the loan (the interest is paid separately). At the end of five years, you would still owe the $10,000 in principal. It was simple and easy, and usually everyone paid off the balance. The concept of a balloon mortgage allowed you to buy a little bit of time to scrape together the cash to actually purchase the property.

As I explained earlier, balloon mortgages worked fine until the Great Depression, when folks lost all their savings and couldn't pay the interest on the money they borrowed, let alone meet the balloon payments. After World War II, the federal government began a program that offered returning veterans an opportunity to purchase a home and pay it off over thirty years. That was the beginning of the thirty-year fixed mortgage. When the thirty-year mortgage was successful and took off, the balloon mortgage became an infrequently used financial vehicle.

Who Could Benefit from a Balloon Mortgage?

With so many financing tools available today, only a few people choose to purchase a home with a balloon mortgage. Sometimes, co-ops (remember, you don't buy a co-op, you buy shares in a corporation that owns the building) may be purchased with a balloon mortgage or other special financing tool because the shares held are personal property (like a refrigerator, clothes, or your typewriter), not real property (like real estate). In addition, the interest rate on a five-year (some banks offer a ten-year or fifteen-year balloon mortgage) balloon might be less than some other financing options. So a few buyers will choose it, especially if they know they might sell within that time period.

QUESTION 78
What Is an FHA Mortgage?

An FHA loan is often called "the first-time buyer's mortgage." The reason for that is clear: FHA loans require a much smaller down payment than conventional loans. It's common to have an FHA loan with only 5 percent down, whereas conventional lenders prefer to see a 20 percent cash down payment, which is often too steep for most first-time buyers. (Conventional lenders will allow you to purchase a home for less than 20 percent down, but you'll have to pay private mortgage insurance.)

But some mortgage seekers wrongly assume that an FHA loan is a government-sponsored handout; that is, you have to be of a certain income level to qualify. That's not true. There are no income requirements for obtaining a loan from the Federal Housing Administration. And you don't have to be a first-time buyer. Instead, the only restriction is the amount of money you can borrow. FHA loans are restricted to a maximum of about $125,000, although that number can change on a yearly basis (for current numbers, check with your local FHA office). But that number is deceptive because it's limited to certain counties within metropolitan areas. For example, Chicago's metropolitan area includes six principal counties: Cook, Du Page, Lake, Kane, McHenry, and Will. The maximum loan amount for Cook (which includes Chicago), Du Page, and McHenry Counties is $120,500; Lake and Kane County dwellers can borrow up to $124,875; and Will County buyers can borrow up to $107,600. Generally, expensive suburbs have higher loan amounts, while more rural areas (where prices are assumed to be lower) are allowed smaller loan amounts.

Of course, the most attractive feature of FHAs is that the borrower needs only 5 percent of the loan amount as a down payment. If the property is a single-family house, however, the loan comes along with a steep mortgage insurance premium. But just because these government-backed loans are available to all home owners doesn't mean an FHA loan is a freebie. In fact, it can be more expensive than a conventional loan. FHA lenders require the same debt-to-income ratio as for other loans, such as a fixed-interest or ARM. The big difference is that home owners have to come up with only a 5 percent down payment. So if a house costs $100,000, an FHA loan would require the buyer to come up with $5,000 in cash, far less than the 10 to 20 percent usually required for other types of loans.

Who Could Benefit from an FHA Loan?

Cash-strapped first-time buyers are the logical choice. Another benefit is that FHA loans are assumable, which allows the next buyer to have lower costs in purchasing the property because he or she isn't taking out a new loan. When buyers assume an FHA loan, lenders are allowed by law to charge up to $500 plus regular loan origination points and fees, such as a credit report. There is typically no appraisal, however, which can save you around $300.

FHA loans are also a good avenue for people who have had credit problems or bankruptcies in their past, because the government does not regard these past financial problems in the same light as a private lender would. As long as the loan-to-income ratios are met, and the borrower can pay the mortgage insurance premium (which can be steep), former bankruptees can qualify. As one lender puts it, an FHA loan is a good way to begin to rebuild a credit history. The idea behind the FHA loan is to provide an outlet for people who do not have access to other financial outlets.

What Is a VA Loan?

One of the many benefits that comes along with joining a branch of the armed forces is the helping hand Uncle Sam offers when it comes time to buy your house. The Department of Veterans Affairs in Washington, D.C. guarantees loans for veterans, allowing them to purchase homes at favorable lending terms with no down payment.

The VA started the program at the end of World War II, and since the program began in 1945, more than 13 million veterans have obtained loans worth more than $360 billion. A spokesman for the VA estimates that there are currently more than 4 million VA loans outstanding. Although the program has changed some since its inception, VA loans generally restrict the amount of money the veteran is obliged to pay for his or her loan. However, the veteran is required to pay some closing costs including a VA appraisal, credit report, survey title, recording fees, a 1 percent loan-origination fee, and a VA funding fee.

The VA funding fee is the expensive part. Except for a brief period during the 1960s, when it was used to distinguish "Cold War" veterans from those who had put in wartime service, there used to be no funding fee for obtaining a VA loan. However, in 1981, a .5 percent funding fee was reinstated, although disabled veterans who receive compensation were, and continue to be, exempt from the fee. In 1984, the funding fee was increased to 1 percent, and it was again raised in 1990 to 1.25 percent. As part of the Clinton administration's 1993 budget package, VA loan funding fees were increased three quarters of a percent. As of October 1, 1993, veterans who are taking out their first no-down-payment loan must pay a 2 percent funding fee to the Department of Veterans Affairs. Veterans who are taking out their second or third no-down-payment loan must pay a funding fee of 3 percent. If the veteran chooses to put down 5 or 10 percent of the sales price, the funding fee is reduced.

Although the new funding fee, coupled with the 1 percent loan-origination fee and the closing costs that the veteran is obliged to pay, makes a VA loan more expensive, the Department of Veterans Affairs maintains it is the only no-down-payment loan on the market. In addition, VA loans are assumable, meaning a buyer can take it over from the seller for very little money, an added incentive for the veteran-as-seller. Finally, the VA has a policy of "forbearance," which means "worthy" veterans experiencing a temporary economic setback are somewhat protected against foreclosure. In rare instances, where a lender has decided to foreclose on such a "worthy" veteran, the VA has stepped in and paid off the lender, putting the loan in its portfolio.

Other changes in lending policy should help guide the VA through the end of the century. For example, the VA used to offer only one kind of loan: a thirty-year fixed-rate mortgage, with a mandated rate that was just below what you could get on the open market. Today, the VA permits adjustable-rate mortgages (ARMs), and allows lenders, veterans, and sellers to negotiate who will pay the loan's discount points. In the past, the veteran was not allowed to pay any points to the lender.

Who Might Benefit from a VA Loan?

While they're expensive, a VA loan might be just the ticket, especially if you're running short on cash. And though you still must qualify for this amount, the upper loan limit is $184,000, which can help you buy a very nice home. (That upper limit may soon be stretched to $203,000.) If you're a reservist with six years of duty behind you, you're now eligible for a VA loan—the catch is, you'll pay a funding fee that's three quarters of a percent higher than your active-duty compatriots.

To apply for a VA loan, simply take your eligibility certificate to a lender. You're eligible for a VA loan if you served ninety days of wartime service in World War II, the Korean conflict, the Vietnam era, and the Persian Gulf War, and were not dishonorably discharged. You are also eligible if you served between six and twenty-four months of continuous active duty from 1981 through today, and were not dishonorably discharged. Check with your loan VA office for more details on eligibility.

QUESTION 80
What Is a Graduated-Payment Mortgage?

Demand for complicated, expensive mortgages like the graduated-payment mortgage has fallen along with interest rates. Moreover, some of the newly invented mortgages—like the two-step loans and ARMs—are easier to work with and require far less paperwork and attention.

A graduated-payment mortgage is a step-payment mortgage that starts out with a low interest rate that increases a certain number of percentage points each year until the loan levels out at a higher, fixed rate. The problem with GPMs is that they require a lot of individual calculations, and each loan must be structured to the specifics of each borrower. That's not cost effective. Mountains of paperwork made these loans expensive to maintain and adjust. They have essentially been replaced by the 5/25, 7/23, and one-year ARMs.

Who Could Benefit from a GPM?

With affordability at its highest levels in twenty-five years, there is hardly any interest for this mortgage, a trend that real estate banking experts believe will continue. People used to want a GPM because it meant that they could qualify for the loan at the lower interest rate. The problems started when the loan would readjust upward. Essentially, borrowers were locking themselves into higher payments down the road. If their projected income didn't match the actual increase in interest payments, the borrower had trouble.

Many families couldn't handle the steep interest payment shock, so the problem of nonpayment of additional interest was solved with programs like negative amortization. With negative amortization (an arcane financial technique), the actual payment increase was limited and anything that was due over the fixed payment was added to the total amount of the loan. But with negative amortization, the borrower would end up paying interest on interest in a potentially never-ending cycle. It was bad for banking and depressing for the home owner, who felt he or she would always be in debt.

SPECIAL FINANCING

QUESTION 81
What Is Seller Financing?

One of the most flexible sources of real estate financing can be the seller of the property you want to buy. Why are sellers interested in providing financing? For many sellers the return on their investment (in your mortgage) will be far greater than what they can get in the open marketplace. In addition, sellers who provide financing sometimes sell their property more quickly.

Home buyers should be interested in seller financing because it eliminates any potential red tape that could slow down or mar the closing, you can close more quickly, and you might get financing at a below-market interest rate. Not every seller will help you purchase his or her home. Look for a seller who is ready to trade down to a smaller property or, perhaps, retire to a rental community. Otherwise, it's likely the seller will need your cash to purchase his or her other home.

First-time buyers Judith and Scott fell in love with a house. Unfortunately, with their salary (at the time, she sold advertising for a magazine and he was a doctor in his second year of residency), they couldn't qualify for a large enough mortgage to quite make ends meet. Although Judith and Scott knew it meant scrimping and saving, they were sure they could afford the payments. So they went to their seller and asked her to take back a second mortgage. She agreed and offered them a rate that was a half point cheaper than the rate they got for their first mortgage. They closed on the house. A year and a half later, when interest rates dropped, Judith and Scott refinanced and paid off the seller.

Seller financing comes in many forms. The seller can:

- Provide all the financing and take a straight first mortgage (eliminating the need for a commercial lender). This is called a purchase money mortgage;
- Take back a second mortgage that will help you scrape together the down payment;
- Buy down your mortgage, to enable you to qualify for more house;

- Arrange a purchase by articles of agreement (also known as an installment purchase), in which you receive an interest in the home, which becomes yours after you pay off the seller in full.

Whatever form the seller financing takes, it's in your best interest to explore this possibility. However, beware the difficult seller who will constantly call you for his or her money. That kind of overbearance is difficult to stomach. If you do opt for seller financing, it would be in your best interest to keep the transaction at an arm's-length distance.

What Is a Buy-Down Mortgage? What Is a Purchase Money Mortgage? What Are Articles of Agreement?

In addition to the regular conventional loans, there are a few other options that might prove helpful as you explore which mortgage is right for you.

A Buy-Down Mortgage

A buy down is a financing technique that lets someone other than the buyer pay cash up front to the lender so the first few years of the loan will be less costly. As they have become more popular through the years, more lenders across the country have begun to offer their own tailor-made versions.

The principle is simple. The seller (it's usually the seller, although it might also be the developer if you're buying new construction, or a relative) buys down the mortgage rate, allowing the buyer to qualify for a below-market mortgage. With a 3-2-1 buy-down mortgage, the first year would be assessed at 3 percentage points below the note rate, although that rate is good only for the first year. The second year, the buyer pays interest at a mortgage rate two points below the note rate; then, in the third year, the mortgage rate is one point below the note rate. Thereafter, the mortgage interest rate is set at the original note rate.

The concept of buy downs is similar to both the ARM and the two-step mortgages, in that the rate starts lower and goes higher. Unlike these mortgages, the buy down is artificially deflated by the seller or another third-party source. The seller makes up the discount that is given to the buyer. But this type of mortgage does offer another option for the first-time buyer, who can often combine the buy down with an option like the ARM for a super-cheap first few years. If you get a buy down and combine it with a 5/25, it can put you significantly ahead of the market.

Here's how it works for simple interest loans: If the buyer takes out a $100,000 at 8 percent interest, the annual interest payment would be $8,000, or $666.67 per month. But with a 3-2-1 mortgage, the buyer would pay only 5 percent interest the first year ($5,000 per year or $416.67 per month), 6 percent interest the second year ($6,000 or $500 per month), and 7 percent interest the third year ($7,000 or $583.33 per month). The total savings would be $6,000 for the buyer. The seller picks up that additional mortgage cost, which is generally paid in cash to the lender at closing. Then, every month for the first three years, the lender takes a portion of the money and adds it to the amount the buyer sends in. The buy down is still primarily used by developers, but more and more sellers are using this financing option to entice first-time buyers, who will likely earn more money down the road, and will be able to afford larger mortgage payments.

Eric, a certified public accountant, said he and his wife offered a 3-2-1 buy-down mortgage and ended up selling it to Steve, a first-time buyer, who didn't really understand the concept at first. Steve refused Eric's offer for the buy down, but later saw the benefit and accepted.

A Purchase Money Mortgage

A purchase money mortgage is another type of seller-provided financing. With a purchase money mortgage, the seller offers to give a first mortgage to you, the buyer. In taking over the role normally played by a bank or savings and loan, the seller would secure the loan with a down payment, and you would pay the seller monthly installments of principal and interest. Although you get title to the property, the seller has a lien on the property. That way, if you default on the mortgage, the seller can reclaim the property. Purchase money mortgages can work well for buyers because you don't pay any points or other costs to obtain the loan. The seller enjoys an excellent return on his or her funds.

Articles of Agreement

With the articles of agreement, you enter into an installment agreement to buy the home over a specified period of time. The seller keeps legal title, and you receive equitable title, which means you receive an interest in the property but do not own it. The benefit to you, the first-time buyer, is that the seller will usually accept a much smaller down payment (perhaps 5 percent of the sales price of the home) and yet will still feel comfortable with the arrangement. Because the seller retains title to the property until you've paid off the loan, if you default on the property, the seller need only evict you to reclaim possession.

Howard and Emily had owned a condo for years, but when they wanted to sell, they couldn't get any interest in the area, which had fallen on hard times. So they put an ad in the newspaper offering to sell the property for $3,000 down. Sally saw the ad, checked her bankbook, and realized she had the cash to buy the apartment. She moved in and paid Howard and Emily as if they were the bank. Over time, she was able to afford a regular loan and paid off Howard and Emily. In the meantime, Sally got a tax deduction, which helped her save more money. (Although the articles-of-agreement purchase seems similar to a lease with an option to buy, the two methods of buying a home are completely different. With the articles of agreement, Sally does not own the home but since she is paying the real estate taxes and making payments to the seller with interest, she gains the tax benefits: the real estate taxes and interest are tax deductible. If Sally leased the home with an option to buy, Howard and Emily would also have retained ownership of the home until Sally had exercised her option. But because they would have paid the taxes, they would have had the tax benefits, not Sally.)

First-Time Buyer Tip: Purchasing a home through an articles of agreement can work very well for some home buyers. But it is extremely important that the buyer consult with an attorney to look after his or her interests. Documents will need to be recorded to protect the buyer's ownership interest in the property that he or she is building up through regular principal and interest payments.

What Is Private Mortgage Insurance (PMI)?

Private mortgage insurance (PMI) is often a necessary expense that accompanies buying a house with less than 20 percent down in cash. Although expensive, PMI allows you to purchase a home with a small down payment, and helps the lender resell your mortgage on the secondary market to an institutional investor.

By definition, PMI is additional insurance designed to protect the lender from individuals who default on their loans and who have less than 20 percent equity in their property. Mortgage experts say that home buyers who make small down payments are more likely to default on their home loans than those who put down the traditional 20 percent of the purchase price. Therefore, lenders require those buyers to purchase PMI to insure the lender against the extra risk—and ensuing cost—of foreclosure.

In fact, most states have regulations prohibiting lenders from making a loan in excess of 80 percent of the purchase price without PMI. The difference between putting down 20 percent and, say, 15 percent or even 10 percent, wouldn't seem to make such a substantial difference on the surface, but Brian Chappelle, of the Mortgage Bankers Association of America (MBA), says that 20 percent provides a necessary cushion for both home buyers and lenders: "If I put down twenty percent and lose my job, and the house has declined in value, I can still sell it and pay off the mortgage and come out even or with a little bit of cash. But if I've only put down five percent in the same set of circumstances, then I'll come out of the deal owing money."

PMI has its up side for buyers, too. About 30 percent of home buyers, most of them first-timers, can't put together enough cash for a 20 percent down payment. PMI allows many people to purchase property years earlier than they otherwise would have been able to. Buyers who are required to purchase PMI have to pay for that additional security, but they gain from being able to get a mortgage with much less cash up front, which is considered a plus by many real estate experts, who argue that you should buy a home with as little cash as possible.

First-time buyers often wonder if everyone charges PMI, because not all lenders advertise it. "If a customer calls me and says [a lender] doesn't charge PMI, I ask them to check the interest rate," says Ray, a mortgage banker, "It's always one quarter or three-eighths of a percent higher than ours. And you'll be paying it for the life of the loan."

Some buyers confuse PMI with other types of insurance, including mortgage insurance that pays off the loan in the event of the purchaser's death or disability. Like many types of home insurance, however, PMI is paid in monthly installments a year in advance; a twelve-month reserve is paid in advance, at closing. The premium price depends on the purchase price of the home and the type of mortgage you've selected (for example, fixed thirty-year, fixed fifteen-year, ARM, 7/23, or balloon) and the first year is usually a little more expensive than subsequent years. For example, Mary Carol Arado, an Illinois mortgage broker, says for the first year of a fixed-rate mortgage, the prepaid premium can run between .4 and .5 of 1 percent of the buyer's loan amount. An ARM (Adjustable-Rate Mortgage) is more expensive, running from .44 to .6 of 1 percent of the loan amount.

So if you need a $100,000 loan to purchase your $110,000 property, in the first year, your PMI premium would cost between $400 to $500 for a fixed-rate loan. In subsequent years, the premium drops to between .34 to .44 of 1 percent of the loan amount, which is then broken into twelve pieces and attached to the monthly mortgage payment. For the same $100,-000 loan, the PMI annual fee would fall to $340 per year, which is $28.33 per month.

Canceling Your PMI Premiums

Although it may seem like a lead weight, you don't have to pay PMI throughout the whole life of the loan. When you have accumulated 20 percent equity in your house, you can approach the lender to cancel your PMI premiums. (Upon canceling, you should receive the twelve-month cushion back.) Just be sure that the cancelation agreement is spelled out in writing before you sign the policy. If you ask up front which conditions must occur for the PMI to be canceled, then everyone knows from day one what the story is. You'll know how to plan and won't be shocked by any requests the lender makes.

When you're ready to cancel your PMI, contact the lender and ask what steps are required. Don't go to the mortgage servicing company, because they can't make the decision. The company that purchased your mortgage on the secondary market decides if and when PMI can be dropped, and they usually have specific rules about canceling PMI. If the lender self-insures (meaning it funds its own insurance programs) it may have its own set of rules.

Many lenders ask the home owner to meet certain requirements and will look at the following:

- *An appraisal.* The lender will want to see an appraisal
  that shows the value of the home has increased enough

to give you the 20 percent equity you must have to cancel PMI. But if you live in a neighborhood with volatile swings in home values, the lender may be hesitant to cancel your PMI even if your home has appreciated beyond the 20 percent equity mark.

- *Payment history.* Lenders want to see a clean mortgage payment history for the preceding twelve to twenty-four months.
- *Length of ownership.* Most lenders will not allow you to cancel your PMI within the first two years of home ownership. This period allows the home owner to develop a track record of on-time mortgage payments.

Today, many buyers are asking their lenders for a letter stating that the PMI payments will stop automatically when the equity level reaches 20 percent. Asking the lender for a disclosure statement at the time of closing should tell you just how much you can expect to shell out for PMI over the life of the loan. The most important thing to remember is that it is up to you to contact the lender. Unless it has been spelled out in a contract signed at the closing, the lender will not contact you when you have reached the magic 20 percent in equity.

QUESTION 84
What if I'm Rejected for My Loan?

After all the hours spent searching for the perfect home, negotiating the purchase price, working with your attorney to perfect the contract, and applying for a mortgage, it's extremely disappointing and frustrating to be rejected for a loan. But before you give up and decide you'll never be able to afford a home, you should know that hundreds of people get rejected for loans every day. Sometimes it's their fault, and sometimes lenders reject them for reasons that seem to defy logic or comprehension.

Sam once had a client who was rejected for a loan by several lenders. Her ex-husband had declared bankruptcy, but because her name was on some of the credit card accounts, she was tarnished along with his fall. Another first-time buyer was rejected because she had just bought a new car and the lender decided her debt-to-income ratios were out of whack. A third first-time buyer couple was rejected by a handful of lenders because the husband truthfully stated that his business was being sued for $100,000. As the lawsuit was ongoing, the lenders decided it was too big a risk.

Let's look at the reasons why you might be rejected for a loan:

- *Credit Report Problems.* When you go to get a mortgage, or any other type of loan, the bank or mortgage broker will pull up your credit report. This report includes all of your financial information, including every credit card, card balances, and your payment record; current and past addresses; any bankruptcies or other credit problems; bank and money market accounts; any outstanding loans; and a host of other credit information. The credit report is used to determine whether or not you're a good credit risk.

  There are numerous types of credit report problems (which may or may not be your fault) that would cause a lender to reject your application for a loan. First, if you've ever missed a credit card payment, or been late with a credit card payment, or defaulted on a prior mortgage or school or car loan, it will probably show up on your credit report. If you've filed for bankruptcy within the past seven years, that will show up on your credit report. If you haven't paid your taxes, or there has been a judgment filed against you (perhaps for nonpayment of spousal or child support), it will also show up. Failure to pay your landlord, doctor, or hospital may turn into a black spot on your credit report.

Credit report companies get their information about you from companies that extend credit, like department stores, lenders, banks, and credit card companies. The information is updated on a periodic basis. Since people actually enter in the information into the company computer, there is a good chance that a mistake has been made somewhere along the line.

If you feel that your credit report is wrong, experts say it's best to take it up with the organization or company that is claiming you owe them money. Try to find documentation that proves the mistake and have it corrected as quickly as possible. If there is a more serious problem, such as a bankruptcy filing, judgment, or if you've not filed your income taxes or "forgotten" to pay back a school loan, you may have a more difficult time getting the lender to approve your loan application. If you've been late paying your bills, regroup by paying in full and on time for six months to a year to prove to the lender that the late payments were an aberration. Be sure all your taxes are paid in full and on time.

- *Inconsistencies in Information.* Sometimes lenders will find inconsistencies between what you've told them on the application and information the loan officer discovers. If you say your income is $45,000 annually and the lender calls your employer for verification and finds out that it's only $30,000, that's probably grounds for rejection. The lender figures if you've lied about something as basic and easily checkable as your income, you may have lied about something more important. Most lenders, upon discovering minor inconsistencies (if you say your income is $45,000 and it's really $44,500), will ask you about them and give you a chance to explain. Others won't. The bottom line is this: Be straight with the lender. Answer his or her questions honestly and if you don't know the answer to a question, say so. Don't make anything up. If you get rejected for providing false or misleading information, consider the lost application fee a cheap lesson that honesty is always the best policy.

• *Employed Less than Two Years.* Lenders like to see that you're earning a stable income. They like consistency. They like knowing that someone has been employing you and will continue to employ you. That's why most lenders will generally reject you for a loan if you've been employed less than two years. As with most rules, however, there are exceptions. If you're a secretary making $25,000 and the company across the hall offers you a job as an executive secretary for $35,000, most lenders will be delighted to see you take the job and earn the extra income, even if it's a couple of weeks before closing. Why? Because lenders like lateral moves (that is, the same job for better pay at a competing company) or a step up the corporate ladder (from vice president to president). Although you're changing jobs, you're changing for the better, and the lender should be understanding. If, however, you spend a year as a mechanic, then become a short-order chef for six months, then move into used-car sales, the lender will probably shake his or her head and reject your application, even if you've moved up in income. Too much movement; not enough consistency.

What if you're self-employed? Being self-employed adds an extra twist to the process of getting a mortgage because lenders don't view self-employed workers as being as stable as those who are employed by others (although the good news is, you can't be fired!). Lenders will rarely approve a mortgage unless you have been self-employed for at least two years. When you apply for the mortgage, you'll have to bring profit-and-loss statements, as well as your last two tax returns. The lender won't look at your gross income. Net income (that is, gross income minus expenses) is what's important. (This is important to remember when looking for a home, because you may be grossly overestimating the amount of money you'll be able to borrow. For example, if you have gross earnings of $75,000 and $50,000 in expenses, a lender will consider your income to be $25,000, even though you may feel you can spend more. Some mortgage brokers specialize in getting loans for self-employed people, and work with lenders who keep these loans in their portfolio, and therefore have more relaxed lending policies.)

If you're self-employed for less than two years, back away from the application and wait until you have been running your own business for at least two years. Or find a lender who specializes in placing loans of this type. If you're employed but all or most of your salary is from commission, you may also be a good candidate for rejection, especially if you've been at it less than two years. Or you can speak to your mortgage lender ahead of time. Also, avoid paying any fees up front, so that in case you aren't approved, you won't lose any money.

Sam recently worked with a man who had taken a new commission-only sales job about six months before making an offer on a home. Although the man was pulling in an excellent salary, he couldn't find a lender who would approve a mortgage. After several weeks of making the rounds to no avail, the man was offered a better job for even more money, in Boston. Thanks to his mortgage contingency, he backed out of the purchase (without penalty) and decided to move his family to Boston.

- *Losing Your Job.* If you lose your job before the closing, it can mean an instant rejection of your loan application. If you're married, and your spouse earns enough money to support the mortgage payments, then the lender may approve the loan anyway. If your application is denied based on job loss, wait until your job prospects change and you've found a new job. Try to find something in the same field, for about the same (or more) money, otherwise you may be subjected to the two-year employment rule.

- *Unapproved Condo Building or New Development.* Sometimes you'll get rejected for a loan and you won't even be the problem. Institutions that buy loans on the secondary market have a specific set of guidelines that lenders must follow. One of these rules is the *70 percent rule* for condominiums. Lenders like their home buyers to purchase condos in buildings in which owners occupy at least 70 percent of the building. Why? It's that stability issue. Lenders believe that home owners will take better care of property than renters. This makes sense, as owners have more of a stake in a property than renters. Historically, condo buildings that have a high percentage of renters can lose their value. If you're rejected because of the 70 percent rule, you may want to seek out other lenders who may ease up a little (say, to 68 or 65 percent). If the building is less than 50 percent owner occupied, you may want to rethink your purchase. Or you may want to seek out a lender that has made loans to home owners in that building.

Those buyers who purchase new-construction town houses and condominiums may also have a tough time finding a lender who will approve their loan. Conventional lenders like to see development projects that have been in existence for more than two years. They like to see a new-construction project more than 50 percent owner occupied before they'll grant a loan, otherwise the project could go into default and the properties might drop in value (an anathema to a lender, who wants to protect the investment). If you get rejected for a loan for your new town house or condo purchase, check with the developer. A developer will usually arrange for some sort of financing package from a lender who will keep the loans in-house for one to two years, and then resell them on the secondary market.

- *Low Appraisal.* Another reason people get rejected for loans is that it doesn't "appraise out." When lenders say a home doesn't "appraise out," they mean that the bank appraisers have determined that the home is worth less than you contracted to pay for it. Let's say you offered $150,000 for a home, with 20 percent ($30,000) as a cash down payment, which is all the savings you have in the world. You're counting on the bank lending you the additional $120,000 to purchase the home. But when the bank actually sends in the appraiser, the home is appraised at $120,000, and the bank will only lend you 80 percent (or $96,000). You need to come up with an additional $24,000 in cash to close on the home:

$120,000	–	$96,000	=	$24,000
What you needed		What the bank will lend you		The difference

If you can't come up with the $24,000 to close on the house, the lender will reject your loan application.

• *Adding New Debt.* Sometimes buyers think they'll be able to get away with making a large purchase after they've been approved for a mortgage. For example, if you get approved for your loan and then two weeks before closing you go out and buy a new Corvette, with hefty monthly installments, the lender's going to know. How? What few people realize is that lenders may do two credit checks: before they approve your loan and before you close on it. Lenders are increasingly watching out for folks who incur large new debts that may interfere with their repayment of the mortgage. So don't buy that new car just before closing. Wait until after you close.

• *Refusal to Provide New Documentation.* If the loan officer calls you up and asks for additional documentation, by all means provide it. Not providing information is grounds for loan application rejection. If the loan officer continually asks for additional information, or asks you to send material you've already sent, this may be indicative of an extremely disorganized and pressed office. Or you may have another problem.

The Gambling Game

As I discussed earlier, this isn't an official scam, but it happens often enough that first-time buyers, repeat buyers, and home owners looking to refinance their loans should be aware of it. As you have now seen, there are a half-dozen reasons or more why a loan application might not be approved. One problem that doesn't get much media attention is this: Some loan officers gamble with your locked-in interest rates, hoping to put more money in their own pockets. Although that sounds surprising (it is) and perhaps illegal (technically it is, but it's isn't enforced as long as the lender lives up to his lock agreement), a little explanation might help you understand why loan officers might gamble with your rate.

To eliminate the uncertainty of changeable interest rates, borrowers may pay their prospective lender for the privilege of locking in a specific interest rate and number of points (a point is equal to 1 percent of the loan amount). The lock is good for a predefined time, usually thirty to sixty days. When you lock in your rate, you must close on your mortgage before the lock expires, or you lose the preset interest rate. Experts say that the mortgage loan process can easily go awry, particularly when interest rates are headed up. Lenders, nervous about their investments and eager to charge the highest interest rate possible, are not as eager to close on their loans as when interest rates are dropping.

According to the Office of the Commissioner of Savings and Residential Finance, which regulates and monitors mortgage brokers, mortgage bankers, and financial institutions in Illinois, lenders often "play the float" with your mortgage interest rate. Although you think you've locked in at a certain rate with a certain number of points, lenders will, in essence, gamble with the rate rather than actually lock it in, hoping that interest rates will slip further. The loan officer and the mortgage company will then pocket the difference between the new current interest rate the rate you locked in to.

The problems start when interest rates begin to go up instead of down. If the loan officer has been playing the float with your loan, and the rate goes up, he will have to pay the difference between your locked-in interest rate and the current market rate out of his pocket to close on the loan. And because loan officers are loath to pay out, they will often find something "wrong" with your application at the last minute (such as new documentation that's needed, etc.), forcing you to accept a higher interest rate or more points, says one loan officer.

If you feel as if your loan rejection is without merit, and can prove that you sent all the information required, you may want to complain to your state regulatory body. Again, the squeaky wheel gets the grease. Make sure you are heard loud and clear.

Racial Rejection

Recent investigations and surveys of the mortgage banking industry seem to prove that minorities, specifically African-Americans, are twice as likely to be rejected for a loan as Caucasians. And that makes people very angry. If you feel you've been rejected for a loan simply because you're African-American, you will want to file a complaint with your state attorney general's office, the state office that regulates the mortgage banking industry, and other regulatory agencies, including the Department of Housing and Urban Development (HUD). If the rejection is for an FHA loan, notify your local housing authority office.

PART IV

The Closing

When Should I Schedule My Preclosing Inspection? And What Do I Do if I Discover Something Is Damaged or Missing?

Patty and Frank agreed to buy a $300,000 condominium from David and Marla. When they negotiated the contract, David and Marla agreed to leave all the fixtures, including light fixtures, refrigerator, sconces, and bookcases that were attached to the wall. Everything was so friendly that Patty and Frank decided to forgo the preclosing inspection. They didn't need to walk through the apartment because David and Marla assured them that everything was in order. So after closing, everyone shook hands, and David and Marla handed over the keys. Patty and Frank went over to their new condo, opened the door, and discovered that it had been stripped bare: no light fixtures, no refrigerator, no sconces, and huge holes in the wall where the bookcases had been ripped out. They were, understandably, heartbroken. And while David and Marla certainly should have lived up to the contract (they could be sued), Patty and Frank should have taken it upon themselves to have a final walk-through of the apartment before closing.

Most first-time buyers don't realize that they should ask for a preclosing inspection. Sure, most folks understand that they can ask for an initial inspection, and bring a licensed house inspector along to point out what's wrong with the home. But too many first-time buyers aren't told that *they should request the right to a second, preclosing inspection.*

To avoid getting burned, schedule the walk-through as close to the actual closing as possible, certainly within the twenty-four to forty-eight hours prior to closing. The whole point of the walk-through is to protect yourself and your future property from sellers who aren't as nice as they seem to be, or who are actually as nasty as they appear. By inspecting the premises, you're making sure the seller has lived up to his or her agreements in the sales contract. And if he or she hasn't, you want to know about it in advance of the closing so remedies (both monetary and otherwise) can be agreed upon before money changes hands.

What should you look for in a preclosing inspection? You basically want to make sure that the condition of the home hasn't changed since you signed the contract several months earlier. Remember, you probably negotiated for the home some sixty to ninety days ago and have spent the past weeks arranging for your mortgage, packing, and preparing to move. As Patty and Frank discovered, a lot can change in sixty days. And you don't want any surprises at closing.

There are several requisites about walk-throughs:

Turn on every appliance.

Open every door.

Make sure nothing's broken.

Be certain everything the seller agreed to leave is actually there.

Be certain that when the sellers moved out, they did no damage to the home.

It's vital that you turn on every appliance that's being left in the home, including the dishwasher. As you may recall from an earlier question, Sam and I learned the hard way. But the story bears repeating.

When Sam and I were closing on our co-op, we decided to have a final walk-through. We had been in the unit several times, and knew that we were going to make some significant cosmetic improvements, so we weren't too worried about the condition of the walls and wallpaper, flooring, etc. The apartment was a mess. Our sellers were a retired couple who had lived in the unit for twenty-five years and had a huge accumulation of stuff. Boxes were stacked everywhere. Clothes had been taken from closets and laid down. Furniture had been moved. It was difficult to actually walk through the apartment and look at things. But we plodded along. When we got to the kitchen, we opened the fridge, and it seemed cold and relatively clean, though at least twenty years old. When we got to the dishwasher, we said to ourselves, "Well, we'll probably replace this soon after closing, so why bother testing it out?" Our sellers, hovering over us, assured us everything worked. We felt as if we were in the way, so we left.

I'm sure you can guess what happened next. We closed on the unit and moved our stuff in that afternoon. That night, after unwrapping a stack of dishes, Sam suggested we test out the dishwasher. So we put a load in, started to run it, and nothing happened. So Sam reached under the sink and found the water valve. Sure enough, it had been shut off. ("Now why would they shut off the water?" Sam said to himself.) Sam turned on the water and started the dishwasher. It was about 3:00 A.M. We woke up around 7:00 A.M. to banging on the door. In our bathrobes, we opened the door to find one of the engineers and our new downstairs neighbor complaining that we'd ruined her ceiling and window shade, and who knows what else, all because our dishwasher leaked. (It cost us around $150 to replace our neighbor's window treatment.) It's been years, but Sam and I still discuss whether or not our old sellers actually knew that the dishwasher leaked. Regardless, we know we should have tested the dishwasher while we were there, and let it run a full cycle.

It's equally important to open every door. Don't be afraid to poke your head into your seller's messy closets. You're looking for anything unusual or broken. Finally, be certain that everything the seller agreed to leave is actually in place and in the apartment. Check your contract if you're not sure if that window air conditioner was part of the agreement. Are the window shades or curtains supposed to be left? Or did the seller want to take them? If the seller asks you at the preclosing inspection if he or she can take additional items, say "I have to check with my attorney." That will give you time to think about whether or not you want to give away that chandelier.

If you're buying new construction, you'll be looking for different things on your walk-through. You want to be sure that everything the developer promised would be done and put in is actually there before closing. This includes any sod or plantings, doorknobs, doorbell, window screens, fixtures, appliances, etc. You also want to be sure that everything works in every room. Take a hair dryer or radio with you and test out the electrical sockets in each room. Make sure everything has been painted and is in working condition. Turn on the water in the showers and sinks, and flush the toilets. If there is a garage, make sure the electric door opener works.

With new construction, there are always a few last-minute items that need to be finished, and it may not be possible for the contractor or developer to get them finished before closing. That's why you need a *punch list*. A punch list is a list of all items that need to be fixed in the home before you consider it completely finished. During your preclosing inspection, write down all of the items that need attention: That loose tile in the master bath; the wall that wasn't painted; the electrical outlet that doesn't work; the tree that should have been planted in the side yard. Have your attorney or broker present the punch list to the developer at closing, or before closing, and have the developer agree to fix these items before you actually close. Most developers should be happy to comply with any reasonable request.

Who should go to your walk-through? My mother, Susanne, makes it a point to go to almost all of her clients' walk-throughs. She says she helps the buyer remember what was where amid the mess and muck of moving. It goes without saying that you, the buyer (or buyers, if you're buying with someone else), should attend the walk-through. You should ask your broker to be there. Beyond that, the seller or the seller's broker may attend. If the seller attends and you notice that certain things are missing, try to avoid a confrontation. Have your broker speak to the seller or seller's broker to confirm what was written in the contract.

Some buyers like to have a professional house inspector attend the preclosing inspection. I think that's overkill in most cases. The preclosing inspection isn't about finding a leaky oil tank. You should be looking for things like a gash in the wall caused by the L-shaped sofa as it was moved out of the home. That gash is something you could ask the sellers to fix before closing, or they could give you a credit at closing for the damage.

What should you do if you discover something's missing or damaged during the preclosing inspection? Make a list of anything that doesn't seem right to you and call your attorney immediately after you leave the home. You can also call your broker. Your attorney may telephone the seller's attorney before closing, or may present a list of items at closing. Either way, the list will have to be resolved before you'll agree to close on the house. The list gives you some leverage, because as anxious as you are to move, the sellers are equally anxious and have most likely found another place to live. Perhaps they are scheduled to close on a new home shortly after you buy theirs. At this point, most sellers, and the attorneys, will find a way to make everyone happy. The seller may offer you $45 instead of fixing the back door. He or she might offer you $600 for the washer and dryer their movers took "by accident." Or the seller might say, "Forget it, I'm not fixing the east window screen."

The bottom line is this: The preclosing inspection or walk-through gives you your last opportunity to make sure that the property is in the same condition (except for normal wear and tear) as the day you bought it. It's important that you take full advantage of that opportunity.

When Should the Seller Move Out?

Unless there are some extraordinary circumstances, you want to make sure the seller is completely out of the home before you close on the home. That doesn't mean the end of the business day of closing, as in, you close at 10:00 A.M. and the seller's out by 5:00 P.M.; after all, your new home isn't a business. Getting the seller out by the closing means that if you're scheduled to close at 10:00 A.M., the seller is packed and gone by 9:59 A.M. After closing (when the seller gets all of his or her money) there's no incentive to move out. If you close and pay money to the seller, and then the seller decides not to leave, well, then, you might have a real problem getting the seller out. Also, the seller no longer has any interest in the property once the deed changes hands. An unscrupulous seller might be inclined to inflict damage (if the transaction has been a bit hostile), or may be less than careful when moving his or her items out of the home. You want to protect your property, and the best way to do that is to make sure the seller is out before money changes hands.

This said, sometimes buyers and sellers make other arrangements. For example, let's say the seller has had his home on the market for a long time, say, a year. And within the year, the seller went out and bought another home and moved. So the house you're buying is vacant and perhaps empty of furniture. The seller, unless he has Ross Perot's money, will want to close as quickly as possible because he or she is paying two mortgages (on your house and the new house). You don't want to close until your apartment lease is up (so you avoid paying both rent and mortgage), but you do want to get in a little early to do some painting, and would the seller mind? It doesn't hurt to ask. If the seller seems to hesitate, offer to "rent" the house for a few days before closing for a nominal daily fee.

The earliest the seller would probably want to let you into a house would be two to three weeks before closing. Still, there's not much risk for a seller in this situation, as time marches forward to the closing.

There's greater risk for you, the buyer, if the seller wants to stay in the house *after* closing. Let's look at why a seller might want to do this:

- First, the seller may not have found anywhere to live. This is the most dangerous for you because there is no end in sight for when the seller might leave. It could be in a few days, a few months, or never. Also, you're going to be coming from somewhere and will want to, or have to, move into *your* house.
- Second, the seller isn't scheduled to close on his or her new home until a few days after closing. Most sellers are going to turn around and buy something new because of the tax laws that allow you to postpone any capital gains profit you may have when you sell by buying a new home for at least the same price as the one you just sold. (You have two years to buy the replacement home, but most sellers purchase a new home shortly after selling their old home.) So unless your sellers are retirees, it's likely they'll be buying something new. In a perfect world, the sellers would attend your closing while they simultaneously closed on their new house. However, this isn't a perfect world, and the sellers will usually want to close first on your home (because then they'll be able to use the funds to purchase the new home). So you

might be scheduled to close on your house on a Friday, and the seller is scheduled to close on his new place on Monday and may ask to "rent" your house for the weekend. If this is the case, and you have a few extra days you can spend in your current place of abode and the seller will pay you the daily rate you want, then that's fine. (Just so you know, the seller could close on his new place a few days ahead of your closing by using a financial product known as a "bridge loan." A bridge loan is a short-term loan that allows the seller to borrow enough money to close on his new home before he sells his old home. Some sellers get into trouble, however, by buying a new home before trying to sell their original home. If that happens, and they use a bridge loan to fund the new purchase, they could end up paying the equivalent of three mortgages simultaneously: their original home mortgage, the new home mortgage, and their bridge loan.)

How much should you charge for each day the seller stays in the home? The first thing to do is to calculate exactly how much the home costs per day. Add up your monthly mortgage (principal and interest), taxes, and insurance premiums, then divide by thirty (unless we're talking February). That number is your minimum out-of-pocket cost to own and maintain the home each day. Let's say you have a $100,000 mortgage at 8 percent annually. That's $8,000 ÷ 12 = $666.67 per month. And let's say your real estate tax bill is $3,000 per year or $250 per month. Your insurance premium is $35 per month.

$666.67 + $250 + $35 = $951.67 (monthly cost of the home)
$951.67 ÷ 30 = $31.72 (daily cost of the home)

If this were your home, you can see it would cost $31.72 per day for PITI (principal, interest, taxes, and insurance), which is generally the most expensive part of home ownership. If you think that $31.72 is too cheap for a daily fee to adequately encourage the seller to make his or her after-closing stay a short one, you may increase the daily fee by as much as you think is necessary. Certainly, a few dollars more per day for electricity, heat, gas, water, sewer, and garbage pickup wouldn't be out of line. Also, if there are any assessments (for condos, co-ops, and town houses), those fees should also be covered. When all's said and done, $50 or $75 per day starts to add up pretty quickly.

First-Time Buyer Tip: The daily fee and the length of the after-closing stay should be negotiated before the closing. There should also be a stiff daily penalty for each day the seller stays in the house past the agreed-upon deadline. You, or your attorney, should make it completely clear to the seller and his or her attorney that the seller will not receive all the proceeds from the closing until he or she has moved out of the house and you've had a chance to walk through the house to make sure that the house is still in good condition and the appliances and plumbing are still in working order.

How much money should be held back at closing? It's a good idea to retain enough cash to cover the payment due for the after-closing stay, plus at least another ten days' worth. *Usually, this amount is equal to 2 to 3 percent of the purchase price of the home.* If you give all the money at closing, you may have to sue to collect your daily fee from the seller. The money should be given to your real estate broker, the title company, or an unassociated third party.

What Exactly Is the Closing? And Where Is It Held?

By now you've probably heard about "The Closing." Real estate industry professionals talk about The Closing as if it were (a) a big show on Broadway, and (b) some huge black hole in outer space, sucking buyers, sellers, brokers, lawyers, inspectors, money, and mortgages into a netherworld blender out of which pops a deed that now has your name on it. Those are the two extremes. After it's over, you and your broker will either describe your closing as a dream or a nightmare. Rarely have I heard them described as being somewhere in the middle.

So let's start at the top. Why do we have the closing? Well, one attorney put it this way: If you were the seller, would you take the buyer's personal check, fold it up, and put it in your pocket, and then hand the buyer the deed to your house? Of course not. You would want some security that that check was really going to clear. Conversely, you, the buyer, want some reassurance that the deed you're being given is actually the seller's to give. Your lender, worried that you will take bad title to the home, which could mean trouble down the pike for his loan, also wants that same reassurance. The broker wants some security that he or she will actually get paid the commission. The attorney wants to know his or her fee will be paid.

Everyone wants to be protected. It is from this point that today's closing evolved. Closing a transaction has always meant that point in time when the deal is completed. One party has paid another for certain rights, privileges, property, or other goods and services. When the passing of money or other consideration has occurred, and the goods and services been received, a deal is deemed closed. Kaput. Finished.

Around the country, closings are generally held at the title company, which issues title insurance for the buyer and the lender. The title company researches the chain of title to the home. Your attorney reviews the information furnished by the title company to make sure you will get "good" title to the home when you close. Once the title issues have been resolved (that is, if they need to be resolved), then the title company will insure title in your name—with any exception shown on the policy—in the amount of the purchase price. But remember, lender's title insurance covers the *lender's* losses on the property, if some outside claim to the title is eventually upheld. If you want to protect *your* interests, you will have to purchase a separate title policy that insures your losses.

Title companies facilitate the closing by providing a forum for the free exchange of documents and releasing of funds. Generally, the title company acts as an agent for the lender, meaning that the title company works to protect the lender's best interest. However, usually the seller selects which title company will be used, because he or she is the party that generally pays for title insurance. (Of course, who pays for the title policy is dictated by local custom.) If the title company can act as agent for the lender, and close the transaction, the closing will take place at the offices of the title company. Otherwise, the closing may take place of the office of the lender, or another location acceptable to the lender.

In several states, including California and New York, it's more common to have what's known as an escrow closing. In this case, the title company acts for the benefit of both parties, using a document called an "escrow agreement." The title company will only disburse money after certain steps take place. For example, in an escrow closing, the title company will send someone to the recorder's office (where deeds are recorded). Once the name on the deed has been verified as being that of the sellers, and the transfer of title has been accomplished, the title company will allow the closing to take place. If there are any problems along the way, the title company returns the closing funds to the buyer and seller, and records a deed from the buyer back to the seller.

From the buyer's perspective, the closing can be generally broken into three pieces:

1. *Review and signing of loan documents.* In the first phase of the closing, you, the buyer, must review and sign all the loan documents provided by the lender. There may be seven to twenty documents or more, including the actual mortgage, note, affidavits, Truth-in-Lending statements, estimate of closing costs, and the escrow statement letter that outlines how much will be paid in to the real estate tax and insurance escrows.

2. *Exchange of documents between buyer and seller and title company.* The second phase of the closing deals with the relationship between you and the seller and the title company. There is an exchange of documents that must be signed by you and the seller, and then other documents that require the additional signature of the title company.

   Depending on your local customs, the seller will provide certain documents for your inspection to verify that they are correct:

   - The deed;
   - Bill of sale;
   - Affidavit of title;
   - Any documentation that may have been required in

the contract, including paid water bills, certificates of compliance with laws pertaining to smoke-detection equipment, lead paint, termite or radon inspection (these items will vary from state to state, and even county to county);

- Condo assessment full-payment certificate;
- Co-op assessment full-payment certificate;
- Insurance certificate;
- Property survey (except for condos and co-ops).

You may have anywhere from a handful of documents to a dozen or more that will require both your (and your spouse's or partner's) signature and the seller's. After you have finished with these documents, the title company will have more papers for you to sign. These documents generally relate to the title, or are papers the title company must send to the Internal Revenue Service regarding the purchase and sale of the home. Your documentation may include these:

- The RESPA (Real Estate Settlement Procedures Act) "HUD-1" statement outlines who provides the money and from which sources, and details how the money gets paid out. This document is signed by you, the seller, and the title company;
- Disclosure statements about construction contracts or any agreements entered into within the past three to six months for work to be done on the property. This is to ensure that there will be no outstanding mechanics' liens placed on the property;
- Disclosure statement about any tenants who have

access to the property other than the buyer or seller;

- Statements about any other matters that could ultimately affect the title to the property, such as lawsuits;
- Internal Revenue Service form 1099, which relates the sales price of the home. Once signed, it will be used to cross-check your IRS form with documentation signed by the title company regarding the purchase and sale of the home.

Many of these documents are signed and notarized. (Each state and county has little particular quirks regarding documentation. For example, any document that will be recorded in Hawaii must be typed and signed in black ink only. Otherwise, it will not be accepted. In other parts of the country, the notary stamp must be embossed.) Once the documents are notarized, the closing can proceed to the final step: disbursement.

3. *Disbursement of funds.* Once all the documents have been signed, dated, and notarized, the title company can proceed with the disbursement of funds. It will take the money from you, the buyer, and cut checks to the seller, the seller's lender (if applicable), the brokers, the title company, and the attorneys. Since everyone usually gets paid out of the closing proceeds, it's easy to see why the title company doesn't accept personal checks, even for a few pennies. Title companies accept only cashier's or certified checks, or a wire transfer, because that's like accepting cash.

What if There's No Lender Involved?

Good question. Almost all first-time buyers will have some sort of financing involved with their purchase simply because it's expensive to buy a home (even a home that costs $30,000), and most first-time buyers don't have that kind of cash stuffed inside their mattresses. (Oh, I'm sure there are one or two, but we're talking majority here.) If there's no lender, or if the seller is acting as lender through seller financing, the buyer and seller can sit down together and exchange and sign documents. Or, they can have the title company act as intermediary between seller and buyer in an "Escrow Closing." The closing may take less time (most closings that involve financing generally take between thirty minutes and two hours) and will certainly have fewer steps overall.

In the next few questions, I'll dissect some of the more complicated pieces of the closing, and explain in a bit more detail why they're important.

QUESTION 88
What Are My Closing Costs Likely to Be?

As I explained in Questions 61 and 62, lenders charge certain fees for giving you a mortgage. Every lender won't charge every fee, but they can certainly add up. In addition to the lender's fees, there are other closing costs to be added up, including title fees, recording fees, city and state transfer taxes, and so on. Of course, the lion's share of the buyer's closing costs are generated by the mortgage. The lender's points—a point equals 1 percent of the loan amount—which are also referred to as the service charge, are the largest fees paid to the lender and usually run between 1 and 3 percent of the loan amount. Occasionally, the points will run more than 3 percent, and there are some loans available with zero points.

(Remember that for every extra point you pay up front, the lender will decrease the interest rate of the loan. If you have the cash and are planning to stay in the home for a long time, you might want to pay three points to get the lowest interest rate possible. The points are fully deductible on your income tax return in the year you buy your home. On the other hand, if you're strapped for cash today, but know that down the line your prospects are for a higher income, you may want to go with zero points and a slightly higher interest rate, then refinance down the line.)

If you've been reading this book start to finish, you know that when it comes to calculating closing costs, your lender is supposed to make it easier for you by giving you a written, Good Faith Estimate of all closing costs. And this estimate is supposed to accurately reflect the buyer's closing costs. "But a lot of times, people are surprised when they actually get to the closing," says Neil, a real estate attorney. "The Truth-in-Lending law is supposed to take the surprise away, but it doesn't require that the lender explain what the costs are used for and where they are going." If the loan officer taking your application doesn't do a good job of explaining what happens at the closing and what the charges are going to be, you might not feel so good when the big day arrives.

Here's a list of your closing cost responsibilities. Remember, not every charge will apply to your loan, and your actual fee may be higher or lower depending on your specific situation. Ask your real estate attorney or broker to help you go over this list and identify how much each item might cost. On page 246 is a worksheet that you can fill in when you get your finalized closing costs.

- Lender's points, loan origination, or loan service fees— usually 0 to 3 percent of the loan, or more.
- Loan application fee—$0 to $350.
- Lender's credit report—$40 to $60.
- Lender's processing fee—$75 to $125.
- Lender's document preparation fee—$50 to $200.
- Lender's appraisal fee—$225 to $275.
- Prepaid interest on the loan—paid per day until the end of the month in which the closing occurs.
- Lender's insurance escrow—runs about 15 to 20 percent of the cost of the home owner's insurance policy for one year.
- Lender's tax escrow—about 33 to 50 percent of annual property taxes, depending on the time of year you close. (This is just at closing. After closing, you will begin to make regular real estate tax and insurance escrow payments as part of your monthly mortgage payment.)
- Lender's tax escrow service fee, a fee to set up the tax escrow—$40 to $65.
- Title insurance cost for the lender's policy—$170 to $300, based on the dollar amount of the home you buy. The cost to the buyer for title insurance may be relatively small because the seller may have paid a basic fee to the title company and the lender's policy is issued simultaneously. In many parts of the country, it is the seller's responsibility to ensure that the home is owned free and clear. So the seller picks up most of the cost of title insurance. When you refinance, you'll find that the

cost for title insurance goes up substantially. If you purchase a $100,000 house, your title insurance cost might be a flat $150. If you refinance that house, your title insurance may skyrocket to $415. That reflects the additional $265 that the seller paid to ensure that you received good title to his or her home.

- Special endorsements to the title—$15 to $50 each. Depending on the type of property you pick, your lender may request that special endorsements be added to the title. If the lender requires an environmental lien endorsement, it may cost $15. A location endorsement proves the house is located where the documents say it is. If you choose an adjustable-rate mortgage, that may be another $50 endorsement, depending on the title company. If the property is a condominium, there may be a condo endorsement. For a town house, there may be a PUD (planned-unit development) endorsement. As you can see, three or four extra endorsements can really add to your closing cost tab.
- Any outstanding house inspection fees—$225 to $275.
- Title company closing fee—runs from $150 to $400.
- Recording fees, of deed or mortgage—$50 to $75.
- Local city, town, or village property transfer tax; county transfer tax; state transfer tax. The charges that you, the buyer, will pay vary from city to city, and state to state. In Illinois, for example, the seller picks up the county tax ($.50 per $1,000 of sales price) and the state tax ($1.00 per $1,000 of sales price). In Chicago, the buyer picks up the city transfer tax (a hefty $3.75 per $500 of sales price). There may be other special taxes on high-end property. And certain kinds of property, such as co-ops, may under certain circumstances be exempt from prop-

erty transfer taxes. In general, property transfer taxes can range from nothing to $5.00 per $1,000 of sales price, or you may be assessed a flat fee of $25 or $50 per transaction.

- Attorney's fee—if you need an attorney, fees generally start at $250. Although some attorneys in large firms work solely on an hourly rate, there are loads of real estate attorneys who do house closings for a flat fee, and then may charge a small amount extra depending on whether your deal turns out to be particularly complicated or difficult.
- Condo move-in fee—a building charge that can run from nothing to more than $400.
- Association transfer fees—often required for condominium and town house buyers. This fee can range from nothing to more than $200.
- Co-op apartment fees—sometimes, small fees are required by co-op associations for transferring shares of stock (remember, with a co-op you're not buying an apartment, you're buying shares in a corporation that owns the building in which your apartment is located), or doing name searches. These fees can range from $50 to more than $200.
- Credit checks for condo and co-op buildings by the board.

(Just so you don't think the seller gets off scot-free, he or she will also pay a long list of closing costs, including: survey, $150 to $300; title insurance, $150 to $500 plus; recording release charges for the mortgage, $23 to $45; broker's commission, usually 5 to 7 percent of the sales price; state, county, and city transfer taxes; paid utility bills, including water, sewer, or electricity, $10 to $25; credit to the buyer of unpaid real estate taxes for prior year or current year, depending on the way your state collects property taxes; attorney's fee, $250 and up; and FHA fees and costs, depending on the loan amount.)

On the following page is a blank closing-cost sheet for you to use to figure out exactly how much you'll be paying in closing costs.

QUESTION 89
What Is a Title Search? What Is Title Insurance? And Why Do I Need Them?

How do you prove you own something? Generally, you have a bill of sale, or the certificate title to the item—let's say it's a car—that's registered in your name with the state. So if anyone inquires who owns that cherry red Ford Mustang, the state can tell them it's you. Proving that a seller owns a particular home, however, is a little more difficult. And lenders will not allow you to purchase a home without knowing it actually belongs to the person actually selling it. How do you prove the seller owns the home you want to buy? You conduct a title search.

During a title search, the examiner looks at the chain of title of a home, working backwards from owner to owner until it reaches the point where the land was originally granted or sold from the government to the original owners or developers. If the title has been recorded correctly, you should be able to trace the lineage of a piece of land all the way back to when that area of the country was settled. (As with many of our laws, we derive our methods of recording title from our English cousins, whose records of property ownership stretch back one thousand years or more in some cases.)

Closing-Cost Sheet

Name _____

Property Address _____

Closing Date _____

Lender's points, loan origination, or loan service fees	_____
Loan application fee	_____
Lender's credit report	_____
Lender's processing fee	_____
Lender's document preparation fee	_____
Lender's appraisal fee	_____
Second appraisal (if required)	_____
Prepaid interest on the loan	_____
Lender's insurance escrow	_____
Lender's tax escrow	_____
Lender's tax escrow service fee	_____
Title insurance cost for lender's policy	_____
Special endorsements to the title	_____
House inspection fees	_____
House reinspection fee	_____
Title company closing fee	_____
Recording fees, of deed or mortgage	_____
City, town, or village transfer tax	_____
County transfer tax	_____
State transfer tax	_____
Capital gains or other tax	_____
Attorney's fee	_____
Other fees and charges:	
_____	_____
_____	_____
_____	_____
_____	_____
_____	_____
_____	_____

Total Closing Costs _____

How the title search is carried out varies from city to city, and depends on what kinds of records have been kept. Public records that may affect a property's title include records of deaths, divorces, court judgments, liens, taxes, and wills. Public records in a wide variety of county and city offices must be examined, including those in the recorders of deeds, county courts, tax assessors, and surveyors. Since many local governments have not yet computerized their records, the majority of title searches are performed manually, with someone spending hours, in many cases, poring over different documents in various offices. If the municipality in which you are buying is computerized, title searches can be done in a matter of minutes.

What are they looking for? Title searches are conducted by lawyers, title companies, or title specialists, to discover if there are any problems—called "clouds" in the industry—with the title. The lender wants to know if there have been any liens (a claim made against a property by a person or tax assessor for payment of a debt) or judgments (by a court of law) or easements (known or unknown rights) filed against the property, which might prevent you from receiving good title.

For example, Roberta and Dave bought a house in a suburb of Chicago. They had the land surveyed. When they actually moved into the house, they discovered that years earlier a neighbor had built a garage that took about ten feet off the back end of their property. The survey should have noted that the garage encroached on their property. The title Roberta and Dave received to the land wasn't "good" title because the encroachment created a defect on their title. In other words, someone was making use of their land without their permission. If Roberta and Dave had bought title insurance, their insurer would have reimbursed them for the portion of land that they paid for but to which they didn't receive good title, had the insurer failed to catch the encroachment.

If the insurer notes the encroachment, you, the buyer, are considered to have been notified of the defect and must approach the seller about it before the closing. A title search looks for any clouds on the title to the home. Title insurance protects you and the lender against any mistakes or errors or omissions made by the individual performing the search. If you buy a home from Dan and Shelly, and a long-lost relative turns up with irrefutable evidence (say, a recorded deed from the property's original owner) that she actually owns the home, you'll have to turn over the home to the long-lost relative. Now, the title search should have turned up this information, but whoever conducted the search missed this important piece of evidence. What happens in a case like this is the lender finds it has lent you money to purchase a property from someone who didn't really own it. Title insurance protects you, the buyer, from any losses associated with the cost of any errors made. It also protects the lender's interest.

Title insurance is paid as a onetime premium; the cost is based entirely on the sales price of the home. In many communities, the seller pays for the cost of the title search, since he or she wants to guarantee that you, the buyer, will receive good title to the home. The lender will insist that you pay for, or obtain from the seller, title insurance that covers the lender. The lender may not insist that you get an owner's policy (which will compensate you if there is an error—title insurance insures the lender against errors), but it's a good idea. If you purchase the owner's policy at the same place you buy title insurance for the lender, you may be able to get a discounted rate. In addition, ask your real estate attorney if there is a title company he works with regularly. Your attorney may be able to use his or her economic muscle (he or she probably does a lot of house closings and the title company may be eager to encourage the business) to get you a discounted rate. Finally, if the seller has owned the home for only a short period of time, say, a few years, you may be able to get a discounted policy by checking with the seller's original title company. They may be able to give you a "reissue" rate, which may have a significantly lower premium.

QUESTION 90
What Is RESPA? And What Does the RESPA Statement Look Like?

In 1974, Congress decided Americans were suffering from abuses in the title industry. Title companies were giving kickbacks to real estate agents and brokers who referred buyers to settlement agencies. Congress decided buyers should be free to choose their own title company or settlement agency. So the Real Estate Settlement Procedures Act (RESPA) was passed to address these issues.

Section 8 in the RESPA code is the kickback provision according to the Mortgage Bankers Association of America (MBA). It makes it a crime to pay or receive any money, or give or receive anything of value, to another person for the referral of any real estate settlement services, which includes making a mortgage loan. (This means your broker cannot legally receive money for referring you to Jones Mortgage Company down the street.) Sections 4 and 5 of the RESPA code deal with disclosure. Mortgage companies must tell you how many loans they resell on the secondary market before you take their mortgage. Then they are required to tell you when they are actually selling your mortgage. Finally, the company that buys your mortgage must disclose all sorts of information, including a telephone number and a name you can contact if there is trouble with your loan.

RESPA, which is regulated by the department of Housing and Urban Development (HUD), also requires that lenders give their prospective borrowers a copy of a HUD information booklet within three days of receiving the application. Lenders must also give the Good Faith Estimate (GFE) within three days, in which the lender estimates what the buyer's closing costs will be. There's another disclosure that mortgage companies are required to make: the HUD-1 settlement statement, which outlines exactly what monies come in and how they are distributed. This is a closing document that you will have to sign. It is filled out by the title company once all the numbers have been called in. The HUD-1 statement is instructive for both buyers and sellers because you can see exactly where the money comes from and where it is going. The buyer's and seller's costs are itemized side by side. It also neatly wraps up a lot of the issues we've been talking about. (See Appendix IV for a complete form.)

The first line of the "Summary of Borrower's Transaction"

A. Settlement Statement	U.S.Department of Housing and Urban Development	
		OMB No. 2502-0265

B. Type of Loan

1. ☐ FHA 2. ☐ FmHA 3. ☐ Conv. Unins.	6. File Number	7. Loan Number	8. Mortgage Insurance Case Number
4. ☐ VA 5. ☐ Conv. Ins.			

C. Note: This form is furnished to give you a statement of actual settlement costs. Amounts paid to and by the settlement agent are shown. Items marked "(p.o.c.)" were paid outside the closing; they are shown here for informational purposes and are not included in the totals.

D. Name and Address of Borrower	E. Name and Address of Seller	F. Name and Address of Lender

G. Property Location	H. Settlement Agent	I. Settlement Date
	Place of Settlement	

	K. Summary of Seller's Transaction	
	400. Gross Amount Due to Seller	

250

indicates the contract sales price. The settlement charges, or closing costs, are on the next line. On the middle of the page, there is a line for the deposit or earnest money, and another line detailing the principal amount of the new loan. Your application fee will also be listed. Finally, any extra city, county, and perhaps real estate taxes will be listed. Everything is totaled up at the bottom, where you see what cash you'll need to close the deal.

On the seller's side, we see the contract sales price at the top. Then comes his or her settlement charges, or closing costs. Then there is a line detailing the payoff of the seller's first mortgage loan (including who holds that loan). Then the earnest money is listed (it's been paid to the seller), and the title indemnity charge (title insurance). Finally, there are adjustments for items unpaid by seller, including any city, county, or real estate property taxes. The bottom line indicates how much cash the seller will receive from the deal.

Page two details exactly what settlement charges, or closing costs, the buyer and seller are paying and to whom. For example, there may be a $225 charge paid to Randy Appraisal Company for a home appraisal. You may have paid $45 for a credit report and $300 for a mortgage application. (The problem with finding all of this out at the closing is that it's a little too late to start shopping around for another mortgage company if you find yours has added onerous charges that it didn't disclose on the Good Faith Estimate. Of course, wonders one first-time buyer, once you go through all the work and actually get to the closing, who's going to quash the deal for an extra $100 here or there?

A separate page, which isn't part of the HUD-1, but is given out by some title companies, looks at disbursements. Who gets what money. Whose name is on the check. There will be maybe ten to fifteen checks written at the closing, including ones for title insurance, for city or county stamp taxes, for inspections, to the real estate broker, for the mortgage insurance premium, to the real estate attorney, to pay off any other mortgages or liens, and others. Usually within 30 days of closing, the bank releases the real estate tax and insurance escrow proceeds (if any) to the sellers. After all, they won't be needing real estate tax and insurance escrow for a property they've sold.

Some folks feel that RESPA is a waste of time. Others find the disclosures and HUD-1 statement to be useful to consumers. Once you get to the closing, you can decide for yourself.

QUESTION 91

Will I Need Home Owner's Insurance? What Should It Cover?

If you need a loan to buy your home, you will need to have home owner's, or hazard, insurance. Lenders want to know that you're protecting their investment from harm. When you take out a mortgage, you're pledging your home as collateral for the loan. The papers you sign say if you default on the mortgage, the lender may begin foreclosure proceedings and take over the home. So the lender's primary concern is protecting the value of the home. Issues of concern to the lender are damage by fire, water, tornado, flood, or a tree crashing in through the roof. Let's say you have no insurance and you have a $100,000 loan and there's a fire. In a few hours, the lender's $100,000 has disappeared in a puff of smoke.

There's almost no way (unless you have seller financing and the seller does not insist upon it) that you'll get a mortgage without having to purchase enough home or hazard insurance to cover at least the amount of money the lender has given you. (In fact, you'll have to turn up at the closing with a piece of paper that says you've purchased a policy for at least a year that's effective the day of closing or earlier.) Of course, if you have a $100,000 loan, that probably also represents a significant investment on your part. You probably put down $20,000 in cash. You may have paid between $3,000 to $5,000 in closing costs. Plus, you may have decorated the interior of the home, or renovated, or built an addition. You have personal possessions. What goes up in flames can be worth double or triple what you actually owe the lender.

It's important to keep your policy current as well. Dan and Cindy buy a nice house for $125,000. They owe $100,000 to their lender, and have home insurance worth $150,000, should anything happen. For many years, nothing happens. One day, disaster strikes, and the house burns to the ground. The insurer pays Dan and Cindy $50,000 and the lender gets $100,000. The problem is that the house has escalated in value and before burning down was worth $250,000. To rebuild it and refurnish it would cost nearly $300,000. But Dan and Cindy get only $50,000 because they never added onto their policy's value. They didn't realize the home and its contents were worth so much.

What kind of coverage should you get? Most people purchase a general policy that covers the house and its contents. Condominium and co-op owners need their own unique policies, but they still cover the unit and its contents. The standard policy you'll buy is probably based on the "HO-3" forms developed by the New York City–based Insurance Services Office (ISO), a nonprofit industry group that provides statistics and rate-making services to underwriters. According to the Insurance Information Institute, a nonprofit information group for the property/casualty insurance industry, your home owner's policy should cover the eighteen listed "perils" as defined by the ISO:

1. Fire or lightning.
2. Loss of property removed from premises endangered by fire or other perils.
3. Windstorm or hail.
4. Explosion.
5. Riot or civil commotion.
6, Aircraft.
7. Vehicles.
8. Smoke.
9. Vandalism and malicious mischief.
10. Theft.
11. Breakage of glass constituting part of the building (windows, skylights).
12. Falling objects.
13. Weight of ice, snow, or sleet.
14. Collapse of building(s) or any part thereof.
15. Sudden and accidental searing asunder, cracking, burning, or bulging of a steam or hot water heating system or of appliances for heating water.
16. Accidental discharge, leakage, or overflow of water or steam from within a plumbing, heating, or air-conditioning system or domestic appliance.
17. Freezing of plumbing, heating, and air-conditioning systems and domestic appliances.
18. Sudden and accidental injury from artificially generated currents to electrical appliances, devices, fixtures, and wiring (TV and radio tubes not included).

In addition to these "perils" you're protected from everything that may cause damage to your house except those events specifically excluded by the underwriter: nuclear accident, earthquakes, flood, and war. If you are in a flood plain, and you know that when it rains your house will flood, you would do well to purchase additional flood insurance. If you live on the San Andreas fault in California, you'd better have earthquake insurance. It would probably be prohibitively expensive to get insurance to cover every possible calamity; the idea is to get the best coverage possible at the best price.

Your lender will expect that you will continue to pay your premiums, and will expect that as you change, modify, or make additions to the home over the years, you will keep your policy updated and increasing in value. Remember, if something happens and you can't meet your monthly mortgage payments, your lender gets the first chunk of the insurance proceeds. (The Insurance Information Institute publishes a small book called *How to Get Your Money's Worth in Auto and Home Insurance*, which describes the process of buying the proper insurance coverage. See Appendix VI for information on how to receive this useful booklet.)

QUESTION 92
How Should We Hold Title to Our New Home?

When Janet and Scott recently bought a house in a suburb north of Chicago, they wondered how they should hold title. Scott, a pediatrician just starting his own practice, is well aware of the litigious nature of society. Industry statistics tell him it's likely he may be targeted in a medical malpractice suit over the course of his career as a doctor. Scott was worried someone could sue him and take away their home.

Other home owners have the same concerns. Whatever business you're in, there may come a time when your home may be in jeopardy. If you declare bankruptcy, your creditors may be able to attach a lien against your house, possibly even forcing you to sell it. There may be a judgment against you. The time to think about how to protect your home, your largest investment to date, is now, before you buy it. Here are some of the ways you can hold title to your home:

Individual

If you're a single person buying a home, your options for the way you hold title are limited. You may hold title to your property as an individual. In some states, very few, you may hold title in a land trust. A land trust is a legal invention where the sole asset in the trust is the property you are buying, and the beneficiary of the trust is you. At one time, you could use a land trust to completely obscure the identity of the beneficiary. Today, the veil of the land trust has been lifted.

Two or More Buyers or a Married Couple

If you're married, you can hold property in one of four ways: as joint tenants, tenants in common, tenancy by the entirety, or a land trust.

Joint tenancy with rights of survivorship is the most common way married couples hold property. You each own the property as a whole. If you or your spouse dies, that person's share in the property is immediately transferred to the spouse. You share and share alike in the entire property.

If you hold the property as tenants in common, your share in the property can be broken down into percentages; for example, you might own 30 percent of a house, your spouse may own 30 percent, and your parents may own 40 percent. While you may use and enjoy the whole property—you cannot be restricted to "your" 30 percent—you can sell your share, just as you might sell stock in a company. You may sell your share to whomever you choose.

Tenancy by the entirety is an option that is only available to married couples. It has the same benefits as joint tenancy, with rights of survivorship, but as long as the couple is married, it protects the interest of each spouse. With tenancy by the entirety, both spouses in the marriage must agree before the property is subject to one spouse's creditors. So, no spouse may do anything that would create a claim or lien on the marital property. If, for example, Scott was sued, the creditors could not attach the residence because he and Janet each owns the whole property. Creditors would have to wait until the marriage is severed, or the spouse consented to the claim, or the property is sold. Once the property is sold, a claim can be attached to the proceeds.

Holding property in a land trust is also an option. It works in exactly the same way as it would for an individual.

What's the best way to hold property? That depends on your personal circumstances. Tenancy by the entirety is the best for married couples, but it's not available in every state. The next best option is joint tenancy with rights of survivorship, which is available all over the country.

QUESTION 93
Who Should Attend the Closing? And What Should I Do if I Can't Be There?

The closing contains some of the most important legal contracts you'll sign. You're promising to pay thousands of dollars in exchange for a place to call home. It is likely the largest single investment of your life thus far.

That said, it's probably a good idea for you to attend the closing. In fact, as a buyer, it's more like a command performance. All of the buyers—that means you, your spouse if you have one, or any partners who are going into the transaction with you—must attend. There are two compelling reasons for you to attend: First, you have to sign your name a dozen or more times on various documents; second, you have to read those documents to make sure everything is in order.

Who else generally attends the closing? If you're in a state where attorneys are involved, your attorney and the seller's attorney will generally attend the closing. Also, the seller's broker and the subagent or buyer broker (who are very interested in making sure everything goes smoothly up until the final papers are signed and the final checks—including theirs—are cut) will often attend. There will generally be a title officer (if you are closing at a title company) or other closing agent, and there may be a representative from the lender. Sometimes the lender will bring along an attorney. Whether or not the sellers attend is up to them. While you need to be present to sign documents, sellers' documents can be signed ahead of time.

Despite marking your calendar two to three months in advance, sometimes there's a last minute scheduling conflict with the closing. An important business trip comes up, or someone gets sick, or perhaps a family member passes away and you want to attend the funeral in another state. Whatever comes up, call your attorney and see if you can juggle the closing date. It may be possible, especially if the seller already owns another home, or the seller is taking back financing, or is moving to an interim home before going on somewhere else. Moving the closing up or back a few days is the least onerous way to deal with a scheduling conflict.

If you cannot change the date of closing—if, for example, the seller is closing on his or her new property that same day and requires the proceeds from the sale—then you must give some consideration to assigning a power of attorney to someone who can step into your shoes and sign your name legally at the closing. You're better off giving it to someone who's familiar with the transaction. If the only person who knows it is your attorney, and he or she is willing to accept that designation, then that's who should have it. If a friend or family member is familiar with the transaction, then that person should be designated.

In most cases, it's not smart to give your broker the power of attorney. Most brokers work for and represent the seller, so there's a potential conflict of interest. You wouldn't give power of attorney to the seller, but if you gave it to the seller's broker, in effect you would be doing just that. If your broker is a buyer broker, then you may want to discuss power of attorney. But remember, no matter whose broker it is, he or she is not a disinterested third party. In most cases, the broker has a significant amount of money riding on the outcome of the closing. If something comes up at closing (see Question 96), you want the person with power of attorney to look out for your best interests, not his or her own.

First-Time Buyer Tip: Check with your lender ahead of time to see if he will allow your documents to be signed with a power of attorney. Ask what power-of-attorney form they require.

Many lenders will not accept power-of-attorney signatures on their documents.

What Are Prorations?

Let's say that Ginny makes an offer to purchase Maureen and Mike's home. In the two months up until the closing, some bills come due that must be paid. Maureen and Mike pay the water bill (which comes every six months), the second install-ment of real estate taxes (they're due in March and September), and the gas bill (which comes once every two months). On the day of closing, Maureen and Mike's attorney tells Ginny how much is her share of these prorated expenses.

Almost every closing has some costs prorated, simply be-cause we don't pay for our housing needs on a daily basis. Can you imagine trucking on down to the county clerk's office to pay your real estate taxes *every day?* What about your electric bills? Water bill? Association dues? Many of these costs are spread out over a long period of time. Depending on where you live in the country, you pay your real estate taxes once or twice a year. It isn't fair for Maureen and Mike to have paid an entire year's worth of property taxes, if they only live in the house for nine months of that year before selling to Ginny. Likewise, if Ginny bought the home just before the second installment of taxes was due, it wouldn't be fair for her to pay for six months of taxes, when she would only have three months in the home.

So a little bit of math evens things out for everyone. How do you calculate prorations? Take the number of days covered by the bill and then divide the bill by the number of days. That gives you a daily fee. Then multiply by the number of days up to and including the closing. For example, let's say Maureen and Mike's property taxes are $2,000 for the year, broken into two installments of $1,000 each, half due on March 15 and the other half due on September 15. Each $1,000 represents 183 days per year (it's actually 182.5, but we'll round up).

$$\$1,000 \div 183 = \$5.46 \text{ per day}$$

If the closing is on September 16, Maureen and Mike have already paid the real estate property taxes for the rest of the year. At closing, Ginny would have to reimburse them for the days of that year she's going to live in the house. It's 106 days from September 17 to the end of the year. Multiply 106 by the $5.46 daily fee:

$$106 \text{ days} \times \$5.46 \text{ daily fee} = \$578.76$$

Ginny would owe Maureen and Mike $578.76 at closing. It can work in reverse also. Let's say the closing is on September 14. On September 15, Ginny pays the $1,000 real estate tax bill. It's seventy-six days from July 1 to September 14. Multiply 76 by the $5.46 daily fee:

$$76 \text{ days} \times \$5.46 \text{ daily fee} = \$414.96$$

If the closing was on September 14, Maureen and Mike would owe Ginny $414.96 for their share of property taxes.

In some states, it's common to ask the previous owners to pay a little extra in real estate taxes above the daily fee, because in many areas property taxes rise each year and the exact amount for the next bill may not be known. So instead of asking for the daily fee multiplied by the number of days, the buyer may ask the seller to put up 110 percent of the daily fee to cover any increases. In our example, the daily fee of $5.46 would be increased to $6.01 to cover any increase in taxes.

Real estate lawyers (or your broker, if you're in a state where attorneys are not used for house closings) will calculate prorations for every bill that has some sort of shared time arrangement, including gas bills, water bills, assessments to home owners' associations, and real estate taxes. This includes any insurance policies (above and beyond hazard insurance required by the lender) or service agreements the buyer will have to pay for. Any bill can be prorated using basic math. (Generally, telephone service is shut off when an owner vacates a home and the new owners must start their own account. The local electric company will generally change the name on the service the day of closing, and begin billing the new owners.)

Sometimes attorneys draw up a reproration agreement. If the sellers reimburse the buyer for more than the actual bill, sometimes the buyer and seller agree to recalculate the bill to reflect the actual amount paid. Here's how it works: If you thought the bill was going to be $100 and the seller's share was 25 percent, the seller would have paid you $25. But if the actual bill ends up being only $80, the seller's share is only $20, so you would owe the seller $5 (which is paid after closing when the recalculation is done.)

Sometimes proration money is kept in escrow (by a disinterested third party), which usually happens only with substantial amounts of money. The escrow then makes payments to the buyer based on the bills that come in and will return any extra money to the seller. The important thing with prorations is that the seller pays all his or her costs before closing. Otherwise you may have to chase the seller to get your fair share.

First-Time Buyer Tip: Local custom dictates who pays for, and who receives the benefit for, the day of closing. In Chicago, the buyer pays the expenses associated with the closing date, including taxes, assessments, etc. Your attorney should be able to advise you on local custom.

QUESTION 95
What Do I Need to Bring with Me to the Closing?

The simple answer, "bring yourself," won't quite do here. You also need to bring money. I suppose you could bring cash, but the preferred methods are a cashier's or certified check. You must also bring your home owner's insurance certificate (to prove you have it), and any documents the lender requires (these should have been spelled out in the commitment for the loan).

On the day before the closing, check with your attorney to see how much money you should have the check made out for. It's not a disaster if you bring too much, as the title company can cut a check to you for the difference. The problem comes if you have too little. In that case, you may find the closing stretched out as you run all over town trying to convert a personal check into a cashier's check. You may also wire transfer funds but you'll need to get the proper information to know where, and to what account, to wire the money. And bring a favorite pen. You'll be signing your name quite a few times.

First-Time Buyer Tip: Usually the check you bring to the closing can be made out to your name and endorsed to the title company at closing.

What if Something Goes Wrong at the Closing?

Just when you think you've crossed the finish line, it seems to move farther away. That's what closing feels like sometimes. You solve one problem and another crops up. And another. And another.

When Janet bought her condo, she discovered that the loan amount on the loan document was incorrect. And then she noticed some of the documentation didn't have her correct address! Leo and Genna's loan agreement also had an incorrect amount. At the last minute, the developer who built Bart and Michelle's town house refused to put $1,500 into escrow to cover the sod and landscaping that was supposed to be part of the deal. One buyer refused to close on a condo for twenty-four hours because the sellers—who didn't live there anymore—couldn't find their mailbox key.

There are at least ten reasons why a closing doesn't happen or is delayed for a few days or is stretched out:

1. *Money Problems.* Money problems are one of the most popular reasons home sales may not close on time. For example, if you're transferring money by wire, it's always a possibility that the money will get tied up, or there will be a delay in the processing of the wire transfer. Sometimes the numbers don't add up and a buyer will find that he or she is short. Since lenders and title companies don't take personal checks, you may have to run across town to get that personal check converted into a certified or cashier's check.

2. *Missing Loan Package.* If the lender's documents aren't

there, you're not closing. If the loan package has to come from out of state, and it's shipped via overnight delivery, it's always possible that the package will be lost or delayed. If the loan package is missing documents, they may have to be sent by messenger or faxed over to the closing. In addition to adding more time, the lender may try to charge you for the messenger service or even for use of the fax. You should vigorously deny these charges, particularly if it was the lender who made the mistake.

3. *Disagreement about Documents.* Read all of the documents carefully. It's possible that the loan company may try to slip something in, or has made changes to the documents you didn't agree to.

4. *Incorrect Loan Documents.* Nothing can create problems like incorrect information on loan documents. Check to be sure that you're actually getting the amount of money you agreed to and that your address, phone number, and other personal information is correct. Be certain the interest rate is correct. Bring inconsistencies and wrong information to the attention of the lender. New documents may have to be drawn up, or the lender may try to get by with Wite-Out.

5. *Last-Minute Requests.* Sometimes the lender will make a last-minute request for documentation at the closing. At Leo and Genna's closing, the lender requested a copy of the canceled deposit check. To safeguard against time-wrenching delays, it's a good idea to bring everything with you to the closing.

6. *Walk-Through Problems.* If you do the final walk-through (hopefully after the seller has moved out) and

find that some items are missing or damaged, it must be brought up at the closing. This is the time to negotiate with the seller (or the seller's attorney or broker, if the seller is not at the closing) for remuneration. You and the seller should agree to a settlement before you close.

7. *Title Problems.* Sometimes, last-minute title problems creep up. A long-lost relative turns up, or the title company discovers the real estate taxes haven't been paid. A contractor may have filed a mechanic's lien. You should insist that these title issues are resolved before you'll close on the home. You don't want to inherit someone else's problems.

8. *Someone Dies.* It doesn't happen too often, but you should know what can happen if either you or the seller dies after the contract is signed and before closing. If the seller dies after signing the contract, the estate must go through with the sale. However, it may be difficult to close on time, particularly if the seller dies close to the day of closing, or if the estate is in probate court. If you die, the seller may be able to force your estate to continue with the sale, although in the real world, sellers may not force the issue. Check with an attorney for further details about your rights in your state.

9. *Catastrophe Strikes.* Nearly every first-time buyer has a nightmare about his or her new home being destroyed before the closing. Fire, flood, earthquake, lightning—you name it. What happens if a fire actually consumes the home you're supposed to purchase tomorrow? In most cases, depending on what the contract says, you wouldn't have to close if something

266

major happened to the home. Or you can elect to close and take the insurance proceeds (after the seller's lender has been paid off—if the home is underinsured that could mean little or nothing for you). If you have already taken possession of the home when disaster strikes, you may lose the right to terminate the purchase and be forced to close. Again, have your attorney advise you of your rights.

10. *Seller's Deal Falls Through.* Usually, sellers take the money from the sale of their home and use it to pay for another home. So it's likely your seller will do the same. But if the seller's deal (for any number of reasons) falls through, he may have no place to go and might have second thoughts about your closing. In other words, the seller might refuse to vacate the home. If this happens, you have three options: First, don't close until he moves out. Second, close and force him out, which is emotionally, physically, and legally difficult. Third, hold back money from the closing to ensure that the seller gets out by a certain time, and attach a stiff daily penalty for every day he remains in the home. And make that incentive *very* stiff, so the seller will want to move rather than stay. You actually want the daily penalty to be so stiff it's cheaper for the seller to put all of his or her belongings in storage and go to a hotel.

How long should the closing last? As we discussed early on, most closings take less than an hour. One attorney estimates that 10 percent of his closings take less than a half hour. An additional 50 percent take less than an hour. Another 30 percent take less than an hour and a half. Ten percent take less than two hours. So 90 percent of all closings happen in less than two hours. And the final 10 percent? Well, it could take ten hours, or ten days, or never happen at all. But most closings happen. And when it's over, and the last fire has been put out, you'll own your very own home. Congratulations!

QUESTION 97
What Should I Get from the Sellers at Closing?

You've signed your name so often your arm is about to drop off. You've tallied up the numbers, made fast and furious calls to your office to reassure them you're still living and breathing, and are wired from cup after cup of stale coffee. The last thing to do is to get the keys to your new home from the seller. Keys are pretty important and they require a bit of good faith. After all, when the seller hands you the keys at closing, you don't know if they work or not. You won't find out until much later, perhaps even next spring, that the seller forgot to give you the keys (or combination) to the toolshed lock. Or the combination on the bicycle room. Or the key to your storage locker.

The seller is supposed to turn over all keys to the home at closing. This includes front- and back-door locks, any dead-bolt locks, window locks, interior door locks, shed or storage room locks, or locks on any part of the property. The seller should also give you any combinations you need to open any locks on the property. Finally, mailbox keys and garage-door openers are supposed to be included. Those of you who buy new construction will generally not get keys at closing. The developer, or the developer's representative, will give you a letter indicating where keys can be picked up. Usually the broker for the development will have the keys.

What if the keys don't work? Well, there is that element of good faith. But just in case your seller doesn't have any good faith left at the end of closing, the brokers (if you used one) can be marshaled in to help the situation. If the brokers have participated, it's likely that they have a set of working keys. They should give you those keys to the home, which you can then use to check against the keys the seller has given you. If the seller refuses to turn over the keys, perhaps your first call should be to the local locksmith.

Sam once had a closing where the sellers had moved out of state several months earlier. The sellers' broker had the condo keys, and they left their mailbox key with a neighbor. On the day of closing, the buyer refused to close until the mailbox key had been delivered. The sellers, reached by telephone during the closing, told the buyer to call the neighbor. The buyer did call, but the neighbor wasn't there. After hemming and hawing for the better part of a day and a half, the buyer finally decided to have a locksmith come and make a new key for the mailbox. Fine. But he wanted the sellers to pay for the locksmith. The sellers refused. He closed anyway.

QUESTION 98
How Does My Deed Get Recorded?

What is a deed? A deed is the physical manifestation of the title to your home. Holding title is an amorphous concept—it's not like holding a handful of dirt and saying, "I own this land." To give you something to show for your money and efforts, our legal system has sanctioned deeds, or pieces of paper that say you own a specific piece of property at a specific address.

Part of the process to formalize your ownership is to record the deed. This gives legal recognition—in other words, puts the world on notice—of your ownership of the property. Anyone can go to the office of the recorder of deeds and find out that you own your home. The deed becomes part of the public record. And your ownership becomes part of the property's chain of title. If a title company looked up your property now, after the closing and after the deed has been recorded, your name would come up as the official owner.

How does a deed get recorded? If you're closing at a title company, the title company may record the deed. Or the title company will deliver the deed to you, and you will have to take it to your local recorder of deeds' office. It's as simple as that. But you want to make sure that the deed is recorded properly, and that your correct name, address, and other information is listed. When real estate tax bills are sent out, they are sent to the name and address listed at the recorder's or assessor's office. If there's a problem with your home or with your tax bill, a notice will be sent to the address listed at the recorder's or assessor's office. If the address, or your name, is incorrectly listed, you may never get your property tax bill or any notices and you could lose your property.

First-Time Buyer Tip: Check to make sure your deed is recorded correctly and the information is listed correctly. Verify that the proper authorities have your correct address for tax bills. Mark down the days you're supposed to receive your tax bill. If you don't receive it, call the recorder's (or real estate tax bill collector's) office to find out why. Nonpayment of property taxes is an easy (and quick) way to lose your property. Make sure it doesn't happen to you.

How Should I Prepare for the Move to My New Home?

If it feels as if you're the only family you know moving to a new house, maybe you don't know the right people. One out of every five families moves each year (this includes both owners and renters). Forty-five percent of these moves happen during the summer, according to the American Movers Conference (AMC), the interstate moving industry's national trade association, which represents some twelve hundred moving companies worldwide. There are dozens of details to think about when you move, even if your new house is across town. It pays to plan and be organized. There are several free, or inexpensive (about 50 cents to $1 each), consumer publications about moving that are available to you. *Guide to a Satisfying Move* and *Moving with Pets and Plants* are published by the American Movers Conference. *Helpful Tips in Planning Your Interstate Move* is published by the Interstate Commerce Commission, as is *When You Move: Your Rights and Responsibilities*. Regulated household-goods movers are required to furnish a copy of *When You Move* to prospective customers.

Here are some things to think about when planning a move:

1. Don't take everything with you. Sort through, throw out, give away, or sell things you don't need anymore. When you've gotten to the bare minimum, start packing.
2. As soon as you get your mortgage, start saving your old newspapers for wrapping delicate objects like china and glassware. You may want to double wrap each piece, so make sure you have enough paper.

3. Will your new home be ready on time? Do you need an interim move? Will you be storing your furniture? If you're moving across state lines, it's best to store your belongings near your new home, not your old one. That way, if you need something you might be able to get it quickly and easily.

4. If you need repair, decorating, or renovation work done on your new house, get busy scheduling the work four to six weeks before you move. If you're planning to paint or decorate, you may want to have that work done before you've unpacked most things and settled into your new home.

5. Three weeks before the move, you'll want to contact your local utility companies (telephone, electricity, cable, gas, water) and inform them of your move. Arrange to have these services cut off at the end of moving day (if you're moving in the afternoon, it would be nice to be able to drink water and use the bathroom). Don't forget to arrange the hookup of utilities to your new home.

6. If you're moving to a condominium or a co-op, you'll need to schedule a day to move in with the building's management. Generally, large condos (those with an elevator) require you to "reserve" the freight elevator for your move. There may even be a fee for having the building maintenance men "oversee" your move. Ask your new building personnel about moving-in rules.

7. Two weeks before your move, you'll want to set the day to discontinue your delivery services, like newspapers, milk, dry cleaning, or laundry. If you're moving to a new state, your broker may be able to offer a little advice on employing these services in your new town.

8. Also, around two weeks before your move, you'll have to fill out and mail your change-of-address cards. Your local post office can give you some cards to fill out, or you may want to have change-of-address cards preprinted.

9. If you're moving with pets, you may need to take some special precautions, according to the AMC. Pets cannot be shipped on moving vans. They should travel with you and wear special identification tags with your name, address, telephone number, and the name of an alternative relative, in case you can't be located. If you decide to ship your pet by air, make the arrangements ahead of time. If you move across state lines, nearly every state has laws on the entry of animals. Write to the State Veterinarian, State Department of Animal Husbandry, or other state agency for information. Most states require up-to-date rabies shots for dogs and cats. If you're moving to Hawaii with your pet, you'll have to quarantine the animal for 120 days. Some pets must have an entry permit issued by the destination state's regulatory agency. Finally, your new town may have restrictions on the number of dogs or cats that can live at one residence. If this might be a problem for you, check with your new city or village council.

10. You generally won't have a problem if you're moving house plants, but some states do require you to have an inspection by an authorized state department agriculture inspector. Plants are susceptible to shock when moving, and it may be dangerous to move a plant if the temperature is below 35°F or above 95°F to 100°F for more than an hour. The AMC says plants

can tolerate darkness for up to a week, but it's best not to store them. Cuttings of your favorite houseplants, while convenient, will not last as long or as well as potted plants.

Of course, as many as eight weeks before moving day, you'll probably need to find a moving company. Shop around and compare prices. Try to use a licensed, insured, and bonded mover. Be careful of overcharges, and if you're moving across state lines, find out how much the company charges per mile. It's better to get a flat fee, if that's possible.

Movers are required to prepare an "order for service" for each customer. Keep a copy of this, as it shows the terms of the initial agreement with the mover. Next, the mover must issue a "bill of lading," which is the legal contract between the customer and the mover. It is very important, so keep it handy during the move. The Interstate Commerce Commission warns "not to sign the bill of lading until comparing it with the order of service to be sure that all services ordered are correctly shown."

A "binding estimate" binds the mover to bill only at the price agreed to for the specific services needed. If you make any changes or increase the amount that is being moved, it may void the estimate, which should be in writing and attached to the bill of lading. With a binding estimate, you must pay the mover with cash, certified check, or money order, unless you have prearranged to use a credit card. In a "nonbinding estimate," the final price for the move will not be known until everything has been weighed and transportation charges have been calculated. Request a copy of the mover's policy on inconvenience or delay (in case they get lost) in advance of the move.

Make sure you and the mover understand when he or she is

supposed to pick up your household furniture and when it is supposed to be delivered. Do not accept a promise like, "We'll be there as soon as possible." Get definitive dates and make sure it's in writing. If the mover cannot meet the pickup or delivery dates, he or she is required to notify you by telephone, telegram, or in writing. If you're going across country, be sure to ask the mover to notify you of the charges for the move.

Licensed movers are responsible for loss or damage to your property. You should have a list of all the items being moved. Number your boxes, and label them clearly with your name and new address and telephone number. You and the mover should agree about the contents being shipped, and make sure the inventory list reflects your mutual understanding. At the time of delivery, note any items that are damaged or missing, and ask the mover for a liability claims form. Finally, you and the mover should agree on the amount of liability the mover will assume for loss or damage to your property. The mover's liability is limited to 60 cents per pound, so it's wise to add extra insurance if your goods are particularly valuable. The mover can provide you with added coverage, but be sure you understand what's protected and for how much. Likewise, you must declare the value of your goods with the mover before the move. Otherwise, the mover is required to value them at a lump-sum equivalent to $1.25 times the weight of the shipment. So if your goods weigh four thousand pounds, the mover is only required to value them at $5,000. Check with your home owner's or renter's policy to see what's covered.

What if I Discover the Seller or the Seller's Broker Lied about Something in My Home after I Move in?

In some ways, this is perhaps the most difficult question to answer in the book. It's tough to know if people knowingly "lied" about something or if they just told you the truth about what they knew at the time. The first thing to consider is the problem itself. What happened? Did the boiler blow up? Is a pipe burst? Did the electrical system catch on fire? Is there asbestos in the home? Did you fall through the floor? Did the roof leak? Did the dishwasher break? Did the ceiling paint crack? If you've bought a new home, I think you have a right to believe everything will work beautifully for a long time. But if something goes wrong, your attorney should have negotiated for a new home owner's warranty, which covers various items in the home for different periods of time. For example, if your new dishwasher breaks within the first year, the warranty will cover that. If the roof leaks in five years, it may cover that, too.

If you've bought an older or used home, you have to realize some things are going to break. Others may work, but not work well. Each home is different. Each home has its own rhythms. If something goes wrong, you'll have to fix it, unless your seller or the seller's broker purchased a home owner's warranty plan for your older home (if you live in California, around 50 percent of the homes are sold with a warranty plan). If you have a warranty, then you'll be able to have your problems fixed and all you'll be responsible for is the deductible. (See Question 91 for more specific information on home owner's warranties.)

The next question is, did the seller or seller's broker knowingly lie to me? Or is this a case of puffery, where the broker may have said, "This house is perfect! You'll love it." You should know when the broker says, "This house is perfect," he or she doesn't mean everything in the home is in perfect working order. But if the seller and the seller's broker told you the furnace was new and a week after moving into the home you discover it's old, covered with asbestos, and just had a paint job, that could be a problem. If you were told the house was freshly painted, and you find out it wasn't, that could be a problem. If you were told the house's roof did not leak, and a day after the first rain your living room looks like a swimming pool, that could be a problem.

Although disclosure laws vary from state to state, most sellers are required to tell you about "known, material defects" that could affect the value of the home. In some states, home owners have successfully sued their sellers for not disclosing that someone was murdered in their home, or a former owner died of AIDS.

If you feel you've been wronged, or lied to, in the purchase of your new home, consult your attorney.

Top Ten Mistakes
First-Time Buyers Make

Borrowing a little from one of my favorite performers, David Letterman, I've created a top ten list of things first-time buyers tend to do when searching for a home. Brokers call them "mistakes." While these are not egregious errors, if you don't work out timing problems or if you buy the wrong size home or waste time looking at homes you can't afford, these mistakes may at best make the process of home buying a little more time-consuming and heart-wrenching. At worst, they can cause problems down the line, when you're trying to sell the home (yes, you will sell this home and move to another someday).

I can't tell you how many times I've heard first-time buyers exclaim "Not me!" when faced with the prospect of having made mistakes. My feeling is, reading about them here, in the Appendix, presumably after you've read the whole book, might help you head 'em off at the pass. While you may not see yourself doing everything on this list, brokers agree that the average first-time buyer makes at least one of the following mistakes:

1. *Timing Problems.* Most first-time buyers are renters. As such, the best time to close on a house is when your current lease ends. Don't sign another year-long lease if you expect to buy a home before that lease period expires; otherwise you'll end up with a dent in your pocketbook from writing rent and mortgage checks. If you can't time your closing correctly, approach your landlord about a shorter lease—say, three to six months in length. One alternative is a month-to-month lease. Or you can ask your landlord to include an escape clause in your new lease that will allow you to get out of your lease with 30 or 60 days' notice.

2. *Looking at Homes You Can't Afford.* First-time buyers often hear that they can buy a home up to two and a half times their combined income. Heck, if interest rates stay in the 6 to 7 percent range, you might actually be able to push that number to three or three and a half times your combined income. Still, you have to factor in your debts, property taxes, insurance premiums, private mortgage insurance (PMI), and the down payment. The problem with looking at homes you can't afford is you'll get spoiled. When you finally come to your senses and start looking at homes in your price range, it'll probably be disappointing. For example, if you've been looking at four-bedroom homes with attached garages in plush suburbs, a three-bedroom home in a so-so neighborhood with street parking is going to seem, well, not quite nice enough. In order to save yourself the heartache, get prequalified through a local lender. There's no cost or obligation, and the lender will tell you exactly how much house you can afford to buy.

3. *Buying the Wrong Size Home.* Many first-time buyers, especially those who are single and in their late twenties and early thirties, purchase one-bedroom condominiums. What they don't realize is how likely it is they will meet someone, fall madly in love and marry. Unless the girl next door has a condo you can combine with yours, that one-bedroom, one-bath apartment will soon seem too small. For the same price, and possibly even the same location, your dollars might buy a two-bedroom, two-bath apartment, which would give you additional flexibility. When you buy property, think about how long you intend to live there. Is this a five-year home? A ten-year home? Or, is this the home you intend to die in? The average American family changes residences every five to seven years. If you're in your twenties, it's likely you'll have significantly changed your lifestyle within five to seven years. Smart buyers plan for those changes ahead of time.

4. *Buying in a Neighborhood You Know Nothing About.* Sometimes first-time buyers will fall in love with a house in a neighborhood that is inappropriate for them. Even though you'll live in the house, you'll have to travel through the neighborhood to get there. Is it a nice neighborhood? Is there graffiti on every wall? Are there gangs? Is there a neighborhood crime watch group? Are the neighbors your age? Are there families around the same age as yours? Is it a transient neighborhood, or do families stay there forever? To avoid making this mistake, spend a lot of time in the neighborhood before you buy. Drive to and from the house. Sit in your car and watch your future neigh-

bors come home from work. Listen to how loudly their children play their favorite rock music. Walk to the local bar, restaurant, grocery store, and cleaners. Think about whether or not this neighborhood will make you as happy as the house.

5. *Operating on a First-House-Is-Best Theory.* Coming from a cramped, one-bedroom rental, almost any home will look good. Try to avoid jumping at the first home you see. Look at five, ten, or even twenty houses to see what's on the market. Season your eyes by inspecting different types of homes, including condos, town houses, duplexes, and single-family houses. When you've finally narrowed down your choices to three or four, visit them again. By this time some form of objectivity should have returned. Now make your choice. Although some completely impulsive decisions work out, most do not, and you could wind up paying for this impulsiveness down the road.

6. *Buying a Property That's Difficult to Resell.* Although you say you don't mind that the house backs up to the local railroad, you will when it comes time to sell the home. And it's unlikely you'll be able to easily convince another buyer just how quiet and peaceful life is there. When buying a home, try not to buy one that will be difficult to resell because even though you think you'll be there forever, you won't. Most first-time buyers sell within five to seven years. Think hard about how you would sell this home before you buy it. Walk yourself through and point out all the negatives. Say them out loud. Then ask your agent or broker how long it would take him or her to sell it.

7. *Overextending Your Budget.* Although the lender who

prequalifies you for your loan tells you you're able to afford a $100,000 home, buying in that price range may stretch your budget beyond the comfort zone. To avoid feeling pinched, it's important to understand how you spend your money. You may be comfortable spending 35 percent of your take-home pay on rent, or you may prefer to spend less—say, 25 percent. Write down everything you spend (down to that last piece of bubble gum) for two months. Can you live without buying your favorite group's latest CD? Would you feel uncomfortable knowing you can go out to dinner only once a month? That you must eliminate your yearly vacation? That your children can't have camp or piano lessons? Becoming a homeowner means you'll have additional expenses besides your mortgage payment. There's the maintenance and upkeep of the home, and property taxes. If you live in a condo, you've got assessments. Better to buy something less expensive that will give you greater peace of mind and allow for savings and a few extras.

8. *Being Indecisive.* No one's saying you shouldn't take your time when finding the right house. You should. In fact, take all the time you need. Don't let your broker bully you into making a decision before you're ready to do it. Ask to see five, ten, twenty, or fifty homes if you haven't found one you love. The problem with indecisiveness is finding a home you would like to live in, but being afraid of making the commitment. First-time buyers often lose two or three homes because they can't bring themselves to actually make the offer. Or there might be two wonderful properties, a tough choice. If you're afraid, admit that fear

and conquer it by talking with your broker. You're not the only first-time buyer who's had trouble making up his or her mind. Remember, others have trod this way before.

9. *Choosing the Wrong Mortgage.* Many first-time buyers have heard from their parents that the only mortgage to get is a thirty-year fixed interest rate loan. That's because the generation ahead of you didn't have the tailor-made financial options buyers have today. Consider choosing an adjustable-rate mortgage (ARM) to take advantage of super-low interest rates. Or pick a ten- or fifteen-year fixed interest rate loan to maximize your deduction, and save you hundreds of thousands of dollars in interest. Or you might want to look into a two-step mortgage, which combines a little of the risk of an ARM with the dependability of a fixed-rate loan. Explore all the options. Have your lender show you on paper how much they'll cost you and how they compare with each other.

10. *Underinsuring the Property.* First-time buyers know they have to buy home insurance to cover their mortgage. Sometimes they forget to increase the coverage of that insurance as the neighborhood improves and the home appreciates in value. Sometimes they forget to insure the contents of the house. Think about how much it would cost you to replace your furniture, clothing, books, CDs, artwork, and pots and pans. Add up everything and then tack on the cost of actually rebuilding the home (for single family or town houses) should it burn to the ground. Then add on your mortgage (even if the house burns down you'll still have to repay that money). That's how much insurance you should buy.

APPENDIX II

How You Can Lighten Your Property Tax Load

As a new home owner, you've probably realized that real estate taxes are about as inevitable as death. While you'll eventually get to the end of your mortgage payments, you'll pay property taxes until you sell the house or . . . well, let's just leave it at that.

The good news is, you can do a few things to keep your property taxes as low as possible. According to tax professionals, county and township governments often make loads of mistakes when assessing property. Figures from the nonprofit National Taxpayers Union, a taxpayers advocacy group based in Washington, D.C., indicate that approximately 60 percent of all homeowners are overassessed.

So out of every hundred angry taxpayers, sixty are overpaying. Of those, says the union, only 2 percent appeal their real estate taxes. Of the 2 percent who do appeal, anywhere from 50 to 80 percent of these—the figures vary based on the source—receive some sort of reduction in their property taxes. Those are good odds. Of our 100 original taxpayers, fifty-eight are not appealing their taxes. About half of those who do appeal get some sort of break.

Though it may seem complicated, appealing your property taxes is not a difficult process, say those who have done it. However, it does require a bit of ingenuity, perseverance, and organization. And the reward—a lower tax bill—is eminently worthwhile.

How worthwhile? That depends on each house, but Jim Siudut, an accountant and real estate tax specialist who has produced a video called *Fight Higher Real Estate Taxes and Win*, says he saved himself $1,500 in one year. The next year he saved himself an even greater amount because the rise in his property taxes was keyed to a lower assessed valuation (for an explanation of these terms, see the miniglossary at the end of this section).

The key to successfully fighting your property taxes is solid evidence presented clearly and concisely. Siudut says all homeowners should make sure they're being correctly assessed, especially if their property taxes are high or if they have received steep increases in the last few years. And the time to appeal is when you get your assessment notice—not your tax bill.

The assessment notice details your home's current and past assessed valuation and its current estimated market value. It should also list your property's physical characteristics. In other words, if you have four bedrooms and two bathrooms and an attached two-car garage, the notice should say that.

The estimated market value is the price the assessor's office attaches to your property based on surveys and studies of neighboring properties. The assessment is a percentage of the estimated market value, and that percentage is usually set by law.

It's important to remember that once you receive your assessment notice, you have a limited time to file an appeal, usually thirty to sixty days, depending on the county. If you are not satisfied with your judgment, you may appeal all the way up to your state's Supreme Court.

In North Carolina, for example, any taxpayer dissatisfied with the assessment made by the county assessor should arrange immediately for an informal meeting with the assessor to explain why he or she thinks the assessment is excessive. If a satisfactory conclusion cannot be reached, the taxpayer should file an appeal with the County Board of Equalization and Review (Board of County Commissioners), requesting a hearing. A taxpayer dissatisfied with the decision of the county board may file an appeal with the State Property Tax Commission within thirty days of the mailing of the decision by the county board. That decision may be appealed to the Court of Appeals and ultimately the North Carolina Supreme Court.

To effectively appeal your assessment, you'll need your most recent and prior year's tax bill (for new home owners, this should be available at your local tax assessor's office), your current assessment notice, your current property survey, your purchase contract or closing statements (if you purchased your home within the last five years), a copy of any building plans, and an itemized account of expenses (for any improvements made to the property) and any recent appraisals.

To analyze your assessment, you'll need the following data: your property record card; a list of comparable homes ("comps"); their property record cards, sale dates, and prices. Experts recommend that you check with a local real estate agent or broker for some of this information. Agents and brokers should be happy to oblige because it's a good opportunity for them to market their services to potential customers.

The first step is to go to your county assessor's office and take a look at your property record card. You do this by using the parcel number or permanent real estate index number, which you can find on your tax bill. The card lists the physical characteristics of your property, including the number of bedrooms, bathrooms and fireplaces; garage size; square footage; and lot size.

Many overassessments result from factual errors. That is, the assessor's office may say that your house has four bedrooms when it actually has only three. So check the facts. Factual errors are the easiest to document and the easiest to appeal. If you do find a factual error, you'll need either blueprints or a property survey to "prove" your claim. Your evidence should include recent color photographs of the inside and outside of your house. Or you can also ask the assessor's office to come out and reexamine your house.

In addition to factual errors, Siudut uses four tests to determine whether property has been overassessed: an assessment ratio test, an equity test, a market test, and an environmental factors test. Gary Whalen, a real estate broker and tax consultant who has written a book called *Digging for Gold in Your Own Backyard: The Complete Homeowner's Guide to Lowering Your Real Estate Taxes*, refers to property overassessments due to factors other than factual errors as judgmental errors.

Assessment Ratio Test

"In any county, the assessment is based on the home's market value. The assessment ratio is a percentage of market value. What you want to do is determine whether or not your assessment [ratio] is in line with that of comparable homes in your neighborhood," Siudut says.

Gathering comparable data is the most time-consuming part

of appealing your property taxes. Siudut and Whalen recommend that you check for properties that have sold within the last two years and are similar to yours in size and amenities. Armed with the exact addresses of these comps, ask the assessor's office for the property record cards for them. Compare the assessed valuation of the comps with the sale price to see if the assessor comes close in determining the correct market value. Did the homes sell for less money than their market value? Check to see what percentage the assessor used to determine the assessed valuation (before the multiplier was applied). Compare this with the percentage used on your property.

Experts say the biggest misconception is that homeowners think they can go only on market value. The key test to fairness is not market value, it's uniformity.

Market and Equity Tests

The law of uniformity also helps home owners construct appeals based on market and equity tests. Homes in the same neighborhood should be assessed at the same rate, proportionate to their size and amenities.

Siudut's market test compares your assessment per square foot with those of comps in your neighborhood. To gain an accurate square footage account, measure from your house's exterior walls. Next, find eight to ten comps so that you will end up with at least four that have lower assessments per square foot. To find out the assessment per square foot, simply divide the assessed value by the number of square feet in the property. Like the market test, the equity test compares the value of other homes similar in age and amenities to yours. And again, the idea is to find comps that have been assessed at a lower rate than yours.

Level out the value of the homes by adding and subtracting the value of amenities one house might be missing but another home has. For example, if your house doesn't have a fireplace, but your comps do, then subtract $1,500 from your assessed valuation. A local real estate agent can help you determine the appropriate value for each amenity.

Environmental Test

Did the state recently build a nuclear power plant in your backyard? Did the railroad just add a new switching station down the street? Are a large number of people in your neighborhood out of work because a plant closed down? Is a new garbage dump being planned within a couple of miles of your home?

These are environmental factors that could lower your property's market value. (Of course, as a new home buyer, you've remembered the broker's maxim, "location, location, location," and hopefully not chosen a house next to a garbage dump.) If you put these factors to work for you, Siudut says, you might be able to lower your assessment. Document these changes and how they might work against property values in the neighborhood. Use articles from your local newspapers, editorials, and evidence of any television and radio reports. Clip these together to give added weight to your appeal.

Whalen and Siudut recommend combining any errors— both judgmental and factual—to get the biggest reduction.

"If you're organized and present a clear case, it does not substantially increase the assessor's workload," Siudut says. "The more organized and focused you are, the easier you make their job, and the easier it is to get that reduction."

When researching your case, don't be afraid to ask the person behind the desk for help. Home owners should also apply for all the exceptions to which they're legally entitled: senior citizens, homestead, homestead improvement, disabled, or disabled veterans. The assessor can reduce your equalized assessed valuation anywhere from $2,000 to $50,000, depending on which benefits you're entitled to.

A Glossary of Tax Terms

Here are a few tax terms to help get you going:

- *Assessed Valuation:* The value placed on property for tax purposes and used as a basis for division of the tax burden. It's a percentage of what is deemed the home's fair market value.
- *Assessment Ratio:* The percentage of your home's fair market value that each assessor uses to determine the property's assessed valuation. The ratio can vary from county to county.
- *State Multiplier:* Also known as the state equalization factor, this is a number the state assigns to each county, depending on the assessment ratio the county uses to calculate assessed valuation. The multiplier either raises or lowers the assessed valuation to the state-mandated level of 33.33 percent of market value. The multiplier ensures that taxpayers in each of the state's counties pay the same amount proportionately in property taxes.
- *Tax Rate:* The rate at which property is taxed, usually shown per hundred dollars of the property's value.
- *Notice of Revision:* A notice mailed to the property owner after a property has been reassessed.
- *Uniformity:* The legal principle that governs property tax assessments. It states that all property in a given area

must be assessed at the same level. That is, you should not be assessed at a higher rate than your next-door neighbor. The principle of uniformity is the basis for many successful assessment appeals.

APPENDIX III

Contracts and Contingencies

M ost sellers will expect the contract to be accompanied by the "standard package" of contingencies, including attorney approval, financing or mortgage, and inspection. Because these three contingencies are so common these days, I've included them here. I've also included the condominium, co-op, and single-family home offer to purchase contracts that were discussed in earlier chapters. Though you may want to use these contracts and contingency forms as a guide, they may not include the exact language that will protect you in your state. Have your real estate attorney provide you with the correct forms for your state.

Chicago R Association of Realtors

NOTICE TO PROSPECTIVE PURCHASERS

Thank you for giving us the opportunity to work with you in satisfying your real estate needs. You should be aware that, as members of the Chicago Association of Realtors®/MLS, and as fellow members of this community, we endeavor at all times to provide our customers with fair and honest service.

As a part of providing this service, we believe you should know that:

EITHER AS A LISTING BROKER OR AS A COOPERATING BROKER,

WE ARE THE AGENTS OR SUB-AGENTS OF THE SELLER OF ALL

PROPERTIES THAT WE WILL SHOW YOU.

AS AN AGENT OR SUB-AGENT OF THE SELLER, WE OWE THE

FIDUCIARY DUTIES OF LOYALTY AND FAITHFULNESS TO THE SELLER.

As a part of our service to you, we can and will:

Treat you fairly and honestly.

Show you availabe properties meeting the criteria established by you.

Disclose all material facts of which we are aware, about the properties

you are considering.

Provide you with information about the financing of your transaction.

If you have any questions about our role as a real estate agent, please feel free to ask. We look forward to having the opportunity to work with you, and to provide you with our services.

The undersigned acknowledges receiving and reading the above notice.

_____   _____
(Firm)   (Signature of Prospective Purchaser)

_____   _____
(Agent)   (Print Name)

                                            _____
                                            (Signature)

_____   _____
(Date)   (Print Name)

NOTICE PROVIDED HEREIN IS REQUIRED BY STATE LICENSING LAW. THIS FORM OF NOTICE HAS BEEN APPROVED BY STATE OF ILLINOIS DEPARTMENT OF PROFESSIONAL REGULATION.

6/92

EQUAL HOUSING
OPPORTUNITY

From the Office of:

STANDARD FORM
PURCHASE AND SALE AGREEMENT

This _____ day of _____ 19 ___

1. **PARTIES AND MAILING ADDRESSES**

   (fill in)

   hereinafter called the SELLER, agrees to SELL and

   hereinafter called the BUYER or PURCHASER, agrees to BUY, upon the terms hereinafter set forth, the following described premises:

2. **DESCRIPTION**
   (fill in and include title reference)

3. **BUILDINGS, STRUCTURES, IMPROVEMENTS, FIXTURES**

   (fill in or delete)

   Included in the sale as a part of said premises are the buildings, structures, and improvements now thereon, and the fixtures belonging to the SELLER and used in connection therewith including, if any, all wall-to-wall carpeting, drapery rods, automatic garage door openers, venetian blinds, window shades, screens, screen doors, storm windows and doors, awnings, shutters, furnaces, heaters, heating equipment, stoves, ranges, oil and gas burners and fixtures appurtenant thereto, hot water heaters, plumbing and bathroom fixtures, garbage disposers, electric and other lighting fixtures, mantels, outside television antennas, fences, gates, trees, shrubs, plants, and, ONLY IF BUILT IN, refrigerators, air conditioning equipment, ventilators, dishwashers, washing machines and dryers; and

   but excluding

4. TITLE DEED
(fill in)

* Include here by specific reference any restrictions, easements, rights and obligations in party walls not included in (b), leases, municipal and other liens, other encumbrances, and make provision to protect SELLER against BUYER's breach of SELLER's covenants in leases, where necessary.

Said premises are to be conveyed by a good and sufficient quitclaim deed running to the BUYER, or to the nominee designated by the BUYER by written notice to the SELLER at least seven   days before the deed is to be delivered as herein provided, and said deed shall convey a good and clear record and marketable title thereto, free from encumbrances, except

(a) Provisions of existing building and zoning laws;

(b) Existing rights and obligations in party walls which are not the subject of written agreement;

(c) Such taxes for the then current year as are not due and payable on the date of the delivery of such deed;

(d) Any liens for municipal betterments assessed after the date of this agreement;

(e) Easements, restrictions and reservations of record, if any, so long as the same do not prohibit or materially interfere with the current use of said premises;

*(f)

5. PLANS

If said deed refers to a plan necessary to be recorded therewith the SELLER shall deliver such plan with the deed in form adequate for recording or registration.

6. REGISTERED TITLE

In addition to the foregoing, if the title to said premises is registered, said deed shall be in form sufficient to entitle the BUYER to a Certificate of Title of said premises, and the SELLER shall deliver with said deed all instruments, if any, necessary to enable the BUYER to obtain such Certificate of Title.

7. **PURCHASE PRICE**
   *(fill in); space is
   allowed to write
   out the amounts
   if desired*

The agreed purchase price for said premises is

dollars, of which

$ _____
$ _____ have been paid as a deposit this day and

$ _____ are to be paid at the time of delivery of the deed in cash, or by certified, cashier's, treasurer's or bank check(s).

$ _____
$ _____ TOTAL

8.	**TIME FOR PERFORMANCE; DELIVERY OF DEED** *(fill in)*

Such deed is to be delivered at   o'clock   M. on the   day of   19   , at the

Registry of Deeds, unless otherwise agreed upon in writing. It is agreed that time is of the essence of this agreement.

9.	**POSSESSION AND CONDITION OF PREMISE.** *(attach a list of exceptions, if any)*

Full possession of said premises free of all tenants and occupants, except as herein provided, is to be delivered at the time of the delivery of the deed, said premises to be then (a) in the same condition as they now are, reasonable use and wear thereof excepted, and (b) not in violation of said building and zoning laws, and (c) in compliance with provisions of any instrument referred to in clause 4 hereof. The BUYER shall be entitled personally to inspect said premises prior to the delivery of the deed in order to determine whether the condition thereof complies with the terms of this clause.

10.	**EXTENSION TO PERFECT TITLE OR MAKE PREMISES CONFORM** *(Change period of time if desired).*

If the SELLER shall be unable to give title or to make conveyance, or to deliver possession of the pre-mises, all as herein stipulated, or if at the time of the delivery of the deed the premises do not conform with the provisions hereof, then any payments made under this agreement shall be forthwith refunded and all other obligations of the parties hereto shall cease and this agreement shall be void without recourse to the parties hereto, unless the SELLER elects to use reasonable efforts to remove any defects in title, or to deliver possession as provided herein, or to make the said premises conform to the provisions hereof, as the case may be, in which event the SELLER shall give written notice thereof to the BUYER at or before the time for performance hereunder, and thereupon the time for performance hereof shall be extended for a period of thirty   days.

11.	**FAILURE TO PERFECT TITLE OR MAKE PREMISES CONFORM, etc.**

If at the expiration of the extended time the SELLER shall have failed so to remove any defects in title, deliver possession, or make the premises conform, as the case may be, all as herein agreed, or if at any time during the period of this agreement or any extension thereof, the holder of a mortgage on said pre-mises shall refuse to permit the insurance proceeds, if any, to be used for such purposes, then any pay-ments made under this agreement shall be forthwith refunded and all other obligations of the parties hereto shall cease and this agreement shall be void without recourse to the parties hereto.

12. BUYER's ELECTION TO ACCEPT TITLE

The BUYER shall have the election, at either the original or any extended time for performance, to accept such title as the SELLER can deliver to the said premises in their then condition and to pay therefore the purchase price without deduction, in which case the SELLER shall convey such title, except that in the event of such conveyance in accord with the provisions of this clause, if the said premises shall have been damaged by fire or casualty insured against, then the SELLER shall, unless the SELLER has previously restored the premises to their former condition, either

(a) pay over or assign to the BUYER, on delivery of the deed, all amounts recovered or recoverable on account of such insurance, less any amounts reasonably expended by the SELLER for any partial restoration, or

(b) if a holder of a mortgage on said premises shall not permit the insurance proceeds or a part thereof to be used to restore the said premises to their former condition or to be so paid over or assigned, give to the BUYER a credit against the purchase price, on delivery of the deed, equal to said amounts so recovered or recoverable and retained by the holder of the said mortgage less any amounts reasonably expended by the SELLER for any partial restoration.

13. ACCEPTANCE OF DEED

The acceptance of a deed by the BUYER or his nominee as the case may be, shall be deemed to be a full performance and discharge of every agreement and obligation herein contained or expressed, except such as are, by the terms hereof, to be performed after the delivery of said deed.

14. USE OF MONEY TO CLEAR TITLE

To enable the SELLER to make conveyance as herein provided, the SELLER may, at the time of delivery of the deed, use the purchase money or any portion thereof to clear the title of any or all encumbrances or interests, provided that all instruments so procured are recorded simultaneously with the delivery of said deed.

15. INSURANCE
*Insert amount (list additional types of insurance and amounts as agreed)

Until the delivery of the deed, the SELLER shall maintain insurance on said premises as follows:

Type of Insurance	Amount of Coverage
(a) Fire and Extended Coverage	*$
(b)	

16. ADJUSTMENTS
(list operating expenses, if any, or attach schedule)

Collected rents, mortgage interest, water and sewer use charges, operating expenses (if any) according to the schedule attached hereto or set forth below, and taxes for the then current fiscal year, shall be apportioned and fuel value shall be adjusted, as of the day of performance of this agreement and the net amount thereof shall be added to or deducted from, as the case may be, the purchase price payable by the BUYER at the time of delivery of the deed. Uncollected rents for the current rental period shall be apportioned if and when collected by either party.

17. ADJUSTMENT OF UNASSESSED AND ABATED TAXES

If the amount of said taxes is not known at the time of the delivery of the deed, they shall be apportioned on the basis of the taxes assessed for the preceding fiscal year, with a reapportionment as soon as the new tax rate and valuation can be ascertained; and, if the taxes which are to be apportioned shall thereafter be reduced by abatement, the amount of such abatement, less the reasonable cost of obtaining the same, shall be apportioned between the parties, provided that neither party shall be obligated to institute or prosecute proceedings for an abatement unless herein otherwise agreed.

18. BROKER's FEE
(fill in fee with dollar amount or percentage; also name of Brokerage firm(s))

A Broker's fee for professional services of

is due from the SELLER to

the Broker(s) herein, but if the SELLER pursuant to the terms of clause 21 hereof retains the deposits made hereunder by the BUYER, said Broker(s) shall be entitled to receive from the SELLER an amount equal to one-half the amount so retained or an amount equal to the Broker's fee for professional services according to this contract, whichever is the lesser.

19. BROKER(S) WARRANTY
(fill in name)

The Broker(s) named herein
warrant(s) that the Broker(s) is(are) duly licensed as such by the Commonwealth of Massachusetts.

20. DEPOSIT
(fill in name)

All deposits made hereunder shall be held in escrow by
as escrow agent subject to the terms of this agreement and shall be duly accounted for at the time for performance of this agreement. In the event of any disagreement between the parties, the escrow agent may retain all deposits made under this agreement pending instructions mutually given by the SELLER and the BUYER.

21. BUYER's DEFAULT; DAMAGES

If the BUYER shall fail to fulfill the BUYER's agreements herein, all deposits made hereunder by the BUYER shall be retained by the SELLER as liquidated damages unless within thirty days after the time for performance of this agreement or any extension hereof, the SELLER otherwise notifies the BUYER in writing.

22. RELEASE BY HUSBAND OR WIFE

The SELLER's spouse hereby agrees to join in said deed and to release and convey all statutory and other rights and interests in said premises.

23. BROKER AS PARTY

The Broker(s) named herein join(s) in this agreement and become(s) a party hereto, insofar as any provisions of this agreement expressly apply to the Broker(s), and to any amendments or modifications of such provisions to which the Broker(s) agree(s) in writing.

24. LIABILITY OF TRUSTEE, SHAREHOLDER, BENEFICIARY, etc.

If the SELLER or BUYER executes this agreement in a representative or fiduciary capacity, only the principal or the estate represented shall be bound, and neither the SELLER or BUYER so executing, nor any shareholder or beneficiary of any trust, shall be personally liable for any obligation, express or implied, hereunder.

25. WARRANTIES AND REPRESENTATIONS *(fill in); if none, state "none"; if any listed, indicate by whom each warranty or representation was made*

The BUYER acknowledges that the BUYER has not been influenced to enter into this transaction nor has he relied upon any warranties or representations not set forth or incorporated in this agreement or previously made in writing, except for the following additional warranties and representations, if any, made by either the SELLER or the Broker(s):

26. MORTGAGE CONTINGENCY CLAUSE *(omit if not provided for in Offer to Purchase)*

In order to help finance the acquisition of said premises, the BUYER shall apply for a conventional bank or other institutional mortgage loan of $_____ at prevailing rates, terms and conditions. If despite the BUYER's diligent efforts a commitment for such loan cannot be obtained on or before _____, 19_____ the BUYER may terminate this agreement by written notice to the SELLER and/or the Broker(s), as agent(s) for the SELLER, prior to the expiration of such time, whereupon any payments made under this agreement shall be forthwith refunded and all other obligations of the parties hereto shall cease and this agreement shall be void without recourse to the parties hereto. In no event will the BUYER be deemed to have used diligent efforts to obtain such commitment unless the BUYER submits a complete mortgage loan application conforming to the foregoing provisions on or before_____ 19_____

27. CONSTRUCTION OF AGREEMENT

This instrument, executed in multiple counterparts, is to be construed as a Massachusetts contract, is to take effect as a sealed instrument, sets forth the entire contract between the parties, is binding upon and enures to the benefit of the parties hereto and their respective heirs, devisees, executors, administrators, successors and assigns, and may be cancelled, modified or amended only by a written instrument executed by both the SELLER and the BUYER. If two or more persons are named herein as BUYER their obligations hereunder shall be joint and several. The captions and marginal notes are used only as a matter of convenience and are not to be considered a part of this agreement or to be used in determining the intent of the parties to it.

28. LEAD PAINT LAW

The parties acknowledge that, under Massachusetts law, whenever a child or children under six years of age resides in any residential premises in which any paint, plaster or other accessible material contains dangerous levels of lead, the owner of said premises must remove or cover said paint, plaster or other material so as to make it inaccessible to children under six years of age.

29. SMOKE DETECTORS

The SELLER shall, at the time of the delivery of the deed, deliver a certificate from the fire department of the city or town in which said premises are located stating that said premises have been equipped with approved smoke detectors in conformity with applicable law.

30. ADDITIONAL PROVISIONS

The initialed riders, if any, attached hereto, are incorporated herein by reference.

FOR RESIDENTIAL PROPERTY CONSTRUCTED PRIOR TO 1978, BUYER MUST ALSO HAVE SIGNED LEAD PAINT "PROPERTY TRANSFER NOTIFICATION CERTIFICATION"

NOTICE: This is a legal document that creates binding obligations. If not understood, consult an attorney.

_____   _____
SELLER (or spouse)   SELLER

_____   _____
BUYER   BUYER

_____
Broker(s)

EXTENSION OF TIME FOR PERFORMANCE

Date _____

The time for the performance of the foregoing agreement is extended until _____ o'clock _____ M. on the _____ day of _____ 19_____, time still being of the essence of this agreement as extended.

In all other respects, this agreement is hereby ratified and confirmed.

This extension, executed in multiple counterparts, is intended to take effect as a sealed instrument.

_____
SELLER

_____
BUYER

_____
SELLER (or spouse)

_____
BUYER

_____
Broker(s)

Real Estate Sale Contract

1. _____ (Purchaser) agrees to purchase at a price of $ _____ on the terms set forth herein, the following described real estate in _____ County, Illinois:

(If legal description is not included at time of execution, authorized to insert thereafter.)

commonly known as _____ is

with approximate lot dimensions of _____ × _____ , together with the following property presently located thereon: *(strike items not applicable)* (a) storm and screen doors and windows; (b) awnings; (c) outdoor television antenna; (d) wall-to-wall, hallway and stair carpeting; (e) window shades and draperies and supporting fixtures; (f) venetian blinds; (g) electric, plumbing and other attached fixtures as installed; (h) water softener; (i) refrigerator(s); (j) _____ range(s); (k) garage door opener with _____ transmitters; (l) radiator covers; (m) indoor and outdoor (louvered) shutters; and also

2. _____ (Seller)

(Insert names of all owners and their respective spouses)

agrees to sell the real estate and the property, if any, described above at the price and terms set forth herein, and to convey or cause to be conveyed to Purchaser or nominee title thereto (in joint tenancy) by a recordable _____ deed, with release of homestead rights, and a proper bill of sale, subject only to: (a) covenants, conditions and restrictions of record; (b) private, public and utility easements and roads and highways, if any; (c) party wall rights and agreements, if any; (d) existing leases and tenancies; (e) special taxes or assessments for improvements not yet completed; (f) any unconfirmed special tax or assessment; (g) installments not due at the date hereof of any special tax or assessment for improvements heretofore completed; (h) mortgage or trust deed specified below, if any; (i) general taxes for the year _____ and subsequent years including taxes which may accrue by reason of new or additional improvements during the year(s) _____ ; and to

3. Purchaser has paid $ _____ (and will pay within _____ days the additional sum of $ _____) as earnest money to be applied on the purchase price, and agrees to pay or satisfy the balance of the purchase price, plus or minus prorations, at the time of closing as follows: *(strike subparagraph not applicable)*

(a) The payment of $ _____

(b) The acceptance of the title to the real estate by Purchaser subject to a mortgage (trust deed) of record securing a principal indebtedness (which the Purchaser [does] [does not] agree to assume) aggregating $ _____ bearing interest at the rate of _____ % a year, and the payment of a sum which represents the difference between the amount due on the indebtedness at the time of closing and the balance of the purchase price.

4. This contract is subject to the condition that Purchaser be able to procure within _____ days a firm commitment for a loan to be secured by a mortgage or trust deed on the real estate in the amount of $ _____ , or such lesser sum as Purchaser accepts, with interest not to exceed _____ % a year to be amortized over _____ years, the commission and service charges for such loan not to exceed _____ %. If, after making every reasonable effort, Purchaser is unable to procure such commitment within the time specified herein and so notified Seller thereof within that time, this contract shall become null and void and all earnest money shall be returned to Purchaser; provided that if Seller, at his option, within a like period of time following Purchaser's notice, procures for Purchaser such a commitment or notifies Purchaser that Seller will accept a purchase money mortgage upon the same terms, this contract shall remain in full force and effect. *(Strike paragraph if inapplicable.)*

5. The time of closing shall be on _____, or 20 days after notice that financing has been procured if above paragraph 4 is operative, or on the date, if any, to which such time is extended by reasons of paragraph 2 of the Conditions and Stipulations hereafter becoming operative (whichever date is later), unless subsequently mutually agreed otherwise, at the office of _____ or of the mortgage lender, if any, provided title is shown to be good or is accepted by Purchaser.

6. Seller shall deliver possession to Purchaser on or before _____ days after the sale has been closed. Seller agrees to pay Purchaser the sum of $ _____ for each day Seller remains in possession between the time of closing and the time possession is delivered.

7. Seller agrees to pay a broker's commission to _____
in the amount set forth in the broker's listing contract or as follows: _____

8. The earnest money shall be held by _____
for the mutual benefit of the parties.

9. Seller agrees to deliver possession of the real estate in the same condition as it is at the date of this contract, ordinary wear and tear excepted.

10. A duplicate original of this contract, duly executed by the Seller and his spouse, if any, shall be delivered to the Purchasers within _____ days from the date below, otherwise, at the Purchaser's option, this contract shall become null and void and the earnest money shall be refunded to the Purchaser.

This contract is subject to the Conditions and Stipulations set forth on the back page hereof, which Conditions and Stipulations are made a part of this contract.

Dated _____

Purchaser _____ (Address) _____

Purchaser _____ (Address) _____

Seller _____ (Address) _____

Seller _____ (Address) _____

*Form normally used for sale of residential property of four or fewer units.

F:3772 **R.** 5/87

CONDITIONS AND STIPULATIONS

1. Seller shall deliver or cause to be delivered to Purchaser or Purchaser's agent, not less than 5 days prior to the time of closing, a title commitment for an owner's title insurance policy issued by the Chicago Title Insurance Company in the amount of the purchase price, covering title to the real estate on or after the date hereof, showing title in the intended grantor subject only to (a) the general exceptions contained in the policy unless the real estate is improved with a single family dwelling or an apartment building of four or fewer residential units, (b) the title exceptions set forth above, and (c) title exceptions pertaining to liens or encumbrances of a definite or ascertainable amount which may be removed by the payment of money at the time of closing and which the Seller may so remove at that time by using the funds to be paid upon the delivery of the deed (all of which are herein referred to as the permitted exceptions). The title commitment shall be conclusive evidence of good title as therein shown as to all matters insured by the policy, subject only to the exceptions as therein stated. Seller also shall furnish Purchaser an affidavit of title in customary form covering the date of closing and showing title in Seller subject only to the permitted exceptions in foregoing items (b) and (c) unpermitted exceptions, if any, as to which the title insurer commits to extend insurance in the manner specified in paragraph 2 below.

2. If the title commitment discloses unpermitted exceptions, Seller shall have 30 days from the date of delivery thereof to have the exceptions removed from the commitment or to have the title insurer commit to insure against loss or damage that may be occasioned by such exceptions, and, in such event, the time of closing shall be 35 days after delivery of the commitment or the time specified in paragraph 5 on the front page hereof, whichever is later. If Seller fails to have the exceptions removed, or in the alternative, to obtain the commitment for title insurance specified above as to such exceptions within the specified time, Purchaser may terminate this contract or may elect, upon notice to Seller within 10 days after the expiration of the 30-day period, to take title as it then is with the right to deduct from the purchase price liens or encumbrances of a definite or ascertainable amount. If Purchaser does not so elect, this contract shall become null and void without further actions of the parties.

3. Rents, premiums under assignable insurance policies, water and other utility charges, fuels, prepaid service contracts, general taxes, accrued interest on mortgage indebtedness, if any, and other similar items shall be adjusted ratably as of the time of closing. If the amount of the current general taxes is not then ascertainable, the adjustment thereof shall be on the basis of the amount of the most recent ascertainable taxes. The amount of any general taxes which may accrue by reason of new or additional improvements shall be adjusted as follows: _____

All prorations are final unless otherwise provided herein. Existing leases and assignable insurance policies, if any, shall then be assigned to Purchaser. Seller shall pay the amount of any stamp tax imposed by State law on the transfer of the title, and shall furnish a completed Real Estate Transfer Declaration signed by the Seller or the Seller's agent in the form required pursuant to the Real Estate Transfer Tax Act of the State of Illinois and shall furnish any declaration signed by the Seller or the Seller's agent or meet other requirements as established by any local ordinance with regard to a transfer or transaction tax: such tax required by local ordinance shall be paid by the party upon whom such ordinance places responsibility therefor. If such ordinance does not so place responsibility, the tax shall be paid by the (Purchaser) (Seller). *(strike one.)*

4. The provisions of the Uniform Vendor and Purchaser Risk Act of the State of Illinois shall be applicable to this contract.

5. If this contract is terminated without Purchaser's fault, the earnest money shall be returned to the Purchaser, but if the termination is caused by the Purchaser's fault, then at the option of the Seller and upon notice to the Purchaser, the earnest money shall be forfeited to the Seller and applied first to the payment of Seller's expenses and then to payment of broker's commission; the balance, if any, to be retained by the Seller as liquidated damages.

6. At the election of Seller or Purchaser upon notice to the other party not less than 5 days prior to the time of closing, this sale shall be closed through an escrow with Chicago Title and Trust Company, in accordance with the general provisions of the usual form of Deed and Money Escrow Agreement then in use by Chicago Title and Trust Company, with such special provisions inserted in the escrow agreement as may be required to conform with this contract. Upon the creation of such an escrow, anything herein to the contrary notwithstanding, payment of purchase price and delivery of deed shall be made through the escrow and this contract and the earnest money shall be deposited in the escrow. The cost of the escrow shall be divided equally between Sell and Purchaser. *(Strike paragraphs if inapplicable.)*

7. Time is of the essence of this contract.

8. All notices herein required shall be in writing and shall be served on the parties at the addresses following their signatures. The mailing of a notice registered or certified mail, return receipt requested, shall be sufficient service.

9. Purchaser and Seller hereby agree to make all disclosures and do all things necessary to comply with the applicable provisions of the Real Estate Settlement Procedures Act of 1974. In the event that either party shall fail to make appropriate disclosure when asked, such failure shall be considered a breach on the part of said party.

10. Alternative 1:
Seller represents that he is not a "foreign person" as defined in Section 1445 of the Internal Revenue Code and is therefore exempt from the withholding requirements of said Section. Seller will furnish Purchaser at closing the Exemption Certification set forth in said Section.

Alternative 2:
Purchaser represents that the transaction is exempt from the withholding requirements of Section 1445 of the Internal Revenue Code because Purchaser intends to use the subject real estate as a qualifying residence under said Section and the sales price does not exceed $300,000.

Alternative 3:
With respect to Section 1445 of the Internal Revenue Code, the parties agree as follows: _____

_____

_____

REAL ESTATE SALE CONTRACT — ILLINOIS
(Illinois)

No. 77
APRIL, 1980

GEORGE E. COLE®
LEGAL FORMS

CAUTION: Consult a lawyer before using or acting under this form. *All warranties, including merchantability and fitness, are excluded.*

THIS MEMORANDUM WITNESSETH, THAT seller,_____

hereby agrees to SELL, and purchaser,_____

agrees to PURCHASE, at the price of _____

_____ Dollars,

the following described real estate, situated in _____ County, Illinois:

CHICAGO ASSOCIATION OF REALTORS®/MLS
REAL ESTATE SALE CONTRACT — CONDOMINIUM

1 TO: _____ SELLER _____ Date _____

2   I/We offer to purchase the condominium unit known as:

3 located at: _____
                (Address)   (City)   (State)   (Zip)

4 together with its undivided interest in the common elements and accumulated reserves, together with the following, if any, now in the
5 unit, for which a Bill of Sale is to be given: screens; storm windows and doors; shades; venetian blinds; drapery rods; curtain rods;
6 radiator covers; attached TV antenna; heating, central cooling, unit air conditioners; ventilating, lighting, and plumbing fixtures;
7 attached mirrors, shelving, interior shutters, cabinets and bookcases; awnings; porch shades; tacked down carpeting; draperies;

8 refrigerator; range; dishwasher; disposal; and also _____

9 1. Purchase price $ _____, in the form of _____ .

10 2. Initial earnest money $ _____, to be increased to 10% of purchase price within

11 _____ shall be held by _____. Earnest money shall be returned and this contract shall be void if not accepted by Seller on or before
12 days after acceptance hereof. Said initial earnest money shall be deposited by

13 _____, 19____. Earnest money shall be deposited by
14 as escrowee, for the benefit of the parties hereto in an established escrow account in compliance with the laws of the State of Illinois. An
15 original of this contract shall be held by Listing Broker.

16 3. The balance of the purchase price shall be paid at the closing, plus or minus prorations, as follows (STRIKE THROUGH
17 INAPPLICABLE SUBPARAGRAPHS):

18 (a) **Cash, Cashier's Check or Certified Check, or Any Combination Thereof.**

19 (b) **Assumption of Existing Mortgage** (See Rider 705, if Applicable.)

20 (c) **Mortgage Contingency.** This contract is contingent upon Purchaser securing within _____ days after acceptance hereof a
21 commitment for a fixed rate mortgage, or an adjustable rate mortgage permitted to be made by U.S. or Illinois savings and loan associa-
22 tions or banks, for $ _____, the interest rate (or initial interest rate if an adjustable rate mortgage) not to exceed _____ %, plus ap-
23 _____ % per annum, amortized over _____ years, payable monthly, loan fee not to exceed _____ %, plus ap-
24 praisal and credit report fee, if any. If said mortgage has a balloon payment, it shall be due no sooner than _____ years. Pur-
25 chaser shall pay for private mortgage insurance if required by lending institution. If Purchaser does not obtain such commitment,
26 Purchaser shall notify Seller in writing within said number of days. If Seller is not so notified, it shall be conclusively presumed that
27 Purchaser has secured such commitment or will purchase said property without mortgage financing. If Seller is so notified, Seller may
28 within an equal number of additional days, secure a mortgage commitment for Purchaser upon the same terms, and shall have the
29 option of extending the closing date up to the same number of days. Said commitment may be given by Seller as well as a third
30 party. Purchaser shall furnish all requested credit information, sign customary documents relating to the application and securing of

31 such commitment, and pay one application fee as directed by Seller. If Purchaser notifies Seller as above provided, and
32 neither Purchaser, Seller nor Broker secures such commitment as above provided, this contract shall be null and void and all earnest
33 money shall be returned to Purchaser, and Seller shall not be liable for any sales commission.

34   If an FHA or VA mortgage is to be obtained, Seller agrees to pay the loan discount not to exceed _____ % and other costs
35 customarily chargeable to Seller, provided Seller's initials appear here _____.

36   (d) **Purchase Money Note and Trust Deed or Installment Agreement For Deed.** Purchaser shall pay $_____
37 (which sum includes earnest money) and the balance by (STRIKE THROUGH ONE) : (Purchase Money Note and Trust Deed) (Installment Agree-
38 ment For Deed) in the amount of $_____ with interest at the rate of _____ % per annum to be amortized over
39 _____ years, payable monthly, the final payment due _____, 19____ with unlimited prepayment privi-
40 lege without penalty. Payments into escrow for taxes and insurance shall also be made monthly. If the parties cannot agree on the
41 form of said instrument, Chicago Title & Trust Company Note and Trust Deed No. 7 shall be used, or the George E. Cole Installment
42 Agreement No. 74 shall be used, whichever may be applicable. If Seller requests a credit report, Purchaser shall deliver same to
43 Seller within four days of such request; and Seller may cancel this agreement within three days after receiving said credit report if
44 Seller believes said credit report is unsatisfactory.

45   4. At closing, Seller shall execute and deliver to Purchaser, or cause to be executed and delivered to Purchaser, a recordable Warranty
46 Deed with release of homestead rights (or other appropriate deed if title is in trust or in an estate), or Articles of Agreement for such
47 a deed if that portion of subparagraph 3(d) is applicable, subject only to the following, if any: covenants, conditions and restrictions of
48 record; terms, provisions, covenants and conditions of the Declaration of Condominium and all amendments thereto; private, public and
49 utility easements including any easements established by or implied from the Declaration of Condominium or amendments thereto;
50 roads and highways; party wall rights and agreements; existing leases and tenancies; limitations and conditions imposed by the Condo-
51 minium Property Act; special governmental taxes or assessments for improvements not yet completed; unconfirmed special governmental taxes

52 or assessments; general real estate taxes for the year 19____ and subsequent years; installments of regular assessments due after the date of
53 closing established pursuant to the Declaration of Condominium; the mortgage or trust deed set forth in paragraph 3 and/or Rider 705.

54   Seller represents that the 19____ general real estate taxes are $_____.

55   5. Seller represents that as of the date of acceptance hereof the regular monthly assessment pertaining to this unit is $_____ ; a special
56 assessment has/has not (strike one) been levied. The original amount of the special assessment pertaining to this unit was $_____ ; and the
57 remaining amount due at closing will be $_____ and shall/shall not (strike one) be assumed by the Purchaser as of the closing date. Seller shall
58 furnish Purchaser a statement from the proper condominium representative certifying that Seller is current in payment of assessments, and, if
59 applicable, proof of waiver or termination of any right of first refusal or similar options contained in the Declaration of Condominium or by-laws thereof
60 for the transfer of ownership. Additionally, the Seller shall deliver to Purchaser the Condominium Declaration including all amendments and by-laws

61 thereto, rules and regulations, and the prior and current years' operating budgets within _____ days of acceptance hereof. Seller agrees to pay any
62 applicable processing/moveout/transferring fees as required by the Condominium Association and Purchaser agrees to pay the credit report and move-in
63 fee if required by the Association. If the right of first refusal or similar option is exercised, this contract shall be null and void and the earnest money
64 returned to Purchaser, but the Seller shall pay the commission pursuant to paragraph 8 below.

65   6. Closing or escrow payout shall be on _____, 19____ (except as provided in paragraph 3 c above), provided title
66 has been shown to be good or is accepted by Purchaser, at the office of Purchaser's mortgagee, or at _____.

67. Seller agrees to surrender possession of said unit on or before _____, provided this sale has closed.

68 (a) **Use and Occupancy.** At closing, Seller shall pay to Purchaser $ _____ per day for use and occupancy commenc-
69 ing the first day after closing up to and including the date possession is to be surrendered, or on a monthly basis, whichever period is
70 shorter. Purchaser shall refund any payment made for use and occupancy beyond the date possession is surrendered.

71 (b) **Possession Escrow.** At closing, Seller shall deposit with escrowee designated in paragraph 2 above a sum equal to 2% of the
72 purchase price to guarantee possession on or before date set forth above, which sum shall be held from the net proceeds of the sale on
73 escrowee form of receipt. If Seller does not surrender possession as above, Seller shall pay to Purchaser in addition to the above use
74 and occupancy, the sum of 10% of said possession escrow per day up to and including day possession is surrendered to Purchaser plus
75 any unpaid use and occupancy to the date possession is surrendered, said amount(s) to be paid out of escrow and the balance, if any,
76 to be turned over to Seller; and acceptance of payments by Purchaser shall not limit Purchaser's other legal remedies.

77 8. Seller will pay a Broker's commission per Listing Agreement.

78 Listing Broker is: _____ Cooperating Broker/Buyer Broker
79   (STRIKE THROUGH ONE) if any, is: _____

80 9. THIS CONTRACT IS SUBJECT TO THE PROVISIONS APPEARING ON THE REVERSE SIDE HEREOF.

PURCHASER _____ ADDRESS _____

_____ (Social Security #) _____ (City) _____ (State) _____ (Zip)
(Type or print name)

PURCHASER _____ ADDRESS _____

_____ (Social Security #) _____ (City) _____ (State) _____ (Zip)
(Type or print name)

ACCEPTANCE OF CONTRACT BY SELLER

This _____ day of _____, 19 _____, I/We accept this contract and agree to perform
and convey title or cause title to be conveyed according to the terms of this contract.

SELLER _____ ADDRESS _____

_____ (Social Security #) _____ (City) _____ (State) _____ (Zip)
(Type or print name)

SELLER _____ ADDRESS _____

_____ (City) _____ (State) _____ (Zip)
(Type or print name)

Revised 6/92

PROVISIONS

1. Real estate taxes (based on most recent ascertainable taxes), rent, interest on existing mortgage, if any, water taxes and other proratable items shall be prorated to date of closing. If property herein is improved, but last available tax bill is on vacant land, parties hereto agree to reprorate taxes when bill on improved property is available. Security deposits, if any, shall be paid to Purchaser at closing.

2. The provisions of the Uniform Vendor and Purchaser Risk Act of the State of Illinois shall be applicable to this contract.

3. At least five days prior to closing date, Seller shall show to Purchaser or his agent evidence of merchantable title in the intended grantor: (a) by exhibiting owner's duplicate Certificate of Title or a certified copy thereof, subject to no other exceptions than those listed on the reverse side hereof, and a currently dated Special Tax Report issued by the Registrar of Titles, or (b) by delivering a Commitment For Title Insurance of a title insurance company bearing date on or subsequent to the date of the acceptance of this contract, in the amount of the purchase price subject to no other exceptions than those listed on the reverse side hereof and to general exceptions contained in said commitment. Delay in delivery by Seller of Commitment For Title Insurance due to delay by Purchaser's mortgagee in recording mortgage and bringing down title shall not be a default of this contract. Every Certificate of Title or Commitment For Title Insurance furnished by Seller hereunder shall be conclusive evidence of title as therein shown. If evidence of title discloses other exceptions, Seller shall have thirty days from Seller's receipt of evidence of title to cure such exceptions and notify Purchaser accordingly, and as to those exceptions which may be removed at closing by payment of money, Seller may have same removed at closing by using the proceeds of sale in payment thereof. IF THE PROPERTY IS REGISTERED IN THE TORRENS SYSTEM, AND THE PURCHASER'S MORTGAGEE REQUIRES TITLE INSURANCE, SAID TITLE INSURANCE WILL BE PAID BY SELLER.

4. All notices herein required shall be in writing and shall be served on the parties at the addresses following their signatures. The mailing of a notice by registered or certified mail, return receipt requested, shall be sufficient service when the notice is mailed. Notices may also be served by personal delivery, by mail-o-gram, telegram, or by the use of a facsimile machine with proof of transmission and a copy of the notice with proof of transmission being sent by regular mail on the date of transmission.

5. If this contract is terminated without Purchaser's fault, the earnest money shall be returned to the Purchaser, but such refund shall not release Seller from Seller's obligation under this contract. If the termination is caused by Purchaser's fault, then, at the option of the Seller, and upon notice to Purchaser, the earnest money shall be forfeited and applied first to payment of Broker's commission and any expenses incurred, and the balance paid to Seller. In the event of default, escrowee may give written notice to Seller and Purchaser indicating escrowee's intended disposition of the earnest money. Seller and Purchaser hereby agree that if neither party objects, in writing, to the proposed disposition of the earnest money within thirty days after the date of mailing of said notice, escrowee shall proceed to dispose of the earnest money as previously indicated by the escrowee. If either Seller or Purchaser objects to the intended disposition within the aforementioned thirty day period, then the parties hereto agree that the escrowee may deposit earnest money, less costs, with the Clerk of the Circuit Court by the filing of an action in the nature of interpleader. The parties agree that escrowee may be reimbursed from the earnest money for all costs, including reasonable attorney's fees, related to the filing of the interpleader and do hereby agree to indemnify and hold escrowee harmless from any and all claims and demands, including the payment of reasonable attorney's fees, costs and expenses arising out of such default claims and demands.

6. Seller warrants that no notice from any city, village or other governmental authority of a dwelling code violation which currently exists in the aforesaid premises has been issued and received by Seller or his agent. If a notice is received between date of acceptance of the contract and date of closing, Seller shall promptly notify Purchaser of such notice.

7. At the request of Seller or Purchaser evidenced by notice in writing to the other party at any time prior to the date for delivery of deed hereunder, this sale shall be closed through an escrow with a title insurance company, in accordance with the general provisions of the usual form of Deed and Money Escrow Agreement then furnished and in use by said company, with such special provisions inserted in the escrow agreement as may be required to conform with this contract. Upon the creation of such an escrow, anything herein to the contrary notwithstanding, payment of purchase price and delivery of deed shall be made through the escrow and this contract and the earnest money shall be deposited in the escrow and the Broker shall be made a party to the escrow with regard to commission due. The cost of the escrow shall be divided equally between Purchaser and Seller.

8. Seller agrees to furnish to Purchaser an affidavit of title subject only to those items set forth herein, and an ALTA form if required by Purchaser's mortgagee.

9. Right is reserved by either party to insert correct legal description at any time, without notice, when same is available.

10. Seller shall have the right to pay off any existing mortgage(s) out of the proceeds of this sale.

11. Purchaser may place a mortgage on this property and apply proceeds of such mortgage to the purchase price.

12. Purchaser and Seller hereby agree to make all disclosures and do all things necessary to comply with the applicable provisions of the Real Estate Settlement Procedures Act of 1974, as amended, and the Illinois Responsible Property Transfer Act of 1988, as amended.

13. Seller shall pay the amount of any stamp tax imposed by the state and county on the transfer of title, and shall furnish a completed declaration signed by the Seller or Seller's agent in the form required by the state and county, and shall furnish any declaration signed by Seller or Seller's agent or meet other requirements as established by any local ordinance with regard to a transfer or transaction tax. Such tax required by local ordinance shall be paid by designated party in said ordinance.

14. Seller shall remove from premises by date of possession all debris and Seller's personal property not conveyed by Bill of Sale to Purchaser.

15. Seller agrees to surrender possession of the real estate in the same condition as it is at the date of this contract, ordinary wear and tear excepted.

16. Time is of the essence of this contract.

17. Wherever appropriate, the singular includes the plural and the masculine includes the feminine or the neuter.

REAL ESTATE SALE CONTRACT—CO-OPERATIVE APARTMENT

TO: _____ SELLER   Date _____

I/We offer to purchase [STRIKE THROUGH (a) or (b)] :

(a) _____ shares of common stock in the corporation known as _____

(b) _____ beneficial interest under the trust known as _____

Said common stock or beneficial interest carries with it the right to a proprietary lease to the apartment known as _____ (apartment number).

_____ , _____ .
(garage number)   (parking space number)

_____ , _____ , _____ , _____ , _____
(Street)   (City)   (County)   (State)   (Zip)

together with the following, if any, now in the unit, for which a Bill of Sale is to be given: screens; storm windows and doors; shades; venetian blinds; drapery rods; curtain rods; radiator covers; attached TV antenna; heating, central cooling, unit air conditioners, ventilating, lighting, and plumbing fixtures; attached mirrors, shelving, interior shutters, cabinets and bookcases; awnings; porch shades; tacked down carpeting; draperies; refrigerator; range; dishwasher; disposal; and also _____ .

1. Purchase Price $_____ consisting of $_____ equity and

$_____ being the approximate balance of the mortgage applicable to said shares of stock or beneficial interest as of the date hereof. The equity shall be adjusted to reflect the actual mortgage balance outstanding as of the date of the closing.

2. Initial earnest money $_____ , in the form of _____ , to be increased to 10% of purchase price within _____ days after acceptance hereof. Said initial earnest money shall be returned and this contract shall be void if not accepted on or before _____ , 19 _____ . Earnest money shall be deposited by _____ , as escrowee, for the benefit of the parties hereto in an established escrow account in compliance with the law of the State of Illinois. An original of this contract shall be held by Listing Broker. In the event written approval of Purchaser's application for the consummation of this agreement is not given by the Board of Directors of said corporation or Managing Committee of said trust within _____ days from the date of acceptance hereof by the Seller, the earnest money shall be returned and this contract shall become null and void. Seller and Purchaser shall each use diligent efforts to expedite such approval as quickly as possible.

3. Within _____ days of acceptance by Seller, Purchaser shall at Purchaser's cost furnish such credit information as the Board of Directors or Managing Committee may request.

4. Seller shall pay the stock transfer fee or trustee's fee, if any.

5. Purchase Price, subject to prorations, shall be paid as follows [STRIKE THROUGH (a) or (b)] :

(a) Cash, cashier's check or certified check, or any combination thereof.

(b) $ _____ (which includes earnest money) in cash, cashier's check or certified check, or any combination thereof, and the balance by purchase money Collateral Installment Note for $ _____ with interest on unpaid balance at _____ % per annum, with twelve monthly payments per year (including interest) of $ _____ each, the final payment to be due on _____ and with unlimited prepayment privilege without penalty. The said instrument shall be prepared by the Seller or his attorney in the form to be approved by the Purchaser or his attorney. In the event the parties cannot agree on the form of said instrument, the Seller or his attorney shall prepare purchase money Collateral Installment Note on the printed legal form No. TL-150 UCC by George B. Cole & Co. The said instrument shall be secured by assignment from Purchaser to Seller of the said proprietary lease and stock or beneficial interest.

6. The closing shall be at the office of _____, by Seller's delivery to Purchaser of said lease and stock or beneficial interest with proper and effective assignments of the same, and also Bill of Sale as aforesaid, all free of any encumbrances, liens or security interest in favor of other parties under the Uniform Commercial Code or otherwise, except for mortgage referred to in paragraph 1 above, and payment of purchase price by Purchaser, including earnest money and delivery to Seller of purchase money Collateral Installment Note, if any, together with Purchaser's assignment to Seller of lease and stock or beneficial interest and customary Uniform Commercial Code financing statement covering said assignment. Any such encumbrances, liens or security interest may be paid at closing out of sale proceeds, provided parties entitled to such payments furnish appropriate releases, waivers or other documents at closing. Purchaser may in writing direct the manner in which the shares or beneficial interest and the lease shall be assigned.

7. All proratable items shall be prorated to date of closing, including but not limited to monthly assessments and special or extra assessments, if any.

8. Seller agrees to surrender possession of said unit on or before _____, provided this sale has been closed.

(a) Use and Occupancy. At closing, Seller shall pay to Purchaser the sum of $ _____ per day for monthly assessments and use and occupancy commencing the first day after closing up to and including the date possession is to be surrendered, or on a monthly basis, whichever period is shorter. Purchaser shall refund any payment made for monthly assessments and use and occupancy beyond the date possession is surrendered.

(b) Possession Escrow. At closing, Seller shall deposit with escrowee designated in paragraph 2 above a sum equal to 2% of the purchase price to guarantee possession on or before date set forth above, which sum shall be held form the net proceeds of the sale on escrowee form of receipt. If Seller does not surrender possession as above, Seller shall pay to Purchaser in addition to the above monthly assessments and use and occupancy, the sum of 10% of said possession escrow per day up to and including day possession is surrendered to Purchaser plus any unpaid monthly assessments and use and occupancy to the date possession is surrendered, said amount(s) to be paid out of escrow and the balance, if any, to be turned over to Seller; and acceptance of payments by Purchaser shall not limit Purchaser's other legal remedies.

9. Seller represents that the monthly assessment as of the date of the acceptance hereof is $ _____, which includes operating expenses, taxes, insurance, interest and amortization of mortgage, heat and air conditioning. [STRIKE THROUGH ANY ITEM NOT APPLICABLE].

10. Seller will pay a Broker's commission per Listing Agreement.

Listing Broker is: _____.

Cooperating Broker/Buyer Broker
(STRIKE THROUGH ONE) if any, is: _____.

11. THIS CONTRACT IS SUBJECT TO THE PROVISIONS APPEARING ON THE REVERSE SIDE HEREOF.

PURCHASER _____ ADDRESS _____

_____ (Social Security #) _____ (City) _____ (State) _____ (Zip)
(Type or print name)

PURCHASER _____ ADDRESS _____

_____ _____ (City) _____ (State) _____ (Zip)
(Type or print name)

ACCEPTANCE OF CONTRACT BY SELLER

This _____ day of _____, 19 _____, I/We accept this contract and agree to perform and convey the above stated interest or cause the above stated interest to be conveyed according to the terms of this contract.

SELLER _____ ADDRESS _____

_____ (Social Security #) _____ (City) _____ (State) _____ (Zip)
(Type or print name)

SELLER _____ ADDRESS _____

_____ _____ (City) _____ (State) _____ (Zip)
(Type or print name)

Revised 1/90

THIS RIDER IS MADE A PART OF AND INCORPORATED INTO THAT CERTAIN REAL ESTATE CONTRACT DATED _____

19 ____ FOR THE SALE OF THE PROPERTY COMMONLY KNOWN AS _____ ILLINOIS ENTERED

INTO BY. _____ (SELLER) AND _____ (PURCHASER).

ATTORNEY'S APPROVAL

It is agreed by and between the parties hereto as follows: That their respective attorneys may approve of make modifications, other than price and dates, mutually acceptable to the parties. Approval will not be unreasonably withheld, but, it within _____ days after the date of acceptance of the Contract, it becomes evident agreement cannot be reached by the parties hereto, and written notice thereof is given to either party within the time specified, then this Contract shall become null and void, and all monies paid by the Purchaser shall be refunded. IN THE ABSENCE OF WRITTEN NOTICE WITHIN THE TIME SPECIFIED HEREIN, THIS PROVISION SHALL BE DEEMED WAIVED BY ALL PARTIES HERETO, AND THIS CONTRACT SHALL BE IN FULL FORCE AND EFFECT.

INSPECTION

Purchaser's obligation to purchase under this Contract is subject to the inspection and approval of the condition of the property by the Purchaser or Purchaser's agent, at Purchaser's expense, within _____ days from the date of acceptance of this Contract. Purchaser shall indemnify Seller from and against any loss or damage to the property caused by the acts or omissions of Purchaser or the person performing such inspection. In the event the condition of the property is not so approved, written notice shall be given to the Seller or Seller's agent by the Purchaser within the time specified for approval, and thereupon, Seller's Obligation to sell and Purchaser's obligation to purchase under this contract shall become null and void and all monies paid by the Purchaser shall be refunded. IN THE ABSENCE OF WRITTEN NOTICE WITHIN THE TIME SPECIFIED, THIS CONTRACT SHALL REMAIN IN FULL FORCE AND EFFECT.

MORTGAGE CONTINGENCY ADDENDUM

In order to help finance the acquisition of the property, the BUYER shall apply for a conventional bank or other institutional mortgage loan of $ _____ at prevailing rates, terms and conditions. If despite the BUYER's diligent efforts a commitment for such loan cannot be obtained on or before _____, 19____, then the BUYER shall have the option of revoking this Offer by written notice to the SELLER and/or the Broker(s), as agent(s) for the SELLER, prior to the expiration of such time, whereupon all deposits made by the BUYER shall be forthwith refunded and this Offer shall become null and void and without further recourse to either party. In no event will the BUYER be deemed to have used diligent efforts to obtain such commitment unless the BUYER submits a complete mortgage loan application conforming to the foregoing provisions on or before _____, 19____

INITIALS:

_____   _____
Seller (or spouse)   Seller

_____   _____
Buyer   Buyer

                    _____
                    Broker(s)

SELLER'S DISCLOSURE STATEMENT

1. Seller(s) Name(s): _____

   Property Address: _____

   Is each individual named above a U.S. Citizen or resident alien? Yes ☐ No ☐

   Approximate Age of Property: _____ Date Purchased: _____

2. **NOTICE TO SELLER**

   Each Seller is obligated to disclose to a buyer all known facts that materially and adversely affect the value of the property being sold and that are not readily observable. This disclosure statement is designed to assist Seller in complying with disclosure requirements and to assist Buyer in evaluating the property being considered. The listing real estate broker, the selling real estate broker and their respective agents will also rely upon this information when they evaluate, market and present Seller's property to prospective buyers.

3. **NOTICE TO BUYER**

   This is a disclosure of Seller's knowledge of the condition of the property as of the date signed by Seller and is not a substitute for any inspections or warranties that Buyer may wish to obtain. It is not a warranty of any kind by Seller or a warranty or representation by the listing broker, the selling broker, or their agents.

4. **OCCUPANCY**

   Does Seller currently occupy this property? Yes ☐ No ☐ If not, how long has it been since Seller occupied the property? _____

5. **LAND (SOILS, DRAINAGE AND BOUNDARIES)**

(a) Is there any fill or expansive soil on the property? Yes ☐ No ☐ Unknown ☐

(b) Do you know of any sliding, settling, earth movement, upheaval or earth stability problems that have occurred on the property or in the immediate neighborhood? Yes ☐ No ☐

(c) Is the property located in an earthquake zone? Yes ☐ No ☐ Unknown ☐

(d) Is the property located in a flood zone or wetlands area? Yes ☐ No ☐ Unknown ☐

(e) Do you know of any past or present drainage or flood problems affecting the property or adjacent properties? Yes ☐ No ☐

(f) Do you know of any encroachments, boundary line disputes, or easements affecting the property? Yes ☐ No ☐

If any of your answers in this section are "Yes," explain in detail: _____

6. **ROOF**

(a) Age: _____ years.

(b) Has the roof ever leaked during your ownership? Yes ☐ No ☐

(c) Has the roof been replaced or repaired during your ownership? Yes ☐ No ☐

(d) Do you know of any problems with the roof or rain gutters? Yes ☐ No ☐

If any of your answers in this section are "Yes," explain in detail: _____

7. **TERMITES, DRYROT, PESTS**

(a) Do you have any knowledge of termites, dryrot, or pests on or affecting the property? Yes ☐ No ☐

(b) Do you have any knowledge of any damage to the property caused by termites, dryrot, or pests? Yes ☐ No ☐

(c) Is your property currently under warranty or other coverage by a licensed pest control company? Yes ☐ No ☐

(d) Do you know of any termite / pest control reports or treatments for the property in the last five years? Yes ☐ No ☐

If any of your answers in this section are "Yes," explain in detail: _____

8. **STRUCTURAL ITEMS**

(a) Are you aware of any past or present movement, shifting, deterioration, or other problems with walls or foundations? Yes ☐ No ☐

(b) Are you aware of any past or present cracks or flaws in the walls or foundations? Yes ☐ No ☐

(c) Are you aware of any past or present water leakage in the house? Yes ☐ No ☐

(d) Are you aware of any past or present problems with driveways, walkways, patios, or retaining walls on the property? Yes ☐ No ☐

(e) Have there been any repairs or other attempts to control the cause or effect of any problem described above? Yes ☐ No ☐

If any of your answers in this section are "Yes," explain in detail. When describing repairs or control efforts, describe the location, extent, date, and name of the person who did the repair or control effort: _____

9. **BASEMENTS AND CRAWL SPACES (Complete only if applicable)**

(a) Does the property have a sump pump? Yes ☐ No ☐

(b) Has there ever been any water leakage, accumulation, or dampness within the basement or crawlspace? Yes ☐ No ☐

If "Yes," describe in detail: _____

(c) Have there been any repairs or other attempts to control any water or dampness problem in the basement or crawlspace? Yes ☐ No ☐

If "Yes," describe the location, extent, date, and name of the person who did the repair or control effort: _____

10. **ADDITIONS/REMODELS**

(a) Have you made any additions, structural changes, or other alterations to the property? Yes ☐ No ☐

If "Yes", did you obtain all necessary permits and approvals and was all work in compliance with building codes? Yes ☐ No ☐. If your answer is "No," explain: _____

(b) Did any former owners of the property make any additions, structural changes, or other alterations to the property? Yes ☐ No ☐ Unknown ☐. If "Yes", was all work done with all necessary permits and approvals in compliance with building codes? Yes ☐ No ☐ Unknown ☐. If your answer is "No," explain: _____

11. **PLUMBING-RELATED ITEMS**

   (a) What is your drinking water source: Public _____ Private System _____ Well on Property _____

   (b) If your drinking water is from a well, when was your water last checked for safety and what was the result of the test? _____

   (c) Do you have a water softener? Yes ❑ No ❑ Leased ❑ Owned ❑

   (d) What is the type of sewage system: Public Sewer _____ Private Sewer _____ Septic Tank _____ Cesspool _____

   (e) Is there a sewage pump? Yes ❑ No ❑

   (f) When was the septic tank or cesspool last serviced? _____

   (g) Do you know of any leaks, backups, or other problems relating to any of the plumbing, water, and sewage-related items? Yes ❑ No ❑

   If your answer is "Yes," explain in detail: _____

12. **HEATING AND AIR CONDITIONING**

   (a) Air Conditioning _____ Central Electric _____ Central Gas _____ Window _____ (#) Units Included in Sale

   (b) Heating _____ Electric _____ Fuel Oil _____ Natural Gas _____ Other: _____

   (c) Water Heating _____ Electric _____ Gas _____ Solar _____

   Are you aware of any problems regarding these items? Yes ❑ No ❑ . If "Yes," explain in detail: _____

13. **ELECTRICAL SYSTEM**

   Are you aware of any problems or conditions that affect the value or desirability of the electrical system? Yes ❑ No ❑.

   If "Yes," explain in detail: _____

14. **OTHER EQUIPMENT AND APPLIANCES BEING SOLD**

Mark the items included in the sale of your property:

___ Electric Garage Door Opener ___ Number of Transmitters ___ Security Alarm System (___ Owned ___ Leased)
___ Smoke Detectors ___ How Many? ___ Lawn Sprinklers ___ Automatic Timer
___ Swimming Pool ___ Pool Heater ___ Spa/Hot Tub ___ Pool/Spa Equipment (list): ___
___ Refrigerator ___ Stove ___ Microwave Oven ___ Washer ___ Dryer ___ Dishwasher ___ Trash Compactor
___ Intercom ___ Ceiling Fans ___ Other: ___

Are any of these in need of repair or replacement? Yes ☐ No ☐ . If "Yes," explain in detail: ___

15. **NEIGHBORHOOD**

Are you aware of any condition or proposed change in your neighborhood that could adversely affect the value or desirability of the property, such as noise or other nuisance, threat of condemnation or street changes? Yes ☐ No ☐.
If "Yes," explain in detail: ___

16. **TOXIC SUBSTANCES**

(a) Are you aware of any underground tanks or toxic substances present on the property (structure or soil) such as asbestos, PCBs, accumulated radon, lead paint, or others? Yes ☐ No ☐ . If "Yes," explain in detail: ___

(b) Has the property been tested for radon or any other toxic substances? Yes ☐ No ☐ If "Yes," explain in detail: ___

17. **CONDOMINIUMS AND OTHER HOMEOWNERS ASSOCIATIONS**

(a) Is the property part of a condominium or other common ownership or is it subject to covenants, conditions, and restrictions (CC & R's) of a homeowner's association? Yes ☐ No ☐. (If your answer is "no", you may ignore the remainder of this section).

(b) Is there any defect, damage, or problem with any common elements or common areas which could affect their value or desirability? Yes ☐ No ☐ Unknown ☐

(c) Is there any condition or claim which may result in an increase in assessments or fees? Yes ☐ No ☐ Unknown ☐. If your answer to (b) or (c) is "Yes," explain in detail: ___

18. **OTHER MATTERS**

(a) Is there any existing or threatened legal action affecting the property? Yes ☐ No ☐

(b) Do you know of any violations of local, state, or federal laws or regulations relating to this property?
Yes ☐ No ☐

(c) Is there anything else that you feel you should disclose to a prospective buyer because it may materially and adversely affect the value or desirability of the property, e.g., zoning violation, non-conforming units, setback violations, zoning changes, road changes, etc.? Yes ☐ No ☐.

If any of your answers in this section are "Yes," explain in detail: _____

The undersigned Seller represents that the information set forth in the foregoing disclosure statement is accurate and complete. Seller does not intend this disclosure statement to be a warranty or guaranty of any kind. Seller hereby authorizes Coldwell Banker to provide this information to prospective buyers of the property and to real estate brokers and sales people. Seller understands and agrees that Seller will notify Coldwell Banker in writing immediately if any information set forth in this disclosure statement becomes inaccurate or incorrect in any way through the passage of time.

Seller: _____ Date: _____ Seller: _____ Date: _____

RECEIPT AND ACKNOWLEDGEMENT OF BUYER

1. I HAVE CAREFULLY INSPECTED THE PROPERTY. I HAVE BEEN ADVISED TO HAVE THE PROPERTY EXAMINED BY PROFESSIONAL INSPECTORS. I ACKNOWLEDGE THAT NEITHER ANY BROKER OR AGENT INVOLVED IN THIS TRANSACTION IS AN EXPERT AT DETECTING OR REPAIRING PHYSICAL DEFECTS IN THE PROPERTY.

2. I UNDERSTAND THAT UNLESS STATED OTHERWISE IN MY CONTRACT WITH SELLER, THE PROPERTY IS BEING SOLD IN ITS PRESENT CONDITION ONLY, WITHOUT WARRANTIES OR GUARANTEES OF ANY KIND BY SELLER OR ANY BROKER OR AGENT. I STATE THAT **NO REPRESENTATIONS CONCERNING THE CONDITION OF THE PROPERTY ARE BEING RELIED UPON BY ME EXCEPT AS DISCLOSED ABOVE OR STATED WITHIN THE SALES CONTRACT.**

Buyer: _____ Date: _____ Buyer: _____ Date: _____

THIS IS A LEGALLY BINDING DOCUMENT. IF NOT UNDERSTOOD, CONSULT AN ATTORNEY.

Subject to: (1) existing leases, expiring _____
the purchaser to be entitled to the rents, if any, from the time of delivery of Deed; (2) all taxes and assessments levied after the year 19____; (3) any unpaid special taxes or assessments, levied for improvements not yet made; also subject to:

Purchaser has paid _____ Dollars, as earnest money, to be applied on said purchase when consummated, and agrees to pay, within five days after the title has been examined and found good, the further sum of _____

_____ Dollars, at the office of _____, provided a good and sufficient _____ recordable Warranty Deed, conveying to purchaser a good title to said premises with waiver and conveyance of any and all estates of homestead therein and all rights of dower, inchoate or otherwise, (subject as aforesaid), shall then be ready for delivery. The balance to be paid as follows:

with interest _____ at the rate of _____ per cent per annum, payable semi-annually, to be secured by notes and mortgage, or trust deed, of even date herewith, on said premises, in the form of _____. Seller shall furnish within a reasonable time a certificate of title issued by the Registrar of Titles of _____ County or a complete merchantable abstract of title, or a merchantable copy, brought down to date, or a merchantable title insurance policy (or commitment) of title, or a merchantable copy, brought down to date. In case the title upon examination, is found materially defective, within ten days after said abstract, certificate of title or title insurance policy (or commitment) is furnished, then, unless the material defects be cured within sixty days after written notice thereof, the said earnest money shall be refunded and this contract is to become inoperative.

Seller warrants to purchaser that no notice from any city, village or other governmental authority of a dwelling code violation which existed in the dwelling structure before the execution of this contract has been received by the seller, his principal or his agent within 10 years of the date of execution of this contract.

Should purchaser fail to perform this contract promptly on his part, at the time and in the manner herein specified, the earnest money paid as above shall, at the option of seller, be forfeited as liquidated damages, and this contract shall be and become null and void. Time is of the essence of this contract, and of all the conditions thereof.

This contract and the said earnest money shall be held by _____ for the mutual benefit of the parties hereto.

In testimony whereof, said parties hereto set their hands, this _____ day of _____, 19____.

_____(SEAL)   _____(SEAL)

_____(SEAL)   _____(SEAL)

HUD-1 Settlement Statement

The HUD-1 Settlement Statement defines all closings. It tells you who the players are, where the money comes from, and who gets it.

A. Settlement Statement

U.S. Department of Housing and Urban Development

OMB No. 2502-0265

B. Type of Loan

1. ☐ FHA 2. ☐ FmHA 3. ☐ Conv. Unins. 4. ☐ VA 5. ☐ Conv. Ins

6. File Number	7. Loan Number	8. Mortgage Insurance Case Number

C. Note: This form is furnished to give you a statement of actual settlement costs. Amounts paid to and by the settlement agent are shown. Items marked "(p.o.c.)" were paid outside the closing; they are shown here for informational purposes and are not included in the totals.

D. Name and Address of Borrower	E. Name and Address of Seller	F. Name and Address of Lender

G. Property Location	H. Settlement Agent	
	Place of Settlement	I. Settlement Date

J. Summary of Borrower's Transaction		K. Summary of Seller's Transaction	
100. Gross Amount Due from Borrower		**400. Gross Amount Due to Seller**	
101. Contract sales price		401. Contract sales price	
102. Personal property		402. Personal property	
103. Settlement charges to borrower (line 1400)		403.	
104.		404.	
105.		405.	
Adjustments for Items Paid by Seller in Advance		**Adjustments for Items Paid by Seller in Advance**	
106. City/town taxes	to	406. City/town taxes	to
107. County taxes	to	407. County taxes	to
108. Assessments	to	408. Assessments	to
109.		409.	
110.		410.	
111.		411.	

120.	Gross Amount Due from Borrower		420.	Gross Amount Due to Seller	
200.	**Amounts Paid by or in Behalf of Borrower**		500.	**Reductions in Amount Due to Seller**	
201.	Deposit or earnest money		501.	Excess deposit (see instructions)	
202.	Principal amount of new loan(s)		502.	Settlement charges to seller (line 1400)	
203.	Existing loan(s) taken subject to		503.	Existing loan(s) taken subject to	
204.			504.	Payoff of first mortgage loan	
205.			505.	Payoff of second mortgage loan	
206.			506.		
207.			507.		
208.			508.		
209.			509.		
	Adjustments for Items Unpaid by Seller			**Adjustments for Items Unpaid by Seller**	
210.	City/town taxes to		510.	City/town taxes to	
211.	County taxes to		511.	County taxes to	
212.	Assessments to		512.	Assessments to	
213.			513.		
214.			514.		
215.			515.		
216.			516.		
217.			517.		
218.			518.		
219.			519.		
220.	**Total Paid by/for Borrower**		520.	**Total Reduction Amount Due Seller**	
300.	**Cash at Settlement from/to Borrower**		600.	**Cash at Settlement to/from Seller**	
301.	Gross Amount due from borrower (line 120)		601.	Gross amount due to seller (line 420)	
302.	Less amounts paid by/for borrower (line 220)	( )	602.	Less reductions in amt. due seller (line 520)	( )
303.	**Cash ☐ From ☐ To Borrower**		603.	**Cash ☐ To ☐ From Seller**	

335

L. Settlement Charges

			Paid From Borrower's Funds at Settlement	Paid From Seller's Funds at Settlement
700.	**Total Sales/Broker's Commission Based on Price $**	**@**	**% =**	
	Division of Commission (line 700) as follows:			
701.	$	to		
702.	$	to		
703.	Commission paid at settlement			
704.				
800.	**Items Payable in Connection with Loan**			
801.	Loan origination fee	%		
802.	Loan discount	%		
803.	Appraisal fee	to		
804.	Credit report	to		
805.	Lender's inspection fee			
806.	Mortgage insurance application fee	to		
807.	Assumption fee			
808.				
809.				
810.				
811.				
900.	**Items Required by Lender to be Paid in Advance**			
901.	Interest from	to	@ $	/day	
902.	Mortgage insurance premium for		months to	
903.	Hazard insurance premium for		years to	
904.			years to	
905.				

336

1000. Reserves Deposited with Lender

1001. Hazard insurance	____ months @ $	per month
1002. Mortgage insurance	____ months @ $	per month
1003. City property taxes	____ months @ $	per month
1004. County property taxes	____ months @ $	per month
1005. Annual assessments	____ months @ $	per month
1006.	____ months @ $	per month
1007.	____ months @ $	per month
1008.	____ months @ $	per month

1100. Title Charges

1101. Settlement or closing fee	to
1102. Abstract or title search	to
1103. Title examination	to
1104. Title insurance binder	to
1105. Document preparation	to
1106. Notary fees	to
1107. Attorney's fees	to
(includes above items numbers:)	
1108. Title insurance	to
(includes above items numbers:)	
1109. Lender's coverage	$
1110. Owner's coverage	$
1111.	
1112.	
1113.	

1200. Government Recording and Transfer Charges

1201. Recording fees: Deed $	; Mortgage $	; Releases $	
1202. City/county tax/stamps: Deed $	; Mortgage $		
1203. State tax/stamps: Deed $	; Mortgage $		
1204.			
1205.			

1300. Additional Settlement Charges

1301. Survey	to	
1302. Pest inspection	to	
1303.		
1304.		
1305.		

1400. Total Settlement Charges (enter on lines 103, Section J and 502, Section K)

APPENDIX V

Amortization Tables

The following amortization tables allow you to figure out exactly how much you'll be paying in interest and principal each month. Here's how to use them: First, find the table that reflects the interest rate you're being charged. Next, go to the column that corresponds with the length of your loan. Finally, add up the columns to find the amount of your loan.

For example, let's say you're borrowing $122,000 at 7.5 percent interest for fifteen years. If you go to the 7.5 percent table and find the fifteen-year loan column, move down the column until you find $100,000; it will cost you $927.01 per month. Next, move your finger across the $20,000 column; it will cost you an additional $185.40 per month. Finally, find the $2,000 row, move across until you get to $18.54. Add these numbers up to get your monthly interest and principal payment:

$$\$927.01 + \$185.40 + \$18.54 = \$1,130.95$$

Your monthly amortized principal and interest payment for a fifteen-year $122,000 loan at 7.5 percent would be $1,130.95.

4% RATE

Term of Loan in Years

Amount	10	15	20	25	30
$ 50.00	$ 0.51	$ 0.37	$ 0.30	$ 0.26	$ 0.24
$ 100.00	$ 1.01	$ 0.74	$ 0.61	$ 0.53	$ 0.48
$ 200.00	$ 2.02	$ 1.48	$ 1.21	$ 1.06	$ 0.95
$ 300.00	$ 3.04	$ 2.22	$ 1.82	$ 1.58	$ 1.43
$ 400.00	$ 4.05	$ 2.96	$ 2.42	$ 2.11	$ 1.91
$ 500.00	$ 5.06	$ 3.70	$ 3.03	$ 2.64	$ 2.39
$ 600.00	$ 6.07	$ 4.44	$ 3.64	$ 3.17	$ 2.86
$ 700.00	$ 7.09	$ 5.18	$ 4.24	$ 3.69	$ 3.34
$ 800.00	$ 8.10	$ 5.92	$ 4.85	$ 4.22	$ 3.82
$ 900.00	$ 9.11	$ 6.66	$ 5.45	$ 4.75	$ 4.30
$ 1,000.00	$ 10.12	$ 7.40	$ 6.06	$ 5.28	$ 4.77
$ 2,000.00	$ 20.25	$ 14.79	$ 12.12	$ 10.56	$ 9.55
$ 3,000.00	$ 30.37	$ 22.19	$ 18.18	$ 15.84	$ 14.32
$ 4,000.00	$ 40.50	$ 29.59	$ 24.24	$ 21.11	$ 19.10
$ 5,000.00	$ 50.62	$ 36.98	$ 30.30	$ 26.39	$ 23.87
$ 6,000.00	$ 60.75	$ 44.38	$ 36.36	$ 31.67	$ 28.64
$ 7,000.00	$ 70.87	$ 51.78	$ 42.42	$ 36.95	$ 33.42
$ 8,000.00	$ 81.00	$ 59.18	$ 48.48	$ 42.23	$ 38.19
$ 9,000.00	$ 91.12	$ 66.57	$ 54.54	$ 47.51	$ 42.97
$ 10,000.00	$ 101.25	$ 73.97	$ 60.60	$ 52.78	$ 47.74
$ 20,000.00	$ 202.49	$147.94	$121.20	$105.57	$ 95.48
$ 30,000.00	$ 303.74	$221.91	$181.79	$158.35	$143.22
$ 40,000.00	$ 404.98	$295.88	$242.39	$211.13	$190.97
$ 50,000.00	$ 506.23	$369.84	$302.99	$263.92	$238.71
$ 60,000.00	$ 607.47	$443.81	$363.59	$316.70	$286.45
$ 70,000.00	$ 708.72	$517.78	$424.19	$369.49	$334.19
$ 80,000.00	$ 809.96	$591.75	$484.78	$422.27	$381.93
$ 90,000.00	$ 911.21	$665.72	$545.38	$475.05	$429.67
$100,000.00	$1,012.45	$739.69	$605.98	$527.84	$477.42

4⅛% RATE

Term of Loan in Years

Amount	10	15	20	25	30
$ 50.00	$ 0.51	$ 0.37	$ 0.31	$ 0.27	$ 0.24
$ 100.00	$ 1.02	$ 0.75	$ 0.61	$ 0.53	$ 0.48
$ 200.00	$ 2.04	$ 1.49	$ 1.23	$ 1.07	$ 0.97
$ 300.00	$ 3.06	$ 2.24	$ 1.84	$ 1.60	$ 1.45
$ 400.00	$ 4.07	$ 2.98	$ 2.45	$ 2.14	$ 1.94
$ 500.00	$ 5.09	$ 3.73	$ 3.06	$ 2.67	$ 2.42
$ 600.00	$ 6.11	$ 4.48	$ 3.68	$ 3.21	$ 2.91
$ 700.00	$ 7.13	$ 5.22	$ 4.29	$ 3.74	$ 3.39
$ 800.00	$ 8.15	$ 5.97	$ 4.90	$ 4.28	$ 3.88
$ 900.00	$ 9.17	$ 6.71	$ 5.51	$ 4.81	$ 4.36
$ 1,000.00	$ 10.18	$ 7.46	$ 6.13	$ 5.35	$ 4.85
$ 2,000.00	$ 20.37	$ 14.92	$ 12.25	$ 10.70	$ 9.69
$ 3,000.00	$ 30.55	$ 22.38	$ 18.38	$ 16.04	$ 14.54
$ 4,000.00	$ 40.74	$ 29.84	$ 24.50	$ 21.39	$ 19.39
$ 5,000.00	$ 50.92	$ 37.30	$ 30.63	$ 26.74	$ 24.23
$ 6,000.00	$ 61.10	$ 44.76	$ 36.76	$ 32.09	$ 29.08
$ 7,000.00	$ 71.29	$ 52.22	$ 42.88	$ 37.43	$ 33.93
$ 8,000.00	$ 81.47	$ 59.68	$ 49.01	$ 42.78	$ 38.77
$ 9,000.00	$ 91.66	$ 67.14	$ 55.13	$ 48.13	$ 43.62
$ 10,000.00	$ 101.84	$ 74.60	$ 61.26	$ 53.48	$ 48.46
$ 20,000.00	$ 203.68	$149.19	$122.52	$106.95	$ 96.93
$ 30,000.00	$ 305.52	$223.79	$183.78	$160.43	$145.39
$ 40,000.00	$ 407.36	$298.39	$245.03	$213.91	$193.86
$ 50,000.00	$ 509.20	$372.98	$306.29	$267.38	$242.32
$ 60,000.00	$ 611.04	$447.58	$367.55	$320.86	$290.79
$ 70,000.00	$ 712.88	$522.18	$428.81	$374.33	$339.25
$ 80,000.00	$ 814.72	$596.77	$490.07	$427.81	$387.72
$ 90,000.00	$ 916.56	$671.37	$551.33	$481.29	$436.18
$100,000.00	$1,018.40	$745.97	$612.59	$534.76	$484.65

4¼% RATE

0.0425			Term of Loan in Years					
		10		15		20	25	30
Amount								
$ 50.00	$	0.51	$	0.38	$ 0.31	$ 0.27	$ 0.25
$ 100.00	$	1.02	$	0.75	$ 0.62	$ 0.54	$ 0.49
$ 200.00	$	2.05	$	1.50	$ 1.24	$ 1.08	$ 0.98
$ 300.00	$	3.07	$	2.26	$ 1.86	$ 1.63	$ 1.48
$ 400.00	$	4.10	$	3.01	$ 2.48	$ 2.17	$ 1.97
$ 500.00	$	5.12	$	3.76	$ 3.10	$ 2.71	$ 2.46
$ 600.00	$	6.15	$	4.51	$ 3.72	$ 3.25	$ 2.95
$ 700.00	$	7.17	$	5.27	$ 4.33	$ 3.79	$ 3.44
$ 800.00	$	8.20	$	6.02	$ 4.95	$ 4.33	$ 3.94
$ 900.00	$	9.22	$	6.77	$ 5.57	$ 4.88	$ 4.43
$ 1,000.00	$	10.24	$	7.52	$ 6.19	$ 5.42	$ 4.92
$ 2,000.00	$	20.49	$	15.05	$ 12.38	$ 10.83	$ 9.84
$ 3,000.00	$	30.73	$	22.57	$ 18.58	$ 16.25	$ 14.76
$ 4,000.00	$	40.98	$	30.09	$ 24.77	$ 21.67	$ 19.68
$ 5,000.00	$	51.22	$	37.61	$ 30.96	$ 27.09	$ 24.60
$ 6,000.00	$	61.46	$	45.14	$ 37.15	$ 32.50	$ 29.52
$ 7,000.00	$	71.71	$	52.66	$ 43.35	$ 37.92	$ 34.44
$ 8,000.00	$	81.95	$	60.18	$ 49.54	$ 43.34	$ 39.36
$ 9,000.00	$	92.19	$	67.71	$ 55.73	$ 48.76	$ 44.27
$ 10,000.00	$	102.44	$	75.23	$ 61.92	$ 54.17	$ 49.19
$ 20,000.00	$	204.88	$150.46		$123.85	$108.35	$ 98.39
$ 30,000.00	$	307.31	$225.68		$185.77	$162.52	$147.58
$ 40,000.00	$	409.75	$300.91		$247.69	$216.70	$196.78
$ 50,000.00	$	512.19	$376.14		$309.62	$270.87	$245.97
$ 60,000.00	$	614.63	$451.37		$371.54	$325.04	$295.16
$ 70,000.00	$	717.06	$526.59		$433.46	$379.22	$344.36
$ 80,000.00	$	819.50	$601.82		$495.39	$433.39	$393.55
$ 90,000.00	$	921.94	$677.05		$557.31	$487.56	$442.75
$100,000.00	$1,024.38		$752.28		$619.23	$541.74	$491.94

4⅜% RATE

                          Term of Loan in Years

Amount	10	15	20	25	30
$ 50.00	$ 0.52	$ 0.38	$ 0.31	$ 0.27	$ 0.25
$ 100.00	$ 1.03	$ 0.76	$ 0.63	$ 0.55	$ 0.50
$ 200.00	$ 2.06	$ 1.52	$ 1.25	$ 1.10	$ 1.00
$ 300.00	$ 3.09	$ 2.28	$ 1.88	$ 1.65	$ 1.50
$ 400.00	$ 4.12	$ 3.03	$ 2.50	$ 2.20	$ 2.00
$ 500.00	$ 5.15	$ 3.79	$ 3.13	$ 2.74	$ 2.50
$ 600.00	$ 6.18	$ 4.55	$ 3.76	$ 3.29	$ 3.00
$ 700.00	$ 7.21	$ 5.31	$ 4.38	$ 3.84	$ 3.49
$ 800.00	$ 8.24	$ 6.07	$ 5.01	$ 4.39	$ 3.99
$ 900.00	$ 9.27	$ 6.83	$ 5.63	$ 4.94	$ 4.49
$ 1,000.00	$ 10.30	$ 7.59	$ 6.26	$ 5.49	$ 4.99
$ 2,000.00	$ 20.61	$ 15.17	$ 12.52	$ 10.98	$ 9.99
$ 3,000.00	$ 30.91	$ 22.76	$ 18.78	$ 16.46	$ 14.98
$ 4,000.00	$ 41.21	$ 30.34	$ 25.04	$ 21.95	$ 19.97
$ 5,000.00	$ 51.52	$ 37.93	$ 31.30	$ 27.44	$ 24.96
$ 6,000.00	$ 61.82	$ 45.52	$ 37.56	$ 32.93	$ 29.96
$ 7,000.00	$ 72.13	$ 53.10	$ 43.81	$ 38.41	$ 34.95
$ 8,000.00	$ 82.43	$ 60.69	$ 50.07	$ 43.90	$ 39.94
$ 9,000.00	$ 92.73	$ 68.28	$ 56.33	$ 49.39	$ 44.94
$ 10,000.00	$ 103.04	$ 75.86	$ 62.59	$ 54.88	$ 49.93
$ 20,000.00	$ 206.07	$151.72	$125.18	$109.75	$ 99.86
$ 30,000.00	$ 309.11	$227.59	$187.78	$164.63	$149.79
$ 40,000.00	$ 412.15	$303.45	$250.37	$219.50	$199.71
$ 50,000.00	$ 515.18	$379.31	$312.96	$274.38	$249.64
$ 60,000.00	$ 618.22	$455.17	$375.55	$329.26	$299.57
$ 70,000.00	$ 721.26	$531.03	$438.15	$384.13	$349.50
$ 80,000.00	$ 824.30	$606.90	$500.74	$439.01	$399.43
$ 90,000.00	$ 927.33	$682.76	$563.33	$493.89	$449.36
$100,000.00	$1,030.37	$758.62	$625.92	$548.76	$499.29

4½% RATE

Term of Loan in Years

	10	15	20	25	30
Amount					
$ 50.00	$ 0.52	$ 0.38	$ 0.32	$ 0.28	$ 0.25
$ 100.00	$ 1.04	$ 0.76	$ 0.63	$ 0.56	$ 0.51
$ 200.00	$ 2.07	$ 1.53	$ 1.27	$ 1.11	$ 1.01
$ 300.00	$ 3.11	$ 2.29	$ 1.90	$ 1.67	$ 1.52
$ 400.00	$ 4.15	$ 3.06	$ 2.53	$ 2.22	$ 2.03
$ 500.00	$ 5.18	$ 3.82	$ 3.16	$ 2.78	$ 2.53
$ 600.00	$ 6.22	$ 4.59	$ 3.80	$ 3.33	$ 3.04
$ 700.00	$ 7.25	$ 5.35	$ 4.43	$ 3.89	$ 3.55
$ 800.00	$ 8.29	$ 6.12	$ 5.06	$ 4.45	$ 4.05
$ 900.00	$ 9.33	$ 6.88	$ 5.69	$ 5.00	$ 4.56
$ 1,000.00	$ 10.36	$ 7.65	$ 6.33	$ 5.56	$ 5.07
$ 2,000.00	$ 20.73	$ 15.30	$ 12.65	$ 11.12	$ 10.13
$ 3,000.00	$ 31.09	$ 22.95	$ 18.98	$ 16.67	$ 15.20
$ 4,000.00	$ 41.46	$ 30.60	$ 25.31	$ 22.23	$ 20.27
$ 5,000.00	$ 51.82	$ 38.25	$ 31.63	$ 27.79	$ 25.33
$ 6,000.00	$ 62.18	$ 45.90	$ 37.96	$ 33.35	$ 30.40
$ 7,000.00	$ 72.55	$ 53.55	$ 44.29	$ 38.91	$ 35.47
$ 8,000.00	$ 82.91	$ 61.20	$ 50.61	$ 44.47	$ 40.53
$ 9,000.00	$ 93.27	$ 68.85	$ 56.94	$ 50.02	$ 45.60
$ 10,000.00	$ 103.64	$ 76.50	$ 63.26	$ 55.58	$ 50.67
$ 20,000.00	$ 207.28	$153.00	$126.53	$111.17	$101.34
$ 30,000.00	$ 310.92	$229.50	$189.79	$166.75	$152.01
$ 40,000.00	$ 414.55	$306.00	$253.06	$222.33	$202.67
$ 50,000.00	$ 518.19	$382.50	$316.32	$277.92	$253.34
$ 60,000.00	$ 621.83	$459.00	$379.59	$333.50	$304.01
$ 70,000.00	$ 725.47	$535.50	$442.85	$389.08	$354.68
$ 80,000.00	$ 829.11	$611.99	$506.12	$444.67	$405.35
$ 90,000.00	$ 932.75	$688.49	$569.38	$500.25	$456.02
$100,000.00	$1,036.38	$764.99	$632.65	$555.83	$506.69

0.04625	Term of Loan in Years				
	10	15	20	25	30
Amount					
$ 50.00	$ 0.52	$ 0.39	$ 0.32	$ 0.28	$ 0.26
$ 100.00	$ 1.04	$ 0.77	$ 0.64	$ 0.56	$ 0.51
$ 200.00	$ 2.08	$ 1.54	$ 1.28	$ 1.13	$ 1.03
$ 300.00	$ 3.13	$ 2.31	$ 1.92	$ 1.69	$ 1.54
$ 400.00	$ 4.17	$ 3.09	$ 2.56	$ 2.25	$ 2.06
$ 500.00	$ 5.21	$ 3.86	$ 3.20	$ 2.81	$ 2.57
$ 600.00	$ 6.25	$ 4.63	$ 3.84	$ 3.38	$ 3.08
$ 700.00	$ 7.30	$ 5.40	$ 4.48	$ 3.94	$ 3.60
$ 800.00	$ 8.34	$ 6.17	$ 5.12	$ 4.50	$ 4.11
$ 900.00	$ 9.38	$ 6.94	$ 5.75	$ 5.07	$ 4.63
$ 1,000.00	$ 10.42	$ 7.71	$ 6.39	$ 5.63	$ 5.14
$ 2,000.00	$ 20.85	$ 15.43	$ 12.79	$ 11.26	$ 10.28
$ 3,000.00	$ 31.27	$ 23.14	$ 19.18	$ 16.89	$ 15.42
$ 4,000.00	$ 41.70	$ 30.86	$ 25.58	$ 22.52	$ 20.57
$ 5,000.00	$ 52.12	$ 38.57	$ 31.97	$ 28.15	$ 25.71
$ 6,000.00	$ 62.55	$ 46.28	$ 38.37	$ 33.78	$ 30.85
$ 7,000.00	$ 72.97	$ 54.00	$ 44.76	$ 39.41	$ 35.99
$ 8,000.00	$ 83.39	$ 61.71	$ 51.15	$ 45.04	$ 41.13
$ 9,000.00	$ 93.82	$ 69.43	$ 57.55	$ 50.67	$ 46.27
$ 10,000.00	$ 104.24	$ 77.14	$ 63.94	$ 56.30	$ 51.41
$ 20,000.00	$ 208.48	$154.28	$127.88	$112.59	$102.83
$ 30,000.00	$ 312.73	$231.42	$191.83	$168.89	$154.24
$ 40,000.00	$ 416.97	$308.56	$255.77	$225.18	$205.66
$ 50,000.00	$ 521.21	$385.70	$319.71	$281.48	$257.07
$ 60,000.00	$ 625.45	$462.84	$383.65	$337.77	$308.48
$ 70,000.00	$ 729.69	$539.98	$447.59	$394.07	$359.90
$ 80,000.00	$ 833.94	$617.12	$511.53	$450.36	$411.31
$ 90,000.00	$ 938.18	$694.26	$575.48	$506.66	$462.73
$100,000.00	$1,042.42	$771.40	$639.42	$562.95	$514.14

4¾% RATE

Term of Loan in Years

	10	15	20	25	30
Amount					
$ 50.00	$ 0.52	$ 0.39	$ 0.32	$ 0.29	$ 0.26
$ 100.00	$ 1.05	$ 0.78	$ 0.65	$ 0.57	$ 0.52
$ 200.00	$ 2.10	$ 1.56	$ 1.29	$ 1.14	$ 1.04
$ 300.00	$ 3.15	$ 2.33	$ 1.94	$ 1.71	$ 1.56
$ 400.00	$ 4.19	$ 3.11	$ 2.58	$ 2.28	$ 2.09
$ 500.00	$ 5.24	$ 3.89	$ 3.23	$ 2.85	$ 2.61
$ 600.00	$ 6.29	$ 4.67	$ 3.88	$ 3.42	$ 3.13
$ 700.00	$ 7.34	$ 5.44	$ 4.52	$ 3.99	$ 3.65
$ 800.00	$ 8.39	$ 6.22	$ 5.17	$ 4.56	$ 4.17
$ 900.00	$ 9.44	$ 7.00	$ 5.82	$ 5.13	$ 4.69
$ 1,000.00	$ 10.48	$ 7.78	$ 6.46	$ 5.70	$ 5.22
$ 2,000.00	$ 20.97	$ 15.56	$ 12.92	$ 11.40	$ 10.43
$ 3,000.00	$ 31.45	$ 23.33	$ 19.39	$ 17.10	$ 15.65
$ 4,000.00	$ 41.94	$ 31.11	$ 25.85	$ 22.80	$ 20.87
$ 5,000.00	$ 52.42	$ 38.89	$ 32.31	$ 28.51	$ 26.08
$ 6,000.00	$ 62.91	$ 46.67	$ 38.77	$ 34.21	$ 31.30
$ 7,000.00	$ 73.39	$ 54.45	$ 45.24	$ 39.91	$ 36.52
$ 8,000.00	$ 83.88	$ 62.23	$ 51.70	$ 45.61	$ 41.73
$ 9,000.00	$ 94.36	$ 70.00	$ 58.16	$ 51.31	$ 46.95
$ 10,000.00	$ 104.85	$ 77.78	$ 64.62	$ 57.01	$ 52.16
$ 20,000.00	$ 209.70	$155.57	$129.24	$114.02	$104.33
$ 30,000.00	$ 314.54	$233.35	$193.87	$171.04	$156.49
$ 40,000.00	$ 419.39	$311.13	$258.49	$228.05	$208.66
$ 50,000.00	$ 524.24	$388.92	$323.11	$285.06	$260.82
$ 60,000.00	$ 629.09	$466.70	$387.73	$342.07	$312.99
$ 70,000.00	$ 733.93	$544.48	$452.36	$399.08	$365.15
$ 80,000.00	$ 838.78	$622.27	$516.98	$456.09	$417.32
$ 90,000.00	$ 943.63	$700.05	$581.60	$513.11	$469.48
$100,000.00	$1,048.48	$777.83	$646.22	$570.12	$521.65

4⅞% RATE

Term of Loan in Years

Amount	10	15	20	25	30
$ 50.00	$ 0.53	$ 0.39	$ 0.33	$ 0.29	$ 0.26
$ 100.00	$ 1.05	$ 0.78	$ 0.65	$ 0.58	$ 0.53
$ 200.00	$ 2.11	$ 1.57	$ 1.31	$ 1.15	$ 1.06
$ 300.00	$ 3.16	$ 2.35	$ 1.96	$ 1.73	$ 1.59
$ 400.00	$ 4.22	$ 3.14	$ 2.61	$ 2.31	$ 2.12
$ 500.00	$ 5.27	$ 3.92	$ 3.27	$ 2.89	$ 2.65
$ 600.00	$ 6.33	$ 4.71	$ 3.92	$ 3.46	$ 3.18
$ 700.00	$ 7.38	$ 5.49	$ 4.57	$ 4.04	$ 3.70
$ 800.00	$ 8.44	$ 6.27	$ 5.22	$ 4.62	$ 4.23
$ 900.00	$ 9.49	$ 7.06	$ 5.88	$ 5.20	$ 4.76
$ 1,000.00	$ 10.55	$ 7.84	$ 6.53	$ 5.77	$ 5.29
$ 2,000.00	$ 21.09	$ 15.69	$ 13.06	$ 11.55	$ 10.58
$ 3,000.00	$ 31.64	$ 23.53	$ 19.59	$ 17.32	$ 15.88
$ 4,000.00	$ 42.18	$ 31.37	$ 26.12	$ 23.09	$ 21.17
$ 5,000.00	$ 52.73	$ 39.21	$ 32.65	$ 28.87	$ 26.46
$ 6,000.00	$ 63.27	$ 47.06	$ 39.18	$ 34.64	$ 31.75
$ 7,000.00	$ 73.82	$ 54.90	$ 45.71	$ 40.41	$ 37.04
$ 8,000.00	$ 84.36	$ 62.74	$ 52.25	$ 46.19	$ 42.34
$ 9,000.00	$ 94.91	$ 70.59	$ 58.78	$ 51.96	$ 47.63
$ 10,000.00	$ 105.46	$ 78.43	$ 65.31	$ 57.73	$ 52.92
$ 20,000.00	$ 210.91	$156.86	$130.61	$115.47	$105.84
$ 30,000.00	$ 316.37	$235.29	$195.92	$173.20	$158.76
$ 40,000.00	$ 421.82	$313.72	$261.23	$230.93	$211.68
$ 50,000.00	$ 527.28	$392.15	$326.54	$288.67	$264.60
$ 60,000.00	$ 632.73	$470.58	$391.84	$346.40	$317.52
$ 70,000.00	$ 738.19	$549.01	$457.15	$404.13	$370.45
$ 80,000.00	$ 843.64	$627.44	$522.46	$461.86	$423.37
$ 90,000.00	$ 949.10	$705.87	$587.76	$519.60	$476.29
$100,000.00	$1,054.56	$784.30	$653.07	$577.33	$529.21

5% RATE

Term of Loan in Years

Amount	10	15	20	25	30
$ 50.00	$ 0.53	$ 0.40	$ 0.33	$ 0.29	$ 0.27
$ 100.00	$ 1.06	$ 0.79	$ 0.66	$ 0.58	$ 0.54
$ 200.00	$ 2.12	$ 1.58	$ 1.32	$ 1.17	$ 1.07
$ 300.00	$ 3.18	$ 2.37	$ 1.98	$ 1.75	$ 1.61
$ 400.00	$ 4.24	$ 3.16	$ 2.64	$ 2.34	$ 2.15
$ 500.00	$ 5.30	$ 3.95	$ 3.30	$ 2.92	$ 2.68
$ 600.00	$ 6.36	$ 4.74	$ 3.96	$ 3.51	$ 3.22
$ 700.00	$ 7.42	$ 5.54	$ 4.62	$ 4.09	$ 3.76
$ 800.00	$ 8.49	$ 6.33	$ 5.28	$ 4.68	$ 4.29
$ 900.00	$ 9.55	$ 7.12	$ 5.94	$ 5.26	$ 4.83
$ 1,000.00	$ 10.61	$ 7.91	$ 6.60	$ 5.85	$ 5.37
$ 2,000.00	$ 21.21	$ 15.82	$ 13.20	$ 11.69	$ 10.74
$ 3,000.00	$ 31.82	$ 23.72	$ 19.80	$ 17.54	$ 16.10
$ 4,000.00	$ 42.43	$ 31.63	$ 26.40	$ 23.38	$ 21.47
$ 5,000.00	$ 53.03	$ 39.54	$ 33.00	$ 29.23	$ 26.84
$ 6,000.00	$ 63.64	$ 47.45	$ 39.60	$ 35.08	$ 32.21
$ 7,000.00	$ 74.25	$ 55.36	$ 46.20	$ 40.92	$ 37.58
$ 8,000.00	$ 84.85	$ 63.26	$ 52.80	$ 46.77	$ 42.95
$ 9,000.00	$ 95.46	$ 71.17	$ 59.40	$ 52.61	$ 48.31
$ 10,000.00	$ 106.07	$ 79.08	$ 66.00	$ 58.46	$ 53.68
$ 20,000.00	$ 212.13	$158.16	$131.99	$116.92	$107.36
$ 30,000.00	$ 318.20	$237.24	$197.99	$175.38	$161.05
$ 40,000.00	$ 424.26	$316.32	$263.98	$233.84	$214.73
$ 50,000.00	$ 530.33	$395.40	$329.98	$292.30	$268.41
$ 60,000.00	$ 636.39	$474.48	$395.97	$350.75	$322.09
$ 70,000.00	$ 742.46	$553.56	$461.97	$409.21	$375.78
$ 80,000.00	$ 848.52	$632.63	$527.96	$467.67	$429.46
$ 90,000.00	$ 954.59	$711.71	$593.96	$526.13	$483.14
$100,000.00	$1,060.66	$790.79	$659.96	$584.59	$536.82

5⅛% RATE

Term of Loan in Years

		10	15	20	25	30
Amount						
$	50.00	$ 0.53	$ 0.40	$ 0.33	$ 0.30	$ 0.27
$	100.00	$ 1.07	$ 0.80	$ 0.67	$ 0.59	$ 0.54
$	200.00	$ 2.13	$ 1.59	$ 1.33	$ 1.18	$ 1.09
$	300.00	$ 3.20	$ 2.39	$ 2.00	$ 1.78	$ 1.63
$	400.00	$ 4.27	$ 3.19	$ 2.67	$ 2.37	$ 2.18
$	500.00	$ 5.33	$ 3.99	$ 3.33	$ 2.96	$ 2.72
$	600.00	$ 6.40	$ 4.78	$ 4.00	$ 3.55	$ 3.27
$	700.00	$ 7.47	$ 5.58	$ 4.67	$ 4.14	$ 3.81
$	800.00	$ 8.53	$ 6.38	$ 5.34	$ 4.74	$ 4.36
$	900.00	$ 9.60	$ 7.18	$ 6.00	$ 5.33	$ 4.90
$	1,000.00	$ 10.67	$ 7.97	$ 6.67	$ 5.92	$ 5.44
$	2,000.00	$ 21.34	$ 15.95	$ 13.34	$ 11.84	$ 10.89
$	3,000.00	$ 32.00	$ 23.92	$ 20.01	$ 17.76	$ 16.33
$	4,000.00	$ 42.67	$ 31.89	$ 26.68	$ 23.68	$ 21.78
$	5,000.00	$ 53.34	$ 39.87	$ 33.34	$ 29.59	$ 27.22
$	6,000.00	$ 64.01	$ 47.84	$ 40.01	$ 35.51	$ 32.67
$	7,000.00	$ 74.67	$ 55.81	$ 46.68	$ 41.43	$ 38.11
$	8,000.00	$ 85.34	$ 63.79	$ 53.35	$ 47.35	$ 43.56
$	9,000.00	$ 96.01	$ 71.76	$ 60.02	$ 53.27	$ 49.00
$	10,000.00	$ 106.68	$ 79.73	$ 66.69	$ 59.19	$ 54.45
$	20,000.00	$ 213.36	$159.46	$133.38	$118.38	$108.90
$	30,000.00	$ 320.03	$239.20	$200.06	$177.57	$163.35
$	40,000.00	$ 426.71	$318.93	$266.75	$236.76	$217.79
$	50,000.00	$ 533.39	$398.66	$333.44	$295.95	$272.24
$	60,000.00	$ 640.07	$478.39	$400.13	$355.14	$326.69
$	70,000.00	$ 746.74	$558.12	$466.82	$414.33	$381.14
$	80,000.00	$ 853.42	$637.86	$533.50	$473.52	$435.59
$	90,000.00	$ 960.10	$717.59	$600.19	$532.71	$490.04
$100,000.00		$1,066.78	$797.32	$666.88	$591.90	$544.49

5¼% RATE

0.0525   Term of Loan in Years

Amount	10	15	20	25	30
$ 50.00	$ 0.54	$ 0.40	$ 0.34	$ 0.30	$ 0.28
$ 100.00	$ 1.07	$ 0.80	$ 0.67	$ 0.60	$ 0.55
$ 200.00	$ 2.15	$ 1.61	$ 1.35	$ 1.20	$ 1.10
$ 300.00	$ 3.22	$ 2.41	$ 2.02	$ 1.80	$ 1.66
$ 400.00	$ 4.29	$ 3.22	$ 2.70	$ 2.40	$ 2.21
$ 500.00	$ 5.36	$ 4.02	$ 3.37	$ 3.00	$ 2.76
$ 600.00	$ 6.44	$ 4.82	$ 4.04	$ 3.60	$ 3.31
$ 700.00	$ 7.51	$ 5.63	$ 4.72	$ 4.19	$ 3.87
$ 800.00	$ 8.58	$ 6.43	$ 5.39	$ 4.79	$ 4.42
$ 900.00	$ 9.66	$ 7.23	$ 6.06	$ 5.39	$ 4.97
$ 1,000.00	$ 10.73	$ 8.04	$ 6.74	$ 5.99	$ 5.52
$ 2,000.00	$ 21.46	$ 16.08	$ 13.48	$ 11.98	$ 11.04
$ 3,000.00	$ 32.19	$ 24.12	$ 20.22	$ 17.98	$ 16.57
$ 4,000.00	$ 42.92	$ 32.16	$ 26.95	$ 23.97	$ 22.09
$ 5,000.00	$ 53.65	$ 40.19	$ 33.69	$ 29.96	$ 27.61
$ 6,000.00	$ 64.38	$ 48.23	$ 40.43	$ 35.95	$ 33.13
$ 7,000.00	$ 75.10	$ 56.27	$ 47.17	$ 41.95	$ 38.65
$ 8,000.00	$ 85.83	$ 64.31	$ 53.91	$ 47.94	$ 44.18
$ 9,000.00	$ 96.56	$ 72.35	$ 60.65	$ 53.93	$ 49.70
$ 10,000.00	$ 107.29	$ 80.39	$ 67.38	$ 59.92	$ 55.22
$ 20,000.00	$ 214.58	$160.78	$134.77	$119.85	$110.44
$ 30,000.00	$ 321.88	$241.16	$202.15	$179.77	$165.66
$ 40,000.00	$ 429.17	$321.55	$269.54	$239.70	$220.88
$ 50,000.00	$ 536.46	$401.94	$336.92	$299.62	$276.10
$ 60,000.00	$ 643.75	$482.33	$404.31	$359.55	$331.32
$ 70,000.00	$ 751.04	$562.71	$471.69	$419.47	$386.54
$ 80,000.00	$ 858.33	$643.10	$539.08	$479.40	$441.76
$ 90,000.00	$ 965.63	$723.49	$606.46	$539.32	$496.98
$100,000.00	$1,072.92	$803.88	$673.84	$599.25	$552.20

0.05375	Term of Loan in Years				
	10	15	20	25	30
Amount					
$ 50.00	$ 0.54	$ 0.41	$ 0.34	$ 0.30	$ 0.28
$ 100.00	$ 1.08	$ 0.81	$ 0.68	$ 0.61	$ 0.56
$ 200.00	$ 2.16	$ 1.62	$ 1.36	$ 1.21	$ 1.12
$ 300.00	$ 3.24	$ 2.43	$ 2.04	$ 1.82	$ 1.68
$ 400.00	$ 4.32	$ 3.24	$ 2.72	$ 2.43	$ 2.24
$ 500.00	$ 5.40	$ 4.05	$ 3.40	$ 3.03	$ 2.80
$ 600.00	$ 6.47	$ 4.86	$ 4.09	$ 3.64	$ 3.36
$ 700.00	$ 7.55	$ 5.67	$ 4.77	$ 4.25	$ 3.92
$ 800.00	$ 8.63	$ 6.48	$ 5.45	$ 4.85	$ 4.48
$ 900.00	$ 9.71	$ 7.29	$ 6.13	$ 5.46	$ 5.04
$ 1,000.00	$ 10.79	$ 8.10	$ 6.81	$ 6.07	$ 5.60
$ 2,000.00	$ 21.58	$ 16.21	$ 13.62	$ 12.13	$ 11.20
$ 3,000.00	$ 32.37	$ 24.31	$ 20.43	$ 18.20	$ 16.80
$ 4,000.00	$ 43.16	$ 32.42	$ 27.23	$ 24.27	$ 22.40
$ 5,000.00	$ 53.95	$ 40.52	$ 34.04	$ 30.33	$ 28.00
$ 6,000.00	$ 64.74	$ 48.63	$ 40.85	$ 36.40	$ 33.60
$ 7,000.00	$ 75.54	$ 56.73	$ 47.66	$ 42.47	$ 39.20
$ 8,000.00	$ 86.33	$ 64.84	$ 54.47	$ 48.53	$ 44.80
$ 9,000.00	$ 97.12	$ 72.94	$ 61.28	$ 54.60	$ 50.40
$ 10,000.00	$ 107.91	$ 81.05	$ 68.08	$ 60.66	$ 56.00
$ 20,000.00	$ 215.82	$162.09	$136.17	$121.33	$111.99
$ 30,000.00	$ 323.72	$243.14	$204.25	$181.99	$167.99
$ 40,000.00	$ 431.63	$324.19	$272.34	$242.66	$223.99
$ 50,000.00	$ 539.54	$405.23	$340.42	$303.32	$279.99
$ 60,000.00	$ 647.45	$486.28	$408.51	$363.99	$335.98
$ 70,000.00	$ 755.36	$567.33	$476.59	$424.65	$391.98
$ 80,000.00	$ 863.26	$648.37	$544.68	$485.32	$447.98
$ 90,000.00	$ 971.17	$729.42	$612.76	$545.98	$503.97
$100,000.00	$1,079.08	$810.47	$680.85	$606.65	$559.97

0.055	Term of Loan in Years				
	10	15	20	25	30
Amount					
$ 50.00	$ 0.54	$ 0.41	$ 0.34	$ 0.31	$ 0.28
$ 100.00	$ 1.09	$ 0.82	$ 0.69	$ 0.61	$ 0.57
$ 200.00	$ 2.17	$ 1.63	$ 1.38	$ 1.23	$ 1.14
$ 300.00	$ 3.26	$ 2.45	$ 2.06	$ 1.84	$ 1.70
$ 400.00	$ 4.34	$ 3.27	$ 2.75	$ 2.46	$ 2.27
$ 500.00	$ 5.43	$ 4.09	$ 3.44	$ 3.07	$ 2.84
$ 600.00	$ 6.51	$ 4.90	$ 4.13	$ 3.68	$ 3.41
$ 700.00	$ 7.60	$ 5.72	$ 4.82	$ 4.30	$ 3.97
$ 800.00	$ 8.68	$ 6.54	$ 5.50	$ 4.91	$ 4.54
$ 900.00	$ 9.77	$ 7.35	$ 6.19	$ 5.53	$ 5.11
$ 1,000.00	$ 10.85	$ 8.17	$ 6.88	$ 6.14	$ 5.68
$ 2,000.00	$ 21.71	$ 16.34	$ 13.76	$ 12.28	$ 11.36
$ 3,000.00	$ 32.56	$ 24.51	$ 20.64	$ 18.42	$ 17.03
$ 4,000.00	$ 43.41	$ 32.68	$ 27.52	$ 24.56	$ 22.71
$ 5,000.00	$ 54.26	$ 40.85	$ 34.39	$ 30.70	$ 28.39
$ 6,000.00	$ 65.12	$ 49.03	$ 41.27	$ 36.85	$ 34.07
$ 7,000.00	$ 75.97	$ 57.20	$ 48.15	$ 42.99	$ 39.75
$ 8,000.00	$ 86.82	$ 65.37	$ 55.03	$ 49.13	$ 45.42
$ 9,000.00	$ 97.67	$ 73.54	$ 61.91	$ 55.27	$ 51.10
$ 10,000.00	$ 108.53	$ 81.71	$ 68.79	$ 61.41	$ 56.78
$ 20,000.00	$ 217.05	$163.42	$137.58	$122.82	$113.56
$ 30,000.00	$ 325.58	$245.13	$206.37	$184.23	$170.34
$ 40,000.00	$ 434.11	$326.83	$275.15	$245.63	$227.12
$ 50,000.00	$ 542.63	$408.54	$343.94	$307.04	$283.89
$ 60,000.00	$ 651.16	$490.25	$412.73	$368.45	$340.67
$ 70,000.00	$ 759.68	$571.96	$481.52	$429.86	$397.45
$ 80,000.00	$ 868.21	$653.67	$550.31	$491.27	$454.23
$ 90,000.00	$ 976.74	$735.38	$619.10	$552.68	$511.01
$100,000.00	$1,085.26	$817.08	$687.89	$614.09	$567.79

5⅝% RATE

Amount	10	15	20	25	30
			Term of Loan in Years		
$ 50.00	$ 0.55	$ 0.41	$ 0.35	$ 0.31	$ 0.29
$ 100.00	$ 1.09	$ 0.82	$ 0.69	$ 0.62	$ 0.58
$ 200.00	$ 2.18	$ 1.65	$ 1.39	$ 1.24	$ 1.15
$ 300.00	$ 3.27	$ 2.47	$ 2.08	$ 1.86	$ 1.73
$ 400.00	$ 4.37	$ 3.29	$ 2.78	$ 2.49	$ 2.30
$ 500.00	$ 5.46	$ 4.12	$ 3.47	$ 3.11	$ 2.88
$ 600.00	$ 6.55	$ 4.94	$ 4.17	$ 3.73	$ 3.45
$ 700.00	$ 7.64	$ 5.77	$ 4.86	$ 4.35	$ 4.03
$ 800.00	$ 8.73	$ 6.59	$ 5.56	$ 4.97	$ 4.61
$ 900.00	$ 9.82	$ 7.41	$ 6.25	$ 5.59	$ 5.18
$ 1,000.00	$ 10.91	$ 8.24	$ 6.95	$ 6.22	$ 5.76
$ 2,000.00	$ 21.83	$ 16.47	$ 13.90	$ 12.43	$ 11.51
$ 3,000.00	$ 32.74	$ 24.71	$ 20.85	$ 18.65	$ 17.27
$ 4,000.00	$ 43.66	$ 32.95	$ 27.80	$ 24.86	$ 23.03
$ 5,000.00	$ 54.57	$ 41.19	$ 34.75	$ 31.08	$ 28.78
$ 6,000.00	$ 65.49	$ 49.42	$ 41.70	$ 37.29	$ 34.54
$ 7,000.00	$ 76.40	$ 57.66	$ 48.65	$ 43.51	$ 40.30
$ 8,000.00	$ 87.32	$ 65.90	$ 55.60	$ 49.73	$ 46.05
$ 9,000.00	$ 98.23	$ 74.14	$ 62.55	$ 55.94	$ 51.81
$ 10,000.00	$ 109.15	$ 82.37	$ 69.50	$ 62.16	$ 57.57
$ 20,000.00	$ 218.29	$164.75	$138.99	$124.31	$115.13
$ 30,000.00	$ 327.44	$247.12	$208.49	$186.47	$172.70
$ 40,000.00	$ 436.59	$329.49	$277.99	$248.63	$230.26
$ 50,000.00	$ 545.73	$411.87	$347.48	$310.79	$287.83
$ 60,000.00	$ 654.88	$494.24	$416.98	$372.94	$345.39
$ 70,000.00	$ 764.03	$576.61	$486.48	$435.10	$402.96
$ 80,000.00	$ 873.17	$658.99	$555.97	$497.26	$460.53
$ 90,000.00	$ 982.32	$741.36	$625.47	$559.42	$518.09
$100,000.00	$1,091.47	$823.73	$694.97	$621.57	$575.66

5¾% RATE

                            Term of Loan in Years

Amount	10	15	20	25	30
$ 50.00	$ 0.55	$ 0.42	$ 0.35	$ 0.31	$ 0.29
$ 100.00	$ 1.10	$ 0.83	$ 0.70	$ 0.63	$ 0.58
$ 200.00	$ 2.20	$ 1.66	$ 1.40	$ 1.26	$ 1.17
$ 300.00	$ 3.29	$ 2.49	$ 2.11	$ 1.89	$ 1.75
$ 400.00	$ 4.39	$ 3.32	$ 2.81	$ 2.52	$ 2.33
$ 500.00	$ 5.49	$ 4.15	$ 3.51	$ 3.15	$ 2.92
$ 600.00	$ 6.59	$ 4.98	$ 4.21	$ 3.77	$ 3.50
$ 700.00	$ 7.68	$ 5.81	$ 4.91	$ 4.40	$ 4.09
$ 800.00	$ 8.78	$ 6.64	$ 5.62	$ 5.03	$ 4.67
$ 900.00	$ 9.88	$ 7.47	$ 6.32	$ 5.66	$ 5.25
$ 1,000.00	$ 10.98	$ 8.30	$ 7.02	$ 6.29	$ 5.84
$ 2,000.00	$ 21.95	$ 16.61	$ 14.04	$ 12.58	$ 11.67
$ 3,000.00	$ 32.93	$ 24.91	$ 21.06	$ 18.87	$ 17.51
$ 4,000.00	$ 43.91	$ 33.22	$ 28.08	$ 25.16	$ 23.34
$ 5,000.00	$ 54.88	$ 41.52	$ 35.10	$ 31.46	$ 29.18
$ 6,000.00	$ 65.86	$ 49.82	$ 42.13	$ 37.75	$ 35.01
$ 7,000.00	$ 76.84	$ 58.13	$ 49.15	$ 44.04	$ 40.85
$ 8,000.00	$ 87.82	$ 66.43	$ 56.17	$ 50.33	$ 46.69
$ 9,000.00	$ 98.79	$ 74.74	$ 63.19	$ 56.62	$ 52.52
$ 10,000.00	$ 109.77	$ 83.04	$ 70.21	$ 62.91	$ 58.36
$ 20,000.00	$ 219.54	$166.08	$140.42	$125.82	$116.71
$ 30,000.00	$ 329.31	$249.12	$210.63	$188.73	$175.07
$ 40,000.00	$ 439.08	$332.16	$280.83	$251.64	$233.43
$ 50,000.00	$ 548.85	$415.21	$351.04	$314.55	$291.79
$ 60,000.00	$ 658.62	$498.25	$421.25	$377.46	$350.14
$ 70,000.00	$ 768.38	$581.29	$491.46	$440.37	$408.50
$ 80,000.00	$ 878.15	$664.33	$561.67	$503.29	$466.86
$ 90,000.00	$ 987.92	$747.37	$631.88	$566.20	$525.22
$100,000.00	$1,097.69	$830.41	$702.08	$629.11	$583.57

5⅞% RATE

0.05875	Term of Loan in Years				
	10	15	20	25	30
Amount					
$ 50.00	$ 0.55	$ 0.42	$ 0.35	$ 0.32	$ 0.30
$ 100.00	$ 1.10	$ 0.84	$ 0.71	$ 0.64	$ 0.59
$ 200.00	$ 2.21	$ 1.67	$ 1.42	$ 1.27	$ 1.18
$ 300.00	$ 3.31	$ 2.51	$ 2.13	$ 1.91	$ 1.77
$ 400.00	$ 4.42	$ 3.35	$ 2.84	$ 2.55	$ 2.37
$ 500.00	$ 5.52	$ 4.19	$ 3.55	$ 3.18	$ 2.96
$ 600.00	$ 6.62	$ 5.02	$ 4.26	$ 3.82	$ 3.55
$ 700.00	$ 7.73	$ 5.86	$ 4.96	$ 4.46	$ 4.14
$ 800.00	$ 8.83	$ 6.70	$ 5.67	$ 5.09	$ 4.73
$ 900.00	$ 9.94	$ 7.53	$ 6.38	$ 5.73	$ 5.32
$ 1,000.00	$ 11.04	$ 8.37	$ 7.09	$ 6.37	$ 5.92
$ 2,000.00	$ 22.08	$ 16.74	$ 14.18	$ 12.73	$ 11.83
$ 3,000.00	$ 33.12	$ 25.11	$ 21.28	$ 19.10	$ 17.75
$ 4,000.00	$ 44.16	$ 33.48	$ 28.37	$ 25.47	$ 23.66
$ 5,000.00	$ 55.20	$ 41.86	$ 35.46	$ 31.83	$ 29.58
$ 6,000.00	$ 66.24	$ 50.23	$ 42.55	$ 38.20	$ 35.49
$ 7,000.00	$ 77.28	$ 58.60	$ 49.65	$ 44.57	$ 41.41
$ 8,000.00	$ 88.32	$ 66.97	$ 56.74	$ 50.93	$ 47.32
$ 9,000.00	$ 99.35	$ 75.34	$ 63.83	$ 57.30	$ 53.24
$ 10,000.00	$ 110.39	$ 83.71	$ 70.92	$ 63.67	$ 59.15
$ 20,000.00	$ 220.79	$167.42	$141.85	$127.34	$118.31
$ 30,000.00	$ 331.18	$251.14	$212.77	$191.00	$177.46
$ 40,000.00	$ 441.58	$334.85	$283.70	$254.67	$236.62
$ 50,000.00	$ 551.97	$418.56	$354.62	$318.34	$295.77
$ 60,000.00	$ 662.36	$502.27	$425.54	$382.01	$354.92
$ 70,000.00	$ 772.76	$585.98	$496.47	$445.68	$414.08
$ 80,000.00	$ 883.15	$669.69	$567.39	$509.35	$473.23
$ 90,000.00	$ 993.54	$753.41	$638.31	$573.01	$532.38
$100,000.00	$1,103.94	$837.12	$709.24	$636.68	$591.54

6% RATE

<table>
<tr><td>0.06</td><td colspan="5" align="center">Term of Loan in Years</td></tr>
<tr><td></td><td>10</td><td>15</td><td>20</td><td>25</td><td>30</td></tr>
<tr><td>Amount</td><td></td><td></td><td></td><td></td><td></td></tr>
<tr><td>$ 50.00</td><td>$ 0.56</td><td>$ 0.42</td><td>$ 0.36</td><td>$ 0.32</td><td>$ 0.30</td></tr>
<tr><td>$ 100.00</td><td>$ 1.11</td><td>$ 0.84</td><td>$ 0.72</td><td>$ 0.64</td><td>$ 0.60</td></tr>
<tr><td>$ 200.00</td><td>$ 2.22</td><td>$ 1.69</td><td>$ 1.43</td><td>$ 1.29</td><td>$ 1.20</td></tr>
<tr><td>$ 300.00</td><td>$ 3.33</td><td>$ 2.53</td><td>$ 2.15</td><td>$ 1.93</td><td>$ 1.80</td></tr>
<tr><td>$ 400.00</td><td>$ 4.44</td><td>$ 3.38</td><td>$ 2.87</td><td>$ 2.58</td><td>$ 2.40</td></tr>
<tr><td>$ 500.00</td><td>$ 5.55</td><td>$ 4.22</td><td>$ 3.58</td><td>$ 3.22</td><td>$ 3.00</td></tr>
<tr><td>$ 600.00</td><td>$ 6.66</td><td>$ 5.06</td><td>$ 4.30</td><td>$ 3.87</td><td>$ 3.60</td></tr>
<tr><td>$ 700.00</td><td>$ 7.77</td><td>$ 5.91</td><td>$ 5.02</td><td>$ 4.51</td><td>$ 4.20</td></tr>
<tr><td>$ 800.00</td><td>$ 8.88</td><td>$ 6.75</td><td>$ 5.73</td><td>$ 5.15</td><td>$ 4.80</td></tr>
<tr><td>$ 900.00</td><td>$ 9.99</td><td>$ 7.59</td><td>$ 6.45</td><td>$ 5.80</td><td>$ 5.40</td></tr>
<tr><td>$ 1,000.00</td><td>$ 11.10</td><td>$ 8.44</td><td>$ 7.16</td><td>$ 6.44</td><td>$ 6.00</td></tr>
<tr><td>$ 2,000.00</td><td>$ 22.20</td><td>$ 16.88</td><td>$ 14.33</td><td>$ 12.89</td><td>$ 11.99</td></tr>
<tr><td>$ 3,000.00</td><td>$ 33.31</td><td>$ 25.32</td><td>$ 21.49</td><td>$ 19.33</td><td>$ 17.99</td></tr>
<tr><td>$ 4,000.00</td><td>$ 44.41</td><td>$ 33.75</td><td>$ 28.66</td><td>$ 25.77</td><td>$ 23.98</td></tr>
<tr><td>$ 5,000.00</td><td>$ 55.51</td><td>$ 42.19</td><td>$ 35.82</td><td>$ 32.22</td><td>$ 29.98</td></tr>
<tr><td>$ 6,000.00</td><td>$ 66.61</td><td>$ 50.63</td><td>$ 42.99</td><td>$ 38.66</td><td>$ 35.97</td></tr>
<tr><td>$ 7,000.00</td><td>$ 77.71</td><td>$ 59.07</td><td>$ 50.15</td><td>$ 45.10</td><td>$ 41.97</td></tr>
<tr><td>$ 8,000.00</td><td>$ 88.82</td><td>$ 67.51</td><td>$ 57.31</td><td>$ 51.54</td><td>$ 47.96</td></tr>
<tr><td>$ 9,000.00</td><td>$ 99.92</td><td>$ 75.95</td><td>$ 64.48</td><td>$ 57.99</td><td>$ 53.96</td></tr>
<tr><td>$ 10,000.00</td><td>$ 111.02</td><td>$ 84.39</td><td>$ 71.64</td><td>$ 64.43</td><td>$ 59.96</td></tr>
<tr><td>$ 20,000.00</td><td>$ 222.04</td><td>$168.77</td><td>$143.29</td><td>$128.86</td><td>$119.91</td></tr>
<tr><td>$ 30,000.00</td><td>$ 333.06</td><td>$253.16</td><td>$214.93</td><td>$193.29</td><td>$179.87</td></tr>
<tr><td>$ 40,000.00</td><td>$ 444.08</td><td>$337.54</td><td>$286.57</td><td>$257.72</td><td>$239.82</td></tr>
<tr><td>$ 50,000.00</td><td>$ 555.10</td><td>$421.93</td><td>$358.22</td><td>$322.15</td><td>$299.78</td></tr>
<tr><td>$ 60,000.00</td><td>$ 666.12</td><td>$506.31</td><td>$429.86</td><td>$386.58</td><td>$359.73</td></tr>
<tr><td>$ 70,000.00</td><td>$ 777.14</td><td>$590.70</td><td>$501.50</td><td>$451.01</td><td>$419.69</td></tr>
<tr><td>$ 80,000.00</td><td>$ 888.16</td><td>$675.09</td><td>$573.14</td><td>$515.44</td><td>$479.64</td></tr>
<tr><td>$ 90,000.00</td><td>$ 999.18</td><td>$759.47</td><td>$644.79</td><td>$579.87</td><td>$539.60</td></tr>
<tr><td>$100,000.00</td><td>$1,110.21</td><td>$843.86</td><td>$716.43</td><td>$644.30</td><td>$599.55</td></tr>
</table>

6⅛% RATE

0.06175   Term of Loan in Years

		10		15		20		25		30
Amount										
$	50.00	$ 0.56	$ 0.43	$ 0.36	$ 0.33	$ 0.31
$	100.00	$ 1.12	$ 0.85	$ 0.73	$ 0.66	$ 0.61
$	200.00	$ 2.24	$ 1.71	$ 1.45	$ 1.31	$ 1.22
$	300.00	$ 3.36	$ 2.56	$ 2.18	$ 1.97	$ 1.83
$	400.00	$ 4.48	$ 3.41	$ 2.91	$ 2.62	$ 2.44
$	500.00	$ 5.60	$ 4.27	$ 3.63	$ 3.28	$ 3.05
$	600.00	$ 6.71	$ 5.12	$ 4.36	$ 3.93	$ 3.67
$	700.00	$ 7.83	$ 5.97	$ 5.09	$ 4.59	$ 4.28
$	800.00	$ 8.95	$ 6.83	$ 5.81	$ 5.24	$ 4.89
$	900.00	$ 10.07	$ 7.68	$ 6.54	$ 5.90	$ 5.50
$	1,000.00	$ 11.19	$ 8.53	$ 7.27	$ 6.55	$ 6.11
$	2,000.00	$ 22.38	$ 17.07	$ 14.53	$ 13.10	$ 12.22
$	3,000.00	$ 33.57	$ 25.60	$ 21.80	$ 19.65	$ 18.33
$	4,000.00	$ 44.76	$ 34.13	$ 29.06	$ 26.20	$ 24.43
$	5,000.00	$ 55.95	$ 42.67	$ 36.33	$ 32.75	$ 30.54
$	6,000.00	$ 67.14	$ 51.20	$ 43.59	$ 39.30	$ 36.65
$	7,000.00	$ 78.33	$ 59.73	$ 50.86	$ 45.85	$ 42.76
$	8,000.00	$ 89.52	$ 68.27	$ 58.13	$ 52.40	$ 48.87
$	9,000.00	$ 100.71	$ 76.80	$ 65.39	$ 58.95	$ 54.98
$	10,000.00	$ 111.90	$ 85.33	$ 72.66	$ 65.50	$ 61.08
$	20,000.00	$ 223.80	$170.67	$145.31	$131.01	$122.17
$	30,000.00	$ 335.70	$256.00	$217.97	$196.51	$183.25
$	40,000.00	$ 447.61	$341.34	$290.63	$262.02	$244.34
$	50,000.00	$ 559.51	$426.67	$363.28	$327.52	$305.42
$	60,000.00	$ 671.41	$512.00	$435.94	$393.02	$366.51
$	70,000.00	$ 783.31	$597.34	$508.59	$458.53	$427.59
$	80,000.00	$ 895.21	$682.67	$581.25	$524.03	$488.68
$	90,000.00	$1,007.11	$768.01	$653.91	$589.54	$549.76
$100,000.00		$1,119.01	$853.34	$726.56	$655.04	$610.85

357

6¼% RATE

Term of Loan in Years

Amount	10	15	20	25	30
$ 50.00	$ 0.56	$ 0.43	$ 0.37	$ 0.33	$ 0.31
$ 100.00	$ 1.12	$ 0.86	$ 0.73	$ 0.66	$ 0.62
$ 200.00	$ 2.25	$ 1.71	$ 1.46	$ 1.32	$ 1.23
$ 300.00	$ 3.37	$ 2.57	$ 2.19	$ 1.98	$ 1.85
$ 400.00	$ 4.49	$ 3.43	$ 2.92	$ 2.64	$ 2.46
$ 500.00	$ 5.61	$ 4.29	$ 3.65	$ 3.30	$ 3.08
$ 600.00	$ 6.74	$ 5.14	$ 4.39	$ 3.96	$ 3.69
$ 700.00	$ 7.86	$ 6.00	$ 5.12	$ 4.62	$ 4.31
$ 800.00	$ 8.98	$ 6.86	$ 5.85	$ 5.28	$ 4.93
$ 900.00	$ 10.11	$ 7.72	$ 6.58	$ 5.94	$ 5.54
$ 1,000.00	$ 11.23	$ 8.57	$ 7.31	$ 6.60	$ 6.16
$ 2,000.00	$ 22.46	$ 17.15	$ 14.62	$ 13.19	$ 12.31
$ 3,000.00	$ 33.68	$ 25.72	$ 21.93	$ 19.79	$ 18.47
$ 4,000.00	$ 44.91	$ 34.30	$ 29.24	$ 26.39	$ 24.63
$ 5,000.00	$ 56.14	$ 42.87	$ 36.55	$ 32.98	$ 30.79
$ 6,000.00	$ 67.37	$ 51.45	$ 43.86	$ 39.58	$ 36.94
$ 7,000.00	$ 78.60	$ 60.02	$ 51.16	$ 46.18	$ 43.10
$ 8,000.00	$ 89.82	$ 68.59	$ 58.47	$ 52.77	$ 49.26
$ 9,000.00	$ 101.05	$ 77.17	$ 65.78	$ 59.37	$ 55.41
$ 10,000.00	$ 112.28	$ 85.74	$ 73.09	$ 65.97	$ 61.57
$ 20,000.00	$ 224.56	$171.48	$146.19	$131.93	$123.14
$ 30,000.00	$ 336.84	$257.23	$219.28	$197.90	$184.72
$ 40,000.00	$ 449.12	$342.97	$292.37	$263.87	$246.29
$ 50,000.00	$ 561.40	$428.71	$365.46	$329.83	$307.86
$ 60,000.00	$ 673.68	$514.45	$438.56	$395.80	$369.43
$ 70,000.00	$ 785.96	$600.20	$511.65	$461.77	$431.00
$ 80,000.00	$ 898.24	$685.94	$584.74	$527.74	$492.57
$ 90,000.00	$1,010.52	$771.68	$657.84	$593.70	$554.15
$100,000.00	$1,122.80	$857.42	$730.93	$659.67	$615.72

6⅜% RATE

0.06375			Term of Loan in Years							
		10		15		20		25		30
Amount										
$ 50.00	$	0.56	$	0.43	$	0.37	$	0.33	$	0.31
$ 100.00	$	1.13	$	0.86	$	0.74	$	0.67	$	0.62
$ 200.00	$	2.26	$	1.73	$	1.48	$	1.33	$	1.25
$ 300.00	$	3.39	$	2.59	$	2.21	$	2.00	$	1.87
$ 400.00	$	4.52	$	3.46	$	2.95	$	2.67	$	2.50
$ 500.00	$	5.65	$	4.32	$	3.69	$	3.34	$	3.12
$ 600.00	$	6.77	$	5.19	$	4.43	$	4.00	$	3.74
$ 700.00	$	7.90	$	6.05	$	5.17	$	4.67	$	4.37
$ 800.00	$	9.03	$	6.91	$	5.91	$	5.34	$	4.99
$ 900.00	$	10.16	$	7.78	$	6.64	$	6.01	$	5.61
$ 1,000.00	$	11.29	$	8.64	$	7.38	$	6.67	$	6.24
$ 2,000.00	$	22.58	$	17.29	$	14.76	$	13.35	$	12.48
$ 3,000.00	$	33.87	$	25.93	$	22.15	$	20.02	$	18.72
$ 4,000.00	$	45.17	$	34.57	$	29.53	$	26.70	$	24.95
$ 5,000.00	$	56.46	$	43.21	$	36.91	$	33.37	$	31.19
$ 6,000.00	$	67.75	$	51.86	$	44.29	$	40.05	$	37.43
$ 7,000.00	$	79.04	$	60.50	$	51.68	$	46.72	$	43.67
$ 8,000.00	$	90.33	$	69.14	$	59.06	$	53.39	$	49.91
$ 9,000.00	$	101.62	$	77.78	$	66.44	$	60.07	$	56.15
$ 10,000.00	$	112.91	$	86.43	$	73.82	$	66.74	$	62.39
$ 20,000.00	$	225.83	$172.85		$147.65		$133.48		$124.77	
$ 30,000.00	$	338.74	$259.28		$221.47		$200.23		$187.16	
$ 40,000.00	$	451.65	$345.70		$295.29		$266.97		$249.55	
$ 50,000.00	$	564.57	$432.13		$369.12		$333.71		$311.93	
$ 60,000.00	$	677.48	$518.55		$442.94		$400.45		$374.32	
$ 70,000.00	$	790.39	$604.98		$516.76		$467.19		$436.71	
$ 80,000.00	$	903.30	$691.40		$590.59		$533.93		$499.10	
$ 90,000.00	$1,016.22		$777.83		$664.41		$600.68		$561.48	
$100,000.00	$1,129.13		$864.25		$738.23		$667.42		$623.87	

359

6½% RATE

Term of Loan in Years

Amount	10	15	20	25	30
$ 50.00	$ 0.57	$ 0.44	$ 0.37	$ 0.34	$ 0.32
$ 100.00	$ 1.14	$ 0.87	$ 0.75	$ 0.68	$ 0.63
$ 200.00	$ 2.27	$ 1.74	$ 1.49	$ 1.35	$ 1.26
$ 300.00	$ 3.41	$ 2.61	$ 2.24	$ 2.03	$ 1.90
$ 400.00	$ 4.54	$ 3.48	$ 2.98	$ 2.70	$ 2.53
$ 500.00	$ 5.68	$ 4.36	$ 3.73	$ 3.38	$ 3.16
$ 600.00	$ 6.81	$ 5.23	$ 4.47	$ 4.05	$ 3.79
$ 700.00	$ 7.95	$ 6.10	$ 5.22	$ 4.73	$ 4.42
$ 800.00	$ 9.08	$ 6.97	$ 5.96	$ 5.40	$ 5.06
$ 900.00	$ 10.22	$ 7.84	$ 6.71	$ 6.08	$ 5.69
$ 1,000.00	$ 11.35	$ 8.71	$ 7.46	$ 6.75	$ 6.32
$ 2,000.00	$ 22.71	$ 17.42	$ 14.91	$ 13.50	$ 12.64
$ 3,000.00	$ 34.06	$ 26.13	$ 22.37	$ 20.26	$ 18.96
$ 4,000.00	$ 45.42	$ 34.84	$ 29.82	$ 27.01	$ 25.28
$ 5,000.00	$ 56.77	$ 43.56	$ 37.28	$ 33.76	$ 31.60
$ 6,000.00	$ 68.13	$ 52.27	$ 44.73	$ 40.51	$ 37.92
$ 7,000.00	$ 79.48	$ 60.98	$ 52.19	$ 47.26	$ 44.24
$ 8,000.00	$ 90.84	$ 69.69	$ 59.65	$ 54.02	$ 50.57
$ 9,000.00	$ 102.19	$ 78.40	$ 67.10	$ 60.77	$ 56.89
$ 10,000.00	$ 113.55	$ 87.11	$ 74.56	$ 67.52	$ 63.21
$ 20,000.00	$ 227.10	$174.22	$149.11	$135.04	$126.41
$ 30,000.00	$ 340.64	$261.33	$223.67	$202.56	$189.62
$ 40,000.00	$ 454.19	$348.44	$298.23	$270.08	$252.83
$ 50,000.00	$ 567.74	$435.55	$372.79	$337.60	$316.03
$ 60,000.00	$ 681.29	$522.66	$447.34	$405.12	$379.24
$ 70,000.00	$ 794.84	$609.78	$521.90	$472.65	$442.45
$ 80,000.00	$ 908.38	$696.89	$596.46	$540.17	$505.65
$ 90,000.00	$1,021.93	$784.00	$671.02	$607.69	$568.86
$100,000.00	$1,135.48	$871.11	$745.57	$675.21	$632.07

6⅝% RATE

Term of Loan in Years

Amount	10	15	20	25	30
$ 50.00	$ 0.57	$ 0.44	$ 0.38	$ 0.34	$ 0.32
$ 100.00	$ 1.14	$ 0.88	$ 0.75	$ 0.68	$ 0.64
$ 200.00	$ 2.28	$ 1.76	$ 1.51	$ 1.37	$ 1.28
$ 300.00	$ 3.43	$ 2.63	$ 2.26	$ 2.05	$ 1.92
$ 400.00	$ 4.57	$ 3.51	$ 3.01	$ 2.73	$ 2.56
$ 500.00	$ 5.71	$ 4.39	$ 3.76	$ 3.42	$ 3.20
$ 600.00	$ 6.85	$ 5.27	$ 4.52	$ 4.10	$ 3.84
$ 700.00	$ 7.99	$ 6.15	$ 5.27	$ 4.78	$ 4.48
$ 800.00	$ 9.13	$ 7.02	$ 6.02	$ 5.46	$ 5.12
$ 900.00	$ 10.28	$ 7.90	$ 6.78	$ 6.15	$ 5.76
$ 1,000.00	$ 11.42	$ 8.78	$ 7.53	$ 6.83	$ 6.40
$ 2,000.00	$ 22.84	$ 17.56	$ 15.06	$ 13.66	$ 12.81
$ 3,000.00	$ 34.26	$ 26.34	$ 22.59	$ 20.49	$ 19.21
$ 4,000.00	$ 45.67	$ 35.12	$ 30.12	$ 27.32	$ 25.61
$ 5,000.00	$ 57.09	$ 43.90	$ 37.65	$ 34.15	$ 32.02
$ 6,000.00	$ 68.51	$ 52.68	$ 45.18	$ 40.98	$ 38.42
$ 7,000.00	$ 79.93	$ 61.46	$ 52.71	$ 47.81	$ 44.82
$ 8,000.00	$ 91.35	$ 70.24	$ 60.24	$ 54.64	$ 51.22
$ 9,000.00	$ 102.77	$ 79.02	$ 67.77	$ 61.47	$ 57.63
$ 10,000.00	$ 114.19	$ 87.80	$ 75.30	$ 68.30	$ 64.03
$ 20,000.00	$ 228.37	$175.60	$150.59	$136.61	$128.06
$ 30,000.00	$ 342.56	$263.40	$225.89	$204.91	$192.09
$ 40,000.00	$ 456.74	$351.20	$301.18	$273.22	$256.12
$ 50,000.00	$ 570.93	$439.00	$376.48	$341.52	$320.16
$ 60,000.00	$ 685.11	$526.80	$451.77	$409.82	$384.19
$ 70,000.00	$ 799.30	$614.60	$527.07	$478.13	$448.22
$ 80,000.00	$ 913.48	$702.40	$602.36	$546.43	$512.25
$ 90,000.00	$1,027.67	$790.19	$677.66	$614.73	$576.28
$100,000.00	$1,141.85	$877.99	$752.95	$683.04	$640.31

6¾% RATE

Term of Loan in Years

Amount	10	15	20	25	30
$ 50.00	$ 0.57	$ 0.44	$ 0.38	$ 0.35	$ 0.32
$ 100.00	$ 1.15	$ 0.88	$ 0.76	$ 0.69	$ 0.65
$ 200.00	$ 2.30	$ 1.77	$ 1.52	$ 1.38	$ 1.30
$ 300.00	$ 3.44	$ 2.65	$ 2.28	$ 2.07	$ 1.95
$ 400.00	$ 4.59	$ 3.54	$ 3.04	$ 2.76	$ 2.59
$ 500.00	$ 5.74	$ 4.42	$ 3.80	$ 3.45	$ 3.24
$ 600.00	$ 6.89	$ 5.31	$ 4.56	$ 4.15	$ 3.89
$ 700.00	$ 8.04	$ 6.19	$ 5.32	$ 4.84	$ 4.54
$ 800.00	$ 9.19	$ 7.08	$ 6.08	$ 5.53	$ 5.19
$ 900.00	$ 10.33	$ 7.96	$ 6.84	$ 6.22	$ 5.84
$ 1,000.00	$ 11.48	$ 8.85	$ 7.60	$ 6.91	$ 6.49
$ 2,000.00	$ 22.96	$ 17.70	$ 15.21	$ 13.82	$ 12.97
$ 3,000.00	$ 34.45	$ 26.55	$ 22.81	$ 20.73	$ 19.46
$ 4,000.00	$ 45.93	$ 35.40	$ 30.41	$ 27.64	$ 25.94
$ 5,000.00	$ 57.41	$ 44.25	$ 38.02	$ 34.55	$ 32.43
$ 6,000.00	$ 68.89	$ 53.09	$ 45.62	$ 41.45	$ 38.92
$ 7,000.00	$ 80.38	$ 61.94	$ 53.23	$ 48.36	$ 45.40
$ 8,000.00	$ 91.86	$ 70.79	$ 60.83	$ 55.27	$ 51.89
$ 9,000.00	$ 103.34	$ 79.64	$ 68.43	$ 62.18	$ 58.37
$ 10,000.00	$ 114.82	$ 88.49	$ 76.04	$ 69.09	$ 64.86
$ 20,000.00	$ 229.65	$176.98	$152.07	$138.18	$129.72
$ 30,000.00	$ 344.47	$265.47	$228.11	$207.27	$194.58
$ 40,000.00	$ 459.30	$353.96	$304.15	$276.36	$259.44
$ 50,000.00	$ 574.12	$442.45	$380.18	$345.46	$324.30
$ 60,000.00	$ 688.94	$530.95	$456.22	$414.55	$389.16
$ 70,000.00	$ 803.77	$619.44	$532.25	$483.64	$454.02
$ 80,000.00	$ 918.59	$707.93	$608.29	$552.73	$518.88
$ 90,000.00	$1,033.42	$796.42	$684.33	$621.82	$583.74
$100,000.00	$1,148.24	$884.91	$760.36	$690.91	$648.60

6⅞% RATE

0.06875   Term of Loan in Years

		10	15	20	25	30
Amount						
$	50.00	$ 0.58	$ 0.45	$ 0.38	$ 0.35	$ 0.33
$	100.00	$ 1.15	$ 0.89	$ 0.77	$ 0.70	$ 0.66
$	200.00	$ 2.31	$ 1.78	$ 1.54	$ 1.40	$ 1.31
$	300.00	$ 3.46	$ 2.68	$ 2.30	$ 2.10	$ 1.97
$	400.00	$ 4.62	$ 3.57	$ 3.07	$ 2.80	$ 2.63
$	500.00	$ 5.77	$ 4.46	$ 3.84	$ 3.49	$ 3.28
$	600.00	$ 6.93	$ 5.35	$ 4.61	$ 4.19	$ 3.94
$	700.00	$ 8.08	$ 6.24	$ 5.37	$ 4.89	$ 4.60
$	800.00	$ 9.24	$ 7.13	$ 6.14	$ 5.59	$ 5.26
$	900.00	$ 10.39	$ 8.03	$ 6.91	$ 6.29	$ 5.91
$	1,000.00	$ 11.55	$ 8.92	$ 7.68	$ 6.99	$ 6.57
$	2,000.00	$ 23.09	$ 17.84	$ 15.36	$ 13.98	$ 13.14
$	3,000.00	$ 34.64	$ 26.76	$ 23.03	$ 20.96	$ 19.71
$	4,000.00	$ 46.19	$ 35.67	$ 30.71	$ 27.95	$ 26.28
$	5,000.00	$ 57.73	$ 44.59	$ 38.39	$ 34.94	$ 32.85
$	6,000.00	$ 69.28	$ 53.51	$ 46.07	$ 41.93	$ 39.42
$	7,000.00	$ 80.83	$ 62.43	$ 53.75	$ 48.92	$ 45.99
$	8,000.00	$ 92.37	$ 71.35	$ 61.43	$ 55.91	$ 52.55
$	9,000.00	$ 103.92	$ 80.27	$ 69.10	$ 62.89	$ 59.12
$	10,000.00	$ 115.47	$ 89.19	$ 76.78	$ 69.88	$ 65.69
$	20,000.00	$ 230.93	$178.37	$153.56	$139.77	$131.39
$	30,000.00	$ 346.40	$267.56	$230.34	$209.65	$197.08
$	40,000.00	$ 461.86	$356.74	$307.13	$279.53	$262.77
$	50,000.00	$ 577.33	$445.93	$383.91	$349.41	$328.46
$	60,000.00	$ 692.79	$535.11	$460.69	$419.30	$394.16
$	70,000.00	$ 808.26	$624.30	$537.47	$489.18	$459.85
$	80,000.00	$ 923.72	$713.48	$614.25	$559.06	$525.54
$	90,000.00	$1,039.19	$802.67	$691.03	$628.94	$591.24
$100,000.00		$1,154.65	$891.85	$767.81	$698.83	$656.93

7% RATE

0.07	Term of Loan in Years				
	10	15	20	25	30
Amount					
$ 50.00	$ 0.58	$ 0.45	$ 0.39	$ 0.35	$ 0.33
$ 100.00	$ 1.16	$ 0.90	$ 0.78	$ 0.71	$ 0.67
$ 200.00	$ 2.32	$ 1.80	$ 1.55	$ 1.41	$ 1.33
$ 300.00	$ 3.48	$ 2.70	$ 2.33	$ 2.12	$ 2.00
$ 400.00	$ 4.64	$ 3.60	$ 3.10	$ 2.83	$ 2.66
$ 500.00	$ 5.81	$ 4.49	$ 3.88	$ 3.53	$ 3.33
$ 600.00	$ 6.97	$ 5.39	$ 4.65	$ 4.24	$ 3.99
$ 700.00	$ 8.13	$ 6.29	$ 5.43	$ 4.95	$ 4.66
$ 800.00	$ 9.29	$ 7.19	$ 6.20	$ 5.65	$ 5.32
$ 900.00	$ 10.45	$ 8.09	$ 6.98	$ 6.36	$ 5.99
$ 1,000.00	$ 11.61	$ 8.99	$ 7.75	$ 7.07	$ 6.65
$ 2,000.00	$ 23.22	$ 17.98	$ 15.51	$ 14.14	$ 13.31
$ 3,000.00	$ 34.83	$ 26.96	$ 23.26	$ 21.20	$ 19.96
$ 4,000.00	$ 46.44	$ 35.95	$ 31.01	$ 28.27	$ 26.61
$ 5,000.00	$ 58.05	$ 44.94	$ 38.76	$ 35.34	$ 33.27
$ 6,000.00	$ 69.67	$ 53.93	$ 46.52	$ 42.41	$ 39.92
$ 7,000.00	$ 81.28	$ 62.92	$ 54.27	$ 49.47	$ 46.57
$ 8,000.00	$ 92.89	$ 71.91	$ 62.02	$ 56.54	$ 53.22
$ 9,000.00	$ 104.50	$ 80.89	$ 69.78	$ 63.61	$ 59.88
$ 10,000.00	$ 116.11	$ 89.88	$ 77.53	$ 70.68	$ 66.53
$ 20,000.00	$ 232.22	$179.77	$155.06	$141.36	$133.06
$ 30,000.00	$ 348.33	$269.65	$232.59	$212.03	$199.59
$ 40,000.00	$ 464.43	$359.53	$310.12	$282.71	$266.12
$ 50,000.00	$ 580.54	$449.41	$387.65	$353.39	$332.65
$ 60,000.00	$ 696.65	$539.30	$465.18	$424.07	$399.18
$ 70,000.00	$ 812.76	$629.18	$542.71	$494.75	$465.71
$ 80,000.00	$ 928.87	$719.06	$620.24	$565.42	$532.24
$ 90,000.00	$1,044.98	$808.95	$697.77	$636.10	$598.77
$100,000.00	$1,161.08	$898.83	$775.30	$706.78	$665.30

0.07125	Term of Loan in Years				
	10	15	20	25	30
Amount					
$ 50.00	$ 0.58	$ 0.45	$ 0.39	$ 0.36	$ 0.34
$ 100.00	$ 1.17	$ 0.91	$ 0.78	$ 0.71	$ 0.67
$ 200.00	$ 2.34	$ 1.81	$ 1.57	$ 1.43	$ 1.35
$ 300.00	$ 3.50	$ 2.72	$ 2.35	$ 2.14	$ 2.02
$ 400.00	$ 4.67	$ 3.62	$ 3.13	$ 2.86	$ 2.69
$ 500.00	$ 5.84	$ 4.53	$ 3.91	$ 3.57	$ 3.37
$ 600.00	$ 7.01	$ 5.43	$ 4.70	$ 4.29	$ 4.04
$ 700.00	$ 8.17	$ 6.34	$ 5.48	$ 5.00	$ 4.72
$ 800.00	$ 9.34	$ 7.25	$ 6.26	$ 5.72	$ 5.39
$ 900.00	$ 10.51	$ 8.15	$ 7.05	$ 6.43	$ 6.06
$ 1,000.00	$ 11.68	$ 9.06	$ 7.83	$ 7.15	$ 6.74
$ 2,000.00	$ 23.35	$ 18.12	$ 15.66	$ 14.30	$ 13.47
$ 3,000.00	$ 35.03	$ 27.17	$ 23.48	$ 21.44	$ 20.21
$ 4,000.00	$ 46.70	$ 36.23	$ 31.31	$ 28.59	$ 26.95
$ 5,000.00	$ 58.38	$ 45.29	$ 39.14	$ 35.74	$ 33.69
$ 6,000.00	$ 70.05	$ 54.35	$ 46.97	$ 42.89	$ 40.42
$ 7,000.00	$ 81.73	$ 63.41	$ 54.80	$ 50.03	$ 47.16
$ 8,000.00	$ 93.40	$ 72.47	$ 62.63	$ 57.18	$ 53.90
$ 9,000.00	$ 105.08	$ 81.52	$ 70.45	$ 64.33	$ 60.63
$ 10,000.00	$ 116.75	$ 90.58	$ 78.28	$ 71.48	$ 67.37
$ 20,000.00	$ 233.51	$181.17	$156.56	$142.95	$134.74
$ 30,000.00	$ 350.26	$271.75	$234.85	$214.43	$202.12
$ 40,000.00	$ 467.01	$362.33	$313.13	$285.91	$269.49
$ 50,000.00	$ 583.77	$452.92	$391.41	$357.39	$336.86
$ 60,000.00	$ 700.52	$543.50	$469.69	$428.86	$404.23
$ 70,000.00	$ 817.28	$634.08	$547.97	$500.34	$471.60
$ 80,000.00	$ 934.03	$724.66	$626.26	$571.82	$538.97
$ 90,000.00	$1,050.78	$815.25	$704.54	$643.30	$606.35
$100,000.00	$1,167.54	$905.83	$782.82	$714.77	$673.72

7¼% RATE

Term of Loan in Years

		10	15	20	25	30
Amount						
$	50.00	$ 0.59	$ 0.46	$ 0.40	$ 0.36	$ 0.34
$	100.00	$ 1.17	$ 0.91	$ 0.79	$ 0.72	$ 0.68
$	200.00	$ 2.35	$ 1.83	$ 1.58	$ 1.45	$ 1.36
$	300.00	$ 3.52	$ 2.74	$ 2.37	$ 2.17	$ 2.05
$	400.00	$ 4.70	$ 3.65	$ 3.16	$ 2.89	$ 2.73
$	500.00	$ 5.87	$ 4.56	$ 3.95	$ 3.61	$ 3.41
$	600.00	$ 7.04	$ 5.48	$ 4.74	$ 4.34	$ 4.09
$	700.00	$ 8.22	$ 6.39	$ 5.53	$ 5.06	$ 4.78
$	800.00	$ 9.39	$ 7.30	$ 6.32	$ 5.78	$ 5.46
$	900.00	$ 10.57	$ 8.22	$ 7.11	$ 6.51	$ 6.14
$	1,000.00	$ 11.74	$ 9.13	$ 7.90	$ 7.23	$ 6.82
$	2,000.00	$ 23.48	$ 18.26	$ 15.81	$ 14.46	$ 13.64
$	3,000.00	$ 35.22	$ 27.39	$ 23.71	$ 21.68	$ 20.47
$	4,000.00	$ 46.96	$ 36.51	$ 31.62	$ 28.91	$ 27.29
$	5,000.00	$ 58.70	$ 45.64	$ 39.52	$ 36.14	$ 34.11
$	6,000.00	$ 70.44	$ 54.77	$ 47.42	$ 43.37	$ 40.93
$	7,000.00	$ 82.18	$ 63.90	$ 55.33	$ 50.60	$ 47.75
$	8,000.00	$ 93.92	$ 73.03	$ 63.23	$ 57.82	$ 54.57
$	9,000.00	$ 105.66	$ 82.16	$ 71.13	$ 65.05	$ 61.40
$	10,000.00	$ 117.40	$ 91.29	$ 79.04	$ 72.28	$ 68.22
$	20,000.00	$ 234.80	$182.57	$158.08	$144.56	$136.44
$	30,000.00	$ 352.20	$273.86	$237.11	$216.84	$204.65
$	40,000.00	$ 469.60	$365.15	$316.15	$289.12	$272.87
$	50,000.00	$ 587.01	$456.43	$395.19	$361.40	$341.09
$	60,000.00	$ 704.41	$547.72	$474.23	$433.68	$409.31
$	70,000.00	$ 821.81	$639.00	$553.26	$505.96	$477.52
$	80,000.00	$ 939.21	$730.29	$632.30	$578.25	$545.74
$	90,000.00	$1,056.61	$821.58	$711.34	$650.53	$613.96
$	100,000.00	$1,174.01	$912.86	$790.38	$722.81	$682.18

7⅜% RATE

Term of Loan in Years

Amount	10	15	20	25	30
$ 50.00	$ 0.59	$ 0.46	$ 0.40	$ 0.37	$ 0.35
$ 100.00	$ 1.18	$ 0.92	$ 0.80	$ 0.73	$ 0.69
$ 200.00	$ 2.36	$ 1.84	$ 1.60	$ 1.46	$ 1.38
$ 300.00	$ 3.54	$ 2.76	$ 2.39	$ 2.19	$ 2.07
$ 400.00	$ 4.72	$ 3.68	$ 3.19	$ 2.92	$ 2.76
$ 500.00	$ 5.90	$ 4.60	$ 3.99	$ 3.65	$ 3.45
$ 600.00	$ 7.08	$ 5.52	$ 4.79	$ 4.39	$ 4.14
$ 700.00	$ 8.26	$ 6.44	$ 5.59	$ 5.12	$ 4.83
$ 800.00	$ 9.44	$ 7.36	$ 6.38	$ 5.85	$ 5.53
$ 900.00	$ 10.62	$ 8.28	$ 7.18	$ 6.58	$ 6.22
$ 1,000.00	$ 11.81	$ 9.20	$ 7.98	$ 7.31	$ 6.91
$ 2,000.00	$ 23.61	$ 18.40	$ 15.96	$ 14.62	$ 13.81
$ 3,000.00	$ 35.42	$ 27.60	$ 23.94	$ 21.93	$ 20.72
$ 4,000.00	$ 47.22	$ 36.80	$ 31.92	$ 29.24	$ 27.63
$ 5,000.00	$ 59.03	$ 46.00	$ 39.90	$ 36.54	$ 34.53
$ 6,000.00	$ 70.83	$ 55.20	$ 47.88	$ 43.85	$ 41.44
$ 7,000.00	$ 82.64	$ 64.39	$ 55.86	$ 51.16	$ 48.35
$ 8,000.00	$ 94.44	$ 73.59	$ 63.84	$ 58.47	$ 55.25
$ 9,000.00	$ 106.25	$ 82.79	$ 71.82	$ 65.78	$ 62.16
$ 10,000.00	$ 118.05	$ 91.99	$ 79.80	$ 73.09	$ 69.07
$ 20,000.00	$ 236.10	$183.98	$159.59	$146.18	$138.14
$ 30,000.00	$ 354.15	$275.98	$239.39	$219.26	$207.20
$ 40,000.00	$ 472.20	$367.97	$319.19	$292.35	$276.27
$ 50,000.00	$ 590.25	$459.96	$398.98	$365.44	$345.34
$ 60,000.00	$ 708.30	$551.95	$478.78	$438.53	$414.41
$ 70,000.00	$ 826.35	$643.95	$558.58	$511.62	$483.47
$ 80,000.00	$ 944.40	$735.94	$638.37	$584.70	$552.54
$ 90,000.00	$1,062.45	$827.93	$718.17	$657.79	$621.61
$100,000.00	$1,180.50	$919.92	$797.97	$730.88	$690.68

7½% RATE

Term of Loan in Years

Amount		10		15		20		25		30
$	50.00	$	0.59	$	0.46	$	0.40	$	0.37	$	0.35
$	100.00	$	1.19	$	0.93	$	0.81	$	0.74	$	0.70
$	200.00	$	2.37	$	1.85	$	1.61	$	1.48	$	1.40
$	300.00	$	3.56	$	2.78	$	2.42	$	2.22	$	2.10
$	400.00	$	4.75	$	3.71	$	3.22	$	2.96	$	2.80
$	500.00	$	5.94	$	4.64	$	4.03	$	3.69	$	3.50
$	600.00	$	7.12	$	5.56	$	4.83	$	4.43	$	4.20
$	700.00	$	8.31	$	6.49	$	5.64	$	5.17	$	4.89
$	800.00	$	9.50	$	7.42	$	6.44	$	5.91	$	5.59
$	900.00	$	10.68	$	8.34	$	7.25	$	6.65	$	6.29
$	1,000.00	$	11.87	$	9.27	$	8.06	$	7.39	$	6.99
$	2,000.00	$	23.74	$	18.54	$	16.11	$	14.78	$	13.98
$	3,000.00	$	35.61	$	27.81	$	24.17	$	22.17	$	20.98
$	4,000.00	$	47.48	$	37.08	$	32.22	$	29.56	$	27.97
$	5,000.00	$	59.35	$	46.35	$	40.28	$	36.95	$	34.96
$	6,000.00	$	71.22	$	55.62	$	48.34	$	44.34	$	41.95
$	7,000.00	$	83.09	$	64.89	$	56.39	$	51.73	$	48.95
$	8,000.00	$	94.96	$	74.16	$	64.45	$	59.12	$	55.94
$	9,000.00	$	106.83	$	83.43	$	72.50	$	66.51	$	62.93
$	10,000.00	$	118.70	$	92.70	$	80.56	$	73.90	$	69.92
$	20,000.00	$	237.40	$	185.40	$	161.12	$	147.80	$	139.84
$	30,000.00	$	356.11	$	278.10	$	241.68	$	221.70	$	209.76
$	40,000.00	$	474.81	$	370.80	$	322.24	$	295.60	$	279.69
$	50,000.00	$	593.51	$	463.51	$	402.80	$	369.50	$	349.61
$	60,000.00	$	712.21	$	556.21	$	483.36	$	443.39	$	419.53
$	70,000.00	$	830.91	$	648.91	$	563.92	$	517.29	$	489.45
$	80,000.00	$	949.61	$	741.61	$	644.47	$	591.19	$	559.37
$	90,000.00	$	1,068.32	$	834.31	$	725.03	$	665.09	$	629.29
$100,000.00		$	1,187.02	$	927.01	$	805.59	$	738.99	$	699.21

0.07625			Term of Loan in Years		
	10	15	20	25	30
Amount					
$ 50.00	$ 0.60	$ 0.47	$ 0.41	$ 0.37	$ 0.35
$ 100.00	$ 1.19	$ 0.93	$ 0.81	$ 0.75	$ 0.71
$ 200.00	$ 2.39	$ 1.87	$ 1.63	$ 1.49	$ 1.42
$ 300.00	$ 3.58	$ 2.80	$ 2.44	$ 2.24	$ 2.12
$ 400.00	$ 4.77	$ 3.74	$ 3.25	$ 2.99	$ 2.83
$ 500.00	$ 5.97	$ 4.67	$ 4.07	$ 3.74	$ 3.54
$ 600.00	$ 7.16	$ 5.60	$ 4.88	$ 4.48	$ 4.25
$ 700.00	$ 8.35	$ 6.54	$ 5.69	$ 5.23	$ 4.95
$ 800.00	$ 9.55	$ 7.47	$ 6.51	$ 5.98	$ 5.66
$ 900.00	$ 10.74	$ 8.41	$ 7.32	$ 6.72	$ 6.37
$ 1,000.00	$ 11.94	$ 9.34	$ 8.13	$ 7.47	$ 7.08
$ 2,000.00	$ 23.87	$ 18.68	$ 16.27	$ 14.94	$ 14.16
$ 3,000.00	$ 35.81	$ 28.02	$ 24.40	$ 22.41	$ 21.23
$ 4,000.00	$ 47.74	$ 37.37	$ 32.53	$ 29.89	$ 28.31
$ 5,000.00	$ 59.68	$ 46.71	$ 40.66	$ 37.36	$ 35.39
$ 6,000.00	$ 71.61	$ 56.05	$ 48.80	$ 44.83	$ 42.47
$ 7,000.00	$ 83.55	$ 65.39	$ 56.93	$ 52.30	$ 49.55
$ 8,000.00	$ 95.48	$ 74.73	$ 65.06	$ 59.77	$ 56.62
$ 9,000.00	$ 107.42	$ 84.07	$ 73.19	$ 67.24	$ 63.70
$ 10,000.00	$ 119.36	$ 93.41	$ 81.33	$ 74.71	$ 70.78
$ 20,000.00	$ 238.71	$186.83	$162.65	$149.43	$141.56
$ 30,000.00	$ 358.07	$280.24	$243.98	$224.14	$212.34
$ 40,000.00	$ 477.42	$373.65	$325.30	$298.86	$283.12
$ 50,000.00	$ 596.78	$467.06	$406.63	$373.57	$353.90
$ 60,000.00	$ 716.13	$560.48	$487.95	$448.28	$424.68
$ 70,000.00	$ 835.49	$653.89	$569.28	$523.00	$495.46
$ 80,000.00	$ 954.84	$747.30	$650.60	$597.71	$566.23
$ 90,000.00	$1,074.20	$840.72	$731.93	$672.43	$637.01
$100,000.00	$1,193.55	$934.13	$813.25	$747.14	$707.79

7¾% RATE

0.0775		Term of Loan in Years				
		10	15	20	25	30
Amount						
$ 50.00	$	0.60	$ 0.47	$ 0.41	$ 0.38	$ 0.36
$ 100.00	$	1.20	$ 0.94	$ 0.82	$ 0.76	$ 0.72
$ 200.00	$	2.40	$ 1.88	$ 1.64	$ 1.51	$ 1.43
$ 300.00	$	3.60	$ 2.82	$ 2.46	$ 2.27	$ 2.15
$ 400.00	$	4.80	$ 3.77	$ 3.28	$ 3.02	$ 2.87
$ 500.00	$	6.00	$ 4.71	$ 4.10	$ 3.78	$ 3.58
$ 600.00	$	7.20	$ 5.65	$ 4.93	$ 4.53	$ 4.30
$ 700.00	$	8.40	$ 6.59	$ 5.75	$ 5.29	$ 5.01
$ 800.00	$	9.60	$ 7.53	$ 6.57	$ 6.04	$ 5.73
$ 900.00	$	10.80	$ 8.47	$ 7.39	$ 6.80	$ 6.45
$ 1,000.00	$	12.00	$ 9.41	$ 8.21	$ 7.55	$ 7.16
$ 2,000.00	$	24.00	$ 18.83	$ 16.42	$ 15.11	$ 14.33
$ 3,000.00	$	36.00	$ 28.24	$ 24.63	$ 22.66	$ 21.49
$ 4,000.00	$	48.00	$ 37.65	$ 32.84	$ 30.21	$ 28.66
$ 5,000.00	$	60.01	$ 47.06	$ 41.05	$ 37.77	$ 35.82
$ 6,000.00	$	72.01	$ 56.48	$ 49.26	$ 45.32	$ 42.98
$ 7,000.00	$	84.01	$ 65.89	$ 57.47	$ 52.87	$ 50.15
$ 8,000.00	$	96.01	$ 75.30	$ 65.68	$ 60.43	$ 57.31
$ 9,000.00	$	108.01	$ 84.71	$ 73.89	$ 67.98	$ 64.48
$ 10,000.00	$	120.01	$ 94.13	$ 82.09	$ 75.53	$ 71.64
$ 20,000.00	$	240.02	$188.26	$164.19	$151.07	$143.28
$ 30,000.00	$	360.03	$282.38	$246.28	$226.60	$214.92
$ 40,000.00	$	480.04	$376.51	$328.38	$302.13	$286.56
$ 50,000.00	$	600.05	$470.64	$410.47	$377.66	$358.21
$ 60,000.00	$	720.06	$564.77	$492.57	$453.20	$429.85
$ 70,000.00	$	840.07	$658.89	$574.66	$528.73	$501.49
$ 80,000.00	$	960.09	$753.02	$656.76	$604.26	$573.13
$ 90,000.00	$1,080.10		$847.15	$738.85	$679.80	$644.77
$100,000.00	$1,200.11		$941.28	$820.95	$755.33	$716.41

370

7⅞% RATE

0.07875   Term of Loan in Years

	10	15	20	25	30
Amount					
$ 50.00	$ 0.60	$ 0.47	$ 0.41	$ 0.38	$ 0.36
$ 100.00	$ 1.21	$ 0.95	$ 0.83	$ 0.76	$ 0.73
$ 200.00	$ 2.41	$ 1.90	$ 1.66	$ 1.53	$ 1.45
$ 300.00	$ 3.62	$ 2.85	$ 2.49	$ 2.29	$ 2.18
$ 400.00	$ 4.83	$ 3.79	$ 3.31	$ 3.05	$ 2.90
$ 500.00	$ 6.03	$ 4.74	$ 4.14	$ 3.82	$ 3.63
$ 600.00	$ 7.24	$ 5.69	$ 4.97	$ 4.58	$ 4.35
$ 700.00	$ 8.45	$ 6.64	$ 5.80	$ 5.34	$ 5.08
$ 800.00	$ 9.65	$ 7.59	$ 6.63	$ 6.11	$ 5.80
$ 900.00	$ 10.86	$ 8.54	$ 7.46	$ 6.87	$ 6.53
$ 1,000.00	$ 12.07	$ 9.48	$ 8.29	$ 7.64	$ 7.25
$ 2,000.00	$ 24.13	$ 18.97	$ 16.57	$ 15.27	$ 14.50
$ 3,000.00	$ 36.20	$ 28.45	$ 24.86	$ 22.91	$ 21.75
$ 4,000.00	$ 48.27	$ 37.94	$ 33.15	$ 30.54	$ 29.00
$ 5,000.00	$ 60.33	$ 47.42	$ 41.43	$ 38.18	$ 36.25
$ 6,000.00	$ 72.40	$ 56.91	$ 49.72	$ 45.81	$ 43.50
$ 7,000.00	$ 84.47	$ 66.39	$ 58.01	$ 53.45	$ 50.75
$ 8,000.00	$ 96.53	$ 75.88	$ 66.29	$ 61.08	$ 58.01
$ 9,000.00	$ 108.60	$ 85.36	$ 74.58	$ 68.72	$ 65.26
$ 10,000.00	$ 120.67	$ 94.84	$ 82.87	$ 76.36	$ 72.51
$ 20,000.00	$ 241.34	$189.69	$165.74	$152.71	$145.01
$ 30,000.00	$ 362.00	$284.53	$248.60	$229.07	$217.52
$ 40,000.00	$ 482.67	$379.38	$331.47	$305.42	$290.03
$ 50,000.00	$ 603.34	$474.22	$414.34	$381.78	$362.53
$ 60,000.00	$ 724.01	$569.07	$497.21	$458.13	$435.04
$ 70,000.00	$ 844.68	$663.91	$580.07	$534.49	$507.55
$ 80,000.00	$ 965.34	$758.76	$662.94	$610.84	$580.06
$ 90,000.00	$1,086.01	$853.60	$745.81	$687.20	$652.56
$100,000.00	$1,206.68	$948.45	$828.68	$763.55	$725.07

8% RATE

Term of Loan in Years

Amount	10	15	20	25	30
$ 50.00	$ 0.61	$ 0.48	$ 0.42	$ 0.39	$ 0.37
$ 100.00	$ 1.21	$ 0.96	$ 0.84	$ 0.77	$ 0.73
$ 200.00	$ 2.43	$ 1.91	$ 1.67	$ 1.54	$ 1.47
$ 300.00	$ 3.64	$ 2.87	$ 2.51	$ 2.32	$ 2.20
$ 400.00	$ 4.85	$ 3.82	$ 3.35	$ 3.09	$ 2.94
$ 500.00	$ 6.07	$ 4.78	$ 4.18	$ 3.86	$ 3.67
$ 600.00	$ 7.28	$ 5.73	$ 5.02	$ 4.63	$ 4.40
$ 700.00	$ 8.49	$ 6.69	$ 5.86	$ 5.40	$ 5.14
$ 800.00	$ 9.71	$ 7.65	$ 6.69	$ 6.17	$ 5.87
$ 900.00	$ 10.92	$ 8.60	$ 7.53	$ 6.95	$ 6.60
$ 1,000.00	$ 12.13	$ 9.56	$ 8.36	$ 7.72	$ 7.34
$ 2,000.00	$ 24.27	$ 19.11	$ 16.73	$ 15.44	$ 14.68
$ 3,000.00	$ 36.40	$ 28.67	$ 25.09	$ 23.15	$ 22.01
$ 4,000.00	$ 48.53	$ 38.23	$ 33.46	$ 30.87	$ 29.35
$ 5,000.00	$ 60.66	$ 47.78	$ 41.82	$ 38.59	$ 36.69
$ 6,000.00	$ 72.80	$ 57.34	$ 50.19	$ 46.31	$ 44.03
$ 7,000.00	$ 84.93	$ 66.90	$ 58.55	$ 54.03	$ 51.36
$ 8,000.00	$ 97.06	$ 76.45	$ 66.92	$ 61.75	$ 58.70
$ 9,000.00	$ 109.19	$ 86.01	$ 75.28	$ 69.46	$ 66.04
$ 10,000.00	$ 121.33	$ 95.57	$ 83.64	$ 77.18	$ 73.38
$ 20,000.00	$ 242.66	$191.13	$167.29	$154.36	$146.75
$ 30,000.00	$ 363.98	$286.70	$250.93	$231.54	$220.13
$ 40,000.00	$ 485.31	$382.26	$334.58	$308.73	$293.51
$ 50,000.00	$ 606.64	$477.83	$418.22	$385.91	$366.88
$ 60,000.00	$ 727.97	$573.39	$501.86	$463.09	$440.26
$ 70,000.00	$ 849.29	$668.96	$585.51	$540.27	$513.64
$ 80,000.00	$ 970.62	$764.52	$669.15	$617.45	$587.01
$ 90,000.00	$1,091.95	$860.09	$752.80	$694.63	$660.39
$100,000.00	$1,213.28	$955.65	$836.44	$771.82	$733.76

8⅛% RATE

Term of Loan in Years

Amount	10	15	20	25	30
$ 50.00	$ 0.61	$ 0.48	$ 0.42	$ 0.39	$ 0.37
$ 100.00	$ 1.22	$ 0.96	$ 0.84	$ 0.78	$ 0.74
$ 200.00	$ 2.44	$ 1.93	$ 1.69	$ 1.56	$ 1.48
$ 300.00	$ 3.66	$ 2.89	$ 2.53	$ 2.34	$ 2.23
$ 400.00	$ 4.88	$ 3.85	$ 3.38	$ 3.12	$ 2.97
$ 500.00	$ 6.10	$ 4.81	$ 4.22	$ 3.90	$ 3.71
$ 600.00	$ 7.32	$ 5.78	$ 5.07	$ 4.68	$ 4.45
$ 700.00	$ 8.54	$ 6.74	$ 5.91	$ 5.46	$ 5.20
$ 800.00	$ 9.76	$ 7.70	$ 6.75	$ 6.24	$ 5.94
$ 900.00	$ 10.98	$ 8.67	$ 7.60	$ 7.02	$ 6.68
$ 1,000.00	$ 12.20	$ 9.63	$ 8.44	$ 7.80	$ 7.42
$ 2,000.00	$ 24.40	$ 19.26	$ 16.88	$ 15.60	$ 14.85
$ 3,000.00	$ 36.60	$ 28.89	$ 25.33	$ 23.40	$ 22.27
$ 4,000.00	$ 48.80	$ 38.52	$ 33.77	$ 31.20	$ 29.70
$ 5,000.00	$ 60.99	$ 48.14	$ 42.21	$ 39.01	$ 37.12
$ 6,000.00	$ 73.19	$ 57.77	$ 50.65	$ 46.81	$ 44.55
$ 7,000.00	$ 85.39	$ 67.40	$ 59.10	$ 54.61	$ 51.97
$ 8,000.00	$ 97.59	$ 77.03	$ 67.54	$ 62.41	$ 59.40
$ 9,000.00	$ 109.79	$ 86.66	$ 75.98	$ 70.21	$ 66.82
$ 10,000.00	$ 121.99	$ 96.29	$ 84.42	$ 78.01	$ 74.25
$ 20,000.00	$ 243.98	$192.58	$168.85	$156.02	$148.50
$ 30,000.00	$ 365.97	$288.86	$253.27	$234.03	$222.75
$ 40,000.00	$ 487.96	$385.15	$337.69	$312.05	$297.00
$ 50,000.00	$ 609.95	$481.44	$422.12	$390.06	$371.25
$ 60,000.00	$ 731.93	$577.73	$506.54	$468.07	$445.50
$ 70,000.00	$ 853.92	$674.02	$590.97	$546.08	$519.75
$ 80,000.00	$ 975.91	$770.31	$675.39	$624.09	$594.00
$ 90,000.00	$1,097.90	$866.59	$759.81	$702.10	$668.25
$100,000.00	$1,219.89	$962.88	$844.24	$780.12	$742.50

8¼% RATE

0.0825   Term of Loan in Years

Amount	10	15	20	25	30
$ 50.00	$ 0.61	$ 0.49	$ 0.43	$ 0.39	$ 0.38
$ 100.00	$ 1.23	$ 0.97	$ 0.85	$ 0.79	$ 0.75
$ 200.00	$ 2.45	$ 1.94	$ 1.70	$ 1.58	$ 1.50
$ 300.00	$ 3.68	$ 2.91	$ 2.56	$ 2.37	$ 2.25
$ 400.00	$ 4.91	$ 3.88	$ 3.41	$ 3.15	$ 3.01
$ 500.00	$ 6.13	$ 4.85	$ 4.26	$ 3.94	$ 3.76
$ 600.00	$ 7.36	$ 5.82	$ 5.11	$ 4.73	$ 4.51
$ 700.00	$ 8.59	$ 6.79	$ 5.96	$ 5.52	$ 5.26
$ 800.00	$ 9.81	$ 7.76	$ 6.82	$ 6.31	$ 6.01
$ 900.00	$ 11.04	$ 8.73	$ 7.67	$ 7.10	$ 6.76
$ 1,000.00	$ 12.27	$ 9.70	$ 8.52	$ 7.88	$ 7.51
$ 2,000.00	$ 24.53	$ 19.40	$ 17.04	$ 15.77	$ 15.03
$ 3,000.00	$ 36.80	$ 29.10	$ 25.56	$ 23.65	$ 22.54
$ 4,000.00	$ 49.06	$ 38.81	$ 34.08	$ 31.54	$ 30.05
$ 5,000.00	$ 61.33	$ 48.51	$ 42.60	$ 39.42	$ 37.56
$ 6,000.00	$ 73.59	$ 58.21	$ 51.12	$ 47.31	$ 45.08
$ 7,000.00	$ 85.86	$ 67.91	$ 59.64	$ 55.19	$ 52.59
$ 8,000.00	$ 98.12	$ 77.61	$ 68.17	$ 63.08	$ 60.10
$ 9,000.00	$ 110.39	$ 87.31	$ 76.69	$ 70.96	$ 67.61
$ 10,000.00	$ 122.65	$ 97.01	$ 85.21	$ 78.85	$ 75.13
$ 20,000.00	$ 245.31	$194.03	$170.41	$157.69	$150.25
$ 30,000.00	$ 367.96	$291.04	$255.62	$236.54	$225.38
$ 40,000.00	$ 490.61	$388.06	$340.83	$315.38	$300.51
$ 50,000.00	$ 613.26	$485.07	$426.03	$394.23	$375.63
$ 60,000.00	$ 735.92	$582.08	$511.24	$473.07	$450.76
$ 70,000.00	$ 858.57	$679.10	$596.45	$551.92	$525.89
$ 80,000.00	$ 981.22	$776.11	$681.65	$630.76	$601.01
$ 90,000.00	$1,103.87	$873.13	$766.86	$709.61	$676.14
$100,000.00	$1,226.53	$970.14	$852.07	$788.45	$751.27

8⅜% RATE

Term of Loan in Years

Amount	10	15	20	25	30
$ 50.00	$ 0.62	$ 0.49	$ 0.43	$ 0.40	$ 0.38
$ 100.00	$ 1.23	$ 0.98	$ 0.86	$ 0.80	$ 0.76
$ 200.00	$ 2.47	$ 1.95	$ 1.72	$ 1.59	$ 1.52
$ 300.00	$ 3.70	$ 2.93	$ 2.58	$ 2.39	$ 2.28
$ 400.00	$ 4.93	$ 3.91	$ 3.44	$ 3.19	$ 3.04
$ 500.00	$ 6.17	$ 4.89	$ 4.30	$ 3.98	$ 3.80
$ 600.00	$ 7.40	$ 5.86	$ 5.16	$ 4.78	$ 4.56
$ 700.00	$ 8.63	$ 6.84	$ 6.02	$ 5.58	$ 5.32
$ 800.00	$ 9.87	$ 7.82	$ 6.88	$ 6.37	$ 6.08
$ 900.00	$ 11.10	$ 8.80	$ 7.74	$ 7.17	$ 6.84
$ 1,000.00	$ 12.33	$ 9.77	$ 8.60	$ 7.97	$ 7.60
$ 2,000.00	$ 24.66	$ 19.55	$ 17.20	$ 15.94	$ 15.20
$ 3,000.00	$ 37.00	$ 29.32	$ 25.80	$ 23.90	$ 22.80
$ 4,000.00	$ 49.33	$ 39.10	$ 34.40	$ 31.87	$ 30.40
$ 5,000.00	$ 61.66	$ 48.87	$ 43.00	$ 39.84	$ 38.00
$ 6,000.00	$ 73.99	$ 58.65	$ 51.60	$ 47.81	$ 45.60
$ 7,000.00	$ 86.32	$ 68.42	$ 60.19	$ 55.78	$ 53.21
$ 8,000.00	$ 98.65	$ 78.19	$ 68.79	$ 63.75	$ 60.81
$ 9,000.00	$ 110.99	$ 87.97	$ 77.39	$ 71.71	$ 68.41
$ 10,000.00	$ 123.32	$ 97.74	$ 85.99	$ 79.68	$ 76.01
$ 20,000.00	$ 246.64	$195.49	$171.99	$159.36	$152.01
$ 30,000.00	$ 369.95	$293.23	$257.98	$239.05	$228.02
$ 40,000.00	$ 493.27	$390.97	$343.97	$318.73	$304.03
$ 50,000.00	$ 616.59	$488.71	$429.96	$398.41	$380.04
$ 60,000.00	$ 739.91	$586.46	$515.96	$478.09	$456.04
$ 70,000.00	$ 863.23	$684.20	$601.95	$557.77	$532.05
$ 80,000.00	$ 986.55	$781.94	$687.94	$637.46	$608.06
$ 90,000.00	$1,109.86	$879.68	$773.94	$717.14	$684.07
$100,000.00	$1,233.18	$977.43	$859.93	$796.82	$760.07

8½% RATE

Term of Loan in Years

	10	15	20	25	30
Amount					
$ 50.00	$ 0.62	$ 0.49	$ 0.43	$ 0.40	$ 0.38
$ 100.00	$ 1.24	$ 0.98	$ 0.87	$ 0.81	$ 0.77
$ 200.00	$ 2.48	$ 1.97	$ 1.74	$ 1.61	$ 1.54
$ 300.00	$ 3.72	$ 2.95	$ 2.60	$ 2.42	$ 2.31
$ 400.00	$ 4.96	$ 3.94	$ 3.47	$ 3.22	$ 3.08
$ 500.00	$ 6.20	$ 4.92	$ 4.34	$ 4.03	$ 3.84
$ 600.00	$ 7.44	$ 5.91	$ 5.21	$ 4.83	$ 4.61
$ 700.00	$ 8.68	$ 6.89	$ 6.07	$ 5.64	$ 5.38
$ 800.00	$ 9.92	$ 7.88	$ 6.94	$ 6.44	$ 6.15
$ 900.00	$ 11.16	$ 8.86	$ 7.81	$ 7.25	$ 6.92
$ 1,000.00	$ 12.40	$ 9.85	$ 8.68	$ 8.05	$ 7.69
$ 2,000.00	$ 24.80	$ 19.69	$ 17.36	$ 16.10	$ 15.38
$ 3,000.00	$ 37.20	$ 29.54	$ 26.03	$ 24.16	$ 23.07
$ 4,000.00	$ 49.59	$ 39.39	$ 34.71	$ 32.21	$ 30.76
$ 5,000.00	$ 61.99	$ 49.24	$ 43.39	$ 40.26	$ 38.45
$ 6,000.00	$ 74.39	$ 59.08	$ 52.07	$ 48.31	$ 46.13
$ 7,000.00	$ 86.79	$ 68.93	$ 60.75	$ 56.37	$ 53.82
$ 8,000.00	$ 99.19	$ 78.78	$ 69.43	$ 64.42	$ 61.51
$ 9,000.00	$ 111.59	$ 88.63	$ 78.10	$ 72.47	$ 69.20
$ 10,000.00	$ 123.99	$ 98.47	$ 86.78	$ 80.52	$ 76.89
$ 20,000.00	$ 247.97	$196.95	$173.56	$161.05	$153.78
$ 30,000.00	$ 371.96	$295.42	$260.35	$241.57	$230.67
$ 40,000.00	$ 495.94	$393.90	$347.13	$322.09	$307.57
$ 50,000.00	$ 619.93	$492.37	$433.91	$402.61	$384.46
$ 60,000.00	$ 743.91	$590.84	$520.69	$483.14	$461.35
$ 70,000.00	$ 867.90	$689.32	$607.48	$563.66	$538.24
$ 80,000.00	$ 991.89	$787.79	$694.26	$644.18	$615.13
$ 90,000.00	$1,115.87	$886.27	$781.04	$724.70	$692.02
$100,000.00	$1,239.86	$984.74	$867.82	$805.23	$768.91

8⅝% RATE

Term of Loan in Years

Amount	10	15	20	25	30
$ 50.00	$ 0.62	$ 0.50	$ 0.44	$ 0.41	$ 0.39
$ 100.00	$ 1.25	$ 0.99	$ 0.88	$ 0.81	$ 0.78
$ 200.00	$ 2.49	$ 1.98	$ 1.75	$ 1.63	$ 1.56
$ 300.00	$ 3.74	$ 2.98	$ 2.63	$ 2.44	$ 2.33
$ 400.00	$ 4.99	$ 3.97	$ 3.50	$ 3.25	$ 3.11
$ 500.00	$ 6.23	$ 4.96	$ 4.38	$ 4.07	$ 3.89
$ 600.00	$ 7.48	$ 5.95	$ 5.25	$ 4.88	$ 4.67
$ 700.00	$ 8.73	$ 6.94	$ 6.13	$ 5.70	$ 5.44
$ 800.00	$ 9.97	$ 7.94	$ 7.01	$ 6.51	$ 6.22
$ 900.00	$ 11.22	$ 8.93	$ 7.88	$ 7.32	$ 7.00
$ 1,000.00	$ 12.47	$ 9.92	$ 8.76	$ 8.14	$ 7.78
$ 2,000.00	$ 24.93	$ 19.84	$ 17.52	$ 16.27	$ 15.56
$ 3,000.00	$ 37.40	$ 29.76	$ 26.27	$ 24.41	$ 23.33
$ 4,000.00	$ 49.86	$ 39.68	$ 35.03	$ 32.55	$ 31.11
$ 5,000.00	$ 62.33	$ 49.60	$ 43.79	$ 40.68	$ 38.89
$ 6,000.00	$ 74.79	$ 59.52	$ 52.55	$ 48.82	$ 46.67
$ 7,000.00	$ 87.26	$ 69.45	$ 61.30	$ 56.96	$ 54.45
$ 8,000.00	$ 99.72	$ 79.37	$ 70.06	$ 65.09	$ 62.22
$ 9,000.00	$ 112.19	$ 89.29	$ 78.82	$ 73.23	$ 70.00
$ 10,000.00	$ 124.66	$ 99.21	$ 87.58	$ 81.37	$ 77.78
$ 20,000.00	$ 249.31	$198.42	$175.15	$162.73	$155.56
$ 30,000.00	$ 373.97	$297.62	$262.73	$244.10	$233.34
$ 40,000.00	$ 498.62	$396.83	$350.30	$325.47	$311.12
$ 50,000.00	$ 623.28	$496.04	$437.88	$406.83	$388.89
$ 60,000.00	$ 747.93	$595.25	$525.45	$488.20	$466.67
$ 70,000.00	$ 872.59	$694.46	$613.03	$569.57	$544.45
$ 80,000.00	$ 997.24	$793.66	$700.60	$650.93	$622.23
$ 90,000.00	$1,121.90	$892.87	$788.18	$732.30	$700.01
$100,000.00	$1,246.55	$992.08	$875.75	$813.67	$777.79

8¾% RATE

0.0875			Term of Loan in Years		
	10	15	20	25	30
Amount					
$ 50.00	$ 0.63	$ 0.50	$ 0.44	$ 0.41	$ 0.39
$ 100.00	$ 1.25	$ 1.00	$ 0.88	$ 0.82	$ 0.79
$ 200.00	$ 2.51	$ 2.00	$ 1.77	$ 1.64	$ 1.57
$ 300.00	$ 3.76	$ 3.00	$ 2.65	$ 2.47	$ 2.36
$ 400.00	$ 5.01	$ 4.00	$ 3.53	$ 3.29	$ 3.15
$ 500.00	$ 6.27	$ 5.00	$ 4.42	$ 4.11	$ 3.93
$ 600.00	$ 7.52	$ 6.00	$ 5.30	$ 4.93	$ 4.72
$ 700.00	$ 8.77	$ 7.00	$ 6.19	$ 5.76	$ 5.51
$ 800.00	$ 10.03	$ 8.00	$ 7.07	$ 6.58	$ 6.29
$ 900.00	$ 11.28	$ 9.00	$ 7.95	$ 7.40	$ 7.08
$ 1,000.00	$ 12.53	$ 9.99	$ 8.84	$ 8.22	$ 7.87
$ 2,000.00	$ 25.07	$ 19.99	$ 17.67	$ 16.44	$ 15.73
$ 3,000.00	$ 37.60	$ 29.98	$ 26.51	$ 24.66	$ 23.60
$ 4,000.00	$ 50.13	$ 39.98	$ 35.35	$ 32.89	$ 31.47
$ 5,000.00	$ 62.66	$ 49.97	$ 44.19	$ 41.11	$ 39.34
$ 6,000.00	$ 75.20	$ 59.97	$ 53.02	$ 49.33	$ 47.20
$ 7,000.00	$ 87.73	$ 69.96	$ 61.86	$ 57.55	$ 55.07
$ 8,000.00	$ 100.26	$ 79.96	$ 70.70	$ 65.77	$ 62.94
$ 9,000.00	$ 112.79	$ 89.95	$ 79.53	$ 73.99	$ 70.80
$ 10,000.00	$ 125.33	$ 99.94	$ 88.37	$ 82.21	$ 78.67
$ 20,000.00	$ 250.65	$199.89	$176.74	$164.43	$157.34
$ 30,000.00	$ 375.98	$299.83	$265.11	$246.64	$236.01
$ 40,000.00	$ 501.31	$399.78	$353.48	$328.86	$314.68
$ 50,000.00	$ 626.63	$499.72	$441.86	$411.07	$393.35
$ 60,000.00	$ 751.96	$599.67	$530.23	$493.29	$472.02
$ 70,000.00	$ 877.29	$699.61	$618.60	$575.50	$550.69
$ 80,000.00	$1,002.61	$799.56	$706.97	$657.71	$629.36
$ 90,000.00	$1,127.94	$899.50	$795.34	$739.93	$708.03
$100,000.00	$1,253.27	$999.45	$883.71	$822.14	$786.70

8⅞% RATE

Amount		10		15		20		25		30
$ 50.00	$	0.63	$	0.50	$	0.45	$	0.42	$	0.40
$ 100.00	$	1.26	$	1.01	$	0.89	$	0.83	$	0.80
$ 200.00	$	2.52	$	2.01	$	1.78	$	1.66	$	1.59
$ 300.00	$	3.78	$	3.02	$	2.68	$	2.49	$	2.39
$ 400.00	$	5.04	$	4.03	$	3.57	$	3.32	$	3.18
$ 500.00	$	6.30	$	5.03	$	4.46	$	4.15	$	3.98
$ 600.00	$	7.56	$	6.04	$	5.35	$	4.98	$	4.77
$ 700.00	$	8.82	$	7.05	$	6.24	$	5.81	$	5.57
$ 800.00	$	10.08	$	8.05	$	7.13	$	6.65	$	6.37
$ 900.00	$	11.34	$	9.06	$	8.03	$	7.48	$	7.16
$ 1,000.00	$	12.60	$	10.07	$	8.92	$	8.31	$	7.96
$ 2,000.00	$	25.20	$	20.14	$	17.83	$	16.61	$	15.91
$ 3,000.00	$	37.80	$	30.21	$	26.75	$	24.92	$	23.87
$ 4,000.00	$	50.40	$	40.27	$	35.67	$	33.23	$	31.83
$ 5,000.00	$	63.00	$	50.34	$	44.59	$	41.53	$	39.78
$ 6,000.00	$	75.60	$	60.41	$	53.50	$	49.84	$	47.74
$ 7,000.00	$	88.20	$	70.48	$	62.42	$	58.15	$	55.70
$ 8,000.00	$	100.80	$	80.55	$	71.34	$	66.45	$	63.65
$ 9,000.00	$	113.40	$	90.62	$	80.25	$	74.76	$	71.61
$ 10,000.00	$	126.00	$	100.68	$	89.17	$	83.07	$	79.56
$ 20,000.00	$	252.00	$	201.37	$178.34		$166.13		$159.13
$ 30,000.00	$	378.00	$	302.05	$267.51		$249.20		$238.69
$ 40,000.00	$	504.00	$	402.74	$356.68		$332.26		$318.26
$ 50,000.00	$	630.00	$	503.42	$445.85		$415.33		$397.82
$ 60,000.00	$	756.00	$	604.11	$535.02		$498.39		$477.39
$ 70,000.00	$	882.00	$	704.79	$624.19		$581.46		$556.95
$ 80,000.00	$1,008.00		$	805.48	$713.36		$664.52		$636.52
$ 90,000.00	$1,134.00		$	906.16	$802.53		$747.59		$716.08
$100,000.00	$1,260.00		$1,006.84		$891.70		$830.65		$795.64

9% RATE

Term of Loan in Years

Amount	10	15	20	25	30
$ 50.00	$ 0.63	$ 0.51	$ 0.45	$ 0.42	$ 0.40
$ 100.00	$ 1.27	$ 1.01	$ 0.90	$ 0.84	$ 0.80
$ 200.00	$ 2.53	$ 2.03	$ 1.80	$ 1.68	$ 1.61
$ 300.00	$ 3.80	$ 3.04	$ 2.70	$ 2.52	$ 2.41
$ 400.00	$ 5.07	$ 4.06	$ 3.60	$ 3.36	$ 3.22
$ 500.00	$ 6.33	$ 5.07	$ 4.50	$ 4.20	$ 4.02
$ 600.00	$ 7.60	$ 6.09	$ 5.40	$ 5.04	$ 4.83
$ 700.00	$ 8.87	$ 7.10	$ 6.30	$ 5.87	$ 5.63
$ 800.00	$ 10.13	$ 8.11	$ 7.20	$ 6.71	$ 6.44
$ 900.00	$ 11.40	$ 9.13	$ 8.10	$ 7.55	$ 7.24
$ 1,000.00	$ 12.67	$ 10.14	$ 9.00	$ 8.39	$ 8.05
$ 2,000.00	$ 25.34	$ 20.29	$ 17.99	$ 16.78	$ 16.09
$ 3,000.00	$ 38.00	$ 30.43	$ 26.99	$ 25.18	$ 24.14
$ 4,000.00	$ 50.67	$ 40.57	$ 35.99	$ 33.57	$ 32.18
$ 5,000.00	$ 63.34	$ 50.71	$ 44.99	$ 41.96	$ 40.23
$ 6,000.00	$ 76.01	$ 60.86	$ 53.98	$ 50.35	$ 48.28
$ 7,000.00	$ 88.67	$ 71.00	$ 62.98	$ 58.74	$ 56.32
$ 8,000.00	$ 101.34	$ 81.14	$ 71.98	$ 67.14	$ 64.37
$ 9,000.00	$ 114.01	$ 91.28	$ 80.98	$ 75.53	$ 72.42
$ 10,000.00	$ 126.68	$ 101.43	$ 89.97	$ 83.92	$ 80.46
$ 20,000.00	$ 253.35	$ 202.85	$179.95	$167.84	$160.92
$ 30,000.00	$ 380.03	$ 304.28	$269.92	$251.76	$241.39
$ 40,000.00	$ 506.70	$ 405.71	$359.89	$335.68	$321.85
$ 50,000.00	$ 633.38	$ 507.13	$449.86	$419.60	$402.31
$ 60,000.00	$ 760.05	$ 608.56	$539.84	$503.52	$482.77
$ 70,000.00	$ 886.73	$ 709.99	$629.81	$587.44	$563.24
$ 80,000.00	$1,013.41	$ 811.41	$719.78	$671.36	$643.70
$ 90,000.00	$1,140.08	$ 912.84	$809.75	$755.28	$724.16
$100,000.00	$1,266.76	$1,014.27	$899.73	$839.20	$804.62

9⅛% RATE

Term of Loan in Years

Amount	10	15	20	25	30
$ 50.00	$ 0.64	$ 0.51	$ 0.45	$ 0.42	$ 0.41
$ 100.00	$ 1.27	$ 1.02	$ 0.91	$ 0.85	$ 0.81
$ 200.00	$ 2.55	$ 2.04	$ 1.82	$ 1.70	$ 1.63
$ 300.00	$ 3.82	$ 3.07	$ 2.72	$ 2.54	$ 2.44
$ 400.00	$ 5.09	$ 4.09	$ 3.63	$ 3.39	$ 3.25
$ 500.00	$ 6.37	$ 5.11	$ 4.54	$ 4.24	$ 4.07
$ 600.00	$ 7.64	$ 6.13	$ 5.45	$ 5.09	$ 4.88
$ 700.00	$ 8.91	$ 7.15	$ 6.35	$ 5.93	$ 5.70
$ 800.00	$ 10.19	$ 8.17	$ 7.26	$ 6.78	$ 6.51
$ 900.00	$ 11.46	$ 9.20	$ 8.17	$ 7.63	$ 7.32
$ 1,000.00	$ 12.74	$ 10.22	$ 9.08	$ 8.48	$ 8.14
$ 2,000.00	$ 25.47	$ 20.43	$ 18.16	$ 16.96	$ 16.27
$ 3,000.00	$ 38.21	$ 30.65	$ 27.23	$ 25.43	$ 24.41
$ 4,000.00	$ 50.94	$ 40.87	$ 36.31	$ 33.91	$ 32.55
$ 5,000.00	$ 63.68	$ 51.09	$ 45.39	$ 42.39	$ 40.68
$ 6,000.00	$ 76.41	$ 61.30	$ 54.47	$ 50.87	$ 48.82
$ 7,000.00	$ 89.15	$ 71.52	$ 63.54	$ 59.34	$ 56.95
$ 8,000.00	$ 101.88	$ 81.74	$ 72.62	$ 67.82	$ 65.09
$ 9,000.00	$ 114.62	$ 91.95	$ 81.70	$ 76.30	$ 73.23
$ 10,000.00	$ 127.35	$ 102.17	$ 90.78	$ 84.78	$ 81.36
$ 20,000.00	$ 254.71	$ 204.34	$181.56	$169.55	$162.73
$ 30,000.00	$ 382.06	$ 306.51	$272.33	$254.33	$244.09
$ 40,000.00	$ 509.41	$ 408.69	$363.11	$339.11	$325.45
$ 50,000.00	$ 636.77	$ 510.86	$453.89	$423.89	$406.82
$ 60,000.00	$ 764.12	$ 613.03	$544.67	$508.66	$488.18
$ 70,000.00	$ 891.47	$ 715.20	$635.45	$593.44	$569.54
$ 80,000.00	$1,018.83	$ 817.37	$726.22	$678.22	$650.91
$ 90,000.00	$1,146.18	$ 919.54	$817.00	$763.00	$732.27
$100,000.00	$1,273.53	$1,021.72	$907.78	$847.77	$813.63

9¼% RATE

0.0925	Term of Loan in Years				
	10	15	20	25	30
Amount					
$ 50.00	$ 0.64	$ 0.51	$ 0.46	$ 0.43	$ 0.41
$ 100.00	$ 1.28	$ 1.03	$ 0.92	$ 0.86	$ 0.82
$ 200.00	$ 2.56	$ 2.06	$ 1.83	$ 1.71	$ 1.65
$ 300.00	$ 3.84	$ 3.09	$ 2.75	$ 2.57	$ 2.47
$ 400.00	$ 5.12	$ 4.12	$ 3.66	$ 3.43	$ 3.29
$ 500.00	$ 6.40	$ 5.15	$ 4.58	$ 4.28	$ 4.11
$ 600.00	$ 7.68	$ 6.18	$ 5.50	$ 5.14	$ 4.94
$ 700.00	$ 8.96	$ 7.20	$ 6.41	$ 5.99	$ 5.76
$ 800.00	$ 10.24	$ 8.23	$ 7.33	$ 6.85	$ 6.58
$ 900.00	$ 11.52	$ 9.26	$ 8.24	$ 7.71	$ 7.40
$ 1,000.00	$ 12.80	$ 10.29	$ 9.16	$ 8.56	$ 8.23
$ 2,000.00	$ 25.61	$ 20.58	$ 18.32	$ 17.13	$ 16.45
$ 3,000.00	$ 38.41	$ 30.88	$ 27.48	$ 25.69	$ 24.68
$ 4,000.00	$ 51.21	$ 41.17	$ 36.63	$ 34.26	$ 32.91
$ 5,000.00	$ 64.02	$ 51.46	$ 45.79	$ 42.82	$ 41.13
$ 6,000.00	$ 76.82	$ 61.75	$ 54.95	$ 51.38	$ 49.36
$ 7,000.00	$ 89.62	$ 72.04	$ 64.11	$ 59.95	$ 57.59
$ 8,000.00	$ 102.43	$ 82.34	$ 73.27	$ 68.51	$ 65.81
$ 9,000.00	$ 115.23	$ 92.63	$ 82.43	$ 77.07	$ 74.04
$ 10,000.00	$ 128.03	$ 102.92	$ 91.59	$ 85.64	$ 82.27
$ 20,000.00	$ 256.07	$ 205.84	$183.17	$171.28	$164.54
$ 30,000.00	$ 384.10	$ 308.76	$274.76	$256.91	$246.80
$ 40,000.00	$ 512.13	$ 411.68	$366.35	$342.55	$329.07
$ 50,000.00	$ 640.16	$ 514.60	$457.93	$428.19	$411.34
$ 60,000.00	$ 768.20	$ 617.52	$549.52	$513.83	$493.61
$ 70,000.00	$ 896.23	$ 720.43	$641.11	$599.47	$575.87
$ 80,000.00	$1,024.26	$ 823.35	$732.69	$685.11	$658.14
$ 90,000.00	$1,152.29	$ 926.27	$824.28	$770.74	$740.41
$100,000.00	$1,280.33	$1,029.19	$915.87	$856.38	$822.68

9⅜% RATE

Amount	10	15	20	25	30
		Term of Loan in Years			
$ 50.00	$ 0.64	$ 0.52	$ 0.46	$ 0.43	$ 0.42
$ 100.00	$ 1.29	$ 1.04	$ 0.92	$ 0.87	$ 0.83
$ 200.00	$ 2.57	$ 2.07	$ 1.85	$ 1.73	$ 1.66
$ 300.00	$ 3.86	$ 3.11	$ 2.77	$ 2.60	$ 2.50
$ 400.00	$ 5.15	$ 4.15	$ 3.70	$ 3.46	$ 3.33
$ 500.00	$ 6.44	$ 5.18	$ 4.62	$ 4.33	$ 4.16
$ 600.00	$ 7.72	$ 6.22	$ 5.54	$ 5.19	$ 4.99
$ 700.00	$ 9.01	$ 7.26	$ 6.47	$ 6.06	$ 5.82
$ 800.00	$ 10.30	$ 8.29	$ 7.39	$ 6.92	$ 6.65
$ 900.00	$ 11.58	$ 9.33	$ 8.32	$ 7.79	$ 7.49
$ 1,000.00	$ 12.87	$ 10.37	$ 9.24	$ 8.65	$ 8.32
$ 2,000.00	$ 25.74	$ 20.73	$ 18.48	$ 17.30	$ 16.63
$ 3,000.00	$ 38.61	$ 31.10	$ 27.72	$ 25.95	$ 24.95
$ 4,000.00	$ 51.49	$ 41.47	$ 36.96	$ 34.60	$ 33.27
$ 5,000.00	$ 64.36	$ 51.83	$ 46.20	$ 43.25	$ 41.59
$ 6,000.00	$ 77.23	$ 62.20	$ 55.44	$ 51.90	$ 49.90
$ 7,000.00	$ 90.10	$ 72.57	$ 64.68	$ 60.55	$ 58.22
$ 8,000.00	$ 102.97	$ 82.94	$ 73.92	$ 69.20	$ 66.54
$ 9,000.00	$ 115.84	$ 93.30	$ 83.16	$ 77.85	$ 74.86
$ 10,000.00	$ 128.71	$ 103.67	$ 92.40	$ 86.50	$ 83.17
$ 20,000.00	$ 257.43	$ 207.34	$184.80	$173.00	$166.35
$ 30,000.00	$ 386.14	$ 311.01	$277.20	$259.51	$249.52
$ 40,000.00	$ 514.86	$ 414.68	$369.59	$346.01	$332.70
$ 50,000.00	$ 643.57	$ 518.35	$461.99	$432.51	$415.87
$ 60,000.00	$ 772.28	$ 622.02	$554.39	$519.01	$499.05
$ 70,000.00	$ 901.00	$ 725.69	$646.79	$605.52	$582.22
$ 80,000.00	$1,029.71	$ 829.36	$739.19	$692.02	$665.40
$ 90,000.00	$1,158.43	$ 933.03	$831.59	$778.52	$748.57
$100,000.00	$1,287.14	$1,036.70	$923.96	$865.02	$831.75

9½% RATE

Amount	10	15	20	25	30
$ 50.00	$ 0.65	$ 0.52	$ 0.47	$ 0.44	$ 0.42
$ 100.00	$ 1.29	$ 1.04	$ 0.93	$ 0.87	$ 0.84
$ 200.00	$ 2.59	$ 2.09	$ 1.86	$ 1.75	$ 1.68
$ 300.00	$ 3.88	$ 3.13	$ 2.80	$ 2.62	$ 2.52
$ 400.00	$ 5.18	$ 4.18	$ 3.73	$ 3.49	$ 3.36
$ 500.00	$ 6.47	$ 5.22	$ 4.66	$ 4.37	$ 4.20
$ 600.00	$ 7.76	$ 6.27	$ 5.59	$ 5.24	$ 5.05
$ 700.00	$ 9.06	$ 7.31	$ 6.52	$ 6.12	$ 5.89
$ 800.00	$ 10.35	$ 8.35	$ 7.46	$ 6.99	$ 6.73
$ 900.00	$ 11.65	$ 9.40	$ 8.39	$ 7.86	$ 7.57
$ 1,000.00	$ 12.94	$ 10.44	$ 9.32	$ 8.74	$ 8.41
$ 2,000.00	$ 25.88	$ 20.88	$ 18.64	$ 17.47	$ 16.82
$ 3,000.00	$ 38.82	$ 31.33	$ 27.96	$ 26.21	$ 25.23
$ 4,000.00	$ 51.76	$ 41.77	$ 37.29	$ 34.95	$ 33.63
$ 5,000.00	$ 64.70	$ 52.21	$ 46.61	$ 43.68	$ 42.04
$ 6,000.00	$ 77.64	$ 62.65	$ 55.93	$ 52.42	$ 50.45
$ 7,000.00	$ 90.58	$ 73.10	$ 65.25	$ 61.16	$ 58.86
$ 8,000.00	$ 103.52	$ 83.54	$ 74.57	$ 69.90	$ 67.27
$ 9,000.00	$ 116.46	$ 93.98	$ 83.89	$ 78.63	$ 75.68
$ 10,000.00	$ 129.40	$ 104.42	$ 93.21	$ 87.37	$ 84.09
$ 20,000.00	$ 258.80	$ 208.84	$186.43	$174.74	$168.17
$ 30,000.00	$ 388.19	$ 313.27	$279.64	$262.11	$252.26
$ 40,000.00	$ 517.59	$ 417.69	$372.85	$349.48	$336.34
$ 50,000.00	$ 646.99	$ 522.11	$466.07	$436.85	$420.43
$ 60,000.00	$ 776.39	$ 626.53	$559.28	$524.22	$504.51
$ 70,000.00	$ 905.78	$ 730.96	$652.49	$611.59	$588.60
$ 80,000.00	$1,035.18	$ 835.38	$745.70	$698.96	$672.68
$ 90,000.00	$1,164.58	$ 939.80	$838.92	$786.33	$756.77
$100,000.00	$1,293.98	$1,044.22	$932.13	$873.70	$840.85

Term of Loan in Years

9⅝% RATE

Term of Loan in Years

Amount	10	15	20	25	30
$ 50.00	$ 0.65	$ 0.53	$ 0.47	$ 0.44	$ 0.42
$ 100.00	$ 1.30	$ 1.05	$ 0.94	$ 0.88	$ 0.85
$ 200.00	$ 2.60	$ 2.10	$ 1.88	$ 1.76	$ 1.70
$ 300.00	$ 3.90	$ 3.16	$ 2.82	$ 2.65	$ 2.55
$ 400.00	$ 5.20	$ 4.21	$ 3.76	$ 3.53	$ 3.40
$ 500.00	$ 6.50	$ 5.26	$ 4.70	$ 4.41	$ 4.25
$ 600.00	$ 7.80	$ 6.31	$ 5.64	$ 5.29	$ 5.10
$ 700.00	$ 9.11	$ 7.36	$ 6.58	$ 6.18	$ 5.95
$ 800.00	$ 10.41	$ 8.41	$ 7.52	$ 7.06	$ 6.80
$ 900.00	$ 11.71	$ 9.47	$ 8.46	$ 7.94	$ 7.65
$ 1,000.00	$ 13.01	$ 10.52	$ 9.40	$ 8.82	$ 8.50
$ 2,000.00	$ 26.02	$ 21.04	$ 18.81	$ 17.65	$ 17.00
$ 3,000.00	$ 39.02	$ 31.55	$ 28.21	$ 26.47	$ 25.50
$ 4,000.00	$ 52.03	$ 42.07	$ 37.61	$ 35.30	$ 34.00
$ 5,000.00	$ 65.04	$ 52.59	$ 47.02	$ 44.12	$ 42.50
$ 6,000.00	$ 78.05	$ 63.11	$ 56.42	$ 52.94	$ 51.00
$ 7,000.00	$ 91.06	$ 73.62	$ 65.82	$ 61.77	$ 59.50
$ 8,000.00	$ 104.07	$ 84.14	$ 75.22	$ 70.59	$ 68.00
$ 9,000.00	$ 117.07	$ 94.66	$ 84.63	$ 79.42	$ 76.50
$ 10,000.00	$ 130.08	$ 105.18	$ 94.03	$ 88.24	$ 85.00
$ 20,000.00	$ 260.17	$ 210.36	$188.06	$176.48	$170.00
$ 30,000.00	$ 390.25	$ 315.53	$282.09	$264.72	$255.00
$ 40,000.00	$ 520.33	$ 420.71	$376.12	$352.96	$340.00
$ 50,000.00	$ 650.41	$ 525.89	$470.15	$441.20	$424.99
$ 60,000.00	$ 780.50	$ 631.07	$564.19	$529.44	$509.99
$ 70,000.00	$ 910.58	$ 736.25	$658.22	$617.68	$594.99
$ 80,000.00	$1,040.66	$ 841.42	$752.25	$705.92	$679.99
$ 90,000.00	$1,170.75	$ 946.60	$846.28	$794.16	$764.99
$100,000.00	$1,300.83	$1,051.78	$940.31	$882.40	$849.99

9¾% RATE

Term of Loan in Years

Amount	10	15	20	25	30
$ 50.00	$ 0.65	$ 0.53	$ 0.47	$ 0.45	$ 0.43
$ 100.00	$ 1.31	$ 1.06	$ 0.95	$ 0.89	$ 0.86
$ 200.00	$ 2.62	$ 2.12	$ 1.90	$ 1.78	$ 1.72
$ 300.00	$ 3.92	$ 3.18	$ 2.85	$ 2.67	$ 2.58
$ 400.00	$ 5.23	$ 4.24	$ 3.79	$ 3.56	$ 3.44
$ 500.00	$ 6.54	$ 5.30	$ 4.74	$ 4.46	$ 4.30
$ 600.00	$ 7.85	$ 6.36	$ 5.69	$ 5.35	$ 5.15
$ 700.00	$ 9.15	$ 7.42	$ 6.64	$ 6.24	$ 6.01
$ 800.00	$ 10.46	$ 8.47	$ 7.59	$ 7.13	$ 6.87
$ 900.00	$ 11.77	$ 9.53	$ 8.54	$ 8.02	$ 7.73
$ 1,000.00	$ 13.08	$ 10.59	$ 9.49	$ 8.91	$ 8.59
$ 2,000.00	$ 26.15	$ 21.19	$ 18.97	$ 17.82	$ 17.18
$ 3,000.00	$ 39.23	$ 31.78	$ 28.46	$ 26.73	$ 25.77
$ 4,000.00	$ 52.31	$ 42.37	$ 37.94	$ 35.65	$ 34.37
$ 5,000.00	$ 65.39	$ 52.97	$ 47.43	$ 44.56	$ 42.96
$ 6,000.00	$ 78.46	$ 63.56	$ 56.91	$ 53.47	$ 51.55
$ 7,000.00	$ 91.54	$ 74.16	$ 66.40	$ 62.38	$ 60.14
$ 8,000.00	$ 104.62	$ 84.75	$ 75.88	$ 71.29	$ 68.73
$ 9,000.00	$ 117.69	$ 95.34	$ 85.37	$ 80.20	$ 77.32
$ 10,000.00	$ 130.77	$ 105.94	$ 94.85	$ 89.11	$ 85.92
$ 20,000.00	$ 261.54	$ 211.87	$189.70	$178.23	$171.83
$ 30,000.00	$ 392.31	$ 317.81	$284.56	$267.34	$257.75
$ 40,000.00	$ 523.08	$ 423.75	$379.41	$356.45	$343.66
$ 50,000.00	$ 653.85	$ 529.68	$474.26	$445.57	$429.58
$ 60,000.00	$ 784.62	$ 635.62	$569.11	$534.68	$515.49
$ 70,000.00	$ 915.39	$ 741.55	$663.96	$623.80	$601.41
$ 80,000.00	$1,046.16	$ 847.49	$758.81	$712.91	$687.32
$ 90,000.00	$1,176.93	$ 953.43	$853.67	$802.02	$773.24
$100,000.00	$1,307.70	$1,059.36	$948.52	$891.14	$859.15

0.09875	Term of Loan in Years				
	10	15	20	25	30
Amount					
$ 50.00	$ 0.66	$ 0.53	$ 0.48	$ 0.45	$ 0.43
$ 100.00	$ 1.31	$ 1.07	$ 0.96	$ 0.90	$ 0.87
$ 200.00	$ 2.63	$ 2.13	$ 1.91	$ 1.80	$ 1.74
$ 300.00	$ 3.94	$ 3.20	$ 2.87	$ 2.70	$ 2.61
$ 400.00	$ 5.26	$ 4.27	$ 3.83	$ 3.60	$ 3.47
$ 500.00	$ 6.57	$ 5.33	$ 4.78	$ 4.50	$ 4.34
$ 600.00	$ 7.89	$ 6.40	$ 5.74	$ 5.40	$ 5.21
$ 700.00	$ 9.20	$ 7.47	$ 6.70	$ 6.30	$ 6.08
$ 800.00	$ 10.52	$ 8.54	$ 7.65	$ 7.20	$ 6.95
$ 900.00	$ 11.83	$ 9.60	$ 8.61	$ 8.10	$ 7.82
$ 1,000.00	$ 13.15	$ 10.67	$ 9.57	$ 9.00	$ 8.68
$ 2,000.00	$ 26.29	$ 21.34	$ 19.14	$ 18.00	$ 17.37
$ 3,000.00	$ 39.44	$ 32.01	$ 28.70	$ 27.00	$ 26.05
$ 4,000.00	$ 52.58	$ 42.68	$ 38.27	$ 36.00	$ 34.73
$ 5,000.00	$ 65.73	$ 53.35	$ 47.84	$ 45.00	$ 43.42
$ 6,000.00	$ 78.88	$ 64.02	$ 57.41	$ 53.99	$ 52.10
$ 7,000.00	$ 92.02	$ 74.69	$ 66.97	$ 62.99	$ 60.78
$ 8,000.00	$ 105.17	$ 85.36	$ 76.54	$ 71.99	$ 69.47
$ 9,000.00	$ 118.31	$ 96.03	$ 86.11	$ 80.99	$ 78.15
$ 10,000.00	$ 131.46	$ 106.70	$ 95.68	$ 89.99	$ 86.83
$ 20,000.00	$ 262.92	$ 213.39	$191.35	$179.98	$173.67
$ 30,000.00	$ 394.38	$ 320.09	$287.03	$269.97	$260.50
$ 40,000.00	$ 525.84	$ 426.79	$382.70	$359.96	$347.34
$ 50,000.00	$ 657.30	$ 533.49	$478.38	$449.95	$434.17
$ 60,000.00	$ 788.76	$ 640.18	$574.05	$539.94	$521.01
$ 70,000.00	$ 920.22	$ 746.88	$669.73	$629.93	$607.84
$ 80,000.00	$1,051.68	$ 853.58	$765.40	$719.92	$694.68
$ 90,000.00	$1,183.14	$ 960.27	$861.08	$809.91	$781.51
$100,000.00	$1,314.60	$1,066.97	$956.75	$899.90	$868.35

10% RATE

Term of Loan in Years

Amount	10	15	20	25	30
$ 50.00	$ 0.66	$ 0.54	$ 0.48	$ 0.45	$ 0.44
$ 100.00	$ 1.32	$ 1.07	$ 0.97	$ 0.91	$ 0.88
$ 200.00	$ 2.64	$ 2.15	$ 1.93	$ 1.82	$ 1.76
$ 300.00	$ 3.96	$ 3.22	$ 2.90	$ 2.73	$ 2.63
$ 400.00	$ 5.29	$ 4.30	$ 3.86	$ 3.63	$ 3.51
$ 500.00	$ 6.61	$ 5.37	$ 4.83	$ 4.54	$ 4.39
$ 600.00	$ 7.93	$ 6.45	$ 5.79	$ 5.45	$ 5.27
$ 700.00	$ 9.25	$ 7.52	$ 6.76	$ 6.36	$ 6.14
$ 800.00	$ 10.57	$ 8.60	$ 7.72	$ 7.27	$ 7.02
$ 900.00	$ 11.89	$ 9.67	$ 8.69	$ 8.18	$ 7.90
$ 1,000.00	$ 13.22	$ 10.75	$ 9.65	$ 9.09	$ 8.78
$ 2,000.00	$ 26.43	$ 21.49	$ 19.30	$ 18.17	$ 17.55
$ 3,000.00	$ 39.65	$ 32.24	$ 28.95	$ 27.26	$ 26.33
$ 4,000.00	$ 52.86	$ 42.98	$ 38.60	$ 36.35	$ 35.10
$ 5,000.00	$ 66.08	$ 53.73	$ 48.25	$ 45.44	$ 43.88
$ 6,000.00	$ 79.29	$ 64.48	$ 57.90	$ 54.52	$ 52.65
$ 7,000.00	$ 92.51	$ 75.22	$ 67.55	$ 63.61	$ 61.43
$ 8,000.00	$ 105.72	$ 85.97	$ 77.20	$ 72.70	$ 70.21
$ 9,000.00	$ 118.94	$ 96.71	$ 86.85	$ 81.78	$ 78.98
$ 10,000.00	$ 132.15	$ 107.46	$ 96.50	$ 90.87	$ 87.76
$ 20,000.00	$ 264.30	$ 214.92	$193.00	$181.74	$175.51
$ 30,000.00	$ 396.45	$ 322.38	$289.51	$272.61	$263.27
$ 40,000.00	$ 528.60	$ 429.84	$386.01	$363.48	$351.03
$ 50,000.00	$ 660.75	$ 537.30	$482.51	$454.35	$438.79
$ 60,000.00	$ 792.90	$ 644.76	$579.01	$545.22	$526.54
$ 70,000.00	$ 925.06	$ 752.22	$675.52	$636.09	$614.30
$ 80,000.00	$1,057.21	$ 859.68	$772.02	$726.96	$702.06
$ 90,000.00	$1,189.36	$ 967.14	$868.52	$817.83	$789.81
$100,000.00	$1,321.51	$1,074.61	$965.02	$908.70	$877.57

10⅛% RATE

0.10125   Term of Loan in Years

Amount	10	15	20	25	30
$ 50.00	$ 0.66	$ 0.54	$ 0.49	$ 0.46	$ 0.44
$ 100.00	$ 1.33	$ 1.08	$ 0.97	$ 0.92	$ 0.89
$ 200.00	$ 2.66	$ 2.16	$ 1.95	$ 1.84	$ 1.77
$ 300.00	$ 3.99	$ 3.25	$ 2.92	$ 2.75	$ 2.66
$ 400.00	$ 5.31	$ 4.33	$ 3.89	$ 3.67	$ 3.55
$ 500.00	$ 6.64	$ 5.41	$ 4.87	$ 4.59	$ 4.43
$ 600.00	$ 7.97	$ 6.49	$ 5.84	$ 5.51	$ 5.32
$ 700.00	$ 9.30	$ 7.58	$ 6.81	$ 6.42	$ 6.21
$ 800.00	$ 10.63	$ 8.66	$ 7.79	$ 7.34	$ 7.09
$ 900.00	$ 11.96	$ 9.74	$ 8.76	$ 8.26	$ 7.98
$ 1,000.00	$ 13.28	$ 10.82	$ 9.73	$ 9.18	$ 8.87
$ 2,000.00	$ 26.57	$ 21.65	$ 19.47	$ 18.35	$ 17.74
$ 3,000.00	$ 39.85	$ 32.47	$ 29.20	$ 27.53	$ 26.60
$ 4,000.00	$ 53.14	$ 43.29	$ 38.93	$ 36.70	$ 35.47
$ 5,000.00	$ 66.42	$ 54.11	$ 48.67	$ 45.88	$ 44.34
$ 6,000.00	$ 79.71	$ 64.94	$ 58.40	$ 55.05	$ 53.21
$ 7,000.00	$ 92.99	$ 75.76	$ 68.13	$ 64.23	$ 62.08
$ 8,000.00	$ 106.28	$ 86.58	$ 77.87	$ 73.40	$ 70.95
$ 9,000.00	$ 119.56	$ 97.40	$ 87.60	$ 82.58	$ 79.81
$ 10,000.00	$ 132.84	$ 108.23	$ 97.33	$ 91.75	$ 88.68
$ 20,000.00	$ 265.69	$ 216.45	$194.66	$183.51	$177.36
$ 30,000.00	$ 398.53	$ 324.68	$292.00	$275.26	$266.05
$ 40,000.00	$ 531.38	$ 432.91	$389.33	$367.01	$354.73
$ 50,000.00	$ 664.22	$ 541.13	$486.66	$458.76	$443.41
$ 60,000.00	$ 797.06	$ 649.36	$583.99	$550.52	$532.09
$ 70,000.00	$ 929.91	$ 757.59	$681.32	$642.27	$620.78
$ 80,000.00	$1,062.75	$ 865.81	$778.65	$734.02	$709.46
$ 90,000.00	$1,195.60	$ 974.04	$875.99	$825.77	$798.14
$100,000.00	$1,328.44	$1,082.27	$973.32	$917.53	$886.82

10¼% RATE

Term of Loan in Years

Amount	10	15	20	25	30
$ 50.00	$ 0.67	$ 0.54	$ 0.49	$ 0.46	$ 0.45
$ 100.00	$ 1.34	$ 1.09	$ 0.98	$ 0.93	$ 0.90
$ 200.00	$ 2.67	$ 2.18	$ 1.96	$ 1.85	$ 1.79
$ 300.00	$ 4.01	$ 3.27	$ 2.94	$ 2.78	$ 2.69
$ 400.00	$ 5.34	$ 4.36	$ 3.93	$ 3.71	$ 3.58
$ 500.00	$ 6.68	$ 5.45	$ 4.91	$ 4.63	$ 4.48
$ 600.00	$ 8.01	$ 6.54	$ 5.89	$ 5.56	$ 5.38
$ 700.00	$ 9.35	$ 7.63	$ 6.87	$ 6.48	$ 6.27
$ 800.00	$ 10.68	$ 8.72	$ 7.85	$ 7.41	$ 7.17
$ 900.00	$ 12.02	$ 9.81	$ 8.83	$ 8.34	$ 8.06
$ 1,000.00	$ 13.35	$ 10.90	$ 9.82	$ 9.26	$ 8.96
$ 2,000.00	$ 26.71	$ 21.80	$ 19.63	$ 18.53	$ 17.92
$ 3,000.00	$ 40.06	$ 32.70	$ 29.45	$ 27.79	$ 26.88
$ 4,000.00	$ 53.42	$ 43.60	$ 39.27	$ 37.06	$ 35.84
$ 5,000.00	$ 66.77	$ 54.50	$ 49.08	$ 46.32	$ 44.81
$ 6,000.00	$ 80.12	$ 65.40	$ 58.90	$ 55.58	$ 53.77
$ 7,000.00	$ 93.48	$ 76.30	$ 68.72	$ 64.85	$ 62.73
$ 8,000.00	$ 106.83	$ 87.20	$ 78.53	$ 74.11	$ 71.69
$ 9,000.00	$ 120.19	$ 98.10	$ 88.35	$ 83.37	$ 80.65
$ 10,000.00	$ 133.54	$ 109.00	$ 98.16	$ 92.64	$ 89.61
$ 20,000.00	$ 267.08	$ 217.99	$196.33	$185.28	$179.22
$ 30,000.00	$ 400.62	$ 326.99	$294.49	$277.91	$268.83
$ 40,000.00	$ 534.16	$ 435.98	$392.66	$370.55	$358.44
$ 50,000.00	$ 667.70	$ 544.98	$490.82	$463.19	$448.05
$ 60,000.00	$ 801.23	$ 653.97	$588.99	$555.83	$537.66
$ 70,000.00	$ 934.77	$ 762.97	$687.15	$648.47	$627.27
$ 80,000.00	$1,068.31	$ 871.96	$785.31	$741.11	$716.88
$ 90,000.00	$1,201.85	$ 980.96	$883.48	$833.74	$806.49
$100,000.00	$1,335.39	$1,089.95	$981.64	$926.38	$896.10

10⅜% RATE

Term of Loan in Years

Amount	10	15	20	25	30
$ 50.00	$ 0.67	$ 0.55	$ 0.49	$ 0.47	$ 0.45
$ 100.00	$ 1.34	$ 1.10	$ 0.99	$ 0.94	$ 0.91
$ 200.00	$ 2.68	$ 2.20	$ 1.98	$ 1.87	$ 1.81
$ 300.00	$ 4.03	$ 3.29	$ 2.97	$ 2.81	$ 2.72
$ 400.00	$ 5.37	$ 4.39	$ 3.96	$ 3.74	$ 3.62
$ 500.00	$ 6.71	$ 5.49	$ 4.95	$ 4.68	$ 4.53
$ 600.00	$ 8.05	$ 6.59	$ 5.94	$ 5.61	$ 5.43
$ 700.00	$ 9.40	$ 7.68	$ 6.93	$ 6.55	$ 6.34
$ 800.00	$ 10.74	$ 8.78	$ 7.92	$ 7.48	$ 7.24
$ 900.00	$ 12.08	$ 9.88	$ 8.91	$ 8.42	$ 8.15
$ 1,000.00	$ 13.42	$ 10.98	$ 9.90	$ 9.35	$ 9.05
$ 2,000.00	$ 26.85	$ 21.95	$ 19.80	$ 18.71	$ 18.11
$ 3,000.00	$ 40.27	$ 32.93	$ 29.70	$ 28.06	$ 27.16
$ 4,000.00	$ 53.69	$ 43.91	$ 39.60	$ 37.41	$ 36.22
$ 5,000.00	$ 67.12	$ 54.88	$ 49.50	$ 46.76	$ 45.27
$ 6,000.00	$ 80.54	$ 65.86	$ 59.40	$ 56.12	$ 54.32
$ 7,000.00	$ 93.97	$ 76.84	$ 69.30	$ 65.47	$ 63.38
$ 8,000.00	$ 107.39	$ 87.81	$ 79.20	$ 74.82	$ 72.43
$ 9,000.00	$ 120.81	$ 98.79	$ 89.10	$ 84.17	$ 81.49
$ 10,000.00	$ 134.24	$ 109.77	$ 99.00	$ 93.53	$ 90.54
$ 20,000.00	$ 268.47	$ 219.53	$198.00	$187.05	$181.08
$ 30,000.00	$ 402.71	$ 329.30	$297.00	$280.58	$271.62
$ 40,000.00	$ 536.94	$ 439.06	$396.00	$374.11	$362.16
$ 50,000.00	$ 671.18	$ 548.83	$495.00	$467.63	$452.70
$ 60,000.00	$ 805.42	$ 658.60	$594.00	$561.16	$543.24
$ 70,000.00	$ 939.65	$ 768.36	$693.00	$654.69	$633.78
$ 80,000.00	$1,073.89	$ 878.13	$792.00	$748.21	$724.33
$ 90,000.00	$1,208.12	$ 987.90	$891.00	$841.74	$814.87
$100,000.00	$1,342.36	$1,097.66	$990.00	$935.27	$905.41

10½% RATE

Term of Loan in Years

	10	15	20	25	30
Amount					
$ 50.00	$ 0.67	$ 0.55	$ 0.50	$ 0.47	$ 0.46
$ 100.00	$ 1.35	$ 1.11	$ 1.00	$ 0.94	$ 0.91
$ 200.00	$ 2.70	$ 2.21	$ 2.00	$ 1.89	$ 1.83
$ 300.00	$ 4.05	$ 3.32	$ 3.00	$ 2.83	$ 2.74
$ 400.00	$ 5.40	$ 4.42	$ 3.99	$ 3.78	$ 3.66
$ 500.00	$ 6.75	$ 5.53	$ 4.99	$ 4.72	$ 4.57
$ 600.00	$ 8.10	$ 6.63	$ 5.99	$ 5.67	$ 5.49
$ 700.00	$ 9.45	$ 7.74	$ 6.99	$ 6.61	$ 6.40
$ 800.00	$ 10.79	$ 8.84	$ 7.99	$ 7.55	$ 7.32
$ 900.00	$ 12.14	$ 9.95	$ 8.99	$ 8.50	$ 8.23
$ 1,000.00	$ 13.49	$ 11.05	$ 9.98	$ 9.44	$ 9.15
$ 2,000.00	$ 26.99	$ 22.11	$ 19.97	$ 18.88	$ 18.29
$ 3,000.00	$ 40.48	$ 33.16	$ 29.95	$ 28.33	$ 27.44
$ 4,000.00	$ 53.97	$ 44.22	$ 39.94	$ 37.77	$ 36.59
$ 5,000.00	$ 67.47	$ 55.27	$ 49.92	$ 47.21	$ 45.74
$ 6,000.00	$ 80.96	$ 66.32	$ 59.90	$ 56.65	$ 54.88
$ 7,000.00	$ 94.45	$ 77.38	$ 69.89	$ 66.09	$ 64.03
$ 8,000.00	$ 107.95	$ 88.43	$ 79.87	$ 75.53	$ 73.18
$ 9,000.00	$ 121.44	$ 99.49	$ 89.85	$ 84.98	$ 82.33
$ 10,000.00	$ 134.93	$ 110.54	$ 99.84	$ 94.42	$ 91.47
$ 20,000.00	$ 269.87	$ 221.08	$199.68	$188.84	$182.95
$ 30,000.00	$ 404.80	$ 331.62	$299.51	$283.25	$274.42
$ 40,000.00	$ 539.74	$ 442.16	$399.35	$377.67	$365.90
$ 50,000.00	$ 674.67	$ 552.70	$499.19	$472.09	$457.37
$ 60,000.00	$ 809.61	$ 663.24	$599.03	$566.51	$548.84
$ 70,000.00	$ 944.54	$ 773.78	$698.87	$660.93	$640.32
$ 80,000.00	$1,079.48	$ 884.32	$798.70	$755.35	$731.79
$ 90,000.00	$1,214.41	$ 994.86	$898.54	$849.76	$823.27
$100,000.00	$1,349.35	$1,105.40	$998.38	$944.18	$914.74

10⅝% RATE

Term of Loan in Years

	10	15	20	25	30
Amount					
$ 50.00	$ 0.68	$ 0.56	$ 0.50	$ 0.48	$ 0.46
$ 100.00	$ 1.36	$ 1.11	$ 1.01	$ 0.95	$ 0.92
$ 200.00	$ 2.71	$ 2.23	$ 2.01	$ 1.91	$ 1.85
$ 300.00	$ 4.07	$ 3.34	$ 3.02	$ 2.86	$ 2.77
$ 400.00	$ 5.43	$ 4.45	$ 4.03	$ 3.81	$ 3.70
$ 500.00	$ 6.78	$ 5.57	$ 5.03	$ 4.77	$ 4.62
$ 600.00	$ 8.14	$ 6.68	$ 6.04	$ 5.72	$ 5.54
$ 700.00	$ 9.49	$ 7.79	$ 7.05	$ 6.67	$ 6.47
$ 800.00	$ 10.85	$ 8.91	$ 8.05	$ 7.62	$ 7.39
$ 900.00	$ 12.21	$ 10.02	$ 9.06	$ 8.58	$ 8.32
$ 1,000.00	$ 13.56	$ 11.13	$ 10.07	$ 9.53	$ 9.24
$ 2,000.00	$ 27.13	$ 22.26	$ 20.14	$ 19.06	$ 18.48
$ 3,000.00	$ 40.69	$ 33.39	$ 30.20	$ 28.59	$ 27.72
$ 4,000.00	$ 54.25	$ 44.53	$ 40.27	$ 38.12	$ 36.96
$ 5,000.00	$ 67.82	$ 55.66	$ 50.34	$ 47.66	$ 46.20
$ 6,000.00	$ 81.38	$ 66.79	$ 60.41	$ 57.19	$ 55.45
$ 7,000.00	$ 94.95	$ 77.92	$ 70.48	$ 66.72	$ 64.69
$ 8,000.00	$ 108.51	$ 89.05	$ 80.54	$ 76.25	$ 73.93
$ 9,000.00	$ 122.07	$ 100.18	$ 90.61	$ 85.78	$ 83.17
$ 10,000.00	$ 135.64	$ 111.32	$ 100.68	$ 95.31	$ 92.41
$ 20,000.00	$ 271.27	$ 222.63	$ 201.36	$190.62	$184.82
$ 30,000.00	$ 406.91	$ 333.95	$ 302.04	$285.94	$277.23
$ 40,000.00	$ 542.54	$ 445.26	$ 402.72	$381.25	$369.64
$ 50,000.00	$ 678.18	$ 556.58	$ 503.40	$476.56	$462.05
$ 60,000.00	$ 813.82	$ 667.90	$ 604.07	$571.87	$554.46
$ 70,000.00	$ 949.45	$ 779.21	$ 704.75	$667.19	$646.87
$ 80,000.00	$1,085.09	$ 890.53	$ 805.43	$762.50	$739.28
$ 90,000.00	$1,220.72	$1,001.84	$ 906.11	$857.81	$831.69
$100,000.00	$1,356.36	$1,113.16	$1,006.79	$953.12	$924.10

10¾% RATE

0.1075	Term of Loan in Years				
	10	15	20	25	30
Amount					
$ 50.00	$ 0.68	$ 0.56	$ 0.51	$ 0.48	$ 0.47
$ 100.00	$ 1.36	$ 1.12	$ 1.02	$ 0.96	$ 0.93
$ 200.00	$ 2.73	$ 2.24	$ 2.03	$ 1.92	$ 1.87
$ 300.00	$ 4.09	$ 3.36	$ 3.05	$ 2.89	$ 2.80
$ 400.00	$ 5.45	$ 4.48	$ 4.06	$ 3.85	$ 3.73
$ 500.00	$ 6.82	$ 5.60	$ 5.08	$ 4.81	$ 4.67
$ 600.00	$ 8.18	$ 6.73	$ 6.09	$ 5.77	$ 5.60
$ 700.00	$ 9.54	$ 7.85	$ 7.11	$ 6.73	$ 6.53
$ 800.00	$ 10.91	$ 8.97	$ 8.12	$ 7.70	$ 7.47
$ 900.00	$ 12.27	$ 10.09	$ 9.14	$ 8.66	$ 8.40
$ 1,000.00	$ 13.63	$ 11.21	$ 10.15	$ 9.62	$ 9.33
$ 2,000.00	$ 27.27	$ 22.42	$ 20.30	$ 19.24	$ 18.67
$ 3,000.00	$ 40.90	$ 33.63	$ 30.46	$ 28.86	$ 28.00
$ 4,000.00	$ 54.54	$ 44.84	$ 40.61	$ 38.48	$ 37.34
$ 5,000.00	$ 68.17	$ 56.05	$ 50.76	$ 48.10	$ 46.67
$ 6,000.00	$ 81.80	$ 67.26	$ 60.91	$ 57.73	$ 56.01
$ 7,000.00	$ 95.44	$ 78.47	$ 71.07	$ 67.35	$ 65.34
$ 8,000.00	$ 109.07	$ 89.68	$ 81.22	$ 76.97	$ 74.68
$ 9,000.00	$ 122.70	$ 100.89	$ 91.37	$ 86.59	$ 84.01
$ 10,000.00	$ 136.34	$ 112.09	$ 101.52	$ 96.21	$ 93.35
$ 20,000.00	$ 272.68	$ 224.19	$ 203.05	$192.42	$186.70
$ 30,000.00	$ 409.02	$ 336.28	$ 304.57	$288.63	$280.04
$ 40,000.00	$ 545.35	$ 448.38	$ 406.09	$384.84	$373.39
$ 50,000.00	$ 681.69	$ 560.47	$ 507.61	$481.05	$466.74
$ 60,000.00	$ 818.03	$ 672.57	$ 609.14	$577.26	$560.09
$ 70,000.00	$ 954.37	$ 784.66	$ 710.66	$673.46	$653.44
$ 80,000.00	$1,090.71	$ 896.76	$ 812.18	$769.67	$746.79
$ 90,000.00	$1,227.05	$1,008.85	$ 913.71	$865.88	$840.13
$100,000.00	$1,363.39	$1,120.95	$1,015.23	$962.09	$933.48

10⅞% RATE

Term of Loan in Years

Amount	10	15	20	25	30
$ 50.00	$ 0.69	$ 0.56	$ 0.51	$ 0.49	$ 0.47
$ 100.00	$ 1.37	$ 1.13	$ 1.02	$ 0.97	$ 0.94
$ 200.00	$ 2.74	$ 2.26	$ 2.05	$ 1.94	$ 1.89
$ 300.00	$ 4.11	$ 3.39	$ 3.07	$ 2.91	$ 2.83
$ 400.00	$ 5.48	$ 4.52	$ 4.09	$ 3.88	$ 3.77
$ 500.00	$ 6.85	$ 5.64	$ 5.12	$ 4.86	$ 4.71
$ 600.00	$ 8.22	$ 6.77	$ 6.14	$ 5.83	$ 5.66
$ 700.00	$ 9.59	$ 7.90	$ 7.17	$ 6.80	$ 6.60
$ 800.00	$ 10.96	$ 9.03	$ 8.19	$ 7.77	$ 7.54
$ 900.00	$ 12.33	$ 10.16	$ 9.21	$ 8.74	$ 8.49
$ 1,000.00	$ 13.70	$ 11.29	$ 10.24	$ 9.71	$ 9.43
$ 2,000.00	$ 27.41	$ 22.58	$ 20.47	$ 19.42	$ 18.86
$ 3,000.00	$ 41.11	$ 33.86	$ 30.71	$ 29.13	$ 28.29
$ 4,000.00	$ 54.82	$ 45.15	$ 40.95	$ 38.84	$ 37.72
$ 5,000.00	$ 68.52	$ 56.44	$ 51.18	$ 48.55	$ 47.14
$ 6,000.00	$ 82.23	$ 67.73	$ 61.42	$ 58.27	$ 56.57
$ 7,000.00	$ 95.93	$ 79.01	$ 71.66	$ 67.98	$ 66.00
$ 8,000.00	$ 109.63	$ 90.30	$ 81.90	$ 77.69	$ 75.43
$ 9,000.00	$ 123.34	$ 101.59	$ 92.13	$ 87.40	$ 84.86
$ 10,000.00	$ 137.04	$ 112.88	$ 102.37	$ 97.11	$ 94.29
$ 20,000.00	$ 274.09	$ 225.75	$ 204.74	$194.22	$188.58
$ 30,000.00	$ 411.13	$ 338.63	$ 307.11	$291.33	$282.87
$ 40,000.00	$ 548.17	$ 451.50	$ 409.48	$388.44	$377.16
$ 50,000.00	$ 685.22	$ 564.38	$ 511.85	$485.54	$471.45
$ 60,000.00	$ 822.26	$ 677.26	$ 614.22	$582.65	$565.73
$ 70,000.00	$ 959.30	$ 790.13	$ 716.59	$679.76	$660.02
$ 80,000.00	$1,096.35	$ 903.01	$ 818.96	$776.87	$754.31
$ 90,000.00	$1,233.39	$1,015.88	$ 921.33	$873.98	$848.60
$100,000.00	$1,370.43	$1,128.76	$1,023.70	$971.09	$942.89

11% RATE

Term of Loan in Years

Amount		10		15		20		25		30
$	50.00	$	0.69	$	0.57	$	0.52	$	0.49	$	0.48
$	100.00	$	1.38	$	1.14	$	1.03	$	0.98	$	0.95
$	200.00	$	2.76	$	2.27	$	2.06	$	1.96	$	1.90
$	300.00	$	4.13	$	3.41	$	3.10	$	2.94	$	2.86
$	400.00	$	5.51	$	4.55	$	4.13	$	3.92	$	3.81
$	500.00	$	6.89	$	5.68	$	5.16	$	4.90	$	4.76
$	600.00	$	8.27	$	6.82	$	6.19	$	5.88	$	5.71
$	700.00	$	9.64	$	7.96	$	7.23	$	6.86	$	6.67
$	800.00	$	11.02	$	9.09	$	8.26	$	7.84	$	7.62
$	900.00	$	12.40	$	10.23	$	9.29	$	8.82	$	8.57
$	1,000.00	$	13.78	$	11.37	$	10.32	$	9.80	$	9.52
$	2,000.00	$	27.55	$	22.73	$	20.64	$	19.60	$	19.05
$	3,000.00	$	41.33	$	34.10	$	30.97	$	29.40	$	28.57
$	4,000.00	$	55.10	$	45.46	$	41.29	$	39.20	$	38.09
$	5,000.00	$	68.88	$	56.83	$	51.61	$	49.01	$	47.62
$	6,000.00	$	82.65	$	68.20	$	61.93	$	58.81	$	57.14
$	7,000.00	$	96.43	$	79.56	$	72.25	$	68.61	$	66.66
$	8,000.00	$	110.20	$	90.93	$	82.58	$	78.41	$	76.19
$	9,000.00	$	123.98	$	102.29	$	92.90	$	88.21	$	85.71
$	10,000.00	$	137.75	$	113.66	$	103.22	$	98.01	$	95.23
$	20,000.00	$	275.50	$	227.32	$	206.44	$196.02		$190.46
$	30,000.00	$	413.25	$	340.98	$	309.66	$294.03		$285.70
$	40,000.00	$	551.00	$	454.64	$	412.88	$392.05		$380.93
$	50,000.00	$	688.75	$	568.30	$	516.09	$490.06		$476.16
$	60,000.00	$	826.50	$	681.96	$	619.31	$588.07		$571.39
$	70,000.00	$	964.25	$	795.62	$	722.53	$686.08		$666.63
$	80,000.00	$1,102.00		$	909.28	$	825.75	$784.09		$761.86
$	90,000.00	$1,239.75		$1,022.94		$	928.97	$882.10		$857.09
$100,000.00		$1,377.50		$1,136.60		$1,032.19		$980.11		$952.32

11⅛% RATE

Term of Loan in Years

Amount	10	15	20	25	30
$ 50.00	$ 0.69	$ 0.57	$ 0.52	$ 0.49	$ 0.48
$ 100.00	$ 1.38	$ 1.14	$ 1.04	$ 0.99	$ 0.96
$ 200.00	$ 2.77	$ 2.29	$ 2.08	$ 1.96	$ 1.92
$ 300.00	$ 4.15	$ 3.43	$ 3.12	$ 2.97	$ 2.89
$ 400.00	$ 5.54	$ 4.58	$ 4.16	$ 3.96	$ 3.85
$ 500.00	$ 6.92	$ 5.72	$ 5.20	$ 4.95	$ 4.81
$ 600.00	$ 8.31	$ 6.87	$ 6.24	$ 5.93	$ 5.77
$ 700.00	$ 9.69	$ 8.01	$ 7.28	$ 6.92	$ 6.73
$ 800.00	$ 11.08	$ 9.16	$ 8.33	$ 7.91	$ 7.69
$ 900.00	$ 12.46	$ 10.30	$ 9.37	$ 8.90	$ 8.66
$ 1,000.00	$ 13.85	$ 11.44	$ 10.41	$ 9.89	$ 9.62
$ 2,000.00	$ 27.69	$ 22.89	$ 20.81	$ 19.78	$ 19.24
$ 3,000.00	$ 41.54	$ 34.33	$ 31.22	$ 29.67	$ 28.85
$ 4,000.00	$ 55.38	$ 45.78	$ 41.63	$ 39.57	$ 38.47
$ 5,000.00	$ 69.23	$ 57.22	$ 52.04	$ 49.46	$ 48.09
$ 6,000.00	$ 83.08	$ 68.67	$ 62.44	$ 59.35	$ 57.71
$ 7,000.00	$ 96.92	$ 80.11	$ 72.85	$ 69.24	$ 67.32
$ 8,000.00	$ 110.77	$ 91.56	$ 83.26	$ 79.13	$ 76.94
$ 9,000.00	$ 124.61	$ 103.00	$ 93.66	$ 89.02	$ 86.56
$ 10,000.00	$ 138.46	$ 114.45	$ 104.07	$ 98.92	$ 96.18
$ 20,000.00	$ 276.92	$ 228.89	$ 208.14	$197.83	$192.36
$ 30,000.00	$ 415.38	$ 343.34	$ 312.21	$296.75	$288.53
$ 40,000.00	$ 553.83	$ 457.78	$ 416.28	$395.67	$384.71
$ 50,000.00	$ 692.29	$ 572.23	$ 520.35	$494.58	$480.89
$ 60,000.00	$ 830.75	$ 686.68	$ 624.43	$593.50	$577.07
$ 70,000.00	$ 969.21	$ 801.12	$ 728.50	$692.41	$673.25
$ 80,000.00	$1,107.67	$ 915.57	$ 832.57	$791.33	$769.42
$ 90,000.00	$1,246.13	$1,030.01	$ 936.64	$890.25	$865.60
$100,000.00	$1,384.59	$1,144.46	$1,040.71	$989.16	$961.78

11¼% RATE

Term of Loan in Years

Amount	10	15	20	25	30
$ 50.00	$ 0.70	$ 0.58	$ 0.52	$ 0.50	$ 0.49
$ 100.00	$ 1.39	$ 1.15	$ 1.05	$ 1.00	$ 0.97
$ 200.00	$ 2.78	$ 2.30	$ 2.10	$ 2.00	$ 1.94
$ 300.00	$ 4.18	$ 3.46	$ 3.15	$ 2.99	$ 2.91
$ 400.00	$ 5.57	$ 4.61	$ 4.20	$ 3.99	$ 3.89
$ 500.00	$ 6.96	$ 5.76	$ 5.25	$ 4.99	$ 4.86
$ 600.00	$ 8.35	$ 6.91	$ 6.30	$ 5.99	$ 5.83
$ 700.00	$ 9.74	$ 8.07	$ 7.34	$ 6.99	$ 6.80
$ 800.00	$ 11.13	$ 9.22	$ 8.39	$ 7.99	$ 7.77
$ 900.00	$ 12.53	$ 10.37	$ 9.44	$ 8.98	$ 8.74
$ 1,000.00	$ 13.92	$ 11.52	$ 10.49	$ 9.98	$ 9.71
$ 2,000.00	$ 27.83	$ 23.05	$ 20.99	$ 19.96	$ 19.43
$ 3,000.00	$ 41.75	$ 34.57	$ 31.48	$ 29.95	$ 29.14
$ 4,000.00	$ 55.67	$ 46.09	$ 41.97	$ 39.93	$ 38.85
$ 5,000.00	$ 69.58	$ 57.62	$ 52.46	$ 49.91	$ 48.56
$ 6,000.00	$ 83.50	$ 69.14	$ 62.96	$ 59.89	$ 58.28
$ 7,000.00	$ 97.42	$ 80.66	$ 73.45	$ 69.88	$ 67.99
$ 8,000.00	$ 111.34	$ 92.19	$ 83.94	$ 79.86	$ 77.70
$ 9,000.00	$ 125.25	$ 103.71	$ 94.43	$ 89.84	$ 87.41
$ 10,000.00	$ 139.17	$ 115.23	$ 104.93	$ 99.82	$ 97.13
$ 20,000.00	$ 278.34	$ 230.47	$ 209.85	$199.65	$194.25
$ 30,000.00	$ 417.51	$ 345.70	$ 314.78	$299.47	$291.38
$ 40,000.00	$ 556.68	$ 460.94	$ 419.70	$399.30	$388.50
$ 50,000.00	$ 695.84	$ 576.17	$ 524.63	$499.12	$485.63
$ 60,000.00	$ 835.01	$ 691.41	$ 629.55	$598.94	$582.76
$ 70,000.00	$ 974.18	$ 806.64	$ 734.48	$698.77	$679.88
$ 80,000.00	$1,113.35	$ 921.88	$ 839.40	$798.59	$777.01
$ 90,000.00	$1,252.52	$1,037.11	$ 944.33	$898.42	$874.14
$100,000.00	$1,391.69	$1,152.34	$1,049.26	$998.24	$971.26

11⅜% RATE

Term of Loan in Years

	10	15	20	25	30
Amount					
$ 50.00	$ 0.70	$ 0.58	$ 0.53	$ 0.50	$ 0.49
$ 100.00	$ 1.40	$ 1.16	$ 1.06	$ 1.01	$ 0.98
$ 200.00	$ 2.80	$ 2.32	$ 2.12	$ 2.01	$ 1.96
$ 300.00	$ 4.20	$ 3.48	$ 3.17	$ 3.02	$ 2.94
$ 400.00	$ 5.60	$ 4.64	$ 4.23	$ 4.03	$ 3.92
$ 500.00	$ 6.99	$ 5.80	$ 5.29	$ 5.04	$ 4.90
$ 600.00	$ 8.39	$ 6.96	$ 6.35	$ 6.04	$ 5.88
$ 700.00	$ 9.79	$ 8.12	$ 7.40	$ 7.05	$ 6.87
$ 800.00	$ 11.19	$ 9.28	$ 8.46	$ 8.06	$ 7.85
$ 900.00	$ 12.59	$ 10.44	$ 9.52	$ 9.07	$ 8.83
$ 1,000.00	$ 13.99	$ 11.60	$ 10.58	$ 10.07	$ 9.81
$ 2,000.00	$ 27.98	$ 23.21	$ 21.16	$ 20.15	$ 19.62
$ 3,000.00	$ 41.96	$ 34.81	$ 31.73	$ 30.22	$ 29.42
$ 4,000.00	$ 55.95	$ 46.41	$ 42.31	$ 40.29	$ 39.23
$ 5,000.00	$ 69.94	$ 58.01	$ 52.89	$ 50.37	$ 49.04
$ 6,000.00	$ 83.93	$ 69.62	$ 63.47	$ 60.44	$ 58.85
$ 7,000.00	$ 97.92	$ 81.22	$ 74.05	$ 70.51	$ 68.65
$ 8,000.00	$ 111.91	$ 92.82	$ 84.63	$ 80.59	$ 78.46
$ 9,000.00	$ 125.89	$ 104.42	$ 95.20	$ 90.66	$ 88.27
$ 10,000.00	$ 139.88	$ 116.03	$ 105.78	$ 100.73	$ 98.08
$ 20,000.00	$ 279.76	$ 232.05	$ 211.57	$ 201.47	$196.15
$ 30,000.00	$ 419.64	$ 348.08	$ 317.35	$ 302.20	$294.23
$ 40,000.00	$ 559.53	$ 464.10	$ 423.13	$ 402.94	$392.31
$ 50,000.00	$ 699.41	$ 580.13	$ 528.91	$ 503.67	$490.38
$ 60,000.00	$ 839.29	$ 696.15	$ 634.70	$ 604.40	$588.46
$ 70,000.00	$ 979.17	$ 812.18	$ 740.48	$ 705.14	$686.54
$ 80,000.00	$1,119.05	$ 928.20	$ 846.26	$ 805.87	$784.61
$ 90,000.00	$1,258.93	$1,044.23	$ 952.05	$ 906.61	$882.69
$100,000.00	$1,396.81	$1,160.26	$1,057.83	$1,007.34	$980.77

11½% RATE

Term of Loan in Years

Amount	10	15	20	25	30
$ 50.00	$ 0.70	$ 0.58	$ 0.53	$ 0.51	$ 0.50
$ 100.00	$ 1.41	$ 1.17	$ 1.07	$ 1.02	$ 0.99
$ 200.00	$ 2.81	$ 2.34	$ 2.13	$ 2.03	$ 1.98
$ 300.00	$ 4.22	$ 3.50	$ 3.20	$ 3.05	$ 2.97
$ 400.00	$ 5.62	$ 4.67	$ 4.27	$ 4.07	$ 3.96
$ 500.00	$ 7.03	$ 5.84	$ 5.33	$ 5.08	$ 4.95
$ 600.00	$ 8.44	$ 7.01	$ 6.40	$ 6.10	$ 5.94
$ 700.00	$ 9.84	$ 8.18	$ 7.47	$ 7.12	$ 6.93
$ 800.00	$ 11.25	$ 9.35	$ 8.53	$ 8.13	$ 7.92
$ 900.00	$ 12.65	$ 10.51	$ 9.60	$ 9.15	$ 8.91
$ 1,000.00	$ 14.06	$ 11.68	$ 10.66	$ 10.16	$ 9.90
$ 2,000.00	$ 28.12	$ 23.36	$ 21.33	$ 20.33	$ 19.81
$ 3,000.00	$ 42.18	$ 35.05	$ 31.99	$ 30.49	$ 29.71
$ 4,000.00	$ 56.24	$ 46.73	$ 42.66	$ 40.66	$ 39.61
$ 5,000.00	$ 70.30	$ 58.41	$ 53.32	$ 50.82	$ 49.51
$ 6,000.00	$ 84.36	$ 70.09	$ 63.99	$ 60.99	$ 59.42
$ 7,000.00	$ 98.42	$ 81.77	$ 74.65	$ 71.15	$ 69.32
$ 8,000.00	$ 112.48	$ 93.46	$ 85.31	$ 81.32	$ 79.22
$ 9,000.00	$ 126.54	$ 105.14	$ 95.98	$ 91.48	$ 89.13
$ 10,000.00	$ 140.60	$ 116.82	$ 106.64	$ 101.65	$ 99.03
$ 20,000.00	$ 281.19	$ 233.64	$ 213.29	$ 203.29	$198.06
$ 30,000.00	$ 421.79	$ 350.46	$ 319.93	$ 304.94	$297.09
$ 40,000.00	$ 562.38	$ 467.28	$ 426.57	$ 406.59	$396.12
$ 50,000.00	$ 702.98	$ 584.09	$ 533.21	$ 508.23	$495.15
$ 60,000.00	$ 843.57	$ 700.91	$ 639.86	$ 609.88	$594.17
$ 70,000.00	$ 984.17	$ 817.73	$ 746.50	$ 711.53	$693.20
$ 80,000.00	$1,124.76	$ 934.55	$ 853.14	$ 813.18	$792.23
$ 90,000.00	$1,265.36	$1,051.37	$ 959.79	$ 914.82	$891.26
$100,000.00	$1,405.95	$1,168.19	$1,066.43	$1,016.47	$990.29

11⅝% RATE

Term of Loan in Years

Amount	10	15	20	25	30
$ 50.00	$ 0.71	$ 0.59	$ 0.54	$ 0.51	$ 0.50
$ 100.00	$ 1.41	$ 1.18	$ 1.08	$ 1.03	$ 1.00
$ 200.00	$ 2.83	$ 2.35	$ 2.15	$ 2.05	$ 2.00
$ 300.00	$ 4.24	$ 3.53	$ 3.23	$ 3.08	$ 3.00
$ 400.00	$ 5.65	$ 4.70	$ 4.30	$ 4.10	$ 4.00
$ 500.00	$ 7.07	$ 5.88	$ 5.38	$ 5.13	$ 5.00
$ 600.00	$ 8.48	$ 7.06	$ 6.45	$ 6.15	$ 6.00
$ 700.00	$ 9.89	$ 8.23	$ 7.53	$ 7.18	$ 7.00
$ 800.00	$ 11.30	$ 9.41	$ 8.60	$ 8.20	$ 8.00
$ 900.00	$ 12.72	$ 10.59	$ 9.68	$ 9.23	$ 9.00
$ 1,000.00	$ 14.13	$ 11.76	$ 10.75	$ 10.26	$ 10.00
$ 2,000.00	$ 28.26	$ 23.52	$ 21.50	$ 20.51	$ 20.00
$ 3,000.00	$ 42.39	$ 35.28	$ 32.25	$ 30.77	$ 30.00
$ 4,000.00	$ 56.52	$ 47.05	$ 43.00	$ 41.02	$ 39.99
$ 5,000.00	$ 70.66	$ 58.81	$ 53.75	$ 51.28	$ 49.99
$ 6,000.00	$ 84.79	$ 70.57	$ 64.50	$ 61.54	$ 59.99
$ 7,000.00	$ 98.92	$ 82.33	$ 75.25	$ 71.79	$ 69.99
$ 8,000.00	$ 113.05	$ 94.09	$ 86.00	$ 82.05	$ 79.99
$ 9,000.00	$ 127.18	$ 105.85	$ 96.75	$ 92.31	$ 89.99
$ 10,000.00	$ 141.31	$ 117.61	$ 107.51	$ 102.56	$ 99.98
$ 20,000.00	$ 282.62	$ 235.23	$ 215.01	$ 205.12	$199.97
$ 30,000.00	$ 423.93	$ 352.84	$ 322.52	$ 307.69	$299.95
$ 40,000.00	$ 565.25	$ 470.46	$ 430.02	$ 410.25	$399.94
$ 50,000.00	$ 706.56	$ 588.07	$ 537.53	$ 512.81	$499.92
$ 60,000.00	$ 847.87	$ 705.69	$ 645.03	$ 615.37	$599.90
$ 70,000.00	$ 989.18	$ 823.30	$ 752.54	$ 717.93	$699.89
$ 80,000.00	$1,130.49	$ 940.92	$ 860.04	$ 820.50	$799.87
$ 90,000.00	$1,271.80	$1,058.53	$ 967.55	$ 923.06	$899.86
$100,000.00	$1,413.12	$1,176.15	$1,075.06	$1,025.62	$999.84

11¾% RATE

Amount	10	15	20	25	30
			Term of Loan in Years		
$ 50.00	$ 0.71	$ 0.59	$ 0.54	$ 0.52	$ 0.50
$ 100.00	$ 1.42	$ 1.18	$ 1.08	$ 1.03	$ 1.01
$ 200.00	$ 2.84	$ 2.37	$ 2.17	$ 2.07	$ 2.02
$ 300.00	$ 4.26	$ 3.55	$ 3.25	$ 3.10	$ 3.03
$ 400.00	$ 5.68	$ 4.74	$ 4.33	$ 4.14	$ 4.04
$ 500.00	$ 7.10	$ 5.92	$ 5.42	$ 5.17	$ 5.05
$ 600.00	$ 8.52	$ 7.10	$ 6.50	$ 6.21	$ 6.06
$ 700.00	$ 9.94	$ 8.29	$ 7.59	$ 7.24	$ 7.07
$ 800.00	$ 11.36	$ 9.47	$ 8.67	$ 8.28	$ 8.08
$ 900.00	$ 12.78	$ 10.66	$ 9.75	$ 9.31	$ 9.08
$ 1,000.00	$ 14.20	$ 11.84	$ 10.84	$ 10.35	$ 10.09
$ 2,000.00	$ 28.41	$ 23.68	$ 21.67	$ 20.70	$ 20.19
$ 3,000.00	$ 42.61	$ 35.52	$ 32.51	$ 31.04	$ 30.28
$ 4,000.00	$ 56.81	$ 47.37	$ 43.35	$ 41.39	$ 40.38
$ 5,000.00	$ 71.01	$ 59.21	$ 54.19	$ 51.74	$ 50.47
$ 6,000.00	$ 85.22	$ 71.05	$ 65.02	$ 62.09	$ 60.56
$ 7,000.00	$ 99.42	$ 82.89	$ 75.86	$ 72.44	$ 70.66
$ 8,000.00	$ 113.62	$ 94.73	$ 86.70	$ 82.78	$ 80.75
$ 9,000.00	$ 127.83	$ 106.57	$ 97.53	$ 93.13	$ 90.85
$ 10,000.00	$ 142.03	$ 118.41	$ 108.37	$ 103.48	$ 100.94
$ 20,000.00	$ 284.06	$ 236.83	$ 216.74	$ 206.96	$ 201.88
$ 30,000.00	$ 426.09	$ 355.24	$ 325.11	$ 310.44	$ 302.82
$ 40,000.00	$ 568.12	$ 473.65	$ 433.48	$ 413.92	$ 403.76
$ 50,000.00	$ 710.15	$ 592.07	$ 541.85	$ 517.40	$ 504.70
$ 60,000.00	$ 852.18	$ 710.48	$ 650.22	$ 620.88	$ 605.65
$ 70,000.00	$ 994.21	$ 828.89	$ 758.59	$ 724.36	$ 706.59
$ 80,000.00	$1,136.24	$ 947.31	$ 866.97	$ 827.84	$ 807.53
$ 90,000.00	$1,278.27	$1,065.72	$ 975.34	$ 931.32	$ 908.47
$100,000.00	$1,420.29	$1,184.13	$1,083.71	$1,034.80	$1,009.41

11⅞% RATE

0.11875 Term of Loan in Years

Amount		10		15		20		25		30
$ 50.00	$	0.71	$	0.60	$	0.55	$	0.52	$	0.51
$ 100.00	$	1.43	$	1.19	$	1.09	$	1.04	$	1.02
$ 200.00	$	2.85	$	2.38	$	2.18	$	2.09	$	2.04
$ 300.00	$	4.28	$	3.58	$	3.28	$	3.13	$	3.06
$ 400.00	$	5.71	$	4.77	$	4.37	$	4.18	$	4.08
$ 500.00	$	7.14	$	5.96	$	5.46	$	5.22	$	5.10
$ 600.00	$	8.56	$	7.15	$	6.55	$	6.26	$	6.11
$ 700.00	$	9.99	$	8.34	$	7.65	$	7.31	$	7.13
$ 800.00	$	11.42	$	9.54	$	8.74	$	8.35	$	8.15
$ 900.00	$	12.85	$	10.73	$	9.83	$	9.40	$	9.17
$ 1,000.00	$	14.27	$	11.92	$	10.92	$	10.44	$	10.19
$ 2,000.00	$	28.55	$	23.84	$	21.85	$	20.88	$	20.38
$ 3,000.00	$	42.82	$	35.76	$	32.77	$	31.32	$	30.57
$ 4,000.00	$	57.10	$	47.69	$	43.70	$	41.76	$	40.76
$ 5,000.00	$	71.37	$	59.61	$	54.62	$	52.20	$	50.95
$ 6,000.00	$	85.65	$	71.53	$	65.54	$	62.64	$	61.14
$ 7,000.00	$	99.92	$	83.45	$	76.47	$	73.08	$	71.33
$ 8,000.00	$	114.20	$	95.37	$	87.39	$	83.52	$	81.52
$ 9,000.00	$	128.47	$	107.29	$	98.31	$	93.96	$	91.71
$ 10,000.00	$	142.75	$	119.21	$	109.24	$	104.40	$	101.90
$ 20,000.00	$	285.50	$	238.43	$	218.48	$	208.80	$	203.80
$ 30,000.00	$	428.25	$	357.64	$	327.72	$	313.20	$	305.70
$ 40,000.00	$	571.00	$	476.86	$	436.95	$	417.60	$	407.60
$ 50,000.00	$	713.75	$	596.07	$	546.19	$	522.00	$	509.50
$ 60,000.00	$	856.50	$	715.28	$	655.43	$	626.40	$	611.40
$ 70,000.00	$	999.24	$	834.50	$	764.67	$	730.80	$	713.30
$ 80,000.00	$1,141.99		$	953.71	$	873.91	$	835.20	$	815.20
$ 90,000.00	$1,284.74		$1,072.92		$	983.15	$	939.60	$	917.10
$100,000.00	$1,427.49		$1,192.14		$1,092.38		$1,044.00		$1,019.00

403

12% RATE

Term of Loan in Years

Amount		10		15		20		25		30
$ 50.00	$	0.72	$	0.60	$	0.55	$	0.53	$	0.51
$ 100.00	$	1.43	$	1.20	$	1.10	$	1.05	$	1.03
$ 200.00	$	2.87	$	2.40	$	2.20	$	2.11	$	2.06
$ 300.00	$	4.30	$	3.60	$	3.30	$	3.16	$	3.09
$ 400.00	$	5.74	$	4.80	$	4.40	$	4.21	$	4.11
$ 500.00	$	7.17	$	6.00	$	5.51	$	5.27	$	5.14
$ 600.00	$	8.61	$	7.20	$	6.61	$	6.32	$	6.17
$ 700.00	$	10.04	$	8.40	$	7.71	$	7.37	$	7.20
$ 800.00	$	11.48	$	9.60	$	8.81	$	8.43	$	8.23
$ 900.00	$	12.91	$	10.80	$	9.91	$	9.48	$	9.26
$ 1,000.00	$	14.35	$	12.00	$	11.01	$	10.53	$	10.29
$ 2,000.00	$	28.69	$	24.00	$	22.02	$	21.06	$	20.57
$ 3,000.00	$	43.04	$	36.01	$	33.03	$	31.60	$	30.86
$ 4,000.00	$	57.39	$	48.01	$	44.04	$	42.13	$	41.14
$ 5,000.00	$	71.74	$	60.01	$	55.05	$	52.66	$	51.43
$ 6,000.00	$	86.08	$	72.01	$	66.07	$	63.19	$	61.72
$ 7,000.00	$	100.43	$	84.01	$	77.08	$	73.73	$	72.00
$ 8,000.00	$	114.78	$	96.01	$	88.09	$	84.26	$	82.29
$ 9,000.00	$	129.12	$	108.02	$	99.10	$	94.79	$	92.58
$ 10,000.00	$	143.47	$	120.02	$	110.11	$	105.32	$	102.86
$ 20,000.00	$	286.94	$	240.03	$	220.22	$	210.64	$	205.72
$ 30,000.00	$	430.41	$	360.05	$	330.33	$	315.97	$	308.58
$ 40,000.00	$	573.88	$	480.07	$	440.43	$	421.29	$	411.45
$ 50,000.00	$	717.35	$	600.08	$	550.54	$	526.61	$	514.31
$ 60,000.00	$	860.83	$	720.10	$	660.65	$	631.93	$	617.17
$ 70,000.00	$1,004.30		$	840.12	$	770.76	$	737.26	$	720.03
$ 80,000.00	$1,147.77		$	960.13	$	880.87	$	842.58	$	822.89
$ 90,000.00	$1,291.24		$1,080.15		$	990.98	$	947.90	$	925.75
$100,000.00	$1,434.71		$1,200.17		$1,101.09		$1,053.22		$1,028.61

12⅛% RATE

Term of Loan in Years

Amount	10	15	20	25	30
$ 50.00	$ 0.72	$ 0.60	$ 0.55	$ 0.53	$ 0.52
$ 100.00	$ 1.44	$ 1.21	$ 1.11	$ 1.06	$ 1.04
$ 200.00	$ 2.88	$ 2.42	$ 2.22	$ 2.12	$ 2.08
$ 300.00	$ 4.33	$ 3.62	$ 3.33	$ 3.19	$ 3.11
$ 400.00	$ 5.77	$ 4.83	$ 4.44	$ 4.25	$ 4.15
$ 500.00	$ 7.21	$ 6.04	$ 5.55	$ 5.31	$ 5.19
$ 600.00	$ 8.65	$ 7.25	$ 6.66	$ 6.37	$ 6.23
$ 700.00	$ 10.09	$ 8.46	$ 7.77	$ 7.44	$ 7.27
$ 800.00	$ 11.54	$ 9.67	$ 8.88	$ 8.50	$ 8.31
$ 900.00	$ 12.98	$ 10.87	$ 9.99	$ 9.56	$ 9.34
$ 1,000.00	$ 14.42	$ 12.08	$ 11.10	$ 10.62	$ 10.38
$ 2,000.00	$ 28.84	$ 24.16	$ 22.20	$ 21.25	$ 20.76
$ 3,000.00	$ 43.26	$ 36.25	$ 33.29	$ 31.87	$ 31.15
$ 4,000.00	$ 57.68	$ 48.33	$ 44.39	$ 42.50	$ 41.53
$ 5,000.00	$ 72.10	$ 60.41	$ 55.49	$ 53.12	$ 51.91
$ 6,000.00	$ 86.52	$ 72.49	$ 66.59	$ 63.75	$ 62.29
$ 7,000.00	$ 100.94	$ 84.58	$ 77.69	$ 74.37	$ 72.68
$ 8,000.00	$ 115.36	$ 96.66	$ 88.79	$ 85.00	$ 83.06
$ 9,000.00	$ 129.78	$ 108.74	$ 99.88	$ 95.62	$ 93.44
$ 10,000.00	$ 144.19	$ 120.82	$ 110.98	$ 106.25	$ 103.82
$ 20,000.00	$ 288.39	$ 241.64	$ 221.96	$ 212.49	$ 207.65
$ 30,000.00	$ 432.58	$ 362.47	$ 332.94	$ 318.74	$ 311.47
$ 40,000.00	$ 576.78	$ 483.29	$ 443.93	$ 424.99	$ 415.30
$ 50,000.00	$ 720.97	$ 604.11	$ 554.91	$ 531.24	$ 519.12
$ 60,000.00	$ 865.17	$ 724.93	$ 665.89	$ 637.48	$ 622.95
$ 70,000.00	$1,009.36	$ 845.76	$ 776.87	$ 743.73	$ 726.77
$ 80,000.00	$1,153.56	$ 966.58	$ 887.85	$ 849.98	$ 830.60
$ 90,000.00	$1,297.75	$1,087.40	$ 998.83	$ 956.23	$ 934.42
$100,000.00	$1,441.94	$1,208.22	$1,109.81	$1,062.47	$1,038.24

12¼% RATE

0.1225

	Term of Loan in Years				
	10	15	20	25	30
Amount					
$ 50.00	$ 0.72	$ 0.61	$ 0.56	$ 0.54	$ 0.52
$ 100.00	$ 1.45	$ 1.22	$ 1.12	$ 1.07	$ 1.05
$ 200.00	$ 2.90	$ 2.43	$ 2.24	$ 2.14	$ 2.10
$ 300.00	$ 4.35	$ 3.65	$ 3.36	$ 3.22	$ 3.14
$ 400.00	$ 5.80	$ 4.87	$ 4.47	$ 4.29	$ 4.19
$ 500.00	$ 7.25	$ 6.08	$ 5.59	$ 5.36	$ 5.24
$ 600.00	$ 8.70	$ 7.30	$ 6.71	$ 6.43	$ 6.29
$ 700.00	$ 10.14	$ 8.51	$ 7.83	$ 7.50	$ 7.34
$ 800.00	$ 11.59	$ 9.73	$ 8.95	$ 8.57	$ 8.38
$ 900.00	$ 13.04	$ 10.95	$ 10.07	$ 9.65	$ 9.43
$ 1,000.00	$ 14.49	$ 12.16	$ 11.19	$ 10.72	$ 10.48
$ 2,000.00	$ 28.98	$ 24.33	$ 22.37	$ 21.43	$ 20.96
$ 3,000.00	$ 43.48	$ 36.49	$ 33.56	$ 32.15	$ 31.44
$ 4,000.00	$ 57.97	$ 48.65	$ 44.74	$ 42.87	$ 41.92
$ 5,000.00	$ 72.46	$ 60.81	$ 55.93	$ 53.59	$ 52.39
$ 6,000.00	$ 86.95	$ 72.98	$ 67.11	$ 64.30	$ 62.87
$ 7,000.00	$ 101.44	$ 85.14	$ 78.30	$ 75.02	$ 73.35
$ 8,000.00	$ 115.94	$ 97.30	$ 89.49	$ 85.74	$ 83.83
$ 9,000.00	$ 130.43	$ 109.47	$ 100.67	$ 96.46	$ 94.31
$ 10,000.00	$ 144.92	$ 121.63	$ 111.86	$ 107.17	$ 104.79
$ 20,000.00	$ 289.84	$ 243.26	$ 223.71	$ 214.35	$ 209.58
$ 30,000.00	$ 434.76	$ 364.89	$ 335.57	$ 321.52	$ 314.37
$ 40,000.00	$ 579.68	$ 486.52	$ 447.43	$ 428.70	$ 419.16
$ 50,000.00	$ 724.60	$ 608.15	$ 559.28	$ 535.87	$ 523.95
$ 60,000.00	$ 869.52	$ 729.78	$ 671.14	$ 643.05	$ 628.74
$ 70,000.00	$1,014.44	$ 851.41	$ 783.00	$ 750.22	$ 733.53
$ 80,000.00	$1,159.36	$ 973.04	$ 894.85	$ 857.40	$ 838.32
$ 90,000.00	$1,304.28	$1,094.67	$1,006.71	$ 964.57	$ 943.11
$100,000.00	$1,449.20	$1,216.30	$1,118.56	$1,071.74	$1,047.90

12⅜% RATE

0.12375   Term of Loan in Years

	10	15	20	25	30
Amount					
$ 50.00	$ 0.73	$ 0.61	$ 0.56	$ 0.54	$ 0.53
$ 100.00	$ 1.46	$ 1.22	$ 1.13	$ 1.08	$ 1.06
$ 200.00	$ 2.91	$ 2.45	$ 2.25	$ 2.16	$ 2.12
$ 300.00	$ 4.37	$ 3.67	$ 3.38	$ 3.24	$ 3.17
$ 400.00	$ 5.83	$ 4.90	$ 4.51	$ 4.32	$ 4.23
$ 500.00	$ 7.28	$ 6.12	$ 5.64	$ 5.41	$ 5.29
$ 600.00	$ 8.74	$ 7.35	$ 6.76	$ 6.49	$ 6.35
$ 700.00	$ 10.20	$ 8.57	$ 7.89	$ 7.57	$ 7.40
$ 800.00	$ 11.65	$ 9.80	$ 9.02	$ 8.65	$ 8.46
$ 900.00	$ 13.11	$ 11.02	$ 10.15	$ 9.73	$ 9.52
$ 1,000.00	$ 14.56	$ 12.24	$ 11.27	$ 10.81	$ 10.58
$ 2,000.00	$ 29.13	$ 24.49	$ 22.55	$ 21.62	$ 21.15
$ 3,000.00	$ 43.69	$ 36.73	$ 33.82	$ 32.43	$ 31.73
$ 4,000.00	$ 58.26	$ 48.98	$ 45.09	$ 43.24	$ 42.30
$ 5,000.00	$ 72.82	$ 61.22	$ 56.37	$ 54.05	$ 52.88
$ 6,000.00	$ 87.39	$ 73.46	$ 67.64	$ 64.86	$ 63.45
$ 7,000.00	$ 101.95	$ 85.71	$ 78.91	$ 75.67	$ 74.03
$ 8,000.00	$ 116.52	$ 97.95	$ 90.19	$ 86.48	$ 84.61
$ 9,000.00	$ 131.08	$ 110.20	$ 101.46	$ 97.29	$ 95.18
$ 10,000.00	$ 145.65	$ 122.44	$ 112.73	$ 108.10	$ 105.76
$ 20,000.00	$ 291.29	$ 244.88	$ 225.47	$ 216.21	$ 211.51
$ 30,000.00	$ 436.94	$ 367.32	$ 338.20	$ 324.31	$ 317.27
$ 40,000.00	$ 582.59	$ 489.76	$ 450.94	$ 432.42	$ 423.03
$ 50,000.00	$ 728.24	$ 612.20	$ 563.67	$ 540.52	$ 528.78
$ 60,000.00	$ 873.88	$ 734.64	$ 676.40	$ 648.62	$ 634.54
$ 70,000.00	$1,019.53	$ 857.08	$ 789.14	$ 756.73	$ 740.30
$ 80,000.00	$1,165.18	$ 979.52	$ 901.87	$ 864.83	$ 846.05
$ 90,000.00	$1,310.82	$1,101.96	$1,014.61	$ 972.93	$ 951.81
$100,000.00	$1,456.47	$1,224.40	$1,127.34	$1,081.04	$1,057.57

12½% RATE

Term of Loan in Years

Amount	10	15	20	25	30
$ 50.00	$ 0.73	$ 0.62	$ 0.57	$ 0.55	$ 0.53
$ 100.00	$ 1.46	$ 1.23	$ 1.14	$ 1.09	$ 1.07
$ 200.00	$ 2.93	$ 2.47	$ 2.27	$ 2.18	$ 2.13
$ 300.00	$ 4.39	$ 3.70	$ 3.41	$ 3.27	$ 3.20
$ 400.00	$ 5.86	$ 4.93	$ 4.54	$ 4.36	$ 4.27
$ 500.00	$ 7.32	$ 6.16	$ 5.68	$ 5.45	$ 5.34
$ 600.00	$ 8.78	$ 7.40	$ 6.82	$ 6.54	$ 6.40
$ 700.00	$ 10.25	$ 8.63	$ 7.95	$ 7.63	$ 7.47
$ 800.00	$ 11.71	$ 9.86	$ 9.09	$ 8.72	$ 8.54
$ 900.00	$ 13.17	$ 11.09	$ 10.23	$ 9.81	$ 9.61
$ 1,000.00	$ 14.64	$ 12.33	$ 11.36	$ 10.90	$ 10.67
$ 2,000.00	$ 29.28	$ 24.65	$ 22.72	$ 21.81	$ 21.35
$ 3,000.00	$ 43.91	$ 36.98	$ 34.08	$ 32.71	$ 32.02
$ 4,000.00	$ 58.55	$ 49.30	$ 45.45	$ 43.61	$ 42.69
$ 5,000.00	$ 73.19	$ 61.63	$ 56.81	$ 54.52	$ 53.36
$ 6,000.00	$ 87.83	$ 73.95	$ 68.17	$ 65.42	$ 64.04
$ 7,000.00	$ 102.46	$ 86.28	$ 79.53	$ 76.32	$ 74.71
$ 8,000.00	$ 117.10	$ 98.60	$ 90.89	$ 87.23	$ 85.38
$ 9,000.00	$ 131.74	$ 110.93	$ 102.25	$ 98.13	$ 96.05
$ 10,000.00	$ 146.38	$ 123.25	$ 113.61	$ 109.04	$ 106.73
$ 20,000.00	$ 292.75	$ 246.50	$ 227.23	$ 218.07	$ 213.45
$ 30,000.00	$ 439.13	$ 369.76	$ 340.84	$ 327.11	$ 320.18
$ 40,000.00	$ 585.50	$ 493.01	$ 454.46	$ 436.14	$ 426.90
$ 50,000.00	$ 731.88	$ 616.26	$ 568.07	$ 545.18	$ 533.63
$ 60,000.00	$ 878.26	$ 739.51	$ 681.68	$ 654.21	$ 640.35
$ 70,000.00	$1,024.63	$ 862.77	$ 795.30	$ 763.25	$ 747.08
$ 80,000.00	$1,171.01	$ 986.02	$ 908.91	$ 872.28	$ 853.81
$ 90,000.00	$1,317.39	$1,109.27	$1,022.53	$ 981.32	$ 960.53
$100,000.00	$1,463.76	$1,232.52	$1,136.14	$1,090.35	$1,067.26

12⅝% RATE

0.12625   Term of Loan in Years

	10	15	20	25	30
Amount					
$ 50.00	$ 0.74	$ 0.62	$ 0.57	$ 0.55	$ 0.54
$ 100.00	$ 1.47	$ 1.24	$ 1.14	$ 1.10	$ 1.08
$ 200.00	$ 2.94	$ 2.48	$ 2.29	$ 2.20	$ 2.15
$ 300.00	$ 4.41	$ 3.72	$ 3.43	$ 3.30	$ 3.23
$ 400.00	$ 5.88	$ 4.96	$ 4.58	$ 4.40	$ 4.31
$ 500.00	$ 7.36	$ 6.20	$ 5.72	$ 5.50	$ 5.38
$ 600.00	$ 8.83	$ 7.44	$ 6.87	$ 6.60	$ 6.46
$ 700.00	$ 10.30	$ 8.68	$ 8.01	$ 7.70	$ 7.54
$ 800.00	$ 11.77	$ 9.93	$ 9.16	$ 8.80	$ 8.62
$ 900.00	$ 13.24	$ 11.17	$ 10.30	$ 9.90	$ 9.69
$ 1,000.00	$ 14.71	$ 12.41	$ 11.45	$ 11.00	$ 10.77
$ 2,000.00	$ 29.42	$ 24.81	$ 22.90	$ 21.99	$ 21.54
$ 3,000.00	$ 44.13	$ 37.22	$ 34.35	$ 32.99	$ 32.31
$ 4,000.00	$ 58.84	$ 49.63	$ 45.80	$ 43.99	$ 43.08
$ 5,000.00	$ 73.55	$ 62.03	$ 57.25	$ 54.98	$ 53.85
$ 6,000.00	$ 88.26	$ 74.44	$ 68.70	$ 65.98	$ 64.62
$ 7,000.00	$ 102.97	$ 86.85	$ 80.15	$ 76.98	$ 75.39
$ 8,000.00	$ 117.69	$ 99.25	$ 91.60	$ 87.98	$ 86.16
$ 9,000.00	$ 132.40	$ 111.66	$ 103.05	$ 98.97	$ 96.93
$ 10,000.00	$ 147.11	$ 124.07	$ 114.50	$ 109.97	$ 107.70
$ 20,000.00	$ 294.21	$ 248.13	$ 228.99	$ 219.94	$ 215.39
$ 30,000.00	$ 441.32	$ 372.20	$ 343.49	$ 329.91	$ 323.09
$ 40,000.00	$ 588.43	$ 496.27	$ 457.99	$ 439.88	$ 430.79
$ 50,000.00	$ 735.54	$ 620.33	$ 572.48	$ 549.85	$ 538.48
$ 60,000.00	$ 882.64	$ 744.40	$ 686.98	$ 659.82	$ 646.18
$ 70,000.00	$1,029.75	$ 868.47	$ 801.48	$ 769.78	$ 753.88
$ 80,000.00	$1,176.86	$ 992.53	$ 915.97	$ 879.75	$ 861.57
$ 90,000.00	$1,323.96	$1,116.60	$1,030.47	$ 989.72	$ 969.27
$100,000.00	$1,471.07	$1,240.67	$1,144.96	$1,099.69	$1,076.97

12¾% RATE

Term of Loan in Years

Amount	10	15	20	25	30
$ 50.00	$ 0.74	$ 0.62	$ 0.58	$ 0.55	$ 0.54
$ 100.00	$ 1.48	$ 1.25	$ 1.15	$ 1.11	$ 1.09
$ 200.00	$ 2.96	$ 2.50	$ 2.31	$ 2.22	$ 2.17
$ 300.00	$ 4.44	$ 3.75	$ 3.46	$ 3.33	$ 3.26
$ 400.00	$ 5.91	$ 5.00	$ 4.62	$ 4.44	$ 4.35
$ 500.00	$ 7.39	$ 6.24	$ 5.77	$ 5.55	$ 5.43
$ 600.00	$ 8.87	$ 7.49	$ 6.92	$ 6.65	$ 6.52
$ 700.00	$ 10.35	$ 8.74	$ 8.08	$ 7.76	$ 7.61
$ 800.00	$ 11.83	$ 9.99	$ 9.23	$ 8.87	$ 8.69
$ 900.00	$ 13.31	$ 11.24	$ 10.38	$ 9.98	$ 9.78
$ 1,000.00	$ 14.78	$ 12.49	$ 11.54	$ 11.09	$ 10.87
$ 2,000.00	$ 29.57	$ 24.98	$ 23.08	$ 22.18	$ 21.73
$ 3,000.00	$ 44.35	$ 37.47	$ 34.61	$ 33.27	$ 32.60
$ 4,000.00	$ 59.14	$ 49.95	$ 46.15	$ 44.36	$ 43.47
$ 5,000.00	$ 73.92	$ 62.44	$ 57.69	$ 55.45	$ 54.33
$ 6,000.00	$ 88.70	$ 74.93	$ 69.23	$ 66.54	$ 65.20
$ 7,000.00	$ 103.49	$ 87.42	$ 80.77	$ 77.63	$ 76.07
$ 8,000.00	$ 118.27	$ 99.91	$ 92.30	$ 88.72	$ 86.94
$ 9,000.00	$ 133.06	$ 112.40	$ 103.84	$ 99.81	$ 97.80
$ 10,000.00	$ 147.84	$ 124.88	$ 115.38	$ 110.91	$ 108.67
$ 20,000.00	$ 295.68	$ 249.77	$ 230.76	$ 221.81	$ 217.34
$ 30,000.00	$ 443.52	$ 374.65	$ 346.14	$ 332.72	$ 326.01
$ 40,000.00	$ 591.36	$ 499.53	$ 461.52	$ 443.62	$ 434.68
$ 50,000.00	$ 739.20	$ 624.42	$ 576.91	$ 554.53	$ 543.35
$ 60,000.00	$ 887.04	$ 749.30	$ 692.29	$ 665.43	$ 652.02
$ 70,000.00	$1,034.88	$ 874.19	$ 807.67	$ 776.34	$ 760.69
$ 80,000.00	$1,182.72	$ 999.07	$ 923.05	$ 887.24	$ 869.35
$ 90,000.00	$1,330.56	$1,123.95	$1,038.43	$ 998.15	$ 978.02
$100,000.00	$1,478.40	$1,248.84	$1,153.81	$1,109.05	$1,086.69

12⅞% RATE

0.12875   Term of Loan in Years

	10	15	20	25	30
Amount					
$ 50.00	$ 0.74	$ 0.63	$ 0.58	$ 0.56	$ 0.55
$ 100.00	$ 1.49	$ 1.26	$ 1.16	$ 1.12	$ 1.10
$ 200.00	$ 2.97	$ 2.51	$ 2.33	$ 2.24	$ 2.19
$ 300.00	$ 4.46	$ 3.77	$ 3.49	$ 3.36	$ 3.29
$ 400.00	$ 5.94	$ 5.03	$ 4.65	$ 4.47	$ 4.39
$ 500.00	$ 7.43	$ 6.29	$ 5.81	$ 5.59	$ 5.48
$ 600.00	$ 8.91	$ 7.54	$ 6.98	$ 6.71	$ 6.58
$ 700.00	$ 10.40	$ 8.80	$ 8.14	$ 7.83	$ 7.68
$ 800.00	$ 11.89	$ 10.06	$ 9.30	$ 8.95	$ 8.77
$ 900.00	$ 13.37	$ 11.31	$ 10.46	$ 10.07	$ 9.87
$ 1,000.00	$ 14.86	$ 12.57	$ 11.63	$ 11.18	$ 10.96
$ 2,000.00	$ 29.71	$ 25.14	$ 23.25	$ 22.37	$ 21.93
$ 3,000.00	$ 44.57	$ 37.71	$ 34.88	$ 33.55	$ 32.89
$ 4,000.00	$ 59.43	$ 50.28	$ 46.51	$ 44.74	$ 43.86
$ 5,000.00	$ 74.29	$ 62.85	$ 58.13	$ 55.92	$ 54.82
$ 6,000.00	$ 89.14	$ 75.42	$ 69.76	$ 67.11	$ 65.79
$ 7,000.00	$ 104.00	$ 87.99	$ 81.39	$ 78.29	$ 76.75
$ 8,000.00	$ 118.86	$ 100.56	$ 93.01	$ 89.47	$ 87.72
$ 9,000.00	$ 133.72	$ 113.13	$ 104.64	$ 100.66	$ 98.68
$ 10,000.00	$ 148.57	$ 125.70	$ 116.27	$ 111.84	$ 109.64
$ 20,000.00	$ 297.15	$ 251.41	$ 232.54	$ 223.69	$ 219.29
$ 30,000.00	$ 445.72	$ 377.11	$ 348.80	$ 335.53	$ 328.93
$ 40,000.00	$ 594.30	$ 502.81	$ 465.07	$ 447.37	$ 438.58
$ 50,000.00	$ 742.87	$ 628.51	$ 581.34	$ 559.22	$ 548.22
$ 60,000.00	$ 891.45	$ 754.22	$ 697.61	$ 671.06	$ 657.86
$ 70,000.00	$1,040.02	$ 879.92	$ 813.88	$ 782.90	$ 767.51
$ 80,000.00	$1,188.59	$1,005.62	$ 930.15	$ 894.75	$ 877.15
$ 90,000.00	$1,337.17	$1,131.33	$1,046.41	$1,006.59	$ 986.79
$100,000.00	$1,485.74	$1,257.03	$1,162.68	$1,118.43	$1,096.44

APPENDIX VI

Resources

Special First-Time Buyer Programs

To find out about special programs for first-time buyers, contact your local city, county, and state housing bureaus. Also, contact your local HUD office. Also, neighborhood or community action groups might also be sponsoring low-interest, low-down-payment programs. Also, contact the real estate staff of your local newspaper and ask if they've heard of any new programs (these programs tend to spring up when a wellspring of community development block grant money appears, and then disappear until new funds are obtained).

Department of Housing and Urban Development (HUD)

451 7th Street, SW
Washington, DC 20410

To locate the nearest HUD office to you: (202) 708-1112
To get program information: (202) 708-4374

HUD User, a clearinghouse of information: (800) 245-2691
HUD User, Washington, D.C. area only: (202) 251-5154

This agency provides programs for low-income housing, including public housing and privately owned rental housing. It supports housing-related site development and housing rehabilitation through Community Development Block Grants to state and local governments. It also provides support for the residential mortgage market through the Federal Housing Administration (FHA) mortgage insurance program and Government National Mortgage Association (Ginnie Mae) mortgage-backed securities guarantee program.

There is a local HUD office in nearly every major urban area. If you are located outside of an urban area call the HUD office in your state capital or in Washington, DC to find the office located closest to you.

Consumer Product Safety Commission

Washington, DC 20207
(800) 638-2772

Call this toll-free number to lodge a complaint about the safety of houses and buildings, including smoke alarms, electrical systems, indoor air quality, and home insulation. You can also get recall information and safety tips. If you negotiate the options successfully, an operator will eventually come on the line to take your complaint.

Department of Veterans Affairs (VA)

Loan Guarantee Service
Department of Veterans Affairs

810 Vermont Avenue, NW
Washington, DC 20420
General number: (800) 827-1000

The federal agency that guarantees a portion of home loans to veterans and regulates their distribution. The Department of Veterans Affairs publishes a pamphlet about guaranteed home loans for veterans that's free for the writing. Contact your local VA office (you can call the general number for information) for additional information.

The Department of Veterans Affairs also runs a Vendee Financing program, which provides inexpensive financing (with little or no down payment required, and a discount for a cash purchase) of VA-acquired homes. You need not be a veteran to qualify. Check with the Loan Guarantee Service for more information and current qualifications.

Consumer Publications

For a list of consumer publications that may be useful to you as a first-time (or repeat) home buyer, write to Consumer Publications, Pueblo, Colorado 81003.

National Council for State Housing Agencies

444 N. Capital Street, NW
Suite 438
Washington, DC 20001
(202) 634-7710

NCSHA is an advocacy group for low-income housing in Washington. It represents state housing finance agencies in all fifty states, plus Puerto Rico and the Virgin Islands. If you are unable to find your state housing finance agency, write to this organization.

As of 1990, there were more than 180 public agencies that provide financial assistance to first-time home buyers. Generally, there are home price and family income limitations. Your state housing agency or real estate agent should be able to point you in the right direction.

Consumer Credit Counseling Service (CCCS)

This organization has offices around the country and it provides many services to first-time home buyers, including credit and comprehensive housing counseling. These services are confidential and free of charge. CCCS offices can prequalify buyers and talk about various mortgage types and may be able to tap you into affordable housing programs.

For more information, look in your telephone book for the nearest CCCS office to you.

Federal National Mortgage Association (Fannie Mae)

Headquarters:
3900 Wisconsin Avenue, NW
Washington, DC 20016
(800) 7-FANNIE

Fannie Mae, the nation's largest investor in home mortgages, is a private corporation, federally chartered to provide financial products and services that increase the availability and affordability of housing for low-, moderate-, and middle-income

Americans. Fannie Mae buys residential mortgages for its investment portfolio. If you call the 800 number, you'll get the public information office, and will be able to order information packets on Community Homebuyers programs, as well as other first-time buyer information.

American Homeowners Foundation (AHF)

Headquarters:
6776 Little Falls Rd.
Arlington, VA 22213
(703) 536-7776

This nonprofit educational and research organization represents home owners, prospective home owners, and home investors. For more information on its publications, write or call the Arlington, Virginia, office.

Consumer Federation of America (CFA)

Headquarters:
1424 16th Street NW, Suite 604
Washington, DC 20036
(202) 387-6121

The Consumer Federation of America has 240 pro-consumer organizations with 50 million individual members. It is a lobbying group that represents consumer interests on Capitol Hill. It publishes CFANews eight times each year. Occasionally, it'll copublish a booklet on residential real estate with a related organization.

Council of Better Business Bureaus

Headquarters:
4200 Wilson Boulevard, Suite 800
Arlington, VA 22203
(703) 276-0100

This organization is dedicated to consumers and attempts to be an effective national self-regulation force for business. The headquarters can help you find the bureau nearest you.

Home Information Center, part of the Office of Affordable Housing

PO Box 7189
Gaithersburg, MD 20898-7189
(800) 998-9999

This organization works with two programs: The Home Program and Hope 3. The Home Program gives grant money to nonprofit associations. Hope 3 is a single-family-home buyer program using government help properties. For more information on Hope 3, call the 800 number.

Neighborhood Reinvestment Corporation

Headquarters:
1325 G Street, N.W., Suite 800
Washington, DC 20005
(202) 376-2400

This organization acts as a national network for affordable housing providers. If you contact the headquarters, it can help you locate the neighborhood housing services nearest to you.

The Insurance Information Institute

110 William Street
New York, NY 10038

The Insurance Information Institute is a nonprofit communications, educational and fact-finding organization dedicated to improving the public's understanding of the property/casualty insurance business.

Glossary of Real Estate Terms Every First-Time Buyer Should Know

Abstract (of Title) A summary of the public records affecting the title to a particular piece of land. An attorney or title insurance company officer creates the abstract of title by examining all recorded instruments (documents) relating to a specific piece of property, such as easements, liens, mortgages, etc.

Acceleration Clause A provision in a loan agreement that allows the lender to require the balance of the loan to become due immediately if mortgage payments are not made or there is a breach in your obligation under your mortgage or note.

Addendum Any addition to, or modification of, a contract. Also called an amendment or rider.

Adjustable-Rate Mortgage (ARM) A type of loan whose prevailing interest rate is tied to an economic index (like one-year Treasury Bills), which fluctuates with the market. There are three types of arms, including one-year ARMs, which adjust every year; three-year ARMs, which adjust every three years; and five-year ARMs, which adjust every five years. When the loan adjusts, the lender tacks a margin onto the economic index rate to come up with your loan's new rate. ARMs are considered far riskier than fixed-rate mortgages, but their starting interest rates are extremely low, and in the past five to ten years, people have done very well with them.

Agency A term used to describe the relationship between a seller and a broker, or a buyer and a broker.

Agency Closing The lender's use of a title company or other party to act on the lender's behalf for the purposes of closing on the purchase of a home or refinancing of a loan.

Agent An individual who represents a buyer or a seller in the purchase or sale of a home. Licensed by the state, an agent must work for a broker or a brokerage firm.

Agreement of Sale This document is also known as the contract of purchase, purchase agreement, or sales agreement. It is the agreement by which the seller agrees to sell you his or her property if you pay a certain price. It contains all the provisions and conditions for the purchase, must be written, and is signed by both parties.

Amortization A payment plan which enables the borrower to reduce his debt gradually through monthly payments of principal and interest. Amortization tables (see Appendix V) allow you to see exactly how much you would pay each month in interest and how much you repay in principal, depending on the amount of money borrowed at a specific interest rate.

Annual Percentage Rate (APR) The total cost of your loan, expressed as a percentage rate of interest, which includes not only the loan's interest rate, but factors in all the costs associated with making that loan, including closing costs and fees. The costs are then amortized over the life of the loan. Banks are required by the federal Truth-in-Lending statutes to disclose the APR of a loan, which allows borrowers a common ground for comparing various loans from different lenders.

Application A series of documents you must fill out when you apply for a loan.

Application Fee A one-time fee charged by the mortgage company for processing your application for a loan. Sometimes the application fee is applied toward certain costs, including the appraisal and credit report.

Appraisal The opinion of an appraiser, who estimates the value of a home at a specific point in time.

Articles-of-Agreement Mortgage A type of seller financing which allows the buyer to purchase the home in installments over a specified period of time. The seller keeps legal title to the home until the loan is paid off. The buyer receives an interest in the property—called equitable title—but does not own it. However, because the buyer is paying the real estate taxes and paying interest to the seller, it is the buyer who receives the tax benefits of home ownership.

Assumption of Mortgage If you assume a mortgage when you purchase a home, you undertake to fulfill the obligations of the existing loan agreement the seller made with the lender. The obligations are similar to those that you would incur if you took out a new mortgage. When assuming a mortgage, you become personally liable for the payment of principal and interest. The seller, or original mortgagor, is released from the liability, and should get that release in writing. Otherwise, he or she could be liable if you don't make the monthly payments.

Balloon Mortgage A type of mortgage which is generally short in length, but is amortized over twenty-five or thirty years so that the borrower pays a combination of interest and principal each month. At the end of the loan term, the entire balance of the loan must be repaid at once.

Broker An individual who acts as the agent of the seller or buyer. A real estate broker must be licensed by the state.

Building Line or Setback The distance from the front, back, or side of a lot beyond which construction or improvements may not extend without permission by the proper governmental authority. The building line may be established by a filed plat of subdivision, by restrictive covenants in deeds, by building codes, or by zoning ordinances.

Buy Down An incentive offered by a developer or seller that allows the buyer to lower his or her initial interest rate by putting up a certain amount of money. A buy down also refers to the process of paying extra points upfront at the closing of your loan in order to have a lower interest rate over the life of the loan.

Buyer Broker A buyer broker is a real estate broker who specializes in representing buyers. Unlike a seller broker or conventional broker, the buyer broker has a fiduciary duty to the buyer, because the buyer accepts the legal obligation of paying the broker (see Question 11 regarding payment of buyer brokers). The buyer broker is obligated to find the best property for a client, and then negotiate the best possible purchase price and terms. Buyer brokerage has gained a significant amount of respect in recent years, since the National Association of Realtors has changed its code of ethics to accept this designation.

Buyer's Market Market conditions that favor the buyer. A buyer's market is usually expressed when there are too many homes for sale, and a home can be bought for less money.

Certificate of Title A document or instrument issued by a local government agency to a homeowner, naming the homeowner as the owner of a specific piece of property. At the sale of the property, the certificate of title is transferred to the buyer. The agency then issues a new certificate of title to the buyer.

Chain of Title The lineage of ownership of a particular property.

Closing The day when buyers and sellers sign the papers and actually swap money for title to the new home. The closing finalizes the agreements reached in the sales agreement.

Closing Costs This phrase can refer to a lender's costs for closing on a loan, or it can mean all the costs associated with closing on a piece of property. Considering all closing costs, it's easy to see that closing can be expensive for both buyers and sellers. A home buyer's closing costs might include: lender's points, loan origination or loan service fees; loan application fee; lender's credit report; lender's processing fee; lender's document preparation fee; lender's appraisal fee; prepaid interest on the loan; lender's insurance escrow; lender's real estate tax escrow; lender's tax escrow service fee; cost for the lender's title policy; special endorsements to the lender's title policy; house inspection fees; title company closing fee; deed or mortgage recording fees; local municipal, county, and state taxes; and the attorney's fee. A seller's closing costs might include: survey (which in some parts of the country is paid for by the buyer); title insurance; recorded release of mortgage; broker's commission; state, county, and local municipality transfer taxes; credit to the buyer for unpaid real estate taxes and other bills; attorney's fees; FHA fees and costs.

Cloud (on title) An outstanding claim or encumbrance that adversely affects the marketability of a property.

Commission The amount of money paid to the broker by the seller (or, in some cases, the buyer), as compensation for selling the home. Usually, the commission is a percentage of the sales price of the home, and generally hovers in the 5 to 7 percent range. There is no "set" commission rate. It is always and entirely negotiable.

Condemnation The government holds the right to "condemn" land for public use, even against the will of the owner. The government, however, must pay fair market price for the land. Condemnation may also mean that the government has decided a particular piece of land, or a dwelling, is unsafe for human habitation.

Condominium A dwelling of two or more units in which you individually own the interior space of your unit and jointly own common areas such as the lobby, roof, parking, plumbing, and recreational areas.

Contingency A provision in a contract that sets forth one or more conditions that must be met prior to the closing. If the contingency is not met, usually the party who is benefitting from the contingency can terminate the contract. Some common contingencies include financing, inspection, attorney approval, and toxic substances.

Contract To Purchase Another name for Agreement of Sale.

Contractor In the building industry, the contractor is the individual who contracts to build the property. He or she erects the structure and manages the subcontracting (to the electrician, plumber, etc.) until the project is finished.

Conventional Mortgage A conventional mortgage means that the loan is underwritten by banks, savings and loans, or other types of mortgage companies. There are also certain limitations imposed on conventional mortgages that allow them to be sold to private institutional investors (like pension funds) on the secondary market. For example, as of 1993, the loan must be less than $203,500, otherwise it is considered a "jumbo" loan. Also, if you are buying a condominium, conventional financing decrees that the condo building be more than 70 percent owner-occupied.

Co-op Cooperative housing refers to a building, or a group of buildings, that is owned by a corporation. The shareholders of the corporation are the people who live in the building. They own shares—which gives them the right to lease a specific unit within the building—in the corporation that owns their building and pay "rent" or monthly maintenance assessments for the expenses associated with living in the building. Co-ops are relatively unknown outside of New York, Chicago, and a few other cities. Since the 1970s, condominiums have become much more popular.

Counteroffer When the seller or buyer responds to a bid. If you decide to offer $100,000 for a home listed at $150,000, the seller might counter your offer and propose that you purchase the home for $140,-000. That new proposal, and any subsequent offer, is called a counteroffer.

Covenant Assurances or promises set out in the deed or a legally binding contract, or implied in the law. For example, when you obtain title to a property by warranty, there is the Covenant of Quiet Enjoyment, which gives you the right to enjoy your property without disturbances.

Credit Report A lender will decide whether or not to give you a loan based on your credit history. A credit report lists all of your credit accounts (such as charge cards), and any debts or late payments that have been reported to the credit company.

Cul de Sac A street that ends in a U-shape, leading the driver or pedestrian back to the beginning. The cul de sac has become exceptionally popular with modern subdivision developers, who use the design technique to create quiet streets and give the development a nonlinear feel.

Custom Builder A home builder who builds houses for individual owners to the owners' specification. The home builder may either own a piece of property or build a home on someone else's land.

Debt Service The total amount of debt (credit cards, mortgage, car loan) that an individual is carrying at any one time.

Declaration of Restrictions Developers of condominiums (or any other type of housing unit that functions as a condo) are required to file a condominium declaration, which sets out the rules and restrictions for the property, the division of ownership, and the rights and privileges of the owners. The "condo dec" or "home owner's dec," as it is commonly called, reflects the developer's original intent, and may only be changed by unit-owner vote. There are other types of declarations, including home owners' association and town house association. Co-op dwellers are governed by a similar type of document.

Deed The document used to transfer ownership in a property from seller to buyer.

Deed of Trust A deed of trust or trust deed is an instrument similar to a mortgage that gives the lender the right to foreclose on the property if there is a default under the trust deed or note by the borrower.

Deposit Money given by the buyer to the seller with a signed contract to purchase or offer to purchase, as a show of good faith. Also called the earnest money.

Down Payment The cash put into a purchase by the borrower. Lenders like to see the borrower put at least 20 percent down in cash, because lenders generally believe that if you have a higher cash down payment, it is less likely the home will go into foreclosure. In recent years, however, lenders have become more flexible about cash down payments; recently, lenders have begun accepting cash down payments of as little as 5 percent.

Dual Agency When a real estate broker represents both the buyer and the seller in a single transaction it creates a situation known as dual agency. In most states, brokers must disclose to the buyer and to the seller whom they are representing. Even with disclosure, dual agency presents a conflict of interest for the broker in the transaction.

If the broker is acting as the seller broker and the subagent for the seller (by bringing the buyer), then anything the buyer tells the broker must by law be brought to the seller's attention. If the broker represents the seller as a seller broker and the buyer as a buyer broker in the same transaction, the broker will receive money from both the buyer and the seller, an obvious conflict of interest.

Due on Sale Clause Nearly every mortgage has this clause, which states that the mortgage must be paid off in full upon the sale of the home.

Earnest Money The money the buyer gives the seller up front as a show of good faith. It can be as much as 10 percent of the purchase price. Earnest money is sometimes called a deposit.

Easement A right given by a landowner to a third party to make use of the land in a specific way. There may be several easements on your property, including for passage of utility lines or poles, sewer or water mains, and even a driveway. Once the right is given, it continues indefinitely, or until released by the party who received it.

Eminent Domain The right of the government to condemn private land for public use. The government must, however, pay full market value for the property.

Encroachment When your neighbor builds a garage or a fence, and it occupies your land, it is said to "encroach on" your property.

Encumbrance A claim or lien or interest in a property by another party. An encumbrance hinders the seller's ability to pass good, marketable, and unencumbered title to you.

Escrow Closing A third party, usually a title company, acts as the neutral party for the receipt of documents for the exchange of the deed by the sellers for the buyer's money. The final exchange is completed when the third party determines that certain preset requirements have been satisfied.

Escrow (for Earnest Money) The document that creates the arrangement whereby a third party or broker holds the earnest money for the benefit of the buyer and seller.

Escrow (for Real Estate Taxes and Insurance) An account in which monthly installments for real estate taxes and property insurance are held—usually in the name of the home buyer's lender.

Fee Simple The most basic type of ownership, under which the owner has the right to use and dispose of the property at will.

Fiduciary Duty A relationship of trust between a broker and a seller or a buyer broker and a buyer, or an attorney and a client.

First Mortgage A mortgage that takes priority over all other voluntary liens.

Fixture Personal property, such as a built-in bookcase, furnace, hot water heater, and recessed lights, that becomes "affixed" because it has been permanently attached to the home.

Foreclosure The legal action taken to extinguish a home owner's right and interest in a property, so that the property can be sold in a foreclosure sale to satisfy a debt.

Gift Letter A letter to the lender indicating that a gift of cash has been made to the buyer and that it is not expected to be repaid. The letter must detail the amount of the gift, and the name of the giver.

Good Faith Estimate (GFE) Under RESPA, lenders are required to give potential borrowers a written Good Faith Estimate of closing costs within three days of an application submission.

Grace Period The period of time after a loan payment due date in which a mortgage payment may be made and not be considered delinquent.

Graduated Payment Mortgage A mortgage in which the payments increase over the life of the mortgage, allowing the borrower to make very low payments at the beginning of the loan.

Hazard Insurance Insurance that covers the property from damages that might materially affect its value. Also known as home owner's insurance.

Holdback An amount of money held back at closing by the lender or the escrow agent until a particular condition has been met. If the problem is a repair, the money is kept until the repair is made. If the repair is not made, the lender or escrow agent uses the money to make the repair. Buyers and sellers may also have holdbacks between them, to ensure that specific conditions of the sale are met.

Home Owner Association A group of home owners in a particular subdivision or area who band together to take care of common property and common interests.

Home Owner's Insurance Coverage that includes hazard insurance, as well as personal liability and theft.

Home Warranty A service contract that covers appliances (with exclusions) in working condition in the home for a certain period of time, usually one year. Home owners are responsible for a per-call service fee. There is a home owner's warranty for new construction. Some developers will purchase a warranty from a company specializing in new construction for the homes they sell. A home owner's warranty will warrant the good working order of the appliances and workmanship of a new home for between one and ten years; for example, appliances might be covered for one year while the roof may be covered for several years.

Housing and Urban Development, Department of Also known as HUD, this is the federal department responsible for the nation's housing programs. It also regulates RESPA the Real Estate Settlement Procedures Act, which governs how lenders must deal with their customers.

Inspection The service an inspector performs when he or she is hired to scrutinize the home for any possible structural defects. May also be done in order to check for the presence of toxic substances, such as leaded paint or water, asbestos, radon, or pests, including termites.

Installment Contract The purchase of property in installments. Title to the property is given to the purchaser when all installments are made.

Institutional Investors or Lenders Private or public companies, corporations, or funds (such as pension funds) that purchase loans on the secondary market from commercial lenders such as banks and savings and loans. Or, they are sources of funds for mortgages through mortgage brokers.

Interest Money charged for the use of borrowed funds. Usually expressed as an interest rate, it is the percentage of the total loan charged annually for the use of the funds.

Interest-Only Mortgage A loan in which only the interest is paid on a regular basis (usually monthly), and the principal is owed in full at the end of the loan term.

Interest Rate Cap The total number of percentage points that an adjustable-rate mortgage (ARM) might rise over the life of the loan.

Joint Tenancy An equal, undivided ownership in a property taken by two or more owners. Under joint tenancy there are rights of survivorship, which means that if one of the owners dies, the surviving owner rather than the heirs of the estate inherits the other's total interest in the property.

Landscape The trees, flowers, plantings, lawn, and shrubbery that surround the exterior of a dwelling.

Late Charge A penalty applied to a mortgage payment that arrives after the grace period (usually the 10th or 15th of a month).

Lease with an Option to Buy When the renter or lessee of a piece of property has the right to purchase the property for a specific period of time at a specific price. Usually, a lease with an option to buy allows a first-time buyer to accumulate a down payment by applying a portion of the monthly rent toward the down payment.

Lender A person, company, corporation, or entity that lends money for the purchase of real estate.

Letter of Intent A formal statement, usually in letter form, from the buyer to the seller stating that the buyer intends to purchase a specific piece of property for a specific price on a specific date.

Leverage Using a small amount of cash, say a 10 or 20 percent down payment, to purchase a piece of property.

Lien An encumbrance against property, which may be voluntary or involuntary. There are many different kinds of liens, including a tax lien (for unpaid federal, state, or real estate taxes), a judgment lien (for monetary judgments by a court of law), a mortgage lien (when you take out a mortgage), and a mechanic's lien (for work done by a contractor on the property that has not been paid for). For a lien to be attached to the property's title, it must be filed or recorded with local county government.

Listing A property that a broker agrees to list for sale in return for a commission.

Loan An amount of money that is lent to a borrower, who agrees to repay it plus interest.

Loan Commitment A written document that states that a mortgage company has agreed to lend a buyer a certain amount of money at a certain rate of interest for a specific period of time, which may contain sets of conditions and a date by which the loan must close.

Loan Origination Fee A one-time fee charged by the mortgage company to arrange the financing for the loan.

Loan-to-Value Ratio The ratio of the amount of money you wish to borrow compared to the value of the property you wish to purchase. Institutional investors (who buy loans on the secondary market from your mortgage company) set up certain ratios that guide lending practices. For example, the mortgage company might only lend you 80 percent of a property's value.

Location Where property is geographically situated. "Location, location, location" is a broker's maxim that states that where the property is located is its most important feature, because you can change everything about a house, except its location.

Lock-In When a borrower signals to a mortgage company that he or she has decided to lock in, or take, a particular interest rate for a specific amount of time. The mechanism by which a borrower locks in the interest rate that will be charged on a particular loan. Usually, the lock lasts for a certain time period, such as thirty, forty-five, or sixty days. On a new construction, the lock may be much longer.

Maintenance Fee The monthly or annual fee charged to condo, co-op, or town house owners, and paid to the home owners' association, for the maintenance of common property. Also called an assessment.

Mortgage A document granting a lien on a home in exchange for financing granted by a lender. The mortgage is the means by which the lender secures the loan and has the ability to foreclose on the home.

Mortgage Banker A company or a corporation, like a bank, that lends its own funds to borrowers in addition to bringing together lenders and borrowers. A mortgage banker may also service the loan (i.e., collect the monthly payments).

Mortgage Broker A company or individual that brings together lenders and borrowers and processes mortgage applications.

Mortgagee A legal term for the lender.

Mortgagor A legal term for the borrower.

Multiple Listing Service (MLS) A computerized listing of all properties offered for sale by member brokers. Buyers may only gain access to the MLS by working with a member broker.

Negative Amortization A condition created when the monthly mortgage payment is less than the amount necessary to pay off the loan over the period of time set forth in the note. Because you're paying less than the amount necessary, the actual loan amount increases over time. That's how you end up with negative equity. To pay off the loan, a lump-sum payment must be made.

Option When a buyer pays for the right or option to purchase property for a given length of time, without having the obligation to actually purchase the property.

Origination Fee A fee charged by the lender for allowing you to borrow money to purchase property. The fee—which is also referred to as points—is usually expressed as a percentage of the total loan amount.

Ownership The absolute right to use, enjoy, and dispose of property. You own it!

Package Mortgage A mortgage that uses both real and personal property to secure a loan.

Paper Slang usage that refers to the mortgage, trust deed, installment, or land contract.

Personal Property Moveable property, such as appliances, furniture, clothing, and artwork.

PITI An acronym for Principal-Interest-Taxes-and-Insurance. These are usually the four parts of your monthly mortgage payment.

Pledged Account Borrowers who do not want to have a real estate tax or insurance escrow administered by the mortgage servicer can, in some circumstances, pledge a savings account into which enough money to cover real estate taxes and the insurance premium must be deposited. You must then make the payments for your real estate taxes and insurance premiums from a separate account. If you fail to pay your taxes or premiums, the lender is allowed to use the funds in the pledged account to make those payments.

Point A point is one percent of the loan amount.

Possession Being in control of a piece of property, and having the right to use it to the exclusion of all others.

Power of Attorney The legal authorization given to an individual to act on behalf of another individual.

Prepaid Interest Interest paid at closing for the number of days left in the month after closing. For example, if you close on the 15th, you would prepay the interest for the 16th through the end of the month.

Prepayment Penalty A fine imposed when a loan is paid off before it comes due. Many states now have laws against prepayment penalties, although banks with federal charters are exempt from state laws. If possible, do not use a mortgage that has a prepayment penalty, or you will be charged a fine if you sell your property before your mortgage has been paid off.

Prequalifying for a Loan When a mortgage company tells a buyer in advance of the formal application approximately how much money the buyer can afford to borrow.

Principal The amount of money you borrow.

Private Mortgage Insurance (PMI) Special insurance that specifically protects the top 20 percent of a loan, allowing the lender to lend more than 80 percent of the value of the property. PMI is paid in monthly installments by the borrower.

Property Tax A tax levied by a county or local authority on the value of real estate.

Proration The proportional division of certain costs of home ownership. Usually used at closing to figure out how much the buyer and seller each owe for certain expenditures, including real estate taxes, assessments, and water bills.

Purchase Agreement An agreement between the buyer and seller for the purchase of property.

Purchase Money Mortgage An instrument used in seller financing, a purchase money mortgage is signed by a buyer and given to the seller in exchange for a portion of the purchase price.

Quitclaim Deed A deed that operates to release any interest in a property that a person may have, *without a representation that he or she actually has a right in that property.* For example, Sally may use a quitclaim deed to grant Bill her interest in the White House, in Washington, D.C., although she may not actually own, or have any rights to, that particular house.

Real Estate Land, and anything permanently attached to it, such as buildings and improvements.

Real Estate Agent An individual licensed by the state, who acts on behalf of the seller or buyer. For his or her services, the agent receives a commission, which is usually expressed as a percentage of the sales price of a home and is split with his or her real estate firm. A real estate agent must either be a real estate broker or work for one.

Real Estate Attorney An attorney who specializes in the purchase and sale of real estate.

Real Estate Broker An individual who is licensed by the state to act as an agent on behalf of the seller or buyer. For his or her services, the broker receives a commission, which is usually expressed as a percentage of the sales price of a home.

Real Estate Settlement Procedures Act (RESPA) This federal statute was originally passed in 1974, and contains provisions that govern the way companies involved with a real estate closing must treat each other and the consumer. For example, one section of RESPA requires lenders to give consumers a written Good Faith Estimate within three days of making an application for a loan. Another section of RESPA prohibits title companies from giving referral fees to brokers for steering business to them.

Realist A designation given to an agent or broker who is a member of the National Association of Real Estate Brokers.

Realtor A designation given to a real estate agent or broker who is a member of the National Association of Realtors.

Recording The process of filing documents at a specific government office. Upon such recording, the document becomes part of the public record.

Redlining The slang term used to describe an illegal practice of discrimination against a particular racial group by real estate lenders. Redlining occurs when lenders decide certain areas of a community are too high risk and refuse to lend to buyers who want to purchase property in those areas, regardless of their qualifications or creditworthiness.

Regulation Z Also known as the Truth in Lending Act. Congress determined that lenders must provide a written good faith estimate of closing costs to all borrowers and provide them with other written information about the loan.

Reserve The amount of money set aside by a condo, co-op, or homeowners' association for future capital improvements.

Sale-Leaseback A transaction in which the seller sells property to a buyer, who then leases the property back to the seller. This is accomplished within the same transaction.

Sales Contract The document by which a buyer contracts to purchase property. Also known as the purchase contract or a Contract to Purchase.

Second Mortgage A mortgage that is obtained after the primary mortgage, and whose rights for repayment are secondary to the first mortgage.

Seller Broker A broker who has a fiduciary responsibility to the seller. Most brokers are seller brokers, although an increasing number are buyer brokers, who have a fiduciary responsibility to the buyer.

Settlement Statement A statement that details the monies paid out and received by the buyer and seller at closing.

Shared Appreciation Mortgage A relatively new mortgage used to help first-time buyers who might not qualify for conventional financing. In a shared appreciation mortgage, the lender offers a below-market interest rate in return for a portion of the profits made by the home owner when the property is sold. Before entering into a shared appreciation mortgage, be sure to have your real estate attorney review the documentation.

Special Assessment An additional charge levied by a condo or co-op board in order to pay for capital improvements, or other unforeseen expenses.

Subagent A broker who brings the buyer to the property. Although the subagent would appear to be working for the buyer (a subagent usually ferries around the buyer, showing him or her properties), they are paid by the seller and have a fiduciary responsibility to the seller. Subagency is often confusing to first-time buyers, who think that because the subagent shows them property, the subagent is "their" agent, rather than the seller's.

Subdivision The division of a large piece of property into several smaller pieces. Usually a developer or a group of developers will build single family or duplex homes of a similar design and cost within one subdivision.

Tax Lien A lien that is attached to property if the owner does not pay his or her real estate taxes or federal income taxes. If overdue property taxes are not paid, the owner's property might be sold at auction for the amount owed in back taxes.

Tenancy by the Entirety A type of ownership whereby both the husband and wife each own the complete property. Each spouse has an ownership interest in the property as their marital residence and, as a result, creditors cannot force the sale of the home to pay back the debts of one spouse without the other spouse's consent. There are rights of survivorship whereby upon the death of one spouse, the other spouse would immediately inherit the entire property.

Tenants in Common A type of ownership in which two or more parties have an undivided interest in the property. The owners may or may not have equal shares of ownership, and there are no rights of survivorship. However, each owner retains the right to sell his or her share in the property as he or she sees fit.

Title Refers to the ownership of a particular piece of property.

Title Company The corporation or company that insures the status of title (title insurance) through the closing, and may handle other aspects of the closing.

Title Insurance Insurance that protects the lender and the property owner against losses arising from defects or problems with the title to property.

Torrens Title A system of recording the chain of ownership for property, which takes its name from the man who created it in Australia in 1858, Sir Robert Torrens. While popular in the nineteenth century, most cities have converted to other, less cumbersome, systems of recording.

Trust Account An account used by brokers and escrow agents, in which funds for another individual are held separately, and not commingled with other funds.

Underwriter One who underwrites a loan for another. Your lender will have an investor underwrite your loan.

Variable Interest Rate An interest rate that rises and falls according to a particular economic indicator, such as Treasury Bills.

Void A contract or document that is not enforceable.

Voluntary Lien A lien, such as a mortgage, that a homeowner elects to grant to a lender.

Waiver The surrender or relinquishment of a particular right, claim, or privilege.

Warranty A legally binding promise given to the buyer at closing by the seller, generally regarding the condition of the home, property, or other matter.

Zoning The right of the local municipal government to decide how different areas of the municipality will be used. Zoning ordinances are the laws that govern the use of the land.

Acknowledgments

There are many people without whose help it would have been impossible to start, let alone finish, this book. I am particularly grateful to the dozens of real estate professionals, experts, and industry observers all over the country, who over the course of this book and hundreds of articles gave freely of their advice, guidance, counsel, and wisdom, including: Doug and Joan Anderson, Century 21 Doug Anderson & Associates, Lancaster, California; Neil Anderson; Julie Bleasdale, *Real Estate Today* magazine; Kristine Blomkvest; Don Brown and Mary Fritze, Century 21 Action Realty, San Antonio, Texas; Mary Frances Burleson, Sherry Richards, and Leslie Kempe, Ebby Halliday Realtors, Dallas, Texas; Sol Ellis, Century 21 RTA Associates, Research Triangle Park, North Carolina; Connie Farmer, Prudential Summerson-Burrows, Overland Park, Kansas; Jon Fogg, Centex Homes, Illinois division; Russell Gay, Century 21 Russell Gay & Associates, Raleigh, North Carolina; Tom Hathaway, The Buyer's Agent, Inc.; Joanne Healey, Coldwell Banker Schlott Realtors, Pompton Plains, New Jersey; Kerry Kidwell, Realty Plus, Bloomington, Illinois;

Keith Kline and Mike Wheeler, Century 21 Heritage Realty, York, Pennsylvania; Mark Litner, Much Shelist Freed Denenberg Ament & Eiger, Chicago, Illinois; Semi Mintz, Coldwell Banker Southern Home, Raleigh, North Carolina; Sharon Miraglia, Koenig & Strey, Libertyville, Illinois; Pam Morrell, People's First Realty, Rock Hill, South Carolina; Richard Nash, North Shore Mortgage and Financial Services Evanston, Illinois; Karen Randell, Century 21 Prime Realty, Marquette, Michigan; Andrea Schmidt, Prudential Landmark Real Estate, Champaign, Illinois; Linda Sherrer, Prudential Network Realty, Jacksonville, Florida; Joseph Wallace, Century 21 HG Brown, Laurel, Maryland; Loretta Waters, Insurance Information Institute; Tim Welch, RE/MAX Brandywine, Wilmington, Delaware; and, Billy Woodyard, Century 21 West Teays Realty, Hurricane, West Virginia. Steve Knipstein and Sherry Bale, of Aaron D. Cushman & Associates, adroitly culled the names of several hundred Century 21 brokers in response to a single telephone call. Likewise, Carol Beekman, of Coldwell Banker, and Ron Tepper, of Prudential Real Estate, provided me with the names of more brokers than I could ever contact. Liz Duncan, of the National Association of Realtors, continues to open many doors.

In my hometown of Chicago, there are many people who readily offer their time and energy, and who always open their files in search of ever-elusive anecdotes. I wish to thank the brokers of Kahn Realty, particularly David Robins, Elaine Waxman, Barbara Isaacs, Rick Druker, and especially David Hall, who helped tremendously in the organization and preparation of this book; Jim Kinney of Rubloff Residential; David Arts, of Century 21 Real Estate Corp. of Northern Illinois; Tom Koenig, of Koenig & Strey; Lyle Williamson, of Prudential Preferred Properties; Stephen Baird, of Baird & Warner;

Joyce Burke, of Coldwell Banker/Chicago; and the brokers of Beliard Gordon & Partners.

An idea doesn't become a book by itself. My thanks to my attorney, Ralph Martire; my agent, Alice Martell, who worked through three drafts of the proposal, then sold it in the blink of an eye; and Henry Ferris, my wonderful editor at Times Books, who happily infected the entire house with his overwhelming enthusiasm for this project.

On a personal level, I am grateful for the unwavering support of many friends, including the members of the Tuesday Night Screenwriter's Group, the Galperins, the Schraibers, Ellyn Rosen, Susan Shatkin, Ann Hagedorn, Jack Wilson, J. Linn Allen, Sallie Gaines, Wayne Faulkner, Karen Egolf, Ellen Shubart, Melanie Glover, and Hank Bernstein; Janet Franz, whose vision has sharpened my writing through the years, and my mentors, Phyllis Magida and Thea Flaum, have provided a special guidance.

My family continues to put up with the best and worst of this eclectic life I've chosen, offering only their love and support: Jeanne and Meyer Kraus, who pick through the papers each week looking for my articles, Betty Glink Feinfeld, Richard and Leona Kraus, Brad Tamkin, Mitch and Alice Tamkin, Linda and Simon Waller, Judy Mayer, and my mother-in-law, Marilyn Tamkin. I especially wish to thank my sisters, Shona Glink and Phyllis Glink, who understood when I worked through many a Sunday-night dinner. My mother, Susanne Kraus Glink, one of the best real estate agents in Chicago, introduced me to this crazy business and repeatedly suggested that I write a book. Finally, I would never have finished without the unstinting help of my husband and best friend, Samuel J. Tamkin, the world's best real estate attorney, who has always believed my wildest dreams would come true.

Index

ABOUT THE AUTHOR

ILYCE R. GLINK is an award-winning nationally syndicated journalist who writes about real estate, business, television and film. Her work has been published by *Worth* magazine, *The Chicago Tribune, The Washington Post, Chicago* magazine, *Electronic Media, City & State, Crain's Chicago Business, Crain's New York Business, National Relocation & Real Estate Magazine,* and other publications. Her column, "Real Estate Matters," is syndicated by Chicago-based Crain News Service. In 1992, Glink was named Best Consumer Reporter by the National Association of Real Estate Editors, and in 1990, she was honored by the National Association of Real Estate Editors for an article on Chicago's building boom of the 1980s. She is currently working on a book for home sellers.